CONSIDERING LITERACY

READING AND WRITING THE EDUCATIONAL EXPERIENCE

LINDA ADLER-KASSNER
Eastern Michigan University

PEARSON
Longman

New York   San Francisco   Boston
London   Toronto   Sydney   Tokyo   Singapore   Madrid
Mexico City   Munich   Paris   Cape Town   Hong Kong   Montreal

Senior Acquisitions Editor: Lynn M. Huddon
Executive Marketing Manager: Megan Galvin-Fak
Senior Supplements Editor: Donna Campion
Production Manager: Donna DeBenedictis
Project Coordination, Text Design, and Electronic Page Makeup: Elm Street Publishing Services, Inc.
Cover Design Manager: Wendy Ann Fredericks
Cover Designer: Nancy Sacks
Cover Photo: ©Alix Minde/PhotoAlto/Getty Images
Photo Researcher: Julie Tesser
Manufacturing Buyer: Roy L. Pickering Jr.
Printer and Binder: R.R. Donnelley & Sons Company/Crawfordsville
Cover Printer: Phoenix Color Corporation

For permission to use copyrighted material, grateful acknowledgment is made to the copyright holders on p. 371, which is hereby made part of this copyright page.

Library of Congress Cataloging-in-Publication Data
Adler-Kassner, Linda.
  Considering literacy : reading and writing the educational experience / Linda Adler-Kassner.—1st ed.
    p. cm.
  Includes index.
  ISBN 0-321-11338-1 (alk. paper)
  1. English language—Rhetoric—Study and teaching—United States. 2. Reading (Higher education)—
United States. 3. Academic writing—Study and teaching—United States. 4. Literacy—United States.
I. Title.
PE1405.U6A35 2006
808'.0420711—dc22
                                                                                            2005027552

Please visit us at www.ablongman.com

ISBN 0-321-11338-1

1 2 3 4 5 6 7 8 9 10—DOC—08 07 06 05

CONTENTS

READINGS ABOUT LEARNING (IN AND OUT OF SCHOOL) *221*

PHOTOGRAPHS *359*

Alternative Contents

INSTRUCTOR'S INTRODUCTION

ASKING QUESTIONS

Sometime during the workshop that new graduate instructors and I do at the beginning of each year, I remind them—and myself—that those of us who teach first-year writing are lucky. We get an opportunity that not many other instructors do: we get to work closely with students during a pretty exciting time, their early semesters in college. In the program where I work, we also get to consider an issue that we think is pretty important for students: the context for literacy practices in college and, sometimes, elsewhere. We also have the luxury of spending at least one term working with students who are practicing writing, reading, and critical thinking strategies that they can use to analyze this issue.

Our program—and now, this book—extends some pretty fascinating questions to students. Some are about *context:*

- What are the literacy practices—the ways of reading, writing, thinking, and engaging with ideas—that are expected among different groups in different sites?
- How are "appropriate" and "inappropriate" literacy practices defined in different sites?
- What values do those definitions represent?
- How are "appropriate" and "inappropriate" literacy practices defined, by whom, and why?

And some are about *practice:*

- How can instructors facilitate students' understandings of how to assess an audience's expectations for different (written and non-written) products?
- How can reading, assignments, and class activities facilitate students' analyses of different audiences' definitions of "appropriate" and "inappropriate" literacies?
- How can writing classes help students make conscious choices about how or whether to meet audiences' expectations, and how to use and develop writing, reading, and critical thinking strategies to act on their decisions?

As many literacy studies and composition researchers have noted, the meanings of "good writing" (and its twin, "good reading") have changed dramatically over time and are always linked to the perpetuation of particular ideologies and values. Helping students to think about these definitions and their concomitant ideological implications, as well as helping them to critically consider the practices designed to elicit them (practices cultivated in classes just like this one), is crucially important.

In fact, first-year classes dedicated to helping students develop the writing, reading, and critical thinking strategies that will be useful for them in and out of college often are the only space in college where students can consider the connections between *context* and *practice* in an educational setting, whether that setting is the college or university where your class is being taught, a school in which students were previously enrolled, or even a site where they are observing. These classes also provide remarkable opportunities for students to consider the implications of their understandings in the context of the college/university, and to develop written products that communicate those implications to other audiences. Certainly, these audiences can include the class—you, their instructor, as well as other students—but they also can extend beyond the classroom to students' communities, to decision makers in the university, or to other (real) audiences.

EXCITEMENT AND INVESTMENT

Considering Literacy asks you and your students to take up questions related to connections between context and practice, to be excited about exploring those questions, to be ready to learn things that perhaps you and/or your students had not considered before. (As an instructor, I know that assignments where students write about contexts, situations, or interpretations that I hadn't thought about or didn't know make the best reading, since I'm learning as I go!) Ideally, as students take up these new issues, they will become increasingly invested in thinking through issues related to *this* context—your context, in your institution— and in using writing as a tool for communicating those ideas to audiences who share their interest.

While an edited book asks you and students to "pay no attention to the [wo]man behind the curtain," let me step out for a moment and relay a story that speaks to this approach. In my eighth year of teaching, I moved from a college for students labeled "under-prepared" by my university to a different job at a fairly selective state institution. During my first semester, one of the students in my class came to talk with me about his first paper, the "What is the Purpose of School?" assignment included in this text. The student had formulated a quick-and-easy response to the assignment: the purpose of school was to prepare him for life. But when we talked I pressed him on it. What kind of life? Life as a monk on a Tibetan mountain top? Life as a line worker in an auto plant? Life as a social worker in an impoverished urban area? Something else entirely? After the conversation, the student said, "When I got this assignment I thought, 'I can rattle off 4–5 pages of crap on the purpose of school, no problem. But you don't want crap!" Certainly, it's possible to look at this student's response as indicative of another *kind* of performance that he realized would be necessary for his success in this class—it was, after all, a selective institution, and this was a student who had been extremely successful in school previous to arriving there. However, even if the student had merely shifted his idea of what kind of performance would be necessary for success (and I think that he had in some ways done just that), this is a more *dynamic*, more *enthusiastic*, more *engaged* performance than he had previously offered. While I make no claims that this approach will shift some students' attitudes toward school, I do claim (from experience) that this approach will create opportunities for students to consider questions that might not have been extended to them before, and which they might—for whatever reason—find especially engaging. Reflecting and being reflexive about why things are as they are can prove challenging, energizing, and exciting.

FEATURES OF THE BOOK

The readings and assignments in *Considering Literacy* are designed to help students consider these questions of literacy and context through a semester. You'll find a number of unique features here.

Assignments

The assignments in *Considering Literacy* are designed to build on one another much like a scaffold, both vertically and horizontally. There are four assignment categories here; each category (except the last) includes a number of assignments to choose from, all of which involve developing the same writing strategies. The assumption is that classes will focus on four "large" assignments through the term and that work within each assignment will help students to develop their work with that large assignment. Each assignment category builds on the writing strategies and content knowledge developed in the previous one, so that as students work through these assignments, both their use of different writing strategies, and their thinking about the issues they write about will become increasingly sophisticated. This progression through assignments constitutes the horizontal pieces of the scaffold, as it were.

The vertical pillars of the scaffold are contained within each assignment category. Inside of each prompt for an extended essay are at least two prompts for Developing Work, brainstorming activities where students develop their ideas and content. You and/or class colleagues can provide feedback on these Developing Work assignments for students to take into account as they use this writing as foundations for their extended essays. Thus, within each assignment, students are continuously developing their writing and their thinking about writing.

Readings

Considering Literacy offers a range of readings linked with each assignment and a variety of ways to work with the readings for each assignment. At the beginning of each assignment, you and your students will find a list of possible readings that can be used in conjunction with the writing; you and/or your students can choose from among the readings. *Considering Literacy* also provides a process for working with the readings which always refers back to the extended essay prompts, and asks students to be reflective and reflexive about this process.

You and your students will find a brief discussion of issues related to reading interpretation, particularly the idea of dominant (or "preferred") readings and non-dominant readings at the beginning of this section. Then, you and students will find four kinds of reading questions intended to help students both understand elements of the dominant reading and strike a balance, if one is to be struck, between that interpretation and their own. First are *Pre-Reading Questions* applied to all the readings that ask students to reflect on why they are doing the reading that they are. Second are *Post-Reading Questions* that, again, are to be used with all readings. They ask students to reflect on what they find to be the reading's central theme and why they find that to be the theme, and to identify a significant piece of the reading (a passage, a quote) that strikes them as significant and to reflect on why they have identified it. Used consistently, these *Pre-* and *Post-Reading Questions* will give students opportunity to practice considering their expectations of readings, writing fluently about what they find to be the major points in the readings and why, and finding evidence in readings that they can then use in their writing.

In addition to *Pre-* and *Post-Reading Questions* to be used across all readings, you will also find questions written specifically for *each* reading. The first group of questions, called *Critical Reflections,* is intended to help students to identify the dominant reading of each selection and consider its implications. The second group, *Making Connections,* is intended to facilitate students' reading across selections in the text.

USING CONSIDERING LITERACY

Obviously, you won't be able to use all of the readings or the assignments in *Considering Literacy* during a one-semester course. The "protoype" courses from which this book stemmed are taught in a 14-week semester. The course is portfolio-based; instructors assign four essay projects and ask students to revise two for their final portfolios (which also include a reflective cover letter and process writing).

There are four categories of scaffolded assignments here; certainly, you might choose one from each of the four categories. However, some assignments might seem more appropriate for *your* context than others, and all can be adapted to reflect the writing strategies in the others. Instructors in the "prototype" course typically ask students to read two to three pieces per assignment; sometimes, instructors select all of the readings, sometimes, they assign one to two common readings and ask students to select a third or fourth from a list of possibilities. The important thing is that you tailor the readings and assignments here so that they reflect your goals and invite students to work within your context. Ideally, you will find ways within this text to make that happen.

Of course, this is just a brief introduction to the ways that you might consider using *Considering Literacy.* You'll find other possibilities as well as sample assignment combinations, lesson plans, ideas for working with the readings in this book, and much more in the *Considering Literacy Instructor's Manual* (available to qualified adopters of the book) by Lori Hubbard Higgins, who has personally taught with the readings and approach described in this book.

ACKNOWLEDGMENTS

Considering Literacy grows out of teaching and writing program administration work that I've done at three institutions over the last 16 years. In that time, I've been privileged to work in collaboration with outstandingly talented instructors. The names of all of the teachers to whom I am indebted could fill several pages. In the interests of space, though, I'll focus on just a handful who have developed and/or road-tested the assignments included here. These include Diane Benton (author of the prototype "classroom ethnography" assignment), Tom Ulch (author of the prototype "Alternative Literacy Practices" assignment), Ralph Zerbonia, Diana Agy, Scott Still, Adam Hazlett, Marcy Lehtinen, Michele Fero, David Marquard, Erin Anderson, Cindy Guillean, Alan Dykstra, Clarinda Flannery, and Heidi Estrem. While there's one name on the cover, the ideas of all of these people (and many others) have shaped what is included here. I also owe a debt of gratitude to Greg Glau and Bob Yagelski, both of whom provided valuable advice at the beginning of this project.

Thanks, too, to the reviewers who provided thoughtful commentary on this reader as it developed. These include Janet Badia, Marshall University; Richard Boyd, San Diego State University; JoAnn Dadisman, West Virginia University; Robert E. Donahoo, Sam Houston State University; Patrice Gray, Fitchburg State College; Ted Hovet, Western Kentucky University; Melissa Ianetta, Oklahoma State University; Emily Isaacs, Montclair State University; Martha Kruse, University of Nebraska–Kearney; Michael Mills, Georgia Southern University; Scott Peeples, College of Charleston; Kathleen J. Ryan, West Virginia University; Beth Sherman, San Diego State University; Mary Trachsel, University of Iowa; Tony Trigilio, Columbia College; Debbie J. Williams, Abilene Christian University; and Sherry L. Wynn, Oakland University. I also am grateful to Lynn Huddon at Longman Publishers for her guidance and to Esther Hollander at Longman for keeping all of the many materials associated with this project in order.

Finally, thanks to my spouse, Scott, and to our daughter Nora for listening to me think aloud about this project. Like all else I do, I couldn't have done this without them.

LINDA ADLER-KASSNER

ABOUT THIS BOOK
APPROACH AND ASSIGNMENTS

It's the beginning of the semester, and this is the text you're using for a class—first-year writing, introduction to college, a first-year seminar, or something else. Maybe you're wondering, "What's the class all about?" Maybe your wonderings even go beyond that, to "What is this institution all about? What am I all about in this place?"

If you are asking these questions, you will find ways to explore them in greater detail in *Considering Literacy*. This book asks you to read and write about how you and others define *education* broadly, but also elements of education. For example, how are "appropriate" and "inappropriate" ideas of good writing (or reading) defined in particular contexts, and why are they defined as they are? If you're not asking these questions yet, this book will raise them and ask you to consider why they might be important to you.

It's fairly standard for the author or editor of a textbook like this one to be invisible. Yet that author or editor has made an enormous number of decisions about what should happen in her or his textbook and why, in addition to how the book should be shaped to guide how it is used. That certainly is the case in this book. One of the fundamental ideas in *Considering Literacy* is that we, students and instructors together, need to uncloak these decisions and think about who has made them, what choices they reflect, and why they have been made. Why is something, whether it be an answer, an approach, or a way of thinking, deemed correct? Why is another incorrect? What makes something more right than something else? And whose interests are served by decisions about what is right and less right?

To that end, before you delve into investigations of questions like these through the readings and assignments in this text, let me (the author of this book) uncloak myself for a moment and lay out some of the assumptions about *writing* and *thinking* that affected my choices of readings, assignments, questions, and approaches in this text, then make some connections between those assumptions and what you will find here.

ASSUMPTION ONE: WRITING, READING, AND THINKING ARE LINKED, AND GOOD WRITING SHOULD BE (PARTLY) ABOUT WRESTLING WITH IDEAS.

When you read some of these assignments, your first instinct might be to leap to an answer to the questions they ask. For instance, one assignment here asks you to consider the purpose of school. You might think, "I know that right off! It's

_____." (Many of the students with whom I've used this assignment have said, "It's to prepare you for life," for instance.) That's a great place to start, certainly.

But don't stop there. What kind of life? Life as a line worker? Life as a Buddhist monk? Life as a dumpster diver? Life as a corporate executive, a social worker, a teacher, a homemaker, a sanitation worker? A citizen in a democracy? A parent? "Life" is not one thing, and "you" is not a generic person. *You,* the student using this book, will be asked to use writing through the assignments in this text to really *define* what you mean when you lay down those phrases. You will be asked to think through them carefully, and the best way to do this is through writing. That's why you will find several different kinds of writing in this text. There are *Long Essays,* the kinds of assignments you work on over a period of weeks inside and outside of the classroom. There are *Developing Work* assignments, opportunities for you to work on smaller pieces of the long essays and brainstorm ideas through writing. Hopefully, you will work on those ideas with class colleagues and your instructor too, receiving feedback as you develop your writing. There are *Pre-Reading Questions,* which ask you to consider why you are reading a particular piece and what you think it will be about. There are *Post-Reading Questions* that ask you to consider what has struck you as significant in the readings. Each of these is an invitation to you to use writing to think hard about important questions.

All of these assignments and questions are intended to help you use writing to explore ideas and maybe (hopefully) discover *new* ideas, things you didn't know (or didn't know you knew) before you started writing.

ASSUMPTION TWO: WRITING SHOULD START WITH SMART (AND MESSY) IDEAS AND END WITH PRETTY (AND SMART) PAPERS, AND NOT THE OTHER WAY AROUND.

Using writing to think through serious questions is challenging. Not all writers have the same process, but most writers I know share at least one common characteristic: they start messy and get neater. For instance, I am a *very* messy, speedy writer. To write this introduction, I've gone through nine drafts. (Those don't include the writing and rewriting I've done as I've drafted on the computer—they're just the drafts I've printed out and edited off-screen.) At the beginning, they involved typing lots and lots of text, then tossing most of it. With each draft I kept some of the previous draft, scrapped some (sometimes a lot), added here and there, and changed things. As I liked the ideas better, I began to think about the structure: did I want this paragraph (the one you're reading right now) here? Before the first assumption? After the third? Should these assumptions be in a table format, or in paragraphs like these? This introduction has been reviewed by other readers too, who provided suggestions that helped me to clarify the ideas in it. But a close friend of mine is exactly the opposite. He doesn't "draft" on the screen as I do. Instead, he ponders and thinks and mulls and turns and reflects, all in his head. When he sits down to write, he has already thought through many of his ideas. Rather than writing many drafts, as I do, he might get through what he needs to in four or five. For both of us, the process starts in a jumble. We're working on working through ideas, figuring out what we want to say by using our own writing process to construct ideas as we think. As we get clearer on those ideas *through* our writing, we can start to think about form. First content, then form, and *then*, and only then, do I look at editing. I am an egregious over-user of commas, for instance. Once I was happy with what I said in this introduction, I went over it for word choice and punctuation, paying particular attention to comma use since that's one of my writing issues. I asked others to look for that, too.

Was this introduction pretty when I started writing it? No. Is it pretty now, at the end? I think so. But before I could worry about it being pretty, I had to make sure that it said smart things. If I were to use this introduction as a piece of evidence to answer the questions about appropriateness above, I might say that I think writing is appropriate (or good, which is a phrase I'm more comfortable with) when it says something smart and does so in a style and form that seems appropriate for the audience. I only notice editing when it's a problem; for example, I notice if the misuse of writing conventions (e.g., punctuation, rules of capitalization, etc.) is so glaring that it starts to pull my attention away from the *content* of the essay and I focus instead on the next error.

The assumption about writing starting smart and ending pretty is reflected vertically (within assignments) and horizontally (across assignments) in *Considering Literacy*. Within each assignment, there is a process laid out that asks you to use pre-reading and post-reading questions and Developing Work assignments as places to brainstorm, to mull over, to think through. The expectation is that you will use these to develop your ideas, but not to think about editing. Instead, these different pieces will serve as foundations for your long essay drafts. At the same time, you don't want to make what instructors with whom I teach call a "peanut butter and jelly" draft ("DW.1 here, DW. 2 here, slap together, done!") Instead, as you use writing to think, you will need to also consider how to bring together the ideas in DW assignments so that they cohere around your central analysis, your own ideas. After you develop those ideas, you can work on the connections, the shaping, the smoothing, and the editing. This is a sort of *vertical* process, which happens as you move from beginning of assignment to end.

ASSUMPTION THREE: ASSUMPTIONS ONE AND TWO APPLY TO READING, TOO.

Start smart and messy and get pretty and smart? Wrestle with ideas? What does that have to do with reading? While we sometimes don't think of it, reading should be just as much a process as writing. You'll find that the readings and reading questions here ask you to engage in a process that asks you to start by wading in and mucking around in the complexities of a text to figure out why you're using it and what you think is going on in it. This is a little like brainstorming. Then, perhaps after a second (or third) reading, you'll use the reading questions that follow each piece as you consider how you'll work with the reading in your own writing. The important point to remember here is that reading shouldn't be like a poaching raid, where you dive into a text that you already "get" and take what you need. Instead, you should (and, I hope, will have to) spend some time thinking through the ideas here, some of which might seem challenging initially, to figure out what is going on and whether they're relevant for you.

ASSUMPTION FOUR: SCAFFOLDING WORKS.

In Assumption Two, I mention that the assignments here help you develop ideas vertically, through the process of working on one essay. They also help you develop ideas about the subject of this text, literacy and education, by working horizontally across assignments. Both within individual assignments (as you work through the different components of prewriting, prereading, and drafting), and across assignments (as you work through the different assignments during the course of the term), this process is called scaffolding. As you develop strategies through individual assignments, you are constructing the vertical parts of the scaffold—the sides that support the different layers. Additionally, each assignment here builds on the next one so that you're building one layer at a time. As you use increasingly complex writing strategies, you continue to work on the ones that support those strategies from previous assignments.

In addition to finding scaffolding within individual assignments, you'll also find scaffolding used across assignments in this book. Assignments in this text come in four categories. With the exception of category four, there are at least eight different assignment choices within each category; however, each assignment choice asks you to work with similar writing strategies. For example, all of the Learning from Self assignments ask you to work on analysis, using evidence from texts, thinking about form, and editing. All of the Learning from Others assignments ask you to work with those strategies, in addition to textual interpretation, summarizing, and paraphrasing. Researching the Text assignments build on these strategies and add still more; the Speaking Out, Joining In, Talking Back assignment does the same. (You will read in more detail what strategies you are developing in the introductions to each category of assignment.) Through scaffolding, you will develop a wider repertoire of writing strategies, practice using those strategies in a variety of ways, and learn more about education and literacy in the process.

ASSUMPTION FIVE: STUDENTS (YOU) ARE SMART AND RISE TO A CHALLENGE.

In the reading called "I Just Wanna Be Average" included in this book, there is a line that has powerfully affected my approach to teaching (and the creation of this book). In the chapter, author Mike Rose is describing the mindset of students in the vocational education track where he was placed initially in high school. "Students will float to the mark you set," Rose writes, "and I and the others in the vocation classes were bobbing in pretty shallow water."

This text sets a high mark with the full expectation that you will float to it. You will find evidence of this assumption in several places in *Considering Literacy*. First, you will find it in assignments that challenge you to think hard about ideas in the various readings included here and, perhaps, your own ideas. You will also find it in the approaches to readings included here, described in greater detail on pages 8–14. You won't find fill in the blank questions about what a reading says; instead, you will find questions that ask you to think about who you are as a reader, about your goals for reading, and about how these things are connected to your goals for writing. I hope you won't find the assignments or reading questions here easy—they are intended to challenge you. However, the approach in the text is also designed to support you as you explore these ideas.

ASSUMPTION SIX: STUDENTS (YOU) SHOULD CARE ABOUT THIS STUFF.

This is the assumption that my own students question most vocally, at least initially. But I say to you the same thing I say to them: Literacy practices are always located in, and reflective of, particular places. What is labeled appropriate in school (for instance, writing lengthy explanations like these) would be highly inappropriate in another context (such as an e-mail message to a close friend). This is a class that is designed to help you develop literacy practices in *this* context, so it's in your best interest to learn more about this context, what it's all about, and where you fit in it. You'll find this idea throughout this text—this introduction, in the readings, the assignments, everywhere.

Stepping Into the Discussion

By accepting the invitation extended in these assignments and readings, you are beginning to participate in a national discussion, ongoing for the last 150 years in the U.S., about what is taught to whom and why. As this introduction is being written, this discussion is reflected in:

- Discussions about the influence of No Child Left Behind, the Bush administration's mandate for education, and the possibility of extending NCLB into high schools;
- Concerns about the reading and writing practices of young people most recently reflected in a report authored by the National Endowment for the Humanities called "Reading at Risk," which claims that "literary reading" by people between the ages of 18–24 is "declining precipitously"(x–xi), but doesn't take into account what *other* things people might read;
- The implementation of the revised writing portion of the SAT and ACT exam, beginning in Spring 2005, and the implications of those revisions for students' educations.

But these are only the latest manifestations of this discussion. In your own school (high school or post-secondary), district, or state there are undoubtedly other parallel, perhaps similar, discussions going on that have affected you. The expertise you have developed as a student will help you as you think about the issues raised in these discussions; hopefully, these readings and assignments will facilitate that thinking. As you work through them, you will become better at articulating your questions and positions on these issues, and at developing writing strategies that can help you communicate successfully with broader audiences participating in discussions about them.

By the time you finish the term, I hope you'll agree that at least some of these assumptions about your interests and experiences aren't too far off the mark. I trust that you will have learned more about developing your literacy strategies — your ability to think about the expectations for college-level writing and meet those using strategies that seem appropriate for the job. I also hope you will have thought more about why those strategies are as they are and how they are connected to the questions that you might be asking yourself as the term begins. Let me know about how this approach has or hasn't worked for you by e-mailing me. My e-mail address is Linda.Adler-Kassner@emich.edu—I would like to hear from you.

READING WORDS AND IMAGES

- "Getting" reading

- Reading questions

- Strategic reading

- Reading images

THINK ABOUT READING: WHAT MAKES YOU LIKE SOMETHING? WHAT MAKES YOU SAY SOMETHING IS BORING?

"Getting" Reading

At one level, reading is a cognitive process: you learn how letters make patterns and how to interpret patterns as words. You have made it to college, so undoubtedly you have had some success with this cognitive work. If you hadn't, you couldn't read this. But beyond this level of cognition, reading gets a lot more complicated.

Maybe there are times when you struggle with reading. Sometimes, you might say you "can't get into it"—the reading seems boring, pointless, or hard to understand. When this is the case, it's likely that it's because you can't find a mental framework to put around the reading that helps you to connect it to things that are important for you. When you do "get into a reading," it's meaningful because you are able to *make it mean* something. You are looking at it through your own lenses—that is, your own experiences, cultures, and ideas—and finding a way for it to matter for your world picture. This process of "getting into a reading" has to do with finding a way to engage the text for yourself, making connections between it and you. You might get into a reading because you enjoy it or engage with the content, or you find it to be a useful model for something you are thinking about or doing, for example.

Other times, you might say that you are having a hard time "getting" a reading, or understanding the ideas. "Getting it" is more complicated than "getting into it" because there's almost always at least one other person involved. You have to "get it" because someone else is trying to explain it to you ("Oh! I get it!") or because you want to explain it to someone else ("Don't you get it?"). So while you approach and interpret any reading through your own experiences, cultures, and ideas—those things that come together to form lenses through which you filter your experiences and interpretations of everything—there are also other interpretations, filtered through other lenses, out there.

In school, these other readings can include what is seen as *the* meaning of a reading, or what academics call the "dominant reading." Sometimes, the dominant reading isn't a *single* meaning; there will be several dominant interpretations of a reading, but the different interpretations will have similar features in common. Maybe you have had experiences in school where you really think that one thing is happening in a reading but your teacher says something else entirely is going on, or where you were told that a question you asked wasn't relevant to the text. These might be occasions when your reading might differ, in whole or in part, from the dominant reading. You might say that you don't, or can't, "get it"; as a result of not "getting it," you might sometimes also write off the reading and say that you couldn't get into it.

But you also could look at this experience in another way. Maybe it's an example of a clash between your interpretation and what was understood as *the* meaning, or the dominant interpretation, of a text. Seen this way, moments like this become occasions to look at what is going on between your interpretation and the other one and to think about whether and how you want to bring the two readings closer together. Teacher-researcher Sheridan Blau suggests that for interpretations to be considered valid, they need to share broad, common precepts with other readings that are already accepted. In other words, valid interpretations need to share the same broad understanding of the text's meaning, and be supported by evidence from that text (75). When we talk about this where I teach, we use the metaphor of "being in the ballpark." A ballpark can be a big place (if you are a baseball fan, think of Yankee Stadium), so a reading that is way out in right field might be as valid as one in left field. If it is outside of the park, though, that is another thing entirely. At the same time, part of the goal of many readers (and many teachers) is to push the walls of the ballpark so that more interpretations reflecting more cultures are seen as valid.

In school (whether college, high school, or any other school), you sometimes will have to be able to show that you can arrive at the dominant interpretation of a reading—in other words, that you are in the ballpark. But since interpretation is shaped by experience and culture, you might not have had the same kinds of experiences or be part of the same cultures that those people whose ideas have formed the dominant interpretation have.

This might lead a teacher to discount your interpretation, to think that you just don't or can't "get" the reading, or to give you a lower grade. At the same time, *only* providing the dominant interpretation of a reading in school might mean that you are not finding readings and the work connected with them very meaningful for your own purposes. This could be a problem, too. You might just begin to go through the motions of interpretation as a sort of performance, or think that teachers are not very interested in your ideas, or see school as always about conforming to others' ideas.

Part of the goal of this book, and therefore of the reading activities outlined below, is to help you to find a way to engage with the readings from the book and achieve a balance—or to navigate the tension between—your own individual interpretation and the dominant interpretation. Ideally, by engaging with these questions, you will find that you can enter into a dialogue with the ideas in the readings and speak to the issues with authority as a reader. Hopefully, you will even push on the ballpark with your interpretations.

Reading Questions

Before you delve into the readings here, you should address three pre-reading questions:

Why are you reading this piece?

What is the assignment for which you are reading it?

What do you hope to learn as you read it?

Of course, since you are answering the questions before you read, there is no expectation that you will know anything about the reading. But you do have an assignment, and you can learn a lot about a reading from a quick glance. For what purposes might you be able to draw on this text? For what purposes do you hope to be able to do so?

You also should end each reading with two questions that ask you to consider your reading purposes, and how the reading did or did not facilitate those purposes:

> How is this reading useful or not useful for the purposes for which you intend it?

> If it is useful, what is useful about it, and what in the reading illustrates that use?

For example, if you intended to use a reading to learn about an idea, what did you learn? What in the reading helped you to learn that? If you intended to use it to think about a researcher's process (such as what they looked for during an observation or what they asked during an interview), what did you learn about that and what in the reading helped you to learn it?

As you read, find a passage, a quote, an idea, or some other element from this reading that strikes you as significant, perhaps for the essay you are thinking about writing, or perhaps for your own thinking. What is the passage, quote, idea, or other element, and why is it significant for you?

Your answers here will help you to begin making connections between the reading and your ideas about the purpose(s) for which you read it. Ideally, you can use this response as a starting point to develop those connections in your writing, entering into the kind of dialogue, with the text or about the issue, that is one of the hallmarks of engaging writing.

In addition to working with these pre- and post-reading questions for each reading, after individual readings you will find two kinds of questions that are specific to individual readings: *Critical Reflections* and *Making Connections*. *Critical Reflections* questions pose content- and process-based questions; sometimes, they also ask you to take a position with regard to your interpretation. *Making Connections* questions ask you to work with issues that a dominant reading might identify as central in two or more readings included here.

Strategic Reading

In addition to (or even instead of) using the reading questions included here, you also should think about other reading strategies that will help you to keep a record of your interpretation and develop connections between interpretations and the ideas you will develop in your writing.

Double-Entry Logs

One strategy for reading is to use a **double-entry log.** To create the log, take a piece of notebook paper and divide it into two columns. Write the name of the reading you are writing about across the top and be *sure* to write down page numbers for anything you quote. In one column, write down anything from the reading that catches your attention, seems significant, bores you silly, confuses you, or otherwise causes you to take note (or to stop taking note). On the other side, write about what led you to write it down. Here's an example:

Paolo Freire, "The Banking Concept of Education"

"Education thus becomes an act of depositing, in which the students are the depositories and the teacher issues communiqués and makes deposits which the students patiently receive, memorize, and repeat. This is the 'banking' concept of education, in which the scope of the action allowed to the students extends only as far as receiving, filing, and storing the deposits. They do, it is true, have the opportunity to become collectors of cataloguers of the things they store. But in the last analysis, it is men themselves who are filed away through the lack of creativity, transformation, and knowledge in this misguided system" (74-75).

The banking concept really rings a bell with me. I had **so** many classes like this, where we were expected to sit quietly and absorb, absorb, absorb. I remember one in particular: my 10th grade English class. We had to read *Macbeth* out loud for what seemed like a year. We didn't talk about what we were reading, though. Instead, my teacher, Ms. Krabopple,* would lecture to us about the themes of the play that we had covered in that day's reading for the last 10 minutes of class. Boring! Wow! I had to make sure I remembered everything — in Freire's words, that I "collected the information," because otherwise I wouldn't do well on the tests. In fact, because I wasn't a very good collector, I didn't do very well. This reminds me of some of what I read in Mike Rose's "I Just Wanna Be Average," too. In a lot of the classes he describes there, it seems like students were expected to just sit quietly and absorb the information. Maybe that is why some of them were sometimes disruptive. Would this model of learning lead to behavioral things? Something to think about.

*Not her real name, but this is a real experience from my 10th grade English class.

In this log entry I've reflected on how I *feel* about the reading (it resonated with me); it also gets at my interpretation of the text (how I understand the banking concept). To make these connections, I needed to interpret the reading in particular ways. That interpretation is implied here, but I start to make it more explicit when I begin thinking about how I was a collector of information. Near the end, I also try to make connections to another reading in this book where I see similar kinds of things happening. I also raise a question that I want to think about as I continue thinking about education through the reading and writing I am doing here.

Annotating the Text

Another strategy for keeping track of your interpretations, considering connections, and raising questions about readings is annotating readings as you go. This means writing comments, questions, and ideas as you read. It sounds simple, but there are lots of different kinds of comments you can make. To illustrate, below are some excerpts from David Barton and Mary Hamilton's "Literacy Practices."

You might want to *restate important ideas* in your own words:

> Our interest is in social practices in which literacy has a role; hence the basic unit of a social theory of unit is that of *literacy practices*. Literacy practices are the general cultural ways of utilizing written language which people draw upon in their lives. In the simplest sense literacy practices are what people do with literacy. However practices are not observable units of behaviour since they also involve values, attitudes, feelings and social relationships (see Street 1993, p. 12).

Literacy practices— ways of using (written) language that people draw on—what people do with literacy.

This kind of annotation makes it easier for you to go back to the reading and remember what you found to be key ideas; the act of writing out the ideas in your own words also helps you interpret the ideas for yourself.

You also might want to *note what interests you and why* in the margins:

> Looking at different literacy events it is clear that literacy is not the same in all contexts; rather, there are different *literacies*. The notion of different literacies has several senses: for example, practices which involve different media or symbolic systems, such as a film or computer, can be regarded as different literacies, as in *film literacy* or *computer literacy*. Another sense is that practices in different cultures and languages can be regarded as different literacies.

Different literacies! Can be more literate in one area—like visual literacy—but not as literate in another— computer literacy, for example. This could explain Cedric's struggles at Brown in "Fierce Intimacies"???

This kind of annotation means that you are making connections between the reading and other ideas, such as your own experiences, other readings, and so on. This also can be useful when you are looking for material to use in your own writing.

Of course, you'll want to note *questions about the reading* and, perhaps, *places where you struggled with the reading* (e.g., where you found it confusing or boring):

> Socially powerful institutions, such as education, tend to support dominant literacy practices. These dominant practices can be seen as part of whole discourse formations, institutionalized configurations of power and knowledge which are embodied in social relationships. Other vernacular literacies which exist in people's every-

What do they mean here? How is education a socially powerful institution? How does

day lives are less visible and supported. This means that *literacy practices are patterned by social institutions and power relationships, and some literacies are more dominant, visible, and influential than others.*

education—which is a BIG thing (and not even one thing, since there are loads of schools) support dominant practices? And what is a discourse formation?

Noting these spots helps you locate them when you want to return to them or when you want to ask questions about them with class colleagues or your instructor.

The key to annotating a reading is *writing in the book.* If you are thinking of preserving these pristine pages because you want to sell the book back at the end of the term, remember that it's unlikely that you will get less for a book if it's written in. On the other hand, you will be very glad as you go through the term when you have notes that make it easier for you to find reading you want to use in your writing.

Reading Images

In the same way that readers interpret words and entire texts to make meanings of them, the same happens with images. Although you might not think about it, when you look at a photograph or other graphic, you move at blazing speed through a process that helps you make that image mean something to you. Reading visual images can help you develop your ideas *for* writing in lots of ways; photographs or other visual images can also provide incredibly compelling evidence for the analysis in your writing.

In this book, several of the assignments ask you to choose photographs that resonate with you, to refer to them in your writing, and/or to use evidence from them. Implied in these requests are two ways that you can use these photographs for pre-writing and as evidence.

For Prewriting

Sometimes, looking at and thinking about your interpretation of an image can help you to get at how you understand the idea behind the image, and you will be surprised at the differences in how people interpret these pictures! For instance, a student once used the photograph entitled "Boys Read Storybooks in the Shade" in conjunction with the Category Two assignment, The Purpose of Education and Literacy. In her DW.2a, she wrote that these boys seemed to be reading for escape, to be alone with their ideas and thoughts. She then went on to write a long essay about how, as a student growing up in wartime Beirut, Lebanon, education both served as an opportunity to escape the realities of her everyday life and, later as a student in the U.S., to retreat from the struggles she had with assimilating into a new culture. Another student looked at the same picture and saw two boys being punished by being sent to read in isolation be-cause they had violated a rule or a norm. She went on to write a long essay about how education represented a form of isolation and punishment for her. In both of these cases, the photographs helped students to think through their own ideas about education and literacy. Their instructors also pressed them to think about what, in their own experiences, led them to interpret the photographs as they had. This is a helpful activity not only for thinking about interpreting pho-tographs, but *any* text.

As Evidence

Most of the time, evidence for academic writing comes from written sources. But that's not always the case, and the conventions of writing in various disciplines are constantly changing. History textbooks, for instance, include a number of photographs and other visual images to support their interpretations. Using photographs as evidence also gives you a great chance to practice writing fully about what you see, and what evidence from your source (in this case, a photo-graph) helps you see that. When you can't use words from the text to help read-ers see what you mean, you have to generate those words yourself.

The photographs included here come from two sources. Most of them come from a collection held at the Library of Congress in Washington, D.C., called "America from the Great Depression to World War II: Photographs from the FSA [Farm Security Administration]-OWI [Office of War Information], 1935–1945." The Farm Security Administration was part of President Franklin Delano Roosevelt's Works Progress Administration (WPA), a program designed to bring the American economy out of the Great Depression, in which it was mired when Roosevelt was elected in 1932. Among other things, the WPA employed thou-sands of artists—writers, photographers, poets, and others—to document the condition of Americans. The photographs included in the FSA/OWI collection come from those efforts, as hundreds of photographers travelled around the country to take pictures of Americans living in difficult conditions. As you look at these photographs, remember that they reflect the time period from which they come. For instance, you will note that the titles of two refer to "Negroes," which was then the preferred term for referring to African-Americans.

Many of the other photographs included here come from a book called *School* by Nicholas Nixon, a photographer, and Robert Coles, a psychiatrist who has long worked with children. Nixon and Coles were both interested in document-ing the experiences of students at different kinds of schools: a public school (Tobin School), an elite private, preparatory school (The Boston Latin School), and a private school for children with special needs (The Perkins School for the Blind). Still others are contemporary photos of activities and spaces connected with school-based activities like reading and writing.

ASSIGNMENTS

- "Learning from Self" Assignments

- "Learning from Others" Assignments

- "Learning Through Research" Assignments

- "Speaking Out, Joining In, Talking Back" Assignment

"LEARNING FROM SELF" ASSIGNMENTS

Before you begin to look at definitions of literacy and education in other contexts and for other people, it's important for you to consider your own ideas about literacy and education—what you know, where you learned it, what you think is important, and why. The assignments in this section ask you to consider these questions by analyzing your own literacy experiences inside and/or outside of school.

As you analyze these experiences, you will develop writing strategies that form the foundation for the other work in this text and this course, strategies that you will also use in writing situations inside and outside of school. These include reading a text to analyze it (whether that text is an experience, a reading, a photograph, or something else); helping readers understand your interpretation of a text by providing abundant detail necessary for them to "see what you mean"; analyzing evidence from text (here, your own experience); considering questions of form, structure, and voice; and, ultimately, some practice with editing.

▨ EXPECTATIONS AND EXPERIENCES

Possible readings for this assignment:

Mark Edmundson, "On the Purposes of a Liberal Education: I. As Lite Entertainment for Bored College Students"

Andrea Fishman, "Becoming Literate: A Lesson from the Amish"

Mike Rose, "I Just Wanna Be Average"

Ron Suskind, "Fierce Intimacies"

Whenever anyone encounters a new situation, we do so with a set of expectations about that situation. Often, our satisfaction with it is based on the ways that the situation meets, or does not meet, those expectations. This first assignment asks you to take up the issue of "expectations and experiences" in conjunction with your presence in college. Specifically, you should address the questions: **What were your expectations for 2–3 specific aspects of college life? How have those expectations shaped your experience of college thus far?**

When you address this question, you'll want to be very *specific* in your approach. Ground it in particular expectations that were formed by (or among) particular people and experiences. How were those expectations formed, who helped, and how did those who helped contribute? Now that you are in college, what *have* been your experiences with these aspects? Have they fulfilled your expectations? Have they not fulfilled them? How and why or why not? Finally, what is the relevance of your reflections on expectations/experiences? Have you learned new things? Discovered others? Why are your experiences important, and for whom?

When you respond to this assignment, you should primarily draw on evidence from your own expectations and experiences. You should also use evidence from at least one of the readings for this assignment to develop your response in some way.

Developing Work

DW.1a   Focus on one expectation that you are thinking of including in this essay. What was it? How was it formed? Who (and/or what experiences) contributed to this expectation, and how did it/they contribute? When you write about this person or experience, do so in as much detail as possible—remember that the readers of your essay are not familiar with your experiences, so the more detail you can provide for them the better. Try to write at least 1 1/2–2 pages. If you still have time within the hour or so you're taking for this DW also write about the experiences you have had with this aspect of college thus far. Again, try for as much detail as possible. Your instructor's comments on this work will help you to develop the details and make connections between expectation and experience.

DW.1b   Here, work with the reading that you are going to use to develop your ideas. Find a quote, a passage, an idea from that reading that strikes you as significant, and write about why it resonated with you, what it might have to do with one (or more) of the expectations or experiences you are going to write about in the essay. Be sure to include the quote or a summary of the idea from the reading, and to write very thoroughly about the connection to your ideas—readers of your work might not interpret the reading as you do, and this will help them understand it from your perspective. Remember, too, that you can use readings in many different ways: to support your ideas, to stand against your ideas, as a frame for something you have seen, and so on. As you develop your long essay, you can also work to incorporate these ideas into your paper.

▨ INFLUENCING YOUR LITERACY DEVELOPMENT

Possible readings for this assignment:

Kate Daniels, "Self-Portrait with Politics"

Frederick Douglass, from *Narrative of the Life of Frederick Douglass, An American Slave*

Andrea Fisher, "Becoming Literate: A Lesson from the Amish"

Robert Louthan, "Heavy Machinery"

Michael Ryan, "The Ditch"

Earl Shorris, "On the Uses of a Liberal Education: II. As a Weapon in the Hands of the Restless Poor"

Ron Suskind, "Fierce Intimacies"

Photographs from FSA/OWI collection

Photographs from *School*

Ideally, learning takes place both in and out of school, and the people whom we come across every day help to develop different literacies for different situations. In this assignment, you will focus on one specific person or event important for your literacy development, then represent the work in two ways.

Choose a person or event that helped you to learn something significant and describe what you learned, and how this person or event was involved in that education. The essay you write in response to this question should be very specific, rather than very general. Consider these questions to help you: Who, or what situation, helped you to develop the thing that you learned? How did the person or event influence the way you learned, and what you learned, and in what context did the influence occur? How has what you learned been important to you, in what context, and why? (Only the one where it was developed? Other ones, as well?) How do you anticipate that your learning will continue to help you in college? You will want to be very specific about this person or event—you are writing to an audience unfamiliar with you, so you will need to provide very full details. Remember, too, that the person or event that you focus on does not need to be school–connected in any way. When you respond to this assignment, you should primarily draw on evidence from your own expectations and experiences. You should also use evidence from at least one of the readings for this assignment to develop your response in some way.

After you have completed the written portion of your assignment, either find or create something that represents the person or event you have written about. For instance, you might use a photograph of a person, create a scrapbook page of an event, put together a collage or a poem, or another creative endeavor. The idea here is to think about an *alternative* representation of how the event or person helped you to develop.

Developing Work

DW.1a Focus on the person or event that helped you learn something significant, and develop one aspect of what you learned in detail. For example, if you are writing about a coach who helped you learn how to be a great soccer player, what is one aspect of your game that she helped to develop? If you are writing about a cousin who helped you learn to be a great rapper, how did he help you to develop one important aspect of that? The idea here is not to write about *all* of the literacy that this person helped you to develop, but to think about, then focus on, a particular *component* of that literacy. (To do this, you might first think about the different components of the literacy that this figure helped you to develop.) Don't worry here about spelling, punctuation, grammar, or form—you are brainstorming and developing details that you can expand, analyze closely, and otherwise work with later on.

DW.1b Work with the reading that you are going to use to develop the ideas here. Find a quote, a passage, an idea from that reading that strikes you as significant, and write about why it resonated with you, what it might have to do with the significant person you are going to write about in this essay. Be sure to include the quote or a summary of the idea from the reading, and to write very thoroughly about the connection to your ideas—readers of your work might not interpret the reading as you do, and this will help them understand it from your perspective. Remember, too, that you can use readings in many different ways: to support your ideas, to stand against your ideas, as a frame for something you have seen, and so on. As you develop your long essay, you can also work to incorporate these ideas into your paper.

▨ THE PURPOSES OF SCHOOLING

Possible readings for this assignment:

Frederick Douglass, from *The Narrative of the Life of Frederick Douglass, An American Slave*

Darcy Frey, "The Last Shot"

June Jordan, "Nobody Mean More to Me Than You and the Future Life of Willie Jordan"

Theresa McCarty, "Community and Culture"

Mike Rose, "I Just Wanna Be Average"

Ron Suskind, "Fierce Intimacies"

Theodore Sizer, "What High School Is"

Photographs from Farm Security Administration—Office of War Information collection

Photographs from *School*

In this assignment, you will begin thinking about these issues by working with two questions: **What was the purpose of your previous schooling? What do you think the purpose of school should be?**

When you address these questions, you will want to spend the bulk of your paper focusing on the material at the center of your analysis: your previous schooling. And because you want this analysis to be grounded in extremely specific, compelling evidence, you will likely want to focus on *one* part of your previous education, not the entire span (from kindergarten through college). If you are just out of high school, for instance, it might make sense to focus on that period; if you think a specific year gets at it, you could even stick to that. You will also want to make connections to at least one of the readings for this assignment.

When you write this essay, remember that the questions here focus on the purpose of *your,* specific, education, not the purpose of school for all students. Think specifically about your own, real experiences—good and bad—and create a purpose based on those. Remember, too, that you want to spend most of the essay writing about what the purpose *was,* not what it should be (though you will want to reflect on that at some point). Also, remember that among other things, writing is a tool for discovery. As you write and think, the idea is that you "discover" a purpose of school that you perhaps had not thought of before. If you do not have a purpose in mind before you begin, that might even be for the better—rather than working from an idea you already have, try writing down experiences from school (good and bad) that really stick out for you, and work to form an overarching purpose from there. (Your instructor can help.)

Developing Work

DW.1a   If you have arrived at a possible purpose, help your readers to understand one experience, event, or individual that embodies or in some way stands for what you see as the purpose of school as you are thinking about it thus far. Remember that while the experience, event, or individual you are writing about might be familiar to you, your readers won't know about it or them, so be sure to provide the kind of detail necessary for readers to really *know* your subject as you do. At the end of your Developing Work, help readers understand connections between what you have written about and the possible purpose you are working with. How does this person, event, or experience represent your purpose? If you have not yet arrived at a specific purpose, use this essay as an opportunity to work through an experience, event, or individual who strikes you as particularly significant, and write as fully as possible, keeping in mind all of the same ideas about your readers as above. Then, at the end of your Developing Work, brainstorm some possible connections to a purpose. What did this person, event, or experience have to do with an idea about what school is about? How did the person or event contribute to some pattern in school? Even if you cannot settle on a single idea, put down some thoughts about this for your readers to respond to.

DW.1b   Work with the readings and, if appropriate, photographs that resonate with you for this assignment. Find a quote, a passage, or an idea from that reading that strikes you as significant, and write here about why it resonated with you and what it might have to do with the purpose of school that you are going to write about in the essay. Be sure to include the quote or a summary of the idea from the reading, and to write very thoroughly about the connection to your ideas—readers of your work might not interpret the reading as you do, and this will help them understand it from your perspective. Remember, too, that you can use readings in many different ways: to support your ideas, to stand against your ideas, as a frame for something you have seen, and so on. As you develop your long essay, you can also work to incorporate these ideas into your paper.

▨▨▨ WHY ARE YOU HERE?

Possible readings for this assignment:

Kate Daniels, "Self-Portrait with Politics"

Mark Edmundson, "On the Uses of a Liberal Education: I. As Lite Entertainment for Bored College Students"

Andrea Fishman, "Becoming Literate: A Lesson from the Amish"

Robert Louthan, "Heavy Machinery"

Michael Moffatt, "What College is REALLY Like"

Mike Rose, "I Just Wanna Be Average"

Michael Ryan, "The Ditch"

Ron Suskind, "Fierce Intimacies"

Photographs from FSA-OWI collection

Photographs from *School*

Since you are in this class, it's clear that you have made a decision to be here, in college. In this essay, address the question: **Why are you here?** What do you mean by that "why," and how did you develop it? Who helped, in what situations, and how? When you respond to this question, be sure to press yourself—if your first response is, "I'm here because I want to earn a good living," ask yourself, "What does that mean? And how did I develop the definition of 'a good living' that I hold?"

In your response to this essay, you will need to include abundant evidence from your own experiences, since your "why" is clearly based in them. You will want to be as specific as possible, too—if people or experiences influenced your "why," name them! Who was that twelfth grade English teacher? What was the experience in that dreadful chemistry class, and how did that influence your "why"? How did that summer working in the restaurant affect your decision? You also should draw on evidence from at least one of the readings for this assignment to develop your ideas in the essay.

Developing Work

DW.1a Here, focus on one significant person or event that significantly influenced your "why." Who or what was it, what happened, and why was it important? When you write this DW assignment, remember that your readers don't know you, so you will need to provide lots of detail for them to understand how the person or event influenced your decision.

DW.1b In this DW assignment, work with the reading that you're going to use to develop the ideas here. Find a quote, a passage, an idea from that reading that strikes you as significant, and write about why it resonated with you, what it might have to do with one (or more) of the reasons you are going to write about in the essay. Be sure to include the quote or a summary of the idea from the reading, and to write very thoroughly about the connection to your ideas—readers of your work might not interpret the reading as you do, and this will help them understand it from your perspective. Remember, too, that you can use readings in many different ways: to support your ideas, to stand against your ideas, as a frame for something you have seen, and so on. As you develop your long essay, you can also work to incorporate these ideas into your paper.

"YOUR" CAMPUS

Possible readings for this assignment:

Mark Edmundson, "On the Uses of a Liberal Education: I. As Lite Entertainment for Bored College Students"

Michael Moffatt, "What College is REALLY Like"

Ron Suskind, "Fierce Intimacies"

As part of Michael Moffatt's efforts to understand how his ethnographic subjects (his students) understood the Rutgers University campus, Moffatt had them make maps of the campus. In this assignment, you will begin with the same idea, then move on to analyze what you have done. Ultimately, your essay should address the question: **What does your campus map say about what is valued on your campus? What kinds of education does the map suggest are more and less important to you (or to the campus designers) on this campus?**

The first step here is to make a map of your campus. The idea here is not to make an objective map that would be useful for others to navigate the buildings, but to make a *personal* map that helps others to understand how *you* understand this site. What is "big" in your campus experience? Perhaps you want to make that place large on your map. What is remote? Should that be very distant from the other places on campus? The idea here, as in the maps included in the chapter entitled "What College is REALLY Like," is to create a visual representation of how you understand this place.

After you have finished, analyze the work you have done and use ideas from at least one of the readings for this assignment to develop your own ideas. What is important, and why is it? What is not, and why isn't it?

Developing Work

DW.1a Write about a typical day in your life on campus, focusing specifically on where you go and why you go there. You will want to be sure and go beyond simple explanations here (e.g., "I go to the student union to get lunch because that's where the Wendy's is.") and think hard about why you go there, and how this place is part of your education. For example, you might write, "I go to the student union to get lunch because Wendy's is there. I like eating Wendy's food because I've always done it, and it makes this place seem a little less foreign and more familiar. Right now, seeming not-so-different is an important part of my education—everything here is pretty strange." Don't worry here about spelling, punctuation, grammar, or form—you are brainstorming and developing details that you can expand, analyze closely, and otherwise work with later on.

DW.1b   Work with the reading that you are going to use to develop the ideas here. Find a quote, a passage, or an idea from that reading that strikes you as significant, and write about why it resonated with you, and what it might have to do with the kinds of education that are more or less important to you. Be sure to include the quote or a summary of the idea from the reading, and to write very thoroughly about the connection to your ideas—readers of your work might not interpret the reading as you do, and this will help them understand it from your perspective. Remember, too, that you can use readings in many different ways: to support your ideas, to stand against your ideas, as a frame for something you have seen, and so on. As you develop your long essay, you can also work to incorporate these ideas into your paper.

▨ YOUR LITERACY HISTORY AND ITS SIGNIFICANCE

Possible readings for this assignment:

David Barton and Mary Hamilton, "Literacy Practices"

David Barton and Mary Hamilton, "How They've Fared in Education"

Kate Daniels, "Self-Portrait with Politics"

Andrea Fishman, "Becoming Literate: A Lesson from the Amish"

Darcy Frey, "The Last Shot"

Robert Louthan, "Heavy Machinery"

Mike Rose, "I Just Wanna Be Average"

Michael Ryan, "The Ditch"

When you approach any literacy situation—like a required writing class, for instance—you bring with you an enormously rich history formed by experiences with writing and reading. Some of this might have taken place, or even been developed, in school. But chances are that a lot of it took place outside of school in writing and reading that you did on your own time. That work may or may not have been connected with the work that you did in school and the work you did in school may or may not have found its way into those outside of school activities.

In this assignment, you will reflect on your reading and writing (in and out of school) up to this point and ultimately address the question: **What kinds of reading and writing (in and out of school) have been or will be particularly useful for college, and how do you think they have been or will be helpful?**

To address this question, you will need to carefully consider and define some key ideas here. First, you will need to consider the kinds of writing and reading that you have done inside and outside of school. Think about this broadly— "writing" doesn't just mean writing papers (it could include everything from writing poetry to writing graffiti to writing e-mail or instant messages); "reading" doesn't just mean reading school-related books (it could include romance novels, mysteries, comic books, magazines, web sites, e-mails, or instant messages), or even reading books at all. (You also read people, clothing, television shows—any situation where you have to interpret something and make it mean something to you.) Second, you will need to consider what kinds of reading and writing strategies you developed by engaging in this writing and reading. Then, you will need to think about what kinds of reading and writing strategies you think will be or have been required in college thus far. Again, think broadly here: you do not just read and write in classes. Have you "read" social situations, thinking about how to fit in (or not fit in) to them? Have you written letters or e-mails to family or friends about your college experience, wanting to represent it a particular way? Have you written notes to an instructor explaining something about the class or an assignment?

Of course, once you realize just how many occasions for reading and writing you have had and encountered, you will also realize you will not be able to fit them all into this essay. Thus, you will need to focus on a few, perhaps 2–3, that seem particularly significant. You will want to use abundant evidence about the writing and reading strategies you developed, how you developed them (Who helped? Where were they developed? Why?), and how you have drawn or will draw on them in college (In what situation, specifically? How? How will they be useful or not useful?). You will also want to draw on at least one of the readings for this assignment to develop your ideas.

Developing Work

DW.1a   Use this DW assignment to focus on one reading or writing activity that you think was particularly useful for you. What was it? What kinds of strategies did it help you develop? Write about this activity in as much detail as possible. Who was involved? What did they do? What was the situation? How were the strategies that you developed useful in that situation? How do you think they will be useful for you in college? Push yourself for the fullest detail you can here. Remember, you are writing to an audience that does not know you or your ideas, so you will need to be as thorough as possible!

DW.1b   Work with the reading that you are going to use to develop the ideas here. Find a quote, a passage, or an idea from that reading that strikes you as significant, and write about why it resonated with you and how it helps to clarify your ideas about literacy development. Be sure to include the quote or a summary of the idea from the reading, and to write very thoroughly about the connection to your ideas—readers of your work might not interpret the reading as you do, and this will help them understand it from your perspective. Remember, too, that you can use readings in many different ways: to support your ideas, to stand against your ideas, as a frame for something you have seen, and so on. As you develop your long essay, you can also work to incorporate these ideas into your paper.

▨▨ YOUR LITERACY DEVELOPMENT

Possible readings for this assignment:

David Barton and Mary Hamilton, "Literacy Practices"

David Barton and Mary Hamilton, "How They've Fared in Education"

Kate Daniels, "Self-Portrait with Politics"

Darcy Frey, "The Last Shot"

Robert Louthan, "Heavy Machinery"

Theresa McCarthy, "Community and Culture"

Michael Ryan, "The Ditch"

Ron Suskind, "Fierce Intimacies"

Booker T. Washington, "The Atlanta Exposition Address"

As many of the readings included here demonstrate, "literacy" is a term that is closely linked to particular places and activities. Before looking at what kinds of literacies exist in other places, this assignment asks you to consider your own literacies, where they come from, where you used them, and why they are important for you in those places.

Ultimately, when you finish this assignment, you should have a paper that addresses the question: **What are your most important literacies?** Where and how did you develop them? Who helped you develop them, what does it take to maintain them, and why are they important for you? You will need to use abundant evidence from your own experiences here; you also should use evidence from at least one reading for this assignment to develop your ideas and analysis.

To respond to this question, you will need to begin by identifying what you consider to be your most important literacies. Then, you will need to consider where and how you developed them, who helped you, what it takes to maintain them, and why they are important.

As you write, remember that although the literacies, places, people, and reasons you are writing about here are familiar to you, your readers will not be familiar with them. Be sure to include the kind of specific details that will help these things seem real and alive to readers. Also, remember that even though you are responding to a list of questions, you do not want your submission draft to read like a list. After you have got a pretty full draft responding to these questions, you will need to consider how to make this reflection engaging for readers.

Developing Work

DW.1a   Focus on one of the most important literacies that you will include in this essay. What is it, how and where did you develop it, and who helped? When you do this DW, remember that you should focus on getting down to as much about the questions as you can in about an hour. Don't worry about spelling, punctuation, grammar, or form—you are brainstorming and developing details that you can expand, analyze closely, and otherwise work with later on.

DW.1b   Work with the reading that you are going to use to develop the ideas here. Find a quote, a passage, or an idea from that reading that strikes you as significant, and write about why it resonated with you, what it might have to do with one (or more) of the expectations or experiences you are going to write about in the essay. Be sure to include the quote or a summary of the idea from the reading, and to write very thoroughly about the connection to your ideas— readers of your work might not interpret the reading as you do, and this will help them understand it from your perspective. Remember, too, that you can use readings in many different ways: to support your ideas, to stand against your ideas, as a frame for something you have seen, and so on. As you develop your long essay, you can also work to incorporate these ideas into your paper.

"LEARNING FROM OTHERS" ASSIGNMENTS

"Learning from Self" assignments asked you to begin thinking through your own definitions of education and literacy primarily by analyzing your own experiences. Here, you will read about the education and literacy experience of others described in the readings in this book and begin to think critically about those. As you do so, you will move to analyze *written* text—the readings. You will read both to develop and support your own interpretation and to ensure that you at least understand the dominant interpretation of a text (for more on this see "Introduction to Reading Questions" on page 9–10). You will consider how best to use the readings to develop your own thinking. As you incorporate your interpretation of these readings into your own work, you will also work on strategies useful for weaving together others' ideas and your own: developing transitions, summarizing, paraphrasing, and citing evidence. Depending on how you use those sources, you also may work on comparing and contrasting different elements of text and continue to practice with issues related to form, voice, and editing.

▨▨▨ WHAT IS THE PURPOSE OF EDUCATION AND LITERACY?

Possible readings for this assignment: listed at the end of each "Purpose" option.

Now that you have formed a foundation to think about your schooling, you can build on that foundation by thinking about what you see as your *individual* purpose for all of this. **Ultimately, in this assignment you will write about what you see as the purpose of education and literacy**—however, you will do that only *after* you work through a series of reading and writing activities that help you to narrow the scope of that purpose so that it is specific to your ideas and your experiences.

First, look at the photographs on pages 359–370. Choose 2–3 that you like— that strike you as interesting, relevant, or meaningful in some way. Then do some writing for yourself, or possibly as a class assignment, reflecting on *why* these are meaningful. Once you have done that, look at the descriptions of "Purposes of Literacy" listed below, which are borrowed and adapted from a reading by Sylvia Scribner called "Three Metaphors for Literacy." Choose the one that you *most* agree with. You do not have to agree with every element of it, but choose one that best reflects what you think literacy and education are about. After each purpose, you will see a list of 2–3 readings below. Do the readings that are connected to your purpose.

Once you have chosen your photo and done the readings, you should have a very specific purpose that education and literacy serve *for you*. When you write about this purpose, be sure to incorporate evidence from the photos you have chosen and from at least one of the readings included in your category. Again, be creative about how you do this. Since you have chosen this material, there should be connections there for you.

Purpose 1: Literacy and education as adaptation
The purpose of school is to help people learn how to fit and function well in the everyday world—that is, the dominant culture of the place where they live. Literacy is important because it helps people to participate in the daily life of this (dominant) culture. What people should learn in school is how to master the tasks of daily life in this culture, whether those tasks are associated with the daily life, like computer literacy, basic reading and writing, and basic numeracy (math skills), or how to weave rugs and tend sheep. The degree to which people learn these things should also depend on what they want to do with their lives. If they want to work in jobs that do not require a lot of school–based knowledge, they should not have to learn things that are not important for them. On the other hand, if they decide they do want to do things that require this knowledge, the opportunity to develop it should be available to them. It all depends on what the individual person wants to do.

> **Readings:**
> Lorene Cary, from *Black Ice*
> Andrea Fishman, "Becoming Literate: A Lesson from the Amish"
> Nicholas Lemann, "The President's Big Test"
> Robert Louthan, "Heavy Machinery"
> Theresa McCarty, "Community and Classroom"
> Theodore Sizer, "What High School Is"
> Booker T. Washington, "The Atlanta Exposition Address"
> Photographs from FSA-OWI collection
> Photographs from *School*

Purpose 2: Literacy and education as a state of grace
Education and schooling are not really about developing specific sets of literacy skills. Instead, they are about developing the ability to think, to approach new situations, and to exercise the mind in meaningful ways. There is always a link between these kinds of "mind exercises" and specific actions in everyday life because those actions stem from, and are related to, the ideas that one is exposed to in one's education. Therefore, literacy is not really about the ability to do particular things, but is instead about the ability to think creatively, solve problems in interesting ways, and face new situations knowing that one has the mental faculties to deal with them appropriately.

> **Readings:**
> Frederick Douglass, from *Narrative of the Life of Frederick Douglass, An American Slave*
> Stanley Kaplan, "My 54-Year Love Affair with the SAT"
> Earl Shorris, "On the Purposes of a Liberal Education: II. As a Weapon in the Hands of the Restless Poor"

Photographs from FSA-OWI collection

Photographs from *School*

Purpose 3: Literacy and education as separation

Education and literacy are valuable, but they are also problematic. As individuals become more educated, they develop skills and ideas that mark them as somehow different from the people around them, like their co-workers, and even their families. Literacy and education can even lead people to become alienated or estranged from the people with whom they grew up, or the people with whom they live. For this reason, education seems particularly complex. The benefits that it provides are important, but it also brings with it potentially unanticipated challenges.

Readings:

Lorene Cary, from *Black Ice*

Kate Daniels, "Self-Portrait with Politics"

June Jordan, "Nobody Mean More to Me Than You and the Future Life of Willie Jordan"

Mike Rose, "I Just Wanna Be Average"

Ron Suskind, "Fierce Intimacies"

Photographs from FSA-OWI collection

Photographs from *School*

Purpose 4: Literacy and education as power

Literacy and education are all about gaining power. When people are educated they are more powerful and they can use this power to help themselves and people or communities with whom they are associated. Education is important because it helps to redistribute power among people, as well.

Readings:

Lorene Cary, from *Black Ice*

Frederick Douglass, from *Narrative of the Life of Frederick Douglass, An American Slave*

Stanley Kaplan, "My 54-Year Love Affair With the SAT"

Theresa McCarty, "Community and Classroom"

Earl Shorris, "On the Purposes of a Liberal Education: II. As a Weapon in the Hands of the Restless Poor"

Photographs from FSA-OWI collection

Photographs from *School*

Purpose 5: Literacy and education as indoctrination

Education and literacy, as defined in schools, reflect the values of a particular culture. In order to be defined as successful in school, students must make these values their own and/or demonstrate that they have assimilated the values successfully. Thus, being considered "educated" primarily shows that students have successfully conformed to an existing, dominant culture, whether or not these values reflect their own.

Readings:
Lorene Cary, from *Black Ice*

Andrea Fishman, "Becoming Literate: A Lesson from the Amish"

Nicholas Lemann, "The President's Big Test"

Theodore Sizer, "What High School Is"

Ron Suskind, "Fierce Intimacies"

Photographs from FSA-OWI collection

Photographs from *School*

Purpose 6: Develop your own purpose and readings

Perhaps none of the purposes above reflect what you have taken away from your analysis of the photographs included here. In this case, come up with your own purpose, and your instructor will help you to locate readings that will help you develop that purpose.

Developing Work

DW.2a   Focus on the photographs you have chosen for this assignment. What is going on in them? What draws you to them? As in Long Essay One, remember that one of the most important parts of your writing will be to help readers see what you do in the photograph you have chosen, since that seeing comes from your experiences and your readers have not *had* those. Thus, you will need to describe the photographs thoroughly. This is doubly true when it comes to using evidence from text, and triply so when you use evidence from visual sources (because the assumption is that pictures are pictures, and we all see them the same way). But remember: the same holds true here. "There's a guy sitting on a couch in an alleyway reading a book," means nothing. Instead, something like this helps readers see what you do:

> In the photo there is an African-American man sitting on a couch in what appears to be an alleyway. The man is tall, so his frame is awkwardly folded onto the couch—he seems to be leaning to the left just to get his body to fit against the back of the couch. In his right hand, he holds a book which he is staring at intently, seemingly reading carefully. Behind the couch is a door, and surrounding the door are gray walls. To the right of the couch is a set of garbage cans.

If you have already worked with a tentative purpose for education and literacy, end by helping readers understand the connection between the photos and that tentative purpose. If you have not, don't worry about it yet.

DW.2b   Since your work with the photos led you to a decision about purposes for education and literacy, here you want to work with ideas from at least one of the readings included in your category. First, summarize something that strikes you from one of those readings—as in your "Learning from Self" DW work, write about something that you strongly concur with, or something with which you adamantly disagree. Then, write about the connection between the piece of the reading you have written about and your idea about the purpose of education and literacy, perhaps taken from the definitional statements you read to make the choice that you did. When you refer to anything from the reading (whether it is an exact quote, a summary, or a paraphrase), **be sure** to include the page number(s) where the material appears. This will make it MUCH easier for you to include the material, correctly cited, in your long essay and will save you time because you will not need to go back through the readings and locate it again.

▄▄▄ LITERACY PRACTICES AND SCHOOLING

Possible readings for this assignment:

David Barton and Mary Hamilton, "Literacy Practices"

Lorene Cary, from *Black Ice*

Andrea Fishman, "Becoming Literate: A Lesson from the Amish"

Darcy Frey, "The Last Shot"

June Jordan, "Nobody Mean More to Me Than You and the Future Life of Willie Jordan"

Ron Suskind, "Fierce Intimacies"

Mike Rose, "I Just Wanna Be Average"

James Traub, "The Test Mess"

Photographs from *School*

In "Literacy Practices," David Barton and Mary Hamilton suggest that different literacy practices are valued in different contexts. In this assignment, you will work with their idea by analyzing the experiences of one of the main characters included in readings by Fishman, Frey, Jordan, Suskind, Cary, or Rose, and by analyzing your own experiences. Ultimately, in your analysis of the experiences of one of the characters and of your own experiences, you should address the following questions: **How did the subject of the reading you chose learn which practices were associated with school, and which were not? How did you learn to distinguish between school- and non-school literacy practices? Based on your analysis, do you have recommendations for boundaries between in- and out-of-school literacy practices?**

To begin working on this assignment, you will need to choose a reading on which to focus. "Fierce Intimacies," "I Just Wanna Be Average," "Literacy Among the Amish," "The Last Shot," "Nobody Mean More to Me Than You and the Future Life of Willie Jordan," and "Black Ice" all focus on this issue in some ways, for instance. Ultimately, you will want to choose one reading to work with, and then analyze it closely. You will need to use abundant evidence from the reading to support your analysis of how the subject of the reading defined in- and out-of-school literacy practices.

You will also need to focus on your own literacy practices, and it might be easier to develop a sense of this term by starting with what is more familiar—you—and then moving to readings. Consider your own definition of right and wrong inside of school and out. What practices are right or wrong in what situation?

Finally, when you have finished your analysis of both readings and experiences, you should consider its relevance. Based on it, do you think more or less should be included in appropriate school literacy practices? Why?

Developing Work

DW.2a To begin thinking through this question, focus on your own literacy practices. What do you define as in-school and out-of-school practices, and why? Where did you learn that these practices were appropriate for the locations they were? As with earlier DW assignments, try to get as much detail as possible about these questions down on paper.

DW.2b This time, focus on the reading that you will use for this assignment. What literacy practices are defined as appropriate for in- and out-of-school for the main subjects there? Based on what is included in the chapter, how do you think the character you are focusing on learned that these practices were appropriate for their locations? When you do this DW either include as many examples from the reading as possible, or write (for your own reference) brief summaries of the examples that you can develop in the long essay. Also, remember to include page numbers! It will save you time because you will not have to search through the reading to find something that you remember but can't quite locate. You also will want to make notes in the margin of your book next to the examples you are going to use about how they illustrate what you say they do—this way, you will have a record of your thinking.

▨ TESTING DEFINITIONS: DOMINANT AND VERNACULAR LITERACIES

Possible readings for this assignment:

David Barton and Mary Hamilton, "Literacy Practices"

Lorene Cary, from *Black Ice*

Frederick Douglass, from *Narrative of the Life of Frederick Douglass, An American Slave*

Darcy Frey, "The Last Shot"

June Jordan, "Nobody Mean More to Me Than You and the Future Life of Willie Jordan"

Theresa McCarty, "Community and Culture"

Ron Suskind, "Fierce Intimacies"

Booker T. Washington, "The Atlanta Exposition Address"

In "Literacy Practices," David Barton and Mary Hamilton define two primary categories for literacy practices: dominant and vernacular. In this assignment, you'll use these definitions for two purposes. First, apply them to a reading in this text that you think deals with peoples' literacy practices, such as "The Last Shot," "Fierce Intimacies," Chapter VII of *The Narrative of the Life of Frederick Douglass*, "I Just Wanna Be Average," "Literacy Among the Amish," "Nobody Mean More to Me Than You and the Future Life of Willie Jordan," or another reading. Using Barton and Hamilton's definition, what practices would you identify as dominant, which as vernacular, and why?

Next, take your show on the road. Choose a place where you spend a lot of time—your workplace, your neighborhood, your dorm, or somewhere else— and think about the literacy practices there. Which are dominant, which are vernacular, and why?

Finally, use your analysis of the reading and the site you selected to reflect back on Barton and Hamilton's definitions to address the following questions: **Based on your identification of dominant and vernacular literacy practices, do you think that Barton and Hamilton's definitions of these terms are valid? If you do, what in your analysis supports their definition? If you do not, how do you think that their definitions should be changed, and why is it important that they are?**

Developing Work

DW.2a   One of the keys to writing this essay is using the ideas of dominant and vernacular literacies in a way that reflects Barton and Hamilton's ideas, but makes sense to you. Write your own definitions of these terms and provide as many examples (from the reading you chose or your own experiences) as time allows to illustrate what you mean when you use them.

DW.2b   This time, focus on the reading that you are going to use for this assignment. What illustrations of dominant and vernacular literacies do you find there? When you do this DW, either include as many examples from the reading as possible, or write (for your own reference) brief summaries of the examples that you can develop in the long essay. Also, remember to include page numbers! It will save you time because you will not have to search through the reading to find something that you remember, but cannot quite locate. You also will want to make notes in the margin of your book next to the examples you are going to use about how they illustrate what you say they do—this way, you will have a record of your thinking.

WHAT COUNTS AS "LEARNING," AND FOR WHOM?

Possible readings for this assignment:

bell hooks, "Engaged Pedagogy"

Lorene Cary, from *Black Ice*

"Wendy Darling," "What 'No Child Left Behind' Left Behind"

Frederick Douglass, from *Narrative of the Life of Frederick Douglass,
    An American Slave*

Andrea Fishman, "Becoming Literate: A Lesson from the Amish"

Darcy Frey, "The Last Shot"

Theresa McCarty, "Community and Culture"

No Child Left Behind Act

Mike Rose, "I Just Wanna Be Average"

Ron Suskind, "Fierce Intimacies"

Earl Shorris, "On the Uses of a Liberal Education: II. As a Weapon in the
    Hands of the Restless Poor"

The question of what counts as learning can be quite controversial. In this assignment, you will take up two questions: **What counts as learning, for whom, and why? How is what counts for one of the authors relevant for your own definition of what counts, and how is it not relevant?**

To begin your work with these questions, you will need to focus on 1–2 readings. If you choose something like "The Last Shot," "Fierce Intimacies, "I Just Wanna Be Average," "On the Uses of a Liberal Education II," "Literacy Among the Amish," or other readings that represent the experiences of a person or group, consider focusing on the perspectives of 1–2 characters from the reading. If you choose something like "Engaged Pedagogy," the No Child Left Behind Act, "What 'No Child Left Behind' Left Behind," or other readings that make an argument *for* a particular position on what should count as learning, focus on the author's perspective.

In your analysis of the reading, focus on what counts as learning, for whom, and why. This is a broad question, so you might want to begin thinking through it by recording (in a list or other form), for yourself, what you think the characters in the readings learn. In "The Last Shot," for instance, you might consider what the players learn about race, class, bureaucracy, stereotyping, or other things; then think about why this counts as learning for them.

Next, compare what counts as learning (and for whom) in the reading you have chosen to compare to your own experiences. What has counted for learning, and why, in 1–2 significant incidents in your life? When are the consequences of what has counted as learning (for you and for others for whom this definition of learning is relevant)? In your response, remember that you will need to use abundant evidence from the reading you have chosen to help readers understand what you think counts as learning, and for whom. You will also need to use detailed evidence from your own experiences to help readers understand that as well.

Developing Work

DW.2a   Focus here on the reading that you are going to use for this assignment. Working from your recollections, as well as from notes from reading questions and/or your double–entry log, what do 1–2 characters from the reading learn, and why does it count as learning? In this DW assignment, spend about an hour writing down as much as possible about these questions. If you do not have time to write out the evidence from the reading that helps you know that "this is what the characters learn, and this is why it counts," be *sure* to at least write down summaries (for yourself) of the examples you want to use, and *note the page numbers!* This will save you time, as you will not have to go re-paging through the reading to find an example you have already located once. You might also want to write how this example works for this essay in the margin of your book, so that you do not have to go back through your thinking process.

DW.2b   Focus on 1–2 significant experiences from your own life where you have developed a firm sense of what counts as learning and for whom. What were the events, what counted as learning, and why did it count? As in DW.2a, be sure to use (or, at least to summarize for later development) examples that will help readers understand how and why the events you write about counted as learning, and for whom.

▨▨▨ HOW IS LITERACY AND EDUCATION DEFINED BY YOU AND BY OTHERS?

Possible readings for this assignment:

bell hooks, "Engaged Pedagogy"

W.E.B. DuBois, "On Mr. Booker T. Washington and Others"

Kate Daniels, "Self-Portrait with Politics"

Frederick Douglass, from *Narrative of the Life of Frederick Douglass, An American Slave*

Mark Edmundson, "On the Uses of a Liberal Education: I. As Lite Entertainment for Bored College Students"

Andrea Fisher, "Becoming Literate: A Lesson from the Amish"

Theresa McCarty, "Community and Culture"

Mike Rose, "I Just Wanna Be Average"

Earl Shorris, "On the Uses of a Liberal Education: II. As a Weapon in the Hands of the Restless Poor"

Nicholas Lemann, "The President's Big Test"
Michael Ryan, "The Ditch"
Booker T. Washington, "The Atlanta Exposition Address"

In this assignment, you will analyze how education has been defined by others and consider the relevance of their definitions to your own. There are several parts to this assignment. First, choose 2–4 readings (in consultation with your instructor) and carefully read and take notes to address the questions: How is education defined in these readings? Where does "education" take place in the readings you've selected? Does education take place only in school? Outside as well? Who is involved in education in the readings you have selected? Is it only teachers? Teachers and student together? What are the roles of people involved in education for these sources and for you? Is it the job of teachers to stand and lecture, and students to sit and listen? Something else? In essence, you will want to consider the features that you (or you and your class) feel are relevant for thinking about and defining education. Summarizing each author's stance in your essay will be important—you will need to draw on abundant evidence from each reading because that will give you the material you need to write about in your reaction.

Next, respond to what you have learned. Develop at least one point from the definitions that you have summarized that strikes you as particularly important. You could think it was important because you really agree with it, or because you really disagree, or because it led you to think of something related to education that you had not thought about before, or for some other reason—it's up to you.

As a possible third step (depending on whether you or your instructor wants to continue), take your show on the road. Interview at least one other person (a fellow student, someone from your neighborhood or from your workplace, your roommate, etc.) who you think would also be affected by the point that you have pulled from these other definitions. Does this person also agree or disagree with the point you have? What is his or her take on it?

The paper you write in response to this assignment should reflect all of the work you have done with it. Certainly, it should include your extensive analysis of definitions of education in the 2–4 readings you have chosen; it should also include your response to at least one of the points you have chosen. If you interview someone about this point, it should include evidence from the interview, as well. The shape of this paper is up to you and your instructor. You could write a thesis-driven essay that begins with the points you have developed and uses evidence from the readings to support your thesis. You could write a paper comparing and contrasting the different perspectives on education. You could write an exploratory essay that opens up questions about different definitions of education and possibilities for it. Talk with your instructor about how you might want to shape your work.

Developing Work

DW.2a   To practice with the kind of summary you will need to do here, work with one of the readings you will use for the long essay. How does the author define education? What does he consider to be involved in education? How does she define the roles of people involved? How does the author believe education happens? What else seems relevant? In this DW, you will want to include as much detail from the reading as possible. When you refer to anything from the reading (whether it is an exact quote, a summary, or a paraphrase), **be sure** to include the page number where the material appears. This will make it much easier for you to include the material, correctly cited, in your long essay and will save you time because you will not need to go back through the readings and locate it again. Remember, too, that the material you generate here can serve as a model for the summarization work you do with other authors included in this essay.

DW.2b   Now that you have summarized one of the authors' ideas, it is time to develop your own. What is at least one point that you want to make based on your reading, for whom is this point relevant, and why is it relevant to them? Develop your own ideas (based on the reading) in as much detail as possible. Be sure, too, to explain how your ideas are based on or stem from at least one of the readings for this assignment—it will be important to make that connection clear for readers.

COMMUNITY LITERACIES

Possible readings for this assignment:

David Barton and Mary Hamilton, "Literacy Practices"

Kate Daniels, "Self-Portrait with Politics"

Frederick Douglass, from *Narrative of the Life of Frederick Douglass, An American Slave*

Andrea Fishman, "Becoming Literate: A Lesson from the Amish"

Darcy Frey, "The Last Shot"

June Jordan, "Nobody Mean More to Me Than You and the Future Life of Willie Jordan"

Theresa McCarty, "Community and Culture"

Michael Ryan, "The Ditch"

Theodore Sizer, "What High School Is"

Photographs from FSA-OWI collection

Photographs from *School*

For this assignment, you will need to choose a location that you think requires people to demonstrate that they *belong* in the location in certain ways—through their behavior, dress, speech, or other actions. These ways of behaving, acting, speaking, and so on, can all be considered part of the literacy required to fit in to this place, in other words, the knowledge required to show that people participate in this place.

To collect evidence for this assignment, you will spend 5–6 hours observing and collecting evidence in the location you have selected. The data you collect will help you formulate a response to the question: **What kinds of literacies are required to fit in in this situation, and how do people demonstrate them?** When you consider your response to this question, you will also need to incorporate relevant evidence from at least one reading for this assignment, though how you will do that depends on what you find, which reading you choose, and how you interpret that reading.

The first step here is to choose a location. You will want a spot where people gather, perhaps in a group, on a regular basis. For instance, people attend religious institutions regularly; they also attend leagues (from bowling to softball and everything in between) on a regular basis. How do you (and the people there) know who belongs and who does not? Are there particular clothes people wear? Ways they behave? Things they say? Next, you will need to develop a formal system for taking notes during your observations, so that you have evidence on which to draw for your analysis and for your essay. (Remember that the majority of the evidence supporting your analysis of "what kinds of literacies are required to fit in here" will come from the notes that you take.) For these observations, you will need to adopt the stance of a researcher: your role will be to spend time watching what kinds of literacies are evident in this community. Consider using a double-entry journal for this, described on page 11. At the same time as you conduct these observations, you will also need to work with the readings associated with this assignment in class. As you read, be sure to note ideas, passages, sections, quotes, and so on, that strike you as significant within the scope of your analysis—perhaps something that strikes you as similar or very different, perhaps another researcher who has noted similar patterns, or perhaps a definition from one of the readings that helps you to frame your own understanding of one of the key ideas in your analysis (or in this assignment). Any of these would make great connections between others' analyses and your own.

Developing Work

DW.2a   After you've spent three or so hours observing in your chosen site, use this DW assignment to think through the evidence you have collected thus far. What kinds of literacies have people needed (and/or used) to fit in here? As you write, be sure to include as much detail from your observations as you can—that will help readers to understand what you are seeing thus far, and will help you record examples that you can develop more fully in the long essay.

DW.2b   This time, focus on the reading that you will use to develop this assignment. Choose a portion of the reading, or readings, that you will use with this assignment. Start by writing down the quote, section, or passage that seems significant to you in some way. Be sure to cite your work with a page number—it is important in academic writing, and it will also save you the trouble of having to go back through the reading and find the section again later when you want to develop your work further. When you do this DW, either include as many examples from the reading as possible, or write (for your own reference) brief summaries of the examples that you can develop in the long essay. You also will want to make notes in the margin of your book next to the examples you are going to use about how they illustrate what you say they do—this way, you will have a record of your thinking.

"LEARNING THROUGH RESEARCH" ASSIGNMENTS

Now that you have thought about your own literacy and education experiences and those of others in written text, it's time to begin considering the relevance and applicability of others' ideas in your own research. Research doesn't always mean burying your head in the library—you engage in research every day. When you observe something to figure it out, you are researching. When you interview someone, to learn more about what they know, to find out how to do something, or to hear about their experiences, you are researching. When you check out which computer has the most memory or which on-line site has the best chat room, you are researching. Doing research means gathering information about something and reflecting on what you have gathered, ideally in a systematic way, to learn more about that topic. We all do this pretty frequently.

In this set of assignments, you will choose a focus for research and then use at least one of the readings included here to construct a frame to analyze the evidence you collect. Framing research might sound odd initially, but it's an easy concept. Imagine I have a picture of myself on vacation, say, at a beach. To me, this picture tells a story, like "I went to the beach, read lots of fantastic novels, relaxed, and had a lovely time." The frame for the photo is my description, "a lovely and relaxing time"; the photo is my illustration of that time.

But maybe someone else (who doesn't know me) puts a different frame on the photo. When they see it they say, "Hmmm. . . a lazy and uninspired person lounging around when she should be doing something better." That person's analysis—her frame—is quite different than my own. To her, the photo illustrates something different than it does to me.

Obviously, you are not going to analyze or construct frames around photographs of someone at the beach. But the analogy works for more academic pursuits, too. Researchers construct a frame around their data—the things they have observed or located through research—so that research shows something and makes a bigger point than just "Here's what I saw (or found)." For instance, in the reading called "What High School Is" included here, Theodore Sizer uses the metaphor of cafeteria-style education to frame his interpretation of Mark's (the main subject of the chapter) schooling. Someone else might look at Mark's day and interpret it differently from Sizer; if they did, they would be putting a different frame around the actions that Sizer describes in the reading. Similarly, another researcher might borrow Sizer's frame ("cafeteria-style education") for her own research, her observation of something else. In this case, she would cite Sizer in her work because she borrowed his frame, and then explain how her picture (her evidence) also fits within it.

As a writer and a researcher, frames can be very useful for you in two ways. First, you can use others' frames and insert your own pictures. For instance, one of the assignments included here is a classroom ethnography, where you spend a period of time observing the literacy practices in a class. To frame the evidence you collect in these observations, you could borrow from one of the readings included here. For instance, you might say that "This class provides a cafeteria-style approach to learning" (borrowing from Sizer) or "This class is an example of problem-posing learning" (borrowing from Freire). If you did this, you would be using a frame provided by someone else, inserting your own "picture" (your research) into that frame.

Another way to use the idea of framing is to borrow others' pictures and develop your own frame. For instance, maybe you will start thinking about Sizer's ideas about "cafeteria-style" learning in your observations and decide that it's not really a valid concept, even for Mark's learning. You can point to his picture (Mark's learning) and the data you have collected to support a new frame, something that you have developed on your own. Both are great ways to use the idea of frames and pictures in your own research. An important note, too: *You must cite your sources when you borrow a frame or use evidence (pictures) from another source, **even if you do not quote any words directly***. To avoid being charged with plagiarism, you need to cite even *ideas* developed by others, which is what you will likely do here.

As you work through the assignments in this category, you are getting at the heart of your own subject knowledge, using what you know to learn more about education and literacy in a specific setting. Your study will help deepen your own and others' understandings of the concepts you have learned about in previous work in this class. You will also extend and deepen the reading and writing strategies you have developed thus far with this assignment. You will gather and assess evidence from a variety of sources—written text, but also non-written sources, like physical sites. You will also consider how to apply existing reading strategies to these new texts and develop new strategies to help you work with this new evidence. As with earlier assignments, you will work on analyzing and synthesizing diverse sources into your writing and citing them correctly; you will also work on developing research questions, using writing to work through sources, and considering how and if to use diverse sources in your writing. You may also spend time considering questions of audiences, making decisions about what genres of writing to include in your assignment, and continuing to work with form, voice, and editing.

▨ DEBATING THE PURPOSE OF SCHOOL

Possible readings for this assignment:

bell hooks, "Engaged Pedagogy"

"Wendy Darling," "What 'No Child Left Behind' Left Behind"

Andrea Fishman, "Becoming Literate: A Lesson from the Amish"

Paolo Freire, "The Banking Concept of Education"

Darcy Frey, "The Last Shot"

Nicholas Lemann, "The President's Big Test"

Theresa McCarty, "Classroom and Community"

Earl Shorris, "On the Uses of a Liberal Education: II. As a Weapon in the Hands of the Restless Poor"

Theodore Sizer, "What High School Is"

Ron Suskind, "Fierce Intimacies"

James Traub, "The Test Mess"

Photographs from FSA-OWI collection

Photographs from *School*

A number of the readings here focus on the purpose of school. Even more consider similarities among and differences between what students consider school to be about, and what the rhetoric of schooling makes it *seem* to be about. In this assignment, you will explore those purposes. There are two options that address a common question: **How does each author (or main character) define the purpose of education, and why does he or she define it that way?**

1. *Option One:* Choose three readings where you think the positions regarding the purpose of education are quite different from one another and analyze those positions. How does each reading define the purpose of education? What, in the reading, tells you about why the purpose is framed as it is? Be sure to use abundant evidence from each reading in your response to support your interpretation of each reading's position. Then, consider your own definition of the purpose of education. What experiences have led you to define that purpose as you have? How can these authors' definitions help you to expand, develop, and support your own definition?

2. *Option Two:* Write a dialogue between at least three of the characters from the reading about what *they* see as the purpose of school. Include yourself as a fourth character in that dialogue in some way. You could be another participant in the discussion, a moderator, a judge, or a talk show host—the format is up to you, as is your role. But somehow, you want to have these people talk *to* one another, as well as to you, and represent their views on the purpose of school. If you like (and your teacher agrees), also add one more character not represented in the readings to the dialogue (someone from your workplace, your dorm, your neighborhood, etc.).

Writing an unconventional essay like this one might seem initially simple, but it requires a lot from you. First, you are going to need to be sure that you *really* understand the positions of the individuals whom you choose to include in your dialogue, and make sure that the evidence in the readings supports your interpretation. You should include these positions in a description of the characters that you include in your dialogue, like this:

Cedric Jennings is a first-year student at Brown University, an Ivy League school in Providence, R.I. Cedric comes from an unusual background for a Brown student—he is from southwest Washington, D.C., a very impoverished neighborhood. While Cedric was a strong student in high school, he is finding that Brown is a more challenging academic atmosphere. Additionally, Cedric has not had a lot of experience living around white people, and most of the white students with whom he lives and works closely have not had a lot of experience around African-Americans. Cedric also is not receiving much support for his difficult transition from high school to college at Brown University. Cedric is sorting out how he feels about the purpose of school. He thinks . . . (and then you would summarize his position statement).

Write one of these descriptions for each character you include, and be sure to use evidence from the readings in your description to enhance your interpretation of each character's positions on the purpose of education.

The character descriptions (which will probably occupy about 1–2 pages of your essay) should be followed by dialogue (3–4 pages). You will need to choose an issue, and probably a set of questions, around which your dialogue is going to revolve. Remember, you want this dialogue to have a *point*—you want it to be about the purpose of school, but you do not want to have them just say, "I think it's this," and "I think it's that," and so on. They should engage in a discussion with one another about issues connected with this purpose, so you will need to think about where their opinions about that purpose might converge and diverge. For instance, would Eli Fishman and Nicholas Lemann agree about the purpose of school? Where would Cedric Jennings fall with those two?

Developing Work

DW.3a   Regardless of which option you choose when writing this essay, you will need to have a very clear interpretation of the position of each reading you are going to use and abundant evidence to support your interpretation of the reading. In this DW assignment, summarize the purposes of education that you see represented in the three readings you are going to use for this essay, and use evidence from the readings to show how you have come to the interpretation that you have. If you run short on time, at least list key passages or ideas (along with their pages numbers) from each reading—this will save you the time of going back and re-reading. Also, be sure to note (by writing in the margins of your book, or by logging in a reading log) how the evidence you will use supports your interpretation—this will also save you time.

DW.3b   Use the form of whichever option you choose from above to write about what you see as the primary areas of agreement and disagreement among these authors concerning the purpose of school. As in DW.3a, be sure to use abundant evidence from the text. If you are writing the essay as an exchange between people, write this DW in the voice of the individuals participating in the discussion.

▨ REPRESENTING THE COLLEGE EXPERIENCE

Possible readings for this assignment:

Mark Edmundson, "On the Uses of a Liberal Education: I. As Lite Entertainment for Bored College Students"

June Jordan, "Nobody Mean More to Me Than You and the Future Life of Willie Jordan"

Michael Moffatt, "What College is REALLY Like"

Earl Shorris, "On the Uses of a Liberal Education: II. As a Weapon in the Hands of the Restless Poor"

Ron Suskind, "Fierce Intimacies"

Photographs from the FSA-OWI collection

Photographs from *School*

As you have seen throughout the reading and writing you have done thus far, students and schooling are represented in various ways, in various texts, and for various purposes. In this assignment, you will choose a primary source and use a frame from one of the readings for your own analysis of a representation of students. The question you will ultimately want to address is: **How is the subject you have chosen framed in the sources you analyzed, and what does that tell you and your readers about this representation of students?**

There are really four steps to this assignment. First, you need to find a source to analyze. Be creative here—representations of students and school are everywhere, from college promotional materials to posters and flyers on campus bulleting boards; from videos to CD covers; from films and TV shows to internet sites. Remember, too, that you can also look at historical materials (college libraries often contain a wealth of compelling historical representations of school and students: old textbooks, college materials, photographs, etc.). You are going to spend a lot of time closely studying the source you find, so you will want to choose something that is visually rich and with which you will enjoy working.

Once you have located your source, you will need to decide what subject to focus on in that source. Do you want to look only at students or at something broader, like schooling (which probably includes students as a sub-set)? Once you choose this focus, you are implicitly developing a research question for yourself, like "How is schooling represented in this series of collegiate songs from the 1920s?" Developing these kinds of questions is essential for pursuing any kind of research.

The third step will be to plunge into your analysis. As with the second assignment, one of the most important parts of this analysis will be to find evidence from your source to support what you see there—in other words, evidence that supports your analysis of how your subject is represented.

As you consider this analysis, the fourth step will be to draw on the readings (for this assignment or others from the term) to develop your analysis. Remember that how you use these readings depends on which reading you choose, how you interpret it, and how your analysis is proceeding. Perhaps one or more of the readings can help you develop a frame; perhaps they can help you link your analysis of the readings to other ones, or show you how your representation counters others circulating in the culture. The readings here may also help you to develop your ideas about why your analysis is important, and for whom.

Developing Work

DW.3a   For this DW assignment, focus on the source that you are analyzing for the long essay. What will you focus on, and why will you focus on that thing? What do you see in it? How is the thing you have chosen to analyze represented here, and how do you know it is? As with other DW assignments, try to write as much as possible about the source you have chosen, why you have chosen it, what you see in it, and where and how you see what you do. Ideally, much of the material you generate here will help you develop your ideas and analysis for the long essay. Your reflections about why you chose this source may also help you clarify why you think it is relevant and for whom.

DW.3b   Focus on the readings that you will use as you develop your long essay. What reading will you use here, why will you use this reading, and how will it contribute to your analysis? Please use as much evidence from the reading as possible so that other readers can understand both your interpretation of the reading, and how it contributes to the analysis of your source.

▨ DESIGNING ASSESSMENTS

Readings for this assignment:

"Wendy Darling," "What 'No Child Left Behind' Left Behind"

Stanley Kaplan, "My 54-Year Love Affair with the SAT"

Nicholas Lemann, "The President's Big Test"

Gary Orfield and Johanna Wald, "Testing, Testing"

Peter Sacks, "Do No Harm: Stopping the Damage to America's Schools"

James Traub, "The Test Mess"

You have spent the better part of the term thinking about issues connected with education and literacy: how education is defined, what should and shouldn't be taught, what your education has been. In this assignment, you will extend that by designing a test for one subject that you think measures what *should* be measured when looking for evidence of learning. You will need to consider what subject you want to test—should it be something that is traditionally included in tests (e.g., American history, math, English, science), or a subject that is not traditionally included? For this assignment, **design one section of a standardized test and then analyze the work you have done using readings chosen by you or your instructor.** Why have you constructed the test as you have? Why did you include the questions and prompts that you did? What would correct and incorrect answers look like? Why did you use the form and style for the test that you did, whether you chose to use fill-in-the-bubble forms, short answers, or an extended written essay? Did you include visual elements? What kind of results will your test achieve? Who will do well on it, who will not, and what will be the implications? Which students will it serve, which will it not, and why are these results acceptable?

Developing Work

DW.3a Use this DW assignment to reflect on your ideas before you begin developing test questions. What kind of literacy do you want to test? In what subjects? (Remember that these can be academic, but they don't have to be.) What kinds of literacy will be validated through correct and incorrect answers on your test? Keeping all of this in mind, what do you think will be the best kinds of questions for your test? (Multiple choice? Essay? Demonstration? Something else?) Who will take it, and when?

DW.3b Once you have started to construct your test, use this DW assignment to begin thinking about your analysis. Use significant ideas, passages, or quotes from the readings as a starting place, and then write about how these ideas help you to think about which students your test will serve, which it will not, and why.

▬ WHAT COUNTS, FOR WHAT, AND WHO SAYS?

Possible readings for this assignment:

"Wendy Darling," "What 'No Child Left Behind' Left Behind"

Stanley Kaplan, "My 54-Year Love Affair with the SAT"

Nicholas Lemann, "The President's Big Test"

No Child Left Behind Act

Gary Orfield and Johanna Wald, "Testing, Testing"

Peter Sacks, "Do No Harm: Stopping the Damage to America's Schools"

James Traub, "The Test Mess"

Thus far, assignments in this text have asked you to analyze your experiences in school and what you see as the purpose of schooling for you. Now, you are going to move from your own experiences to consider what should count for learning, and who says it should. Ultimately in the essay that you write, you will want to summarize others' ideas about "What counts, for what, and who says," and then write your own answer to this vexing question.

To address the issue of "what counts, for what, and who says," you are going to read about a raging debate swirling in education over standardized testing and standards-based assessment. If you took the ACT or the SAT (or an Advanced Placement exam), you have had experience with standardized testing. If you have attended or graduated from high school in the last ten years, you are also familiar with standards-based assessment, like the state-mandated standards in which students must demonstrate proficiency.

At the same time as local governments, and even the federal government, pay increasing attention to testing and standards-based assessment, critics of high stakes testing argue that alternatives must be explored. They point to long-standing research demonstrating the inherent biases in standardized tests, saying that what counts in the tests—that is, what is measured by them—reflects a distinct version of American culture and knowledge, and reflects the values, beliefs, and ideologies of a powerful dominant culture, but not the knowledge of other cultures. They also argue that standards-based assessment is changing the shape of American education for the worse; that as teachers, students, and even school systems have to measure up to a standard defined by external agencies (even a state department of education), it forces teachers to "teach to the test," and not to consider what is most appropriate for the students in her classroom, in her school, and in her community. Thus, they claim not only that the "what counts" is misguided, but the "for what" and the "who says" need to be re-shaped.

If you are writing this essay using only the readings incorporated here, analyze the positions in them. What are the positions taken by the authors with regard to the question, "what counts, for what, and who says?" Ultimately, in your essay you should outline the main perspectives represented by the authors of these readings. Next, find examples of either standardized tests (like the ACT or SAT), or a state-sponsored assessment. (Examples of each are available on the web.) Closely analyze **one section** of that exam. What counts there? Based on your reading and your thinking about education and literacy this term, why do you think it does? Do you agree with what counts and what does not? Why or why not? In your response, be sure to draw on and cite evidence from the readings to which you refer, *including* your own earlier writing.

Developing Work

DW.3a Focus on summarizing the positions on testing reflected in the readings associated with this assignment. What are the positions of each on testing, and what evidence does each provide to support its positions? If you have time, move from these statements to parallels that you see between them. What are the main perspectives represented in the reading, who is aligned with each, and how do you know? When you write this DW, either include as many examples from the reading as possible, or write (for your own reference) brief summaries of the examples that you can develop in the long essay. Also, remember to include page numbers! It will save you time because you will not have to search through the reading to find something that you remember, but cannot quite locate. You also will want to make notes in the margin of your book next to the examples you are going to use about how they illustrate what you say they do—this way, you will have a record of your thinking.

DW.3b Focus on your analysis of the standardized test or state-sponsored assessment that you are going to analyze. What do you think counts there, and why? In your analysis, pay close attention to the kinds of questions asked, the method for responding (e.g., short answer, multiple-choice question), and illustrations provided. What do you think these components say about what kind of knowledge counts? As in DW.3a, be sure to cite evidence from the tests in your response.

▨ ANALYZING LITERACY EXPERIENCES

Possible readings for this assignment:

David Barton and Mary Hamilton, "Literacy Practices"

David Barton and Mary Hamilton, "How They've Fared in Education"

Andrea Fishman, "Becoming Literate: A Lesson from the Amish"

Paolo Freire, "The Banking Concept of Education"

Theodore Sizer, "What High School Is"

Ron Suskind, "Fierce Intimacies"

In "Literacy Practices" and "How They've Fared in Education," David Barton and Mary Hamilton first discuss, then show, how particular values are reflected in education that may or may not be similar to the expectations or values of those being educated. This is also a prominent theme in Andrea Fishman's "Literacy Among the Amish" and runs through Cedric's story in "Fierce Intimacies."

In this assignment, you will use the work of these authors as a model for your own study of literacy expectations and experiences. To conduct your study, you will need to choose someone who you know (from school, from home, from elsewhere), and who will agree to both talk with you and to let you accompany him to some setting where his literacy practices come into play. (A class is a convenient site, for instance, but you also could go to a religious service, an athletic event, or any other event where this person participates, as a member, in an activity.) Your work here will be to address the questions: **What are this person's expectations for literacy practices in this site? What practices *are* valued in this site? What are the consequences (for the person you are observing) of the fit, or lack of fit, between her expectations for literacy practices, and her experiences of them?**

Your response to this question should be based on:

- An interview with the person you are studying;
- At least three observation sessions (of at least one hour each) of the literacy practices in a particular site; and
- A response from the person you are studying to your initial analysis of the fit (or lack of fit) between expectations and the expected practices in this site.

Abundant evidence from each of these should be included to help support your analysis.

To systematically begin gathering the evidence to address this question, you will need to first develop a framework for your own analysis. To do this, summarize (in a chart, in paragraph form, or however is most comfortable for you) the literacy experiences of main characters from "How They've Fared in Education" and either "Becoming Literate" or "Fierce Intimacies." What are those experiences? How do they reflect or not reflect the expectations of the contexts where they are used? (For example, when Cedric offers his response in the James Baldwin seminar, does that response match the expectation of the class and professor? What are the consequences of this match or lack of match?) From your analysis of the reading, begin to develop:

1. ideas about what *counts* as a literacy practice,
2. what you might look for in your own analysis, and
3. questions that you might ask study subjects about their literacy expectations for the site where you are studying them.

Once you have collected your data, your job is to analyze it to discover what your study subject's expectations were for literacy practices in the site where you have analyzed them, what *is* emphasized in that site, and whether your subject's expectations match, or do not match, the practices emphasized in the site. For instance, perhaps the person expected a history class to emphasize students' knowledge of important dates, but instead the instructor asked students to make connections between historical events and broader cultural trends of the period. This might be an occasion when your subject's expectations and what was valued differed.

Finally, you will want to use your analysis to arrive at some kind of conclusion (which might also serve as the focus or thesis for the essay) about literacy experiences of your subject. For instance, perhaps you have seen that particular kinds of literacy expectations lead to greater success (in other words, opportunities where students' literacy acts match those expectations) than others—that is a great point to use to shape the essay. Alternatively, maybe you have seen that there are a number of literacy expectations that do not necessarily lead to students' success, and you want to write about those—this is also a terrific point to make with your evidence. Whatever you choose, you will want to use the evidence you have collected from your observations, as well as evidence from relevant readings that supports or helps to develop your analysis in some way.

Developing Work

DW.3a To help clarify your own definition of literacy experiences, in this DW assignment, identify the literacy practices of the main character from one of the readings you listed above. What experiences does the person have? Are they expected in the contexts where they are used? How do you know? When you write about the experiences here, use as much detail from the reading as possible; if you feel you do not have time to include it all, be sure to at least list page numbers for the examples that you want to use and discuss how you will use them (so you will not have to go back and find them again).

DW.3b   After you have conducted your own study of literacy experiences, use this essay to think through what you have seen. What kinds of literacy experiences did your subject have? How did they match (or not) the contexts in which they occurred? And what are the implications of your observations? Use this DW assignment to think through possibilities on your way to reaching a point that you would like to raise in your essay. A note, too: While this DW assignment (as well as DW.3a) will be useful for your long essay, you will likely need to do some rearranging when you use the assignments. It might be that the points you reach when working through these ideas will ultimately serve as the *beginning* point for the long essay you write, and the evidence you describe here will help to support and develop your ideas.

POSITIVE LEARNING EXPERIENCES

Possible readings for this assignment:

David Barton and Mary Hamilton, "How They've Fared in Education"

David Barton and Mary Hamilton, "Literacy Practices"

Frederick Douglass, from *Narrative of the Life of Frederick Douglass, An American Slave*

Paolo Freire, "The Banking Concept of Education"

In this assignment, you will choose a site where you or others have what you consider to be *positive* learning experiences. This can be in school or out—the choice of site is up to you. However, you will want to consider your audience: remember that this is a public document that will circulate widely among a diverse group of class colleagues.

Spend about 4–5 hours (over a span of 1 or 2 weeks) observing the learning that goes on in this site, taking notes in a double-entry journal about what you see (on one side) and recording comments or questions about your observations (on the other). Drawing on the readings by Freire or Barton and Hamilton, use your observations and relevant evidence from the readings to answer the question: **What is the learning experience here like, and for whom, and what is its relevance?**

A note of caution: One of the goals of research and inquiry (like that which this assignment asks you to conduct) is to learn new things and gain new perspective, rather than just confirm what you already know or believe. Since this assignment asks you to observe at a site that you have already come to some conclusions about (i.e., positive learning happens here), you will need to be careful to observe the site objectively so that you do not merely confirm what you already have seen or know. Using the framing readings will help you with this. For instance, if you are drawing on Freire, how is the learning in this site structured? What kind of interactions take place between people in the site? What is considered useful or beneficial knowledge in the site (and, perhaps, what is not)? How are people treated here? If you are using Barton and Hamilton, what kinds of literacies are used here, and what kinds are valued? Are there connections between these literacies and the kinds of literacies that participants use in other contexts? What makes this a site where people have positive experiences? If your impressions of the site change as you observe, that's okay! One of the tricky things about research is that systematic observation can change your interpretation.

Developing Work

DW.3a Before you enter your site, take some time to reflect on what you already know and think about it. Where is it? Why did you choose it? What kind of positive learning do you think happens there, why is it positive, and for whom?

DW.3b After you have observed the site for 2–3 hours, reflect on what you have noticed. What kind of learning have you seen going on, and how has it been positive for those at the site? Have your impressions of the site changed? How and why?

DW.3c Think about the ways the readings you use to develop your analysis of this site will be useful for you. Which will you use, how, and why? You might begin with a significant quote, idea, or passage from one of the readings and then explain its connection to your analysis. If you have another idea about how to make connections between your ideas and the reading, that is also fine.

▨ WHAT IS TAUGHT AND WHY

Possible readings for this assignment:

"Wendy Darling," "What 'No Child Left Behind' Left Behind"

Mark Edmundson, "On the Uses of a Liberal Education: I. As Lite Entertainment for Bored College Students"

Andrea Fishman, "Becoming Literate: A Lesson from the Amish"

Darcy Frey, "The Last Shot"

Gary Orfield and Johanna Wald, "Testing, Testing"

Peter Sacks, "Do No Harm: Stopping the Damage to American Schools"

Earl Shorris, "On the Uses of a Liberal Education: II. As a Weapon in the Hands of the Restless Poor"

A number of the readings included here address the question, **"What is being taught in school, and why?"** In this assignment, your job is to choose a site in your own institution and find out answers to these questions there. When you do, you should include evidence from several sources:

- *A classroom site study.* Spend at least 1–2 hours a week observing another class. In your observations, focus on what is being taught in that class, and why it is being taught. What kinds of literacies are valued, and how do you know? (For these observations, pay close attention to things that you might normally take for granted—the physical arrangement of the room, the location of instructor and students, the ways that class members communicate, the kind of language that is used—in addition to things like correct and incorrect responses.)
- *An interview with either a student in the class or the class instructor.* What does this person believe is being taught in this class, and why does she think the class is focusing on the subjects that it is?
- *An artifact from the class.* (Perhaps a syllabus, an assignment, or something else that you think represents what is being taught in the class and why.) What does this represent about what is being taught and why?

When you write the analysis of "What is taught and why" that comes from these various sources, you should be sure to draw on the readings for this assignment and, if appropriate, others from earlier in the term. Remember that how you use these readings depends on which reading you choose, how you interpret it, and how your analysis is proceeding. Use at least one of the readings to help you develop a frame for your analysis. For example, are you seeing something that looks like problem-posing, and therefore values the same kind of interaction and shared knowledge? Can you link your analysis of what is taught and why to other readings here? Perhaps the class you are studying seems similar in some ways to the Old Order Amish school—do the readings help you to consider why the subject is being taught or being taught as it is? Does the curriculum emphasize certain values? These are possibilities, but not the only ones.

Developing Work

DW.3a After the first week of your classroom site study, use this DW assignment to write about what you have seen. What did you notice that struck you as surprising, unusual, or unexpected? What did you see that you expected to? When you respond to these questions, use as much detail about your observations as you can (e.g., rather than "I wasn't surprised at the arrangement of the space," write about how the space was arranged, and why it did not surprise you). After you have described the space, write as much as you can about what is taught in this classroom, and why you think those things are taught.

DW.3b After you have finished your classroom study and your interview, think through your interpretation of the evidence you have collected in this DW assignment and what evidence from the readings helps you to interpret them. Begin with evidence from the reading that you find useful—a quote, a summary, or a paraphrase of a section, or some other reference. Then, describe how this section of the reading will help you to interpret the data you have collected in your own research.

UNDERREPRESENTED GENRES

Possible readings for this assignment:

Lorene Cary, from *Black Ice*

"Wendy Darling," "What No Child Left Behind Left Behind"

Andrea Fishman, "Becoming Literate: A Lesson from the Amish"

Paolo Freire, "The Banking Concept of Education"

bell hooks, "Engaged Pedagogy"

Theresa McCarty, "Classroom and Community"

No Child Left Behind Executive Summary

Gary Orfield and Joanna Wald, "Testing, Testing"

Earl Shorris, "On the Purposes of a Liberal Education: II. As a Weapon in the Hands of the Restless Poor"

Theodore Sizer, "What High School Is"

One of the themes that runs through a number of readings in this book—those listed above, as well as others—is that learning takes place through a range of genres inside and outside of school. "What's a genre," you might ask? Here, it's used to refer to a *type* of text (and "text" here could be articles, books, movies . . .). Say that your favorite movie is *Men in Black*. What other movies would you say are like it? Will Smith movies? Action-comedy movies? Movies with extraterrestrial aliens in them? All of these bigger categories could be considered genres. Genres have rules, better known as *conventions,* too. These are the things that make the genre what it is. If you think about a romantic comedy, it wouldn't fit in an action-comedy category with *Men in Black,* right? Because they have different conventions, they belong to different genres (at least, if we use the groupings above). Genres are flexible—it certainly would be possible to create one that could hold both *Men in Black* and a romantic comedy—but it would also have its own conventions.

For this assignment, you should think about the genres that you or someone else encounters in a place where you think learning happens. It should be a *specific* place—a classroom is probably the most obvious example, but it could be anywhere else where you think learning takes place. Then, you need to address two questions: **what is an underrepresented genre in this place? Why should it be included?** Your response to the question should include an analysis of what genres *are* included (though this will likely be brief), an analysis *and an example* of a genre that you think is underrepresented here (one you create or locate), and a thorough discussion of *why* you think the genre you've described and created should be included. For this analysis, you're going to need to consider some of the questions raised in readings like those for this assignment. What kind of learning takes place here? What ideas and values does it reflect? What ideas and values *doesn't* it reflect that it should? In your response to these questions you'll need to incorporate evidence from the readings as frames and/or evidence, and consider appropriate points of connection along the way.

The first step you'll need to take here is identifying a place that you want to study. As above, think about someplace specific. You might want to consider (or be required to) spend a dedicated period of time in this place, too —one to two hours—taking careful notes about what happens there. Even if you don't have to do so, remember that your analysis of what is taught and what is (and isn't) represented in the genres here should be grounded in very, very specific evidence from your place.

After you've studied the place and considered what is taught through what genres, you can move on to think about what isn't represented. Again, here you'll want to be very specific and ground your analysis in the example that you find of this genre.

Developing Work

DW.3a   In this DW, describe what you find to be the underrepresented genre here? What kind of learning takes place here? What isn't included that should be? What genre will help that learning happen, and what does that genre look like? You could include an example—one that you create, or one that you locate—of the genre in your DW along with an explanation of what it provides to the place.

DW.3b   Here, focus on the reading/s that you'll use as you develop your long essay. What reading will you use here, why will you use this reading, and how will it contribute to your analysis? Please use as much evidence from the reading as possible so that other readers can understand both your interpretation of the reading, and how it contributes to the analysis of your place and/or your genre.

OBSERVING LITERACY PRACTICES

Possible readings for this assignment:

bell hooks, "Engaged Pedagogy

David Barton and Mary Hamilton, "Literacy Practices"

David Barton and Mary Hamilton, "How They've Fared in Education"

Lorene Cary, from *Black Ice*

Mark Edmundson, "On the Purposes of a Liberal Education: I. As Lite Entertainment for Bored College Students"

Andrea Fishman, "Becoming Literate"

Darcy Frey, "The Last Shot"

Theresa McCarty, "Community and Culture"

Earl Shorris, "On the Purposes of a Liberal Education: II. As a Weapon in the Hands of the Restless Poor"

Ron Suskind, "Fierce Intimacies"

When instructors and curriculum designers create the work that students do in the classroom, they work from a set of beliefs about students and what will most engage them. These beliefs shape everything from assignments to discussions. As instructors teach, they gather information—formal feedback from students on things like evaluations, as well as informal feedback that comes from discussions and observation—that helps them to know whether they need to modify their beliefs and, therefore, their classroom work.

This assignment asks you to engage in analysis in order to reflect on the beliefs that shape this assignment and this text and, possibly, this writing class. To do this, you will analyze the literacy practices of two subjects—yourself, and one of the subjects of a reading in this text—and compare them. **What are your practices? What are those of the subject's in the reading you chose? Then, extend from your analysis to speak to the beliefs that shape assignments like this one. What should people who write curriculum (like this assignment) learn from your study?** If your practices are significantly different, should we consider that when we create assignments? If they are quite similar, what should we take from that?

To complete this assignment, you will need to work through a series of steps. The first one is to conduct your two case studies: one of your own literacy practices, and another of the literacy practices of a main subject in one of the readings listed above. To study your own practices, you should keep a log of your literacy activities for a full, contiguous two days. (You should begin this right away.) Keep in mind the definition of literacy practices in Barton and Hamilton's work here, and work to write your own definition of literacy practices before you begin. To analyze the literacy practices of one of the characters in the readings above, focus on the literacy practices of that subject in the reading.

After you have collected both sets of data, you should first synthesize each. What have you found are the primary and secondary literacy practices of you and your reading subject? What similarities and differences between the two do you find? Be sure to include extensive evidence from both sets of practices—descriptions of what you did and evidence from the readings—to help readers understand the definitions that you write.

Finally, reflect on the results of your analysis. What should curriculum authors learn from it? Should they take into account particularly important literacy practices? Should they ignore others? Why?

Developing Work

DW.3a After you have kept your literacy log, use this DW assignment to think through what you have found. What kinds of literacies do you see evident in your own practices, as recorded over the two days you tracked in your literacy log? In your DW, either include as many examples from your log as possible, or write (for your own reference) brief summaries of the examples that you can develop in the long essay. If you have time, think about the implications of your literacy practices for curriculum planning, as well. Is there something that planners should learn from what you have seen?

DW.3b   For this DW, you will need to have analyzed the text that you have chosen for this assignment (as well as completed your literacy log, of course). Here, reflect on the similarities and differences between your literacy practices and those of the character in the reading you have chosen. As in previous assignments, be sure to include as many examples from the reading as possible, or write (for your own reference) brief summaries of the examples that you can develop in the long essay. Also, remember to include page numbers! It will save you time because you won't have to search through the reading to find something that you remember, but cannot quite locate. You also will want to make notes in the margin of your book next to the examples you are going to use about how they illustrate what you say they do—this way, you will have a record of your thinking.

"SPEAKING OUT, JOINING IN, TALKING BACK" ASSIGNMENT

Earlier assignments in this book extended the invitation to consider a range of questions linked to larger discussions of education and literacy. In this category, there is only one assignment. It asks you to participate, in a public way, in these discussions. It also asks you to reflect on what you have learned through the term both about education and literacy, and about writing.

In this assignment, you will draw on the aspect of education and literacy in which you feel most expert in order to create a public document—a letter, a memo, an advertising campaign, a press release, or some other form of public expression—on the issue most important to you. You will then need to reflect on your choice of audience, form, subject, genre, and content. The expectation is that you will distribute this document to the public for which you intended it, as well.

To create this document, you will need to reflect on and synthesize both what you have come to understand about education and literacy broadly, as well as the issue you have chosen specifically during your work this term. Additionally, you will need to practice two forms of reading that you use often, though perhaps not always consciously. First, you will need to read the audience you have chosen for your document. What kinds of texts and what styles of writing does that audience find to be appropriate and inappropriate? For example, a formal memo would be received quite differently by a group of high school students and a high school principal—one might see it as excessively formal, while the other might think it a useful document for the situation.

Second, you will need to read the conventions (that is, the rules) of the genre you choose to create here and decide which of them you want to use for your written product, as well. Some genres, a press release for instance, typically look quite similar regardless of author—the conventions of this genre, then, are fairly rigid. Other genres, like a web page, are much more flexible and depend on the audience for the page. To create your document, you will need to read your audience, then read the conventions of your genre to make decisions about how and whether to use them. You will also need to make decisions about the language, form, tone, and style of the document you create. All of those decisions should reflect what you know about your audience.

▰▰ SPEAKING OUT, JOINING IN, TALKING BACK: ACTING ON IDEAS ABOUT EDUCATION

Throughout this term, you have moved toward understanding the roots of literacy (your own and others') and their connections to education. In this last assignment, your job is to create a public document for a specific audience who could benefit from what you have learned, and then to get that document to that audience. For instance, perhaps you wrote about literacy in a specific community in "Learning from Others" assignment. Would it benefit someone (members of the community or others) to have a guide to literacies in that community? Perhaps you examined specific curricula in Essay Three. Do you have specific recommendations about broadening or narrowing literacy curricula in schools? Perhaps you conducted a classroom ethnography in Essay Assignment Three and have recommendations for the teacher whom you observed? The direction that your document takes, including subject and form, should take into consideration the audience you have chosen and the results you hope to achieve.

Once you have created this public document, you will also need to write one only for class colleagues reflecting the decisions you made in putting together your document. In a reflective document (an essay, a letter, or any other form you feel is appropriate), address the following questions:

- Who was your audience?
- What was the point you wanted to make to this audience?
- What did you know about this issue before you started working on Essay Four?
- What did you learn about it as you wrote, and how did you learn it?
- What did you learn from the research you conducted? How was it useful (or not)?
- What did you decide to write (e.g., letter, memo, etc.)? Why did you think it would be most effective for your audience?
- What information did you decide to include and why did you include it?

In this reflective document, include references to the public document you produced so that readers will understand your responses to the questions.

Developing Work

DW.4a   Here, focus on the genre that you have decided to use for your communication. What is it? What are its conventions? To answer this question, you will need to look very closely at what makes the genre you have chosen what it is. For instance, what are the characteristics of a business letter? Of a memo? Of a web site? To respond to this DW prompt, you will need to look at, and think hard about, the *form* of these texts, rather than their *content*. Your response here will help you to incorporate those genre conventions in your own text.

READINGS ABOUT USES OF LEARNING

- David Barton and Mary Hamilton, "Literacy Practices"

- bell hooks, "Engaged Pedagogy"

- Paolo Freire, "The Banking Concept of Education"

- Theodor Sizer, "What High School Is"

DAVID BARTON AND MARY HAMILTON

LITERACY PRACTICES

This reading is about a word that you have probably heard so often, you don't even notice it: literacy. In discussions about school, it is used a lot—for example, to bemoan falling literacy standards, or to talk about the kinds of literacy that students need to develop. But in these discussions, the definition of literacy is more often implied than it is made explicit. In this essay (adapted from a chapter of the same book that includes "How They've Fared in Education," also by Barton and Hamilton, which appears on pages 98–113), the authors offer a definition of *literacies* and suggest that several "base concepts"—a social theory of literacy, literacy events, and texts—are central to understanding how literacies function in peoples' lives rather than which literacy people do or do not have, as tends to be discussed more often. The authors suggest that different literacies are used in different contexts (times, places, situations), and that understanding literacies must be done within these contexts.

A SOCIAL THEORY OF LITERACY: PRACTICES AND EVENTS

In this chapter we provide a framework in terms of a theory of literacy. It is a brief overview of a social theory of literacy. This can be seen as the starting-point or orienting theory, which the detailed studies in this book then expand upon, react to and develop. We define what is meant by literacy practices and literacy events and explain some of the tenets of a social theory of literacy. This is pursued in Barton and Hamilton (1998), where a further example of situated literacies not covered in this book can be found.

We present here the theory of literacy as social practice in the form of a set of six propositions about the nature of literacy, as in Figure 1. The starting-point

---

- Literacy is best understood as a set of social practices; these can be inferred from events which are mediated by written texts.
- There are different literacies associated with different domains of life.
- Literacy practices are patterned by social institutions and power relationships, and some literacies are more dominant, visible and influential than others.
- Literacy practices are purposeful and embedded in broader social goals and cultural practices.
- Literacy is historically situated.
- Literacy practices change and new ones are frequently acquired through processes of informal learning and sense making.

FIGURE 1   LITERACY AS SOCIAL PRACTICE

of this approach is the assertion that *literacy is a social practice,* and the propositions are an elaboration of this. The discussion is a development on that in Barton (1994, pp. 34–52), where contemporary approaches to literacy are discussed within the framework of the metaphor of ecology. The notion of *literacy practices* offers a powerful way of conceptualising the link between the activities of reading and writing and the social structures in which they are embedded and which they help shape. When we talk about practices, then, this is not just the superficial choice of a word but the possibilities that this perspective offers for new theoretical understandings about literacy.

Our interest is in social practices in which literacy has a role; hence the basic unit of a social theory of literacy is that of *literacy practices.* Literacy practices are the general cultural ways of utilising written language which people draw upon in their lives. In the simplest sense literacy practices are what people do with literacy. However practices are not observable units of behaviour since they also involve values, attitudes, feelings, and social relationships (see Street 1993, p. 12). This includes people's awareness of literacy, constructions of literacy and discourses of literacy, how people talk about and make sense of literacy. These are processes internal to the individual; at the same time, practices are the social processes which connect people with one another, and they include shared cognitions represented in ideologies and social identities. Practices are shaped by social rules which regulate the use and distribution of texts, prescribing who may produce and have access to them. They straddle the distinction between individual and social worlds, and literacy practices are more usefully understood as existing in the relations between people, within groups and communities, rather than as a set of properties residing in individuals.

To avoid confusion, it is worth emphasising that this usage is different from situations where the word *practice* is used to mean learning to do something by repetition. It is also different from the way the term is used in recent international surveys of literacy, to refer to 'common or typical activities or tasks' (OECD/Statistics Canada 1996). The notion of practices as we have defined it above—cultural ways of utilising literacy—is a more abstract one that cannot wholly be contained in observable activities and tasks.)

Turning to another basic concept, *literacy events* are activities where literacy has a role. Usually there is a written text, or texts, central to the activity and there may be talk around the text. Events are observable episodes which arise from practices and are shaped by them. The notion of events stresses the situated nature of literacy, that it always exists in a social context. It is parallel to ideas developed in sociolinguistics and also, as Jay Lemke has pointed out, to Bahktin's assertion that the starting point for the analysis of spoken language should be 'the social event of verbal interaction', rather than the formal linguistic properties of texts in isolation (Lemke 1995).

5   Many literacy events in life are regular, repeated activities, and these can often be a useful starting-point for research into literacy. Some events are linked into routine sequences and these may be part of the formal procedures and expectations of social institutions like work-places, schools, and welfare agencies. Some events are structured by the more informal expectations and pressures of the

home or peer group. Texts are a crucial part of literacy events and the study of literacy is partly a study of texts and how they are produced and used. These three components, practices, events, and texts, provide the first proposition of a social theory of literacy, that: *literacy is best understood as a set of social practices; these are observable in events which are mediated by written texts.* The local literacies study was concerned with identifying the events and texts of everyday life and describing people's associated practices. Our prime interest there was to analyse events in order to learn about practices. As with the definition of practices, we take a straightforward view of events at this point, as being activities which involve written texts; discussion throughout this book returns to the definitions of these terms. An example of an everyday literacy event, taken from the local literacies study, is that of cooking a pudding; it is described in Figure 2.

* * *

Once one begins to think in terms of literacy events there are certain things about the nature of reading and writing which become apparent. For instance, in many literacy events there is a mixture of written and spoken language. Many studies of literacy practices have print literacy and written texts as their starting

---

When baking a lemon pie in her kitchen, Rita follows a recipe. She uses it to check the amounts of the ingredients. She estimates the approximate amounts, using teacups and spoons chosen specially for this purpose. The recipe is hand written on a piece of note-paper; it was written out from a book by a friend more than ten years ago. The first time she read the recipe carefully at each stage, but now she only looks at it once or twice. The piece of paper is marked and greasy by having been near the cooking surface on many occasions. It is kept in an envelope with other hand-written recipes and ones cut out of magazines and newspapers. The envelope and some cookery books are on a shelf in the kitchen. The books range in age and condition and include some by Robert Carrier. Sometimes she sits and reads them for pleasure.

Rita does not always go through the same set of activities in making the pie. Sometimes she makes double the amount described in the recipe if more people will be eating it. Sometimes she cooks the pie with her daughter Hayley helping her where necessary. Sometimes she enjoys cooking it, at other times it is more of a chore, when time is limited or she has other things she would rather do. Rita has passed the recipe on to several friends who have enjoyed the pie.

Rita does not always follow recipes exactly, but will add herbs and spices to taste; sometimes she makes up recipes; at one point she describes making a vegetable and pasta dish similar to one she had had as a takeaway meal. She exchanges recipes with other people, although she does not lend her books.

FIGURE 2 COOKING LITERACY

point but it is clear that in literacy events people use written language in an integrated way as part of a range of semiotic systems; these semiotic systems include mathematical systems, musical notation, maps, and other non-text based images. The cookery text has numeracy mixed with print literacy and the recipes come from books, magazines, television, and orally from friends and relatives. By identifying literacy as one of a range of communicative resources available to members of a community, we can examine some of the ways in which it is located in relation to other mass media and new technologies. This is especially pertinent at a time of rapidly changing technologies.

Looking at different literacy events it is clear that literacy is not the same in all contexts; rather, there are different *literacies*. The notion of different literacies has several senses: for example, practices which involve different media or symbolic systems, such as a film or computer, can be regarded as different literacies, as in *film literacy* and *computer literacy*. Another sense is that practices in different cultures and languages can be regarded as different literacies. While accepting these senses of the term, the main way in which we use the notion here is to say that literacies are coherent configurations of literacy practices; often these sets of practices are identifiable and named, as in *academic literacy* or *work-place literacy* and they are associated with particular aspects of cultural life.

This means that, within a given culture, *there are different literacies associated with different domains of life.* Contemporary life can be analysed in a simple way into domains of activity, such as home, school, work-place. It is a useful starting-point to examine the distinct practices in these domains, and then to compare, for example, home and school, or school and work-place. We begin with the home domain and everyday life. The home is often identified as a primary domain in people's literacy lives, for example by James Gee (1990), and central to people's developing sense of social identity. Work is another identifiable domain, where relationships and resources are often structured quite differently from in the home. We might expect the practices associated with cooking, for example, to be quite different in the home and in the work-place—supported, learned, and carried out in different ways. The division of labour is different in institutional kitchens, the scale of the operations, the clothing people wear when cooking, the health and safety precautions they are required to take, and so on. Such practices contribute to the idea that people participate in distinct *discourse communities,* in different domains of life. These communities are groups of people held together by their characteristic ways of talking, acting, valuing, interpreting, and using written language. (See discussion in Swales 1990, pp. 23–27.)

Domains, and the discourse communities associated with them, are not clear-cut, however: there are questions of the permeability of boundaries, of leakages and movement between boundaries, and of overlap between domains. Home and community, for instance, are often treated as being the same domain; nevertheless they are distinct in many ways, including the dimension of public and private behaviour. An important part of the local literacies study was to clarify the domain being studied and to tease apart notions of home, household, neighbourhood, and community. Another aspect is the extent to which this domain is a distinct one with its own practices, and the extent to which the practices that exist in the home originate there, or home practices are exported to other domains. In particular, the private home context appears to be infiltrated by practices from many different public domains.

10   Domains are structured, patterned contexts within which literacy is used and learned. Activities within these domains are not accidental or randomly varying: there are particular configurations of literacy practices and there are regular ways in which people act in many literacy events in particular contexts. Various institutions support and structure activities in particular domains of life. These include family, religion, and education, which are all social institutions. Some of these institutions are more formally structured than others, with explicit rules for procedures, documentation and legal penalties for infringement, whilst others are regulated by the pressure of social conventions and attitudes. Particular literacies have been created by and are structured and sustained by these institutions. Part of the study aims to highlight the ways in which institutions support particular literacy practices.

Socially powerful institutions, such as education, tend to support dominant literacy practices. These dominant practices can be seen as part of whole discourse formations, institutionalised configurations of power and knowledge which are embodied in social relationships. Other vernacular literacies which exist in people's everyday lives are less visible and less supported. This means that *literacy practices are patterned by social institutions and power relationships, and some literacies are more dominant, visible, and influential than others.* One can contrast dominant literacies and vernacular literacies; many of the studies in this book are concerned more with documenting the vernacular literacies which exist, and with exploring their relationship to more dominant literacies.

People are active in what they do and *literacy practices are purposeful and embedded in broader social goals and cultural practices.* Whilst some reading and writing is carried out as an end in itself, typically literacy is a means to some other end. Any study of literacy practices must therefore situate reading and writing activities in these broader contexts and motivations for use. In the cooking example, for instance, the aim is to bake a lemon pie, and the reading of a recipe is incidental to this aim. The recipe is incorporated into a broader set of domestic social practices associated with providing food and caring for children, and it reflects broader social relationships and gendered divisions of labour.

* * *

A first step in reconceptualising literacy is to accept the multiple functions literacy may serve in a given activity, where it can replace spoken language, enable communication, solve a practical problem, or act as a memory aid—in some cases, all at the same time. It is also possible to explore the further work which literacy can do in an activity, and the social meanings it takes on. For instance, there are ways in which literacy acts as *evidence,* as *display,* as *threat,* and as *ritual.* Texts can have multiple roles in an activity and literacy can act in different ways for the different participants in a literacy event; people can be incorporated into the literacy practices of others without reading or writing a single word. The acts of reading and writing are not the only ways in which texts are assigned meaning (as in Barton and Hamilton 1998, Chapter 14).

It is important to shift from a conception of literacy located in individuals to examine ways in which people in groups utilise literacy. In this way literacy becomes a community resource, realised in social relationships rather than a property of individuals. This is true at various levels; at the detailed micro level it can refer to the fact that in particular literacy events there are often several participants taking on different roles and creating something more than their individual practices. At a broader macro level it can mean the ways in which whole communities use literacy. There are social rules about who can produce and use particular literacies and we wish to examine this social regulation of texts. Shifting away from literacy as an individual attribute is one of the most important implications of a practice account of literacy, and one of the ways in which it differs most from more traditional accounts. The ways in which literacy acts as a resource for different sorts of groups are a central theme of Barton and Hamilton (1998), which describes some of the ways in which families, local communities, and organisations regulate and are regulated by literacy practices.

* * *

15   A person's practices can also be located in their own history of literacy. In order to understand this we need to take a life history approach, observing the history within a person's life. There are several dimensions to this: people use literacy to make changes in their lives; literacy changes people and people find themselves in the contemporary world of changing literacy practices. The literacy practices an individual engages with change across their lifetime, as a result of changing demands, available resources, as well as the possibilities and their interests.

Related to the constructed nature of literacy, any theory of literacy implies a theory of learning. *Literacy practices change and new ones are frequently acquired through processes of informal learning and sense making* as well as formal education and training. This learning takes place in particular social contexts and part of this learning is the internalisation of social processes. It is therefore important to understand the nature of informal and vernacular learning strategies and the nature of situated cognition, linking with the work of researchers influenced by Lev Vygotsky, such as Sylvia Scribner, Jean Lave, and colleagues (Scribner 1984; Lave and Wenger, 1991). For this it is necessary to draw upon people's insights into how they learn, their theories about literacy and education, the vernacular strategies they use to learn new literacies. We start out from the position that people's understanding of literacy is an important aspect of their learning, and that people's theories guide their actions. It is here that a study of literacy practices has its most immediate links with education.

NOTE

This chapter is adapted from pages 6–13 of D. Barton and M. Hamilton, *Local Literacies: Reading and Writing in One Community,* Routledge, 1998, with permission of the publishers.

REFERENCES

Barton, D. (1994) *Literacy: An Introduction to the Ecology of Written Language*, Oxford: Blackwell.

Barton, D. and Hamilton, M. (1998) *Local Literacies: Reading and Writing in One Community*, London: Routledge.

Clark, R. and Ivanic, R. (1997) *The Politics of Writing*, London: Routledge.

Gee, J. P. (1990) *Social Linguistics and Literacies: Ideology in Discourses*, London: Palmer Press.

Heath, S. (1983) *Ways with Words: Language, Life and Work in Communities and Classrooms*, Cambridge: Cambridge University Press.

Hoggart, R. (1957) *The Uses of Literacy: Aspects of Working-Class Life*, London: Chatto.

Lave, J. and Wenger, E. (1991) *Situated Learning: Legitimate Peripheral Participation*, Cambridge: Cambridge University Press.

Lemke, J. (1995) *Textual Politics: Discourse and Social Dynamics*, London: Taylor and Francis.

OECD/Statistics Canada (1996) *Literacy, Economy and Society*, Ontario: OECD.

Scribner, S. (1984) 'Studying working intelligence', in B. Rogoff and J. Lave (eds) *Everyday Cognition: Its Development in Social Context*, Cambridge, MA: Harvard University Press.

Street, B. (ed.) (1993) *Cross-cultural Approaches to Literacy*, Cambridge: Cambridge University Press.

Swales, J. (1990) *Genre Analysis: English in Academic and Research Settings*, Cambridge: Cambridge University Press.

Taylor, D. and Dorsey-Gaines, C. (1988) *Growing Up Literate: Learning from Inner-city Families*, London: Heinemann.

▰▰ CRITICAL REFLECTIONS

1. Without doing any research at all, think about the ways that you have heard and/or seen the word literacy used and write all of those ways down. Do you find a pattern among them?

2. As the introduction to this reading outlines, literacy and literacies are key concepts here. How do you define literacy and literacies, and why do you define them as you do?

3. To illustrate their definition of literacies, Barton and Hamilton provide an example of Rita's cooking literacy as she makes a lemon pie. Create a representation—a chart, a list, a map, a diagram, or something else—that shows all of the elements of literacy involved in this illustration. Be sure to include connections to other people (like the friend who gave Rita the recipe) in your representation. What are the different elements of cooking literacy?

4. Reflecting on your representation of Rita's cooking literacy, think about the literacies in which you participate, and where you participate in them. (Barton and Hamilton refer to these different places as "domains.") Schooling is obviously one, since you are a student, and there are likely others,

as well (a religious affiliation or a club or fraternal organization membership, for example). How do you show that you have developed literacies in each of these domains? What skills, behaviors, and other factors are involved?

5. Barton and Hamilton's idea of literacy practices and literacy events are key concepts in this reading. How do you understand their definition of each?

⌦ MAKING CONNECTIONS

1. Barton and Hamilton argue that "literacy practices are patterned by social in-stitutions and power relationships, and some literacies are more dominant, visible, and influential than others. . . . Literacy practices are purposeful and embedded in broader social goals and cultural practices" (64). Consider con-nections between this statement and one or more of the readings included here that focus on students' school experiences: "The Last Shot," "Literacy Among the Amish," "I Just Wanna Be Average," "On the Uses of a Liberal Education I/II," "Fierce Intimacies," or other readings. What literacy practices are evident there? Which do you consider to be dominant, and in what do-main? What "social goals and cultural practices" are advanced through those practices?

2. In this reading, Barton and Hamilton ground literacy practices in very specific contexts. Consider this definition against one implied in Nicholas Lemann's argument for a national curriculum. Could such a curriculum incorporate the definition of literacy practices developed by Barton and Hamilton? Should a national curriculum incorporate this definition of literacy practices?

BELL HOOKS

ENGAGED PEDAGOGY

bell hooks is a teacher, writer, and scholar. This chapter, from hooks' first book, *Teaching to Transgress,* takes up some of the themes that run through-out hooks' many books and essays: race, the contradictory tensions of edu-cation, and feminism. bell hooks is the writing name of Gloria Watkins; the name "bell hooks" comes from Watkins' grandmother and mother. hooks says she uses a pen name in part because it connects her to her past, and in part because it can shift readers' focus away from the author and toward the issues in the writing.

To educate as the practice of freedom is a way of teaching that anyone can learn. That learning process comes easiest to those of us who teach who also believe that there is an aspect of our vocation that is sacred; who believe that our work is not merely to share information but to share in the intellectual and spiritual growth of our students. To teach in a manner that respects and cares for the souls of our students is essential if we are to provide the necessary conditions where learning can most deeply and intimately begin.

Throughout my years as student and professor, I have been most inspired by those teachers who have had the courage to transgress those boundaries that would confine each pupil to a rote, assembly-line approach to learning. Such teachers approach students with the will and desire to respond to our unique beings, even if the situation does not allow the full emergence of a relationship based on mutual recognition. Yet the possibility of such recognition is always present.

Paulo Freire and the Vietnamese Buddhist monk Thich Nhat Hanh are two of the "teachers" who have touched me deeply with their work. When I first began college, Freire's thought gave me the support I needed to challenge the "banking system" of education, that approach to learning that is rooted in the notion that all students need to do is consume information fed to them by a professor and be able to memorize and store it. Early on, it was Freire's insistence that education could be the practice of freedom that encouraged me to create strategies for what he called "conscientization" in the classroom. Translating that term to critical awareness and engagement, I entered the classrooms with the conviction that it was crucial for me and every other student to be an active participant, not a passive consumer. Education as the practice of freedom was continually undermined by professors who were actively hostile to the notion of student participation. Freire's work affirmed that education can only be liberatory when everyone claims knowledge as a field in which we all labor. That notion of mutual labor was affirmed by Thich Nhat Hanh's philosophy of engaged Buddhism, the focus on practice in conjunction with contemplation. His philosophy was similar to Freire's emphasis on "praxis"—action and reflection upon the world in order to change it.

In his work Thich Nhat Hanh always speaks of the teacher as a healer. Like Freire, his approach to knowledge called on students to be active participants, to link awareness with practice. Whereas Freire was primarily concerned with the mind, Thich Nhat Hanh offered a way of thinking about pedagogy which emphasized wholeness, a union of mind, body, and spirit. His focus on a holistic approach to learning and spiritual practice enabled me to overcome years of socialization that had taught me to believe a classroom was diminished if students and professors regarded one another as "whole" human beings, striving not just for knowledge in books, but knowledge about how to live in the world.

5 During my twenty years of teaching, I have witnessed a grave sense of dis-ease among professors (irrespective of their politics) when students want us to see them as whole human beings with complex lives and experiences rather than simply as seekers after compartmentalized bits of knowledge. When I was an undergraduate, Women's Studies was just finding a place in the academy. Those classrooms were the one space where teachers were willing to acknowledge a connection between ideas learned in university settings and those learned in life practices. And, despite those times when students abused that freedom in the

classroom by only wanting to dwell on personal experience, feminist classrooms were, on the whole, one location where I witnessed professors striving to create participatory spaces for the sharing of knowledge. Nowadays, most women's studies professors are not as committed to exploring new pedagogical strategies. Despite this shift, many students still seek to enter feminist classrooms because they continue to believe that there, more than in any other place in the academy, they will have an opportunity to experience education as the practice of freedom.

Progressive, holistic education, "engaged pedagogy" is more demanding than conventional critical or feminist pedagogy. For, unlike these two teaching practices, it emphasizes well-being. That means that teachers must be actively committed to a process of self-actualization that promotes their own well-being if they are to teach in a manner that empowers students. Thich Nhat Hanh emphasized that "the practice of a healer, therapist, teacher or any helping professional should be directed toward his or herself first, because if the helper is unhappy, he or she cannot help many people." In the United States it is rare that anyone talks about teachers in university settings as healers. And it is even more rare to hear anyone suggest that teachers have any responsibility to be self-actualized individuals.

Learning about the work of intellectuals and academics primarily from nineteenth-century fiction and nonfiction during my pre-college years, I was certain that the task for those of us who chose this vocation was to be holistically questing for self-actualization. It was the actual experience of college that disrupted this image. It was there that I was made to feel as though I was terribly naive about "the profession." I learned that far from being self-actualized, the university was seen more as a haven for those who are smart in book knowledge but who might be otherwise unfit for social interaction. Luckily, during my undergraduate years I began to make a distinction between the practice of being an intellectual/teacher and one's role as a member of the academic profession.

It was difficult to maintain fidelity to the idea of the intellectual as someone who sought to be whole—well-grounded in a context where there was little emphasis on spiritual well-being, on care of the soul. Indeed, the objectification of the teacher within bourgeois educational structures seemed to denigrate notions of wholeness and uphold the idea of a mind/body split, one that promotes and supports compartmentalization.

This support reinforces the dualistic separation of public and private, encouraging teachers and students to see no connection between life practices, habits of being, and the roles of professors. The idea of the intellectual questing for a union of mind, body, and spirit had been replaced with notions that being smart meant that one was inherently emotionally unstable and that the best in oneself emerged in one's academic work. This meant that whether academics were drug addicts, alcoholics, batterers, or sexual abusers, the only important aspect of our identity was whether or not our minds functioned, whether we were able to do our jobs in the classroom. The self was presumably emptied out the moment the threshold was crossed, leaving in place only an objective mind—free of experiences and biases. There was fear that the conditions of that self would interfere with the teaching process. Part of the luxury and privilege of the role of teacher/professor today is the absence of any requirement that we be self-actualized. Not surprisingly, professors who are not concerned with inner well-being are the most threatened by the demand on the part of students for liberatory education, for pedagogical processes that will aid them in their own struggle for self-actualization.

10 Certainly it was naive for me to imagine during high school that I would find spiritual and intellectual guidance in university settings from writers, thinkers, scholars. To have found this would have been to stumble across a rare treasure. I learned, along with other students, to consider myself fortunate if I found an interesting professor who talked in a compelling way. Most of my professors were not the slightest bit interested in enlightenment. More than anything they seemed enthralled by the exercise of power and authority within their mini-kingdom, the classroom.

This is not to say that there were not compelling, benevolent dictators, but it is true to my memory that it was rare—absolutely, astonishingly rare—to encounter professors who were deeply committed to progressive pedagogical practices. I was dismayed by this; most of my professors were not individuals whose teaching styles I wanted to emulate.

My commitment to learning kept me attending classes. Yet, even so, because I did not conform—would not be an unquestioning, passive student—some professors treated me with contempt. I was slowly becoming estranged from education. Finding Freire in the midst of that estrangement was crucial to my survival as a student. His work offered both a way for me to understand the limitations of the type of education I was receiving and to discover alternative strategies for learning and teaching. It was particularly disappointing to encounter white male professors who claimed to follow Freire's model even as their pedagogical practices were mired in structures of domination, mirroring the styles of conservative professors even as they approached subjects from a more progressive standpoint.

When I first encountered Paulo Freire, I was eager to see if his style of teaching would embody the pedagogical practices he described so eloquently in his work. During the short time I studied with him, I was deeply moved by his presence, by the way in which his manner of teaching exemplified his pedagogical theory. (Not all students interested in Freire have had a similar experience.) My experience with him restored my faith in liberatory education. I had never wanted to surrender the conviction that one could teach without reinforcing existing systems of domination. I needed to know that professors did not have to be dictators in the classroom.

While I wanted teaching to be my career, I believed that personal success was intimately linked with self-actualization. My passion for this quest led me to interrogate constantly the mind/body split that was so often taken to be a given. Most professors were often deeply antagonistic toward, even scornful of, any approach to learning emerging from a philosophical standpoint emphasizing the union of mind, body, and spirit, rather than the separation of these elements. Like many of the students I now teach, I was often told by powerful academics that I was misguided to seek such a perspective in the academy. Throughout my student years I felt deep inner anguish. Memory of that pain returns as I listen to students express the concern that they will not succeed in academic professions if they want to be well, if they eschew dysfunctional behavior or participation in coercive hierarchies. These students are often fearful, as I was, that there are no spaces in the academy where the will to be self-actualized can be affirmed.

15   This fear is present because many professors have intensely hostile responses to the vision of liberatory education that connects the will to know with the will to become. Within professorial circles, individuals often complain bitterly that students want classes to be "encounter groups." While it is utterly unreasonable for students to expect classrooms to be therapy sessions, it is appropriate for them to hope that the knowledge received in these settings will enrich and enhance them.

Currently, the students I encounter seem far more uncertain about the project of self-actualization than my peers and I were twenty years ago. They feel that there are no clear ethical guidelines shaping actions. Yet, while they despair, they are also adamant that education should be liberatory. They want and demand more from professors than my generation did. There are times when I walk into classrooms overflowing with students who feel terribly wounded in their psyches (many of them see therapists), yet I do not think that they want therapy from me. They do want an education that is healing to the uninformed, unknowing spirit. They do want knowledge that is meaningful. They rightfully expect that my colleagues and I will not offer them information without addressing the connection between what they are learning and their overall life experiences.

This demand on the students' part does not mean that they will always accept our guidance. This is one of the joys of education as the practice of freedom, for it allows students to assume responsibility for their choices. Writing about our teacher/student relationship in a piece for the *Village Voice*, "How to Run the Yard: Off-Line and into the Margins at Yale," one of my students, Gary Dauphin, shares the joys of working with me as well as the tensions that surfaced between us as he began to devote his time to pledging a fraternity rather than cultivating his writing:

> People think academics like Gloria [my given name] are all about difference: but what I learned from her was mostly about sameness, about what I had in common as a black man to people of color; to women and gays and lesbians and the poor and anyone else who wanted in. I did some of this learning by reading but most of it came from hanging out on the fringes of her life. I lived like that for a while, shuttling between high points in my classes and low points outside. Gloria was a safe haven . . . Pledging a fraternity is about as far away as you can get from her classroom, from the yellow kitchen where she used to share her lunch with students in need of various forms of sustenance.

This is Gary writing about the joy. The tension arose as we discussed his reason for wanting to join a fraternity and my disdain for that decision. Gary comments, "They represented a vision of black manhood that she abhorred, one where violence and abuse were primary ciphers of bonding and identity." Describing his assertion of autonomy from my influence he writes, "But she must have also known the limits of even her influence on my life, the limits of books and teachers."

Ultimately, Gary felt that the decision he had made to join a fraternity was not constructive, that I "had taught him openness" where the fraternity had encouraged one-dimensional allegiance. Our interchange both during and after this experience was an example of engaged pedagogy.

Through critical thinking—a process he learned by reading theory and actively analyzing texts—Gary experienced education as the practice of freedom. His final comments about me: "Gloria had only mentioned the entire episode once after it was over, and this to tell me simply that there are many kinds of choices, many kinds of logic. I could make those events mean whatever I wanted as long as I was honest." I have quoted his writing at length because it is testimony affirming engaged pedagogy. It means that my voice is not the only account of what happens in the classroom.

20   Engaged pedagogy necessarily values student expression. In her essay, "Interrupting the Calls for Student Voice in Liberatory Education: A Feminist Poststructuralist Perspective," Mimi Orner employs a Foucauldian framework to suggest that

> Regulatory and punitive means and uses of the confession bring to mind curricular and pedagogical practices which call for students to publicly reveal, even confess, information about their lives and cultures in the presence of authority figures such as teachers.

When education is the practice of freedom, students are not the only ones who are asked to share, to confess. Engaged pedagogy does not seek simply to empower students. Any classroom that employs a holistic model of learning will also be a place where teachers grow, and are empowered by the process. That empowerment cannot happen if we refuse to be vulnerable while encouraging students to take risks. Professors who expect students to share confessional narratives but who are themselves unwilling to share are exercising power in a manner that could be coercive. In my classrooms, I do not expect students to take any risks that I would not take, to share in any way that I would not share. When professors bring narratives of their experiences into classroom discussions it eliminates the possibility that we can function as all-knowing, silent interrogators. It is often productive if professors take the first risk, linking confessional narratives to academic discussions so as to show how experience can illuminate and enhance our understanding of academic material. But most professors must practice being vulnerable in the classroom, being wholly present in mind, body, and spirit.

Progressive professors working to transform the curriculum so that it does not reflect biases or reinforce systems of domination are most often the individuals willing to take the risk that engaged pedagogy requires and to make their teaching practices a site of resistance. In her essay, "On Race and Voice: Challenges for Liberation Education in the 1990s," Chandra Mohanty writes that resistance lies in self-conscious engagement with dominant, normative discourses and representations and in the active creation of oppositional analytic and cultural spaces. Resistance that is random and isolated is clearly not as effective as that which is mobilized through systemic politicized practices of teaching and learning. Uncovering and reclaiming subjugated knowledge is one way to lay claims to alternative histories. But these knowledges need to be understood and defined pedagogically, as questions of strategy and practice as well as of scholarship, in order to transform educational institutions radically.

Professors who embrace the challenge of self-actualization will be better able to create pedagogical practices that engage students, providing them with ways of knowing that enhance their capacity to live fully and deeply.

▰ Critical Reflections

1. In the beginning of this chapter, bell hooks writes about "educat[ing] as the practice of freedom" (67). What do you think she means by this?

2. What do you think hooks' college education taught her about how her professors understood education? Do you agree with the position that they took? Why or why not?

3. hooks writes that while in college, she "became estranged from education." Based on your interpretation of this statement, why do you think it happened to her? Do you think the same thing can happen to others? Why or why not?

4. How would you define "engaged pedagogy" that hooks calls for in this chapter?

▰ Making Connections

1. In this chapter, hooks draws on Mimi Orner to question teachers and classes who ask students to share information about their own lives for teaching purposes within the context of the academy. Many of the assignments and reading questions in this book ask you to think about or draw from your own life. Based on your experiences with these questions and assignments, what is your response to Orner and hooks' charge?

2. hooks cites Paolo Freire as a teacher who inspired her in this work. What parallels do you draw between their ideas? What differences do you see?

3. hooks charges that traditionally, education has not left space for students "on the margins." Consider this statement against narratives about other non-mainstream students included here, like Cedric Jennings, Mike Rose, or the students in "The Last Shot." How do their experiences support and/or refute hooks' ideas?

PAOLO FREIRE

THE BANKING CONCEPT OF EDUCATION

"The Banking Concept of Education" is a chapter from Paolo Freire's book, *Pedagogy of the Oppressed*. Freire believed that teachers and students should work together to develop the knowledge and consciousness necessary to overcome oppression. He put this belief into practice when he worked in impoverished areas in Brazil, teaching illiterate adults to read and write so that they could participate in the political system that governed their lives. When the government of Brazil was overthrown in a coup in 1964, Freire was exiled from the country. He returned only in 1988, after working in Chile and as a Professor at Harvard University, to become Minister of Education in Sao Paolo, Brazil, the nation's capital. Until his death in 1997 at the age of 75, Freire travelled widely, speaking with large audiences about liberation education. He remains one of the most frequently studied educators in the world today.

A careful analysis of the teacher-student relationship at any level, inside or outside the school, reveals its fundamentally *narrative* character. This relationship involves a narrating Subject (the teacher) and patient, listening objects (the students). The contents, whether values or empirical dimensions of reality, tend in the process of being narrated to become lifeless and petrified. Education is suffering from narration sickness.

The teacher talks about reality as if it were motionless, static, compartmentalized, and predictable. Or else he expounds on a topic completely alien to the existential experience of the students. His task is to "fill" the students with the contents of his narration—contents which are detached from reality, disconnected from the totality that engendered them and could give them significance. Words are emptied of their concreteness and become a hollow, alienated, and alienating verbosity.

The outstanding characteristic of this narrative education, then, is the sonority of words, not their transforming power. "Four times four is sixteen; the capital of Pará is Belém." The student records, memorizes, and repeats these phrases without perceiving what four times four really means, or realizing the true significance of "capital" in the affirmation "the capital of Pará is Belém," that is, what Belém means for Pará and what Pará means for Brazil.

Narration (with the teacher as narrator) leads the students to memorize mechanically the narrated content. Worse yet, it turns them into "containers," into "receptacles" to be "filled" by the teacher. The more completely he fills the receptacles, the better a teacher he is. The more meekly the receptacles permit themselves to be filled, the better students they are.

5   Education thus becomes an act of depositing, in which the students are the depositories and the teacher is the depositor. Instead of communicating, the

teacher issues communiqués and makes deposits which the students patiently receive, memorize, and repeat. This is the "banking" concept of education, in which the scope of action allowed to the students extends only as far as receiving, filing, and storing the deposits. They do, it is true, have the opportunity to become collectors or cataloguers of the things they store. But in the last analysis, it is men themselves who are filed away through the lack of creativity, transformation, and knowledge in this (at best) misguided system. For apart from inquiry, apart from the praxis, men cannot be truly human. Knowledge emerges only through invention and re-invention, through the restless, impatient, continuing, hopeful inquiry men pursue in the world, with the world, and with each other.

In the banking concept of education, knowledge is a gift bestowed by those who consider themselves knowledgeable upon those whom they consider to know nothing. Projecting an absolute ignorance onto others, a characteristic of the ideology of oppression, negates education and knowledge as processes of inquiry. The teacher presents himself to his students as their necessary opposite; by considering their ignorance absolute, he justifies his own existence. The students, alienated like the slave in the Hegelian dialectic, accept their ignorance as justifying the teacher's existence—but, unlike the slave, they never discover that they educate the teacher.

The *raison d'être* of libertarian education, on the other hand, lies in its drive towards reconciliation. Education must begin with the solution of the teacher-student contradiction, by reconciling the poles of the contradiction so that both are simultaneously teachers *and* students.

This solution is not (nor can it be) found in the banking concept. On the contrary, banking education maintains and even stimulates the contradiction through the following attitudes and practices, which mirror oppressive society as a whole:

(a) the teacher teaches and the students are taught;

(b) the teacher knows everything and the students know nothing;

(c) the teacher thinks and the students are thought about;

(d) the teacher talks and the students listen—meekly;

(e) the teacher disciplines and the students are disciplined;

(f) the teacher chooses and enforces his choice, and the students comply;

(g) the teacher acts and the students have the illusion of acting through the action of the teacher;

(h) the teacher chooses the program content, and the students (who were not consulted) adapt to it;

(i) the teacher confuses the authority of knowledge with his own professional authority, which he sets in opposition to the freedom of the students;

(j) the teacher is the Subject of the learning process, while the pupils are mere objects.

It is not surprising that the banking concept of education regards men as adaptable, manageable beings. The more students work at storing the deposits entrusted to them, the less they develop the critical consciousness which would result from their intervention in the world as transformers of that world. The more completely they accept the passive role imposed on them, the more they tend simply to adapt to the world as it is and to the fragmented view of reality deposited in them.

10   The capability of banking education to minimize or annul the students' creative power and to stimulate their credulity serves the interests of the oppressors, who care neither to have the world revealed nor to see it transformed. The oppressors use their "humanitarianism" to preserve a profitable situation. Thus they react almost instinctively against any experiment in education which stimulates the critical faculties and is not content with a partial view of reality but always seeks out the ties which link one point to another and one problem to another.

Indeed, the interests of the oppressors lie in "changing the consciousness of the oppressed, not the situation which oppresses them";[1] for the more the oppressed can be led to adapt to that situation, the more easily they can be dominated. To achieve this end, the oppressors use the banking concept of education in conjunction with a paternalistic social action apparatus, within which the oppressed receive the euphemistic title of "welfare recipients." They are treated as individual cases, as marginal men who deviate from the general configuration of a "good, organized, and just" society. The oppressed are regarded as the pathology of the healthy society, which must therefore adjust these "incompetent and lazy" folk to its own patterns by changing their mentality. These marginals need to be "integrated," "incorporated" into the healthy society that they have "forsaken."

The truth is, however, that the oppressed are not "marginals," are not men living "outside" society. They have always been "inside"—inside the structure which made them "beings for others." The solution is not to "integrate" them into the structure of oppression, but to transform that structure so that they can become "beings for themselves." Such transformation, of course, would undermine the oppressors' purposes; hence their utilization of the banking concept of education to avoid the threat of student *conscientização*.

The banking approach to adult education, for example, will never propose to students that they critically consider reality. It will deal instead with such vital questions as whether Roger gave green grass to the goat, and insist upon the importance of learning that, on the contrary, Roger gave green grass to the rabbit. The "humanism" of the banking approach masks the effort to turn men into automatons—the very negation of their ontological vocation to be more fully human.

Those who use the banking approach, knowingly or unknowingly (for there are innumerable well-intentioned bank-clerk teachers who do not realize that they are serving only to dehumanize), fail to perceive that the deposits themselves contain contradictions about reality. But, sooner or later, these contradic-

---

[1]Simone de Beauvoir, *La Pensée de Droite, Aujord'hui* (Paris); ST, *El Pensamiento político de la Derecha* (Buenos Aires, 1963), p. 34.

tions may lead formerly passive students to turn against their domestication and the attempt to domesticate reality. They may discover through existential experience that their present way of life is irreconcilable with their vocation to become fully human. They may perceive through their relations with reality that reality is really a *process,* undergoing constant transformation. If men are searchers and their ontological vocation is humanization, sooner or later they may perceive the contradiction in which banking education seeks to maintain them, and then engage themselves in the struggle for their liberation.

15 But the humanist, revolutionary educator cannot wait for this possibility to materialize. From the outset, his efforts must coincide with those of the students to engage in critical thinking and the quest for mutual humanization. His efforts must be imbued with a profound trust in men and their creative power. To achieve this, he must be a partner of the students in his relations with them.

The banking concept does not admit to such partnership—and necessarily so. To resolve the teacher-student contradiction, to exchange the role of depositor, prescriber, domesticator, for the role of student among students would be to undermine the power of oppression and serve the cause of liberation.

Implicit in the banking concept is the assumption of a dichotomy between man and the world: man is merely *in* the world, not *with* the world or with others; man is spectator, not re-creator. In this view, man is not a conscious being (*corpo consciente*); he is rather the possessor of *a* consciousness: an empty "mind" passively open to the reception of deposits of reality from the world outside. For example, my desk, my books, my coffee cup, all the objects before me—as bits of the world which surrounds me—would be "inside" me, exactly as I am inside my study right now. This view makes no distinction between being accessible to consciousness and entering consciousness. The distinction, however, is essential: the objects which surround me are simply accessible to my consciousness, not located within it. I'am aware of them, but they are not inside me.

It follows logically from the banking notion of consciousness that the educator's role is to regulate the way the world "enters into" the students. His task is to organize a process which already occurs spontaneously, to "fill" the students by making deposits of information which he considers to constitute true knowledge.[2] And since men "receive" the world as passive entities, education should make them more passive still, and adapt them to the world. The educated man is the adapted man, because he is better "fit" for the world. Translated into practice, this concept is well suited to the purposes of the oppressors, whose tranquility rests on how well men fit the world the oppressors have created, and how little they question it.

The more completely the majority adapt to the purposes which the dominant minority prescribe for them (thereby depriving them of the right to their own purposes), the more easily the minority can continue to prescribe. The theory

---

[2]This concept corresponds to what Sartre calls the "digestive" or "nutritive" concept of education, in which knowledge is "fed" by the teacher to the students to "fill them out." See Jean-Paul Sartre, "Une idée fundamentale de la phénoménologie de Husserl: L'intentionalité," *Situations 1* (Paris, 1947).

and practice of banking education serve this end quite efficiently. Verbalistic lessons, reading requirements,[3] the methods for evaluating "knowledge," the distance between the teacher and the taught, the criteria for promotion: everything in this ready-to-wear approach serves to obviate thinking.

20   The bank-clerk educator does not realize that there is no true security in his hypertrophied role, that one must seek to live *with* others in solidarity. One cannot impose oneself, nor even merely co-exist with one's students. Solidarity requires true communication, and the concept by which such an educator is guided fears and proscribes communication.

Yet only through communication can human life hold meaning. The teacher's thinking is authenticated only by the authenticity of the students' thinking. The teacher cannot think for his students, nor can he impose his thought on them. Authentic thinking, thinking that is concerned about *reality*, does not take place in ivory tower isolation, but only in communication. If it is true that thought has meaning only when generated by action upon the world, the subordination of students to teachers becomes impossible.

Because banking education begins with a false understanding of men as objects, it cannot promote the development of what Fromm calls "biophily," but instead produces its opposite: "necrophily."

> While life is characterized by growth in a structured, functional manner, the necrophilous person loves all that does not grow, all that is mechanical. The necrophilous person is driven by the desire to transform the organic into the inorganic, to approach life mechanically, as if all living persons were things. . . . Memory, rather than experience; having, rather than being, is what counts. The necrophilous person can relate to an object—a flower or a person—only if he possesses it; hence a threat to his possession is a threat to himself; if he loses possession he loses contact with the world. . . . He loves control, and in the act of controlling he kills life.[4]

Oppression—overwhelming control—is necrophilic; it is nourished by love of death, not life. The banking concept of education, which serves the interests of oppression, is also necrophilic. Based on a mechanistic, static, naturalistic, spatialized view of consciousness, it transforms students into receiving objects. It attempts to control thinking and action, leads men to adjust to the world, and inhibits their creative power.

When their efforts to act responsibly are frustrated, when they find themselves unable to use their faculties, men suffer. "This suffering due to impotence is rooted in the very fact that the human equilibrium has been disturbed."[5] But the inability to act which causes men's anguish also causes them to reject their impotence, by attempting

---

[3]For example, some professors specify in their reading lists that a book should be read from pages 10 to 15—and do this to "help" their students!

[4]Fromm, *op. cit.,* p. 41.

[5]*Ibid.,* p. 31.

. . . to restore [their] capacity to act. But can [they], and how? One way is to submit to and identify with a person or group having power. By this symbolic participation in another person's life, [men have] the illusion of acting, when in reality [they] only submit to and become a part of those who act.[6]

25   Populist manifestations perhaps best exemplify this type of behavior by the oppressed, who, by identifying with charismatic leaders, come to feel that they themselves are active and effective. The rebellion they express as they emerge in the historical process is motivated by that desire to act effectively. The dominant elites consider the remedy to be more domination and repression, carried out in the name of freedom, order, and social peace (that is, the peace of the elites). Thus they can condemn—logically, from their point of view—"the violence of a strike by workers and [can] call upon the state in the same breath to use violence in putting down the strike."[7]

Education as the exercise of domination stimulates the credulity of students, with the ideological intent (often not perceived by educators) of indoctrinating them to adapt to the world of oppression. This accusation is not made in the naïve hope that the dominant elites will thereby simply abandon the practice. Its objective is to call the attention of true humanists to the fact that they cannot use banking educational methods in the pursuit of liberation, for they would only negate that very pursuit. Nor may a revolutionary society inherit these methods from an oppressor society. The revolutionary society which practices banking education is either misguided or mistrusting of men. In either event, it is threatened by the specter of reaction.

Unfortunately, those who espouse the cause of liberation are themselves surrounded and influenced by the climate which generates the banking concept, and often do not perceive its true significance or its dehumanizing power. Paradoxically, then, they utilize this same instrument of alienation in what they consider an effort to liberate. Indeed, some "revolutionaries" brand as "innocents," "dreamers," or even "reactionaries" those who would challenge this educational practice. But one does not liberate men by alienating them. Authentic liberation—the process of humanization—is not another deposit to be made in men. Liberation is a praxis: the action and reflection of men upon their world in order to transform it. Those truly committed to the cause of liberation can accept neither the mechanistic concept of consciousness as an empty vessel to be filled, nor the use of banking methods of domination (propaganda, slogans—deposits) in the name of liberation.

Those truly committed to liberation must reject the banking concept in its entirety, adopting instead a concept of men as conscious beings, and consciousness as consciousness intent upon the world. They must abandon the educational goal of deposit-making and replace it with the posing of the problems of men in their relations with the world. "Problem-posing" education, responding

---

[6]*Ibid.*

[7]Reinhold Niebuhr, *Moral Man and Immoral Society* (New York, 1960), p. 130.

to the essence of consciousness—*intentionality*—rejects communiqués and embodies communication. It epitomizes the special characteristic of consciousness: being *conscious of,* not only as intent on objects but as turned in upon itself in a Jasperian "split"—consciousness as consciousness *of* consciousness.

Liberating education consists in acts of cognition, not transferrals of information. It is a learning situation in which the cognizable object (far from being the end of the cognitive act) intermediates the cognitive actors—teacher on the one hand and students on the other. Accordingly, the practice of problem-posing education entails at the outset that the teacher-student contradiction be resolved. Dialogical relations—indispensable to the capacity of cognitive actors to cooperate in perceiving the same cognizable object—are otherwise impossible.

30　　Indeed, problem-posing education, which breaks with the vertical patterns characteristic of banking education, can fulfill its function as the practice of freedom only if it can overcome the above contradiction. Through dialogue, the teacher-of-the-students and the students-of-the-teacher cease to exist and a new term emerges: teacher-student with students-teachers. The teacher is no longer merely the-one-who-teaches, but one who is himself taught in dialogue with the students, who in turn while being taught also teach. They become jointly responsible for a process in which all grow. In this process, arguments based on "authority" are no longer valid; in order to function, authority must be *on the side of* freedom, not *against* it. Here, no one teaches another, nor is anyone self-taught. Men teach each other, mediated by the world, by the cognizable objects which in banking education are "owned" by the teacher.

The banking concept (with its tendency to dichotomize everything) distinguishes two stages in the action of the educator. During the first, he cognizes a cognizable object while he prepares his lessons in his study or his laboratory; during the second, he expounds to his students about that object. The students are not called upon to know, but to memorize the contents narrated by the teacher. Nor do the students practice any act of cognition, since the object towards which that act should be directed is the property of the teacher rather than a medium evoking the critical reflection of both teacher and students. Hence in the name of the "preservation of culture and knowledge" we have a system which achieves neither true knowledge nor true culture.

The problem-posing method does not dichotomize the activity of the teacher-student: he is not "cognitive" at one point and "narrative" at another. He is always "cognitive," whether preparing a project or engaging in dialogue with the students. He does not regard cognizable objects as his private property, but as the object of reflection by himself and the students. In this way, the problem-posing educator constantly re-forms his reflections in the reflection of the students. The students—no longer docile listeners—are now critical co-investigators in dialogue with the teacher. The teacher presents the material to the students for their consideration, and re-considers his earlier considerations as the students express their own. The role of the problem-posing educator is to create, together with the students, the conditions under which knowledge at the level of the *doxa* is superseded by true knowledge, at the level of the *logos*.

Whereas banking education anesthetizes and inhibits creative power, problem-posing education involves a constant unveiling of reality. The former attempts to maintain the *submersion* of consciousness; the latter strives for the *emergence* of consciousness and *critical intervention* in reality.

Students, as they are increasingly posed with problems relating to themselves in the world and with the world, will feel increasingly challenged and obliged to respond to that challenge. Because they apprehend the challenge as interrelated to other problems within a total context, not as a theoretical question, the resulting comprehension tends to be increasingly critical and thus constantly less alienated. Their response to the challenge evokes new challenges, followed by new understandings; and gradually the students come to regard themselves as committed.

35 Education as the practice of freedom—as opposed to education as the practice of domination—denies that man is abstract, isolated, independent, and unattached to the world; it also denies that the world exists as a reality apart from men. Authentic reflection considers neither abstract man nor the world without men, but men in their relations with the world. In these relations consciousness and world are simultaneous: consciousness neither precedes the world nor follows it.

> La conscience et le monde sont dormés d'un même coup: extérieur par essence à la conscience, le monde est, par essence relatif à elle.[8]

In one of our culture circles in Chile, the group was discussing (based on a codification[9]) the anthropological concept of culture. In the midst of the discussion, a peasant who by banking standards was completely ignorant said: "Now I see that without man there is no world." When the educator responded: "Let's say, for the sake of argument, that all the men on earth were to die, but that the earth itself remained, together with trees, birds, animals, rivers, seas, the stars . . . wouldn't all this be a world?" "Oh no," the peasant replied emphatically. "There would be no one to say: 'This is a world'."

The peasant wished to express the idea that there would be lacking the consciousness of the world which necessarily implies the world of consciousness. *I* cannot exist without a *not-I*. In turn, the *not-I* depends on that existence. The world which brings consciousness into existence becomes the world *of* that consciousness. Hence, the previously cited affirmation of Sartre: "*La conscience et le monde sont dormés d'un même coup.*"

As men, simultaneously reflecting on themselves and on the world, increase the scope of their perception, they begin to direct their observations towards previously inconspicuous phenomena:

> In perception properly so-called, as an explicit awareness [*Gewahren*], I am turned towards the object, to the paper, for instance. I apprehend it as being this here and now. The apprehension is a singling out, every object having a background in experience. Around and about the paper lie books, pencils, ink-well, and so forth,

---

[8]Sartre, *op. cit.*, p. 32.
[9]See Chapter 3.—Translator's note.

and these in a certain sense are also "perceived", perceptually there, in the "field of intuition"; but whilst I was turned towards the paper there was no turning in their direction, nor any apprehending of them, not even in a secondary sense. They appeared and yet were not singled out, were not posited on their own account. Every perception of a thing has such a zone of background intuitions or background awareness, if "intuiting" already includes the state of being turned towards, and this also is a "conscious experience", or more briefly a "consciousness of" all indeed that in point of fact lies in the co-perceived objective background.[10]

That which had existed objectively but had not been perceived in its deeper implications (if indeed it was perceived at all) begins to "stand out," assuming the character of a problem and therefore of challenge. Thus, men begin to single out elements from their "background awarenesses" and to reflect upon them. These elements are now objects of men's consideration, and, as such, objects of their action and cognition.

In problem-posing education, men develop their power to perceive critically *the way they exist* in the world *with which* and *in which* they find themselves; they come to see the world not as a static reality, but as a reality in process, in transformation. Although the dialectical relations of men with the world exist independently of how these relations are perceived (or whether or not they are perceived at all), it is also true that the form of action men adopt is to a large extent a function of how they perceive themselves in the world. Hence, the teacher-student and the students-teachers reflect simultaneously on themselves and the world without dichotomizing this reflection from action, and thus establish an authentic form of thought and action.

40 Once again, the two educational concepts and practices under analysis come into conflict. Banking education (for obvious reasons) attempts, by mythicizing reality, to conceal certain facts which explain the way men exist in the world; problem-posing education sets itself the task of demythologizing. Banking education resists dialogue; problem-posing education regards dialogue as indispensable to the act of cognition which unveils reality. Banking education treats students as objects of assistance; problem-posing education makes them critical thinkers. Banking education inhibits creativity and domesticates (although it cannot completely destroy) the *intentionality* of consciousness by isolating consciousness from the world, thereby denying men their ontological and historical vocation of becoming more fully human. Problem-posing education bases itself on creativity and stimulates true reflection and action upon reality, thereby responding to the vocation of men as beings who are authentic only when engaged in inquiry and creative transformation. In sum: banking theory and practice, as immobilizing and fixating forces, fail to acknowledge men as historical beings; problem-posing theory and practice take man's historicity as their starting point.

Problem-posing education affirms men as beings in the process of *becoming*—as unfinished, uncompleted beings in and with a likewise unfinished reality. Indeed, in contrast to other animals who are unfinished, but not histori-

---

[10]Edmund Husserl, *Ideas—General Introduction to Pure Phenomenology* (London, 1969), pp. 105–106.

cal, men know themselves to be unfinished; they are aware of their incompletion. In this incompletion and this awareness lie the very roots of education as an exclusively human manifestation. The unfinished character of men and the transformational character of reality necessitate that education be an ongoing activity.

Education is thus constantly remade in the praxis. In order to *be*, it must *become*. Its "duration" (in the Bergsonian meaning of the word) is found in the interplay of the opposites *permanence* and *change*. The banking method emphasizes permanence and becomes reactionary; problem-posing education—which accepts neither a "well-behaved" present nor a predetermined future—roots itself in the dynamic present and becomes revolutionary.

Problem-posing education is revolutionary futurity. Hence it is prophetic (and, as such, hopeful). Hence, it corresponds to the historical nature of man. Hence, it affirms men as beings who transcend themselves, who move forward and look ahead, for whom immobility represents a fatal threat, for whom looking at the past must only be a means of understanding more clearly what and who they are so that they can more wisely build the future. Hence, it identifies with the movement which engages men as beings aware of their incompletion—an historical movement which has its point of departure, its Subjects and its objective.

The point of departure of the movement lies in men themselves. But since men do not exist apart from the world, apart from reality, the movement must begin with the men-world relationship. Accordingly, the point of departure must always be with men in the "here and now," which constitutes the situation within which they are submerged, from which they emerge, and in which they intervene. Only by starting from this situation—which determines their perception of it— can they begin to move. To do this authentically they must perceive their state not as fated and unalterable, but merely as limiting—and therefore challenging.

45   Whereas the banking method directly or indirectly reinforces men's fatalistic perception of their situation, the problem-posing method presents this very situation to them as a problem. As the situation becomes the object of their cognition, the naïve or magical perception which produced their fatalism gives way to perception which is able to perceive itself even as it perceives reality, and can thus be critically objective about that reality.

A deepened consciousness of their situation leads men to apprehend that situation as an historical reality susceptible of transformation. Resignation gives way to the drive for transformation and inquiry, over which men feel themselves to be in control. If men, as historical beings necessarily engaged with other men in a movement of inquiry, did not control that movement, it would be (and is) a violation of men's humanity. Any situation in which some men prevent others from engaging in the process of inquiry is one of violence. The means used are not important; to alienate men from their own decision-making is to change them into objects.

This movement of inquiry must be directed towards humanization—man's historical vocation. The pursuit of full humanity, however, cannot be carried out in isolation or individualism, but only in fellowship and solidarity; therefore it cannot unfold in the antagonistic relations between oppressors and oppressed. No one can be authentically human while he prevents others from being so.

Attempting *to be more* human, individualistically, leads to *having more,* egotistically: a form of dehumanization. Not that it is not fundamental *to have* in order *to be* human. Precisely because it *is* necessary, some men's *having* must not be allowed to constitute an obstacle to others' *having,* must not consolidate the power of the former to crush the latter.

Problem-posing education, as a humanist and liberating praxis, posits as fundamental that men subjected to domination must fight for their emancipation. To that end, it enables teachers and students to become Subjects of the educational process by overcoming authoritarianism and an alienating intellectualism; it also enables men to overcome their false perception of reality. The world—no longer something to be described with deceptive words—becomes the object of that transforming action by men which results in their humanization.

Problem-posing education does not and cannot serve the interests of the oppressor. No oppressive order could permit the oppressed to begin to question: Why? While only a revolutionary society can carry out this education in systematic terms, the revolutionary leaders need not take full power before they can employ the method. In the revolutionary process, the leaders cannot utilize the banking method as an interim measure, justified on ground of expediency, with the intention of *later* behaving in a genuinely revolutionary fashion. They must be revolutionary—that is to say, dialogical—from the outset.

⧉ CRITICAL REFLECTIONS

1. In the first paragraph of this reading, Freire writes that teacher-student relationships are "fundamentally *narrative* [in] character," and that "education is suffering from narration sickness" (74). What do you think Freire means by this? Focus on one of your own classes and sketch out the narrative of that class.

2. Two key concepts lie at the center of this reading: banking and problem-posing. How would you define both, and what do you see as the roles of teachers and students in them?

3. One of the challenges of Freire's reading is that banking and problem-posing are theoretical concepts, and the few examples that Freire provides concern Brazil. To ground these theories in a more accessible practice, come up with your own example of what you would consider a banking and a problem-posing learning situation (whether in class or outside).

4. Freire frames his discussion of banking and problem-posing models within the broader issue of oppression and liberation. How do you interpret his connections between banking and oppression, and problem-posing and liberation? Do you agree with his analysis?

5. Discussing the ways that problem-posing education alters relationships between teachers and students, Freire writes that:

> the problem-posing educator constantly re-forms his reflections in the reflection of the students. The students—no longer docile listeners—are now critical co-investigators in dialogue with the teacher. The teacher presents

the material to the students for their consideration, and re-considers his earlier considerations as the students express their own. The role of the problem-posing educator is to create, together with the students, the conditions under which knowledge at the level of the *doxa*[11] is superseded by true knowledge, at the level of the *logos*[12]. (80)

6. For some, this is a different way to think about education. Sketch out (in words, pictures, or otherwise) a class or assignment where this would happen. What would it be like? Would it change relationships between teachers and students? How or how not?

▰▰ MAKING CONNECTIONS

1. In "The Banking Model," Freire writes that "the deposits themselves contain contradictions about reality" (76) Choose another reading in this text that you think reflects elements of the banking concept. What deposits do you think the educators there are trying to make in students? Do you see contradictions in them?

2. Freire writes that the purpose of education is to lead students to particular roles, which are themselves intended to maintain social order and perpetuate the interests of those in power. Consider the experiences of Lorene Cary, Cedric Jennings, Mike Rose, and/or the players in "The Last Shot" along with this statement. How do you think they support and/or refute it?

THEODORE SIZER

WHAT HIGH SCHOOL IS

"What High School Is" is the opening chapter of Theodore Sizer's book *Horace's Compromise: The Dilemma of the American High School*. That book, published in 1984, was the first in a trilogy authored by Sizer that explored the problematic structures surrounding American public education. Through a distinguished career, Sizer has long been concerned with questions of how schools can most effectively work, and what working means. Even after retiring as Professor of Education at Brown University in 1996, he has remained active in education. After his retirement he became headmaster of an independent (private) school in Massachusetts; he also remains the head of the Coalition of Essential Schools, an organization devoted to school reform that he founded in 1983.

Mark, sixteen and a genial eleventh-grader, rides a bus to Franklin High School, arriving at 7:25. It is an Assembly Day, so the schedule is adapted to allow for a

---

[11]Knowledge based on opinion and not necessarily grounded in evidence, reasoning.
[12]Knowledge that reflects logic and human reasoning.

meeting of the entire school. He hangs out with his friends, first outside school and then inside, by his locker. He carries a pile of textbooks and notebooks; in all, it weighs eight and a half pounds.

From 7:30 to 8:19, with nineteen other students, he is in Room 304 for English class. The Shakespeare play being read this year by the eleventh grade is *Romeo and Juliet*. The teacher, Ms. Viola, has various students in turn take parts and read out loud. Periodically, she interrupts the (usually halting) recitations to ask whether the thread of the conversation in the play is clear. Mark is entertained by the stumbling readings of some of his classmates. He hopes he will not be asked to be Romeo, particularly if his current steady, Sally, is Juliet. There is a good deal of giggling in class, and much attention paid to who may be called on next. Ms. Viola reminds the class of a test on this part of the play to be given next week.

The bell rings at 8:19. Mark goes to the boys' room, where he sees a classmate who he thinks is a wimp but who constantly tries to be a buddy. Mark avoids the leech by rushing off. On the way, he notices two boys engaged in some sort of transaction, probably over marijuana. He pays them no attention. 8:24. Typing class. The rows of desks that embrace big office machines are almost filled before the bell. Mark is uncomfortable here: typing class is girl country. The teacher constantly threatens what to Mark is a humiliatingly female future: "Your employer won't like these erasures." The minutes during the period are spent copying a letter from a handbook onto business stationery. Mark struggles to keep from looking at his work; the teacher wants him to watch only the material from which he is copying. Mark is frustrated, uncomfortable, and scared that he will not complete his letter by the class's end, which would be embarrassing.

Nine tenths of the students present at school that day are assembled in the auditorium by the 9:18 bell. The dilatory tenth still stumble in, running down aisles. Annoyed class deans try to get the mob settled. The curtains part; the program is a concert by a student rock group. Their electronic gear flashes under the lights, and the five boys and one girl in the group work hard at being casual. Their movements on stage are studiously at three-quarter time, and they chat with one another as though the tumultuous screaming of their schoolmates were totally inaudible. The girl balances on a stool; the boys crank up the music. It is very soft rock, the sanitized lyrics surely cleared with the assistant principal. The girl sings, holding the mike close to her mouth, but can scarcely be heard. Her light voice is tentative, and the lyrics indecipherable. The guitars, amplified, are tuneful, however, and the drums are played with energy.

5   The students around Mark—all juniors, since they are seated by class—alternately slouch in their upholstered, hinged seats, talking to one another, or sit forward, leaning on the chair backs in front of them, watching the band. A boy near Mark shouts noisily at the microphone-fondling singer, "Bite it...ohhh," and the area around Mark explodes in vulgar male laughter, but quickly subsides. A teacher walks down the aisle. Songs continue, to great applause. Assembly is over at 9:46, two minutes early.

9:53 and biology class. Mark was at a different high school last year and did not take this course there as a tenth-grader. He is in it now, and all but one of his classmates are a year younger than he. He sits on the side, not taking part in the chatter that goes on after the bell. At 9:57, the public address system goes on, with the announcements of the day. After a few words from the principal ("Here's today's cheers and jeers. . ." with a cheer for the winning basketball team and a jeer for the spectators who made a ruckus at the gymnasium), the task is taken over by officers of ASB (Associated Student Bodies). There is an appeal for "bat bunnies." Carnations are for sale by the Girls' League. Miss Indian American is coming. Students are auctioning off their services (background catcalls are heard) to earn money for the prom. Nominees are needed for the ballot for school bachelor and school bachelorette. The announcements end with a "thought for the day. When you throw a little mud, you lose a little ground."

At 10:04 the biology class finally turns to science. The teacher, Mr. Robbins, has placed one of several labeled laboratory specimens—some are pinned in frames, others swim in formaldehyde—on each of the classroom's eight laboratory tables. The three or so students whose chairs circle each of these benches are to study the specimen and make notes about it or drawings of it. After a few minutes each group of three will move to another table. The teacher points out that these specimens are of organisms already studied in previous classes. He says that the period-long test set for the following day will involve observing some of these specimens—then to be without labels—and writing an identifying paragraph on each. Mr. Robbins points out that some of the printed labels ascribe the specimens names different from those given in the textbook. He explains that biologists often give several names to the same organism.

The class now falls to peering, writing, and quiet talking. Mr. Robbins comes over to Mark, and in whispered words asks him to carry a requisition form for science department materials to the business office. Mark, because of his "older" status, is usually chosen by Robbins for this kind of errand. Robbins gives Mark the form and a green hall pass to show to any teacher who might challenge him, on his way to the office, for being out of a classroom. The errand takes Mark four minutes. Meanwhile Mark's group is hard at work but gets to only three of the specimens before the bell rings at 10:42. As the students surge out, Robbins shouts a reminder about a "double" laboratory period on Thursday.

Between classes one of the seniors asks Mark whether he plans to be a candidate for schoolwide office next year. Mark says no. He starts to explain. The 10:47 bell rings, meaning that he is late for French class.

10   There are fifteen students in Monsieur Bates's language class. He hands out tests taken the day before: *"C'est bien fait, Etienne . . . c'est mieux, Marie . . . Tch, tch, Robert . . ."* Mark notes his C+ and peeks at the A– in front of Susanna, next to him. The class has been assigned seats by M. Bates; Mark resents sitting next to prissy, brainy Susanna. Bates starts by asking a student to read a question and give the correct answer. *"James, question un."* James haltingly reads the question and gives an answer that Bates, now speaking English, says is incomplete. In due course: *"Mark, question cinq."* Mark does his bit, and the sequence goes on, the right quiz questions and answers filling about twenty minutes of time.

"Turn to page forty-nine. *Maintenant, lisez après moi . . ."* and Bates reads a sentence and has the class echo it. Mark is embarrassed by this and mumbles with a barely audible sound. Others, like Susanna, keep the decibel count up, so

Mark can hide. This I-say-you-repeat drill is interrupted once by the public address system, with an announcement about a meeting for the cheerleaders. Bates finishes the class, almost precisely at the bell, with a homework assignment. The students are to review these sentences for a brief quiz the following day. Mark takes note of the assignment, because he knows that tomorrow will be a day of busy-work in French class. Much though he dislikes oral drills, they are better than the workbook stuff that Bates hands out. Write, write, write, for Bates to throw away, Mark thinks.

11:36. Down to the cafeteria, talking noisily, hanging out, munching. Getting to Room 104 by 12:17: U.S. history. The teacher is sitting cross-legged on his desk when Mark comes in, heatedly arguing with three students over the fracas that had followed the previous night's basketball game. The teacher, Mr. Suslovic, while agreeing that the spectators from their school certainly were provoked, argues that they should neither have been so obviously obscene in yelling at the opposing cheerleaders nor have allowed Coke cans to be rolled out on the floor. The three students keep saying that "it isn't fair." Apparently they and some others had been assigned "Saturday mornings" (detentions) by the principal for the ruckus.

At 12:34, the argument appears to subside. The uninvolved students, including Mark, are in their seats, chatting amiably. Mr. Suslovic climbs off his desk and starts talking: "We've almost finished this unit, chapters nine and ten . . ." The students stop chattering among themselves and turn toward Suslovic. Several slouch down in their chairs. Some open notebooks. Most have the five-pound textbook on their desks.

Suslovic lectures on the cattle drives, from north Texas to railroads west of St. Louis. He breaks up this narrative with questions ("Why were the railroad lines laid largely east to west?"), directed at nobody in particular and eventually answered by Suslovic himself. Some students take notes. Mark doesn't. A student walks in the open door, hands Mr. Suslovic a list, and starts whispering with him. Suslovic turns from the class and hears out this messenger. He then asks, "Does anyone know where Maggie Sharp is?" Some one answers, "Sick at home"; someone else says, "I thought I saw her at lunch." Genial consternation. Finally Suslovic tells the messenger, "Sorry, we can't help you," and returns to the class: "Now, where were we?" He goes on for some minutes. The bell rings. Suslovic forgets to give the homework assignment.

15   1:11 and Algebra II. There is a commotion in the hallway: someone's locker is rumored to have been opened by the assistant principal and a narcotics agent. In the five-minute passing time, Mark hears the story three times and three ways. A locker had been broken into by another student. It was Mr. Gregory and a narc. It was the cops, and they did it without Gregory's knowing. Mrs. Ames, the mathematics teacher, has not heard anything about it. Several of the nineteen students try to tell her and start arguing among themselves. "O.K., that's enough." She hands out the day's problem, one sheet to each student. Mark sees with dismay that it is a single, complicated "word" problem about some train that, while traveling at 84 mph, due west, passes a car that was going due east at 55 mph. Mark

struggles: Is it $d = rt$ or $t = rd$? The class becomes quiet, writing, while Mrs. Ames writes some additional, short problems on the blackboard. "Time's up." A sigh; most students still writing. A muffled "Shit." Mrs. Ames frowns. "Come on, now." She collects papers, but it takes four minutes for her to corral them all.

"Copy down the problems from the board." A minute passes. "William, try number one." William suggests an approach. Mrs. Ames corrects and cajoles, and William finally gets it right. Mark watches two kids to his right passing notes; he tries to read them, but the handwriting is illegible from his distance. He hopes he is not called on, and he isn't. Only three students are asked to puzzle out an answer. The bell rings at 2:00. Mrs. Ames shouts a homework assignment over the resulting hubbub.

Mark leaves his books in his locker. He remembers that he has homework, but figures that he can do it during English class the next day. He knows that there will be an in-class presentation of one of the *Romeo and Juliet* scenes and that he will not be in it. The teacher will not notice his homework writing, or won't do anything about it if she does.

Mark passes various friends heading toward the gym, members of the basketball teams. Like most students, Mark isn't an active school athlete. However, he is associated with the yearbook staff. Although he is not taking "Yearbook" for credit as an English course, he is contributing photographs. Mark takes twenty minutes checking into the yearbook staff's headquarters (the classroom of its faculty adviser) and getting some assignments of pictures from his boss, the senior who is the photography editor. Mark knows that if he pleases his boss and the faculty adviser, he'll take that editor's post for the next year. He'll get English credit for his work then.

After gossiping a bit with the yearbook staff, Mark will leave school by 2:35 and go home. His grocery market bagger's job is from 4:45 to 8:00, the rush hour for the store. He'll have a snack at 4:30, and his mother will save him some supper to eat at 8:30. She will ask whether he has any homework, and he'll tell her no. Tomorrow, and virtually every other tomorrow, will be the same for Mark, save for the lack of the assembly: each period then will be five minutes longer.

20   Most Americans have an uncomplicated vision of what secondary education should be. Their conception of high school is remarkably uniform across the country, a striking fact, given the size and diversity of the United States and the politically decentralized character of the schools. This uniformity is of several generations' standing. It has, however, two appearances, each quite different from the other, one of words and the other of practice, a world of political rhetoric and Mark's world.

A California high school's general goals, set out in 1979, could serve equally well most of America's high schools, public and private. This school had as its ends:

- Fundamental scholastic achievement . . . to acquire knowledge and share in the traditionally accepted academic fundamentals . . . to develop the ability to make decisions, to solve problems, to reason independently, and to accept responsibility for self-evaluation and continuing self-improvement.

- Career and economic competence . . .
- Citizenship and civil responsibility . . .
- Competence in human and social relations . . .
- Moral and ethical values . . .
- Self-realization and mental and physical health . . .
- Aesthetic awareness . . .
- Cultural diversity . . .[1]

In addition to its optimistic rhetoric, what distinguishes this list is its comprehensiveness. The high school is to touch most aspects of an adolescent's existence—mind, body, morals, values, career. No one of these areas is given especial prominence. School people arrogate to themselves an obligation to all.

An example of the wide acceptability of these goals is found in the courts. Forced to present a detailed definition of "thorough and efficient education," elementary as well as secondary, a West Virginia judge sampled the best of conventional wisdom and concluded that

> there are eight general elements of a thorough and efficient system of education: (a) Literacy, (b) The ability to add, subtract, multiply, and divide numbers, (c) Knowledge of government to the extent the child will be equipped as a citizen to make informed choices among persons and issues that affect his own governance, (d) Self-knowledge and knowledge of his or her total environment to allow the child to intelligently choose life work—to know his or her options, (e) Work-training and advanced academic training as the child may intelligently choose, (f) Recreational pursuits, (g) Interests in all creative arts such as music, theater, literature, and the visual arts, and (h) Social ethics, both behavioral and abstract, to facilitate compatibility with others in this society.[2]

That these eight—now powerfully part of the debate over the purpose and practice of education in West Virginia—are reminiscent of the influential list, "The Seven Cardinal Principles of Secondary Education," promulgated in 1918 by the National Education Association, is no surprise.[3] The rhetoric of high school purpose has been uniform and consistent for decades. Americans agree on the goals for their high schools.

That agreement is convenient, but it masks the fact that virtually all the words in these goal statements beg definition. Some schools have labored long to identify specific criteria beyond them; the result has been lists of daunting pseudo-specificity and numbing earnestness. However, most leave the words undefined and let the momentum of traditional practice speak for itself. That is why analyzing how Mark spends his time is important: from watching him one uncovers the important purposes of education, the ones that shape practice. Mark's day is similar to that of other high school students across the country, as similar as the rhetoric of one goal statement to others'. Of course, there are variations, but the extent of consistency in the shape of school routine for a large and diverse adolescent population is extraordinary, indicating more graphically than any rhetoric the measure of agreement in America about what one does in high school, and, by implication, what it is for.

The basic organizing structures in schools are familiar. Above all, students are grouped by age (that is, freshman, sophomore, junior, senior), and all are expected to take precisely the same time—around 720 school days over four years, to be precise—to meet the requirements for a diploma. When one is out of his grade level, he can feel odd, as Mark did in his biology class. The goals are the same for all, and the means to achieve them are also similar.

25   Young males and females are treated remarkably alike; the schools' goals are the same for each gender. In execution, there are differences, as those pressing sex discrimination suits have made educators intensely aware. The students in metalworking classes are mostly male; those in home economics, mostly female. But it is revealing how much less sex discrimination there is in high schools than in other American institutions. For many young women, the most liberated hours of their week are in school.

School is to be like a job: you start in the morning and end in the afternoon, five days a week. You don't get much of a lunch hour, so you go home early, unless you are an athlete or are involved in some special school or extracurricular activity. School is conceived of as the children's workplace, and it takes young people off parents' hands and out of the labor market during prime-time work hours. Not surprisingly, many students see going to school as little more than a dogged necessity. They perceive the day-to-day routine, a Minnesota study reports, as one of "boredom and lethargy." One of the students summarizes: School is "boring, restless, tiresome, puts ya to sleep, tedious, monotonous, pain in the neck."[4]

The school schedule is a series of units of time: the clock is king. The base time block is about fifty minutes in length. Some schools, on what they call modular scheduling, split that fifty-minute block into two or even three pieces. Most schools have double periods for laboratory work, especially in the sciences, or four-hour units for the small numbers of students involved in intensive vocational or other work-study programs. The flow of all school activity arises from or is blocked by these time units. "How much time do I have with my kids" is the teacher's key question.

Because there are many claims for those fifty-minute blocks, there is little time set aside for rest between them, usually no more than three to ten minutes, depending on how big the school is and, consequently, how far students and teachers have to walk from class to class. As a result, there is a frenetic quality to the school day, a sense of sustained restlessness. For the adolescents, there are frequent changes of room and fellow students, each change giving tempting opportunities for distraction, which are stoutly resisted by teachers. Some schools play soft music during these "passing times," to quiet the multitude, one principal told me.

Many teachers have a chance for a coffee break. Few students do. In some city schools where security is a problem, students must be in class for seven consecutive periods, interrupted by a heavily monitored twenty-minute lunch period for small groups, starting as early as 10:30 A.M. and running to after 1:00 P.M. A high premium is placed on punctuality and on "being where you're supposed to be." Obviously, a low premium is placed on reflection and repose. The student rushes from class to class to collect knowledge. Savoring it is implied, is not to be done much in school, nor is such meditation really much admired. The picture that these familiar patterns yield is that of an academic supermarket. The purpose of going to school is to pick things up, in an organized and predictable way, the faster the better.

30   What is supposed to be picked up is remarkably consistent among all sorts of high schools. Most schools specifically mandate three out of every five courses a student selects. Nearly all of these mandates fall into five areas—English, social studies, mathematics, science, and physical education. On the average, English is required to be taken each year, social studies and physical education three out of the four high school years, and mathematics and science one or two years. Trends indicate that in the mid-eighties there is likely to be an increase in the time allocated to these last two subjects. Most students take classes in these four major academic areas beyond the minimum requirements, sometimes in such special areas as journalism and "yearbook," offshoots of English departments.[5]

Press most adults about what high school is for, and you hear these subjects listed. *High school? That's where you learn English and math and that sort of thing.* Ask students, and you get the same answer. High school is to "teach" these "subjects."

What is often absent is any definition of these subjects or any rationale for them. They are just there, labels. Under those labels lie a multitude of things. A great deal of material is supposed to be "covered"; most of these courses are surveys, great sweeps of the stuff of their parent disciplines.

While there is often a sequence *within* subjects—algebra before trigonometry, "first-year" French before "second-year" French—there is rarely a coherent relationship or sequence *across* subjects. Even the most logically related matters— reading ability as a precondition for the reading of history books, and certain mathematical concepts or skills before the study of some of physics—are only loosely coordinated, if at all. There is little demand for a synthesis of it all; English, mathematics, and the rest are discrete items, to be picked up individually. The incentive for picking them up is largely through tests and, with success at these, in credits earned.

Coverage within subjects is the key priority. If some imaginative teacher makes a proposal to force the marriage of, say, mathematics and physics or to require some culminating challenges to students to use several subjects in the solution of a complex problem, and if this proposal will take "time" away from other things, opposition is usually phrased in terms of what may be thus forgone. If we do that, we'll have to give up colonial history. We won't be able to get to programming. We'll not be able to read *Death of a Salesman*. There isn't time. The protesters usually win out.

35   The subjects come at a student like Mark in random order, a kaleidoscope of worlds: algebraic formulae to poetry to French verbs to Ping-Pong to the War of the Spanish Succession, all before lunch. Pupils are to pick up these things. Tests measure whether the picking up has been successful.

The lack of connection between stated goals, such as those of the California high school cited earlier, and the goals inherent in school practice is obvious and, curiously, tolerated. Most striking is the gap between statements about "self-realization and mental and physical growth" or "moral and ethical values"—common rhetoric in school documents—and practice. Most physical education programs have neither the time nor the focus really to ensure fitness. Mental health is rarely defined. Neither are ethical values, save at the negative extremes, such as opposition to assault or dishonesty. Nothing in the regimen of a day like Mark's signals direct or implicit teaching in this area. The "schoolboy code" (not ratting on a fellow student) protects the marijuana pusher, and a leechlike associate is shrugged off without concern. The issue of the locker search was pushed aside, as not appropriate for class time.

Most students, like Mark, go to class in groups of twenty to twenty-seven students. The expected attendance in some schools, particularly those in low-income areas, is usually higher, often thirty-five students per class, but high absentee rates push the actual numbers down. About twenty-five per class is an average figure for expected attendance, and the actual numbers are somewhat lower. There are remarkably few students who go to class in groups much larger or smaller than twenty-five.[6]

A student such as Mark sees five or six teachers per day; their differing styles and expectations are part of his kaleidoscope. High school staffs are highly specialized: guidance counselors rarely teach mathematics, mathematics teachers rarely teach English, principals rarely do any classroom instruction. Mark, then, is known a little bit by a number of people, each of whom sees him in one specialized situation. No one may know him as a "whole person"—unless he becomes a special problem or has special needs.

Save in extracurricular or coaching situations, such as in athletics, drama, or shop classes, there is little opportunity for sustained conversation between student and teacher. The mode is a one-sentence or two-sentence exchange: *Mark, when was Grover Cleveland president? Let's see, was 1890 . . . or something . . . wasn't he the one . . . he was elected twice, wasn't he? . . . Yes . . . Gloria, can you get the dates right?* Dialogue is strikingly absent, and as a result the opportunity of teachers to challenge students' ideas in a systematic and logical way is limited. Given the rushed, full quality of the school day, it can seldom happen. One must infer that careful probing of students' thinking is not a high priority. How one gains (to quote the California school's statement of goals again) "the ability to make decisions, to solve problems, to reason independently, and to accept responsibility for self-evaluation and continuing self-improvement" without being challenged is difficult to imagine. One certainly doesn't learn these things merely from lectures and textbooks.

40   Most schools are nice places. Mark and his friends enjoy being in theirs. The adults who work in schools generally like adolescents. The academic pressures are limited, and the accommodations to students are substantial. For example, if many members of an English class have jobs after school, the English teacher's expectations for them are adjusted, downward. In a word, school is sensitively accommodating, as long as students are punctual, where they are supposed to be,

and minimally dutiful about picking things up from the clutch of courses in which they enroll.

This characterization is not pretty, but it is accurate, and it serves to describe the vast majority of American secondary schools. "Taking subjects" in a systematized, conveyer-belt way is what one does in high school. That this process is, in substantial respects, not related to the rhetorical purposes of education is tolerated by most people, perhaps because they do not really either believe in those ill-defined goals or, in their heart of hearts, believe that schools can or should even try to achieve them. The students are happy taking subjects. The parents are happy, because that's what they did in high school. The rituals, the most important of which is graduation, remain intact. The adolescents are supervised, safely and constructively most of the time, during the morning and afternoon hours, and they are off the labor market. That is what high school is all about.

ENDNOTES

1. Shasta High School, Redding, California. An eloquent and analogous statement, "The Essentials of Education," one stressing explicitly the "interdependence of skills and content" that is implicit in the Shasta High School statement, was issued in 1980 by a coalition of education associations. Organizations for the Essentials of Education (Urbana, Illinois).

2. Judge Arthur M. Recht, in his order resulting from *Pauley* v. *Kelly,* 1979, as reprinted in *Education Week,* May 26, 1982, p. 10. See also, in *Education Week,* January 16, 1983, pp. 21, 24, Jonathan P. Sher, "The Struggle to Fulfill at Judicial Mandate: How Not to 'Reconstruct' Education in W. Va."

3. Bureau of Education, Department of the Interior, "Cardinal Principles of Secondary Education: A Report of the Commission on the Reorganization of Secondary Education, appointed by the National Education Association," *Bulletin,* no. 35 (Washington: U.S. Government Printing Office, 1918).

4. Diane Hedin, Paula Simon, and Michael Robin, *Minnesota Youth Poll: Youth's Views on School and School Discipline.* Minnesota Report 184 (1983), Agricultural Experiment Station, University of Minnesota, p. 13.

5. I am indebted to Harold F. Sizer and Lyde E. Sizer for a survey of the diploma requirements of fifty representative secondary schools, completed for A Study of High Schools.

6. Education Research Service, Inc. *Class Size: A Summary of Research* (Arlington, Virginia, 1978); and *Class Size Research: A Critique of Recent Meta-Analyses* (Arlington, Virginia, 1980).

▰ CRITICAL REFLECTIONS

1. Chart Mark's schedule using the times and events mentioned by Sizer in this reading. Does Mark's day strike you as typical of high school? Of college?

2. Sizer includes the goals of a California high school from 1979 in this reading, which itself was published over 20 years ago. Do the goals of the high school, or the experience of Mark in the reading, seem dated to you? Why or why not?

If it does or does not seem dated, what are the implications of your response for your own view of education?

3. Consider the definition of "a thorough and efficient education" included on page 90. How is this definition similar or different from your own?

4. In your view, what do you think Sizer believes to be the purpose of a school like Mark's? How is that purpose reflected in Mark's school day?

▆▆ MAKING CONNECTIONS

1. Consider the school day mapped by Sizer in this reading against either Freire's or hooks' ideas about education and learning. How would either or both of them respond to Mark's day, and what in the Sizer reading leads you to that analysis?

2. In "How They've Fared in Education," Harry (the main subject of the reading) discusses what he sees as a distinction between educated and uneducated people. Do you think Harry would define Mark's school day as educating or as something else?

3. Compare the principles underscoring Mark's school day to Booker T. Washington's ideas about education as they are reflected in "The Atlanta Exposition Address." What similarities and/or differences between the positions do you find?

READINGS ABOUT LEARNERS

■ David Barton and Mary Hamilton, "How They've Fared in Education: Harry's Literacy Practices"

■ Lorene Cary, from *Black Ice*

■ Mark Edmundson, "On the Uses of a Liberal Education: I. As Lite Entertainment for Bored College Students"

■ Andrea R. Fishman, "Becoming Literate: A Lesson from the Amish"

■ June Jordan, "Nobody Mean More to Me Than You and the Future Life of Willie Jordan"

■ Robert Louthan, "Heavy Machinery"

■ Mike Rose, "I Just Wanna Be Average"

■ Michael Ryan, "The Ditch"

■ Earl Shorris, "On the Uses of a Liberal Education: II. As a Weapon in the Hands of the Restless Poor"

■ Ron Suskind, "Fierce Intimacies"

DAVID BARTON AND MARY HAMILTON

HOW THEY'VE FARED IN EDUCATION: HARRY'S LITERACY PRACTICES

David Barton and Mary Hamilton both teach literacy studies at Lancaster University, located in northern England. This is a chapter from a book that they co-authored called *Local Literacies*. As part of their work for the book, Barton, Hamilton, and colleagues went door-to-door in a working-class neighborhood in Lancaster that they called Sunnyside. They spoke with whomever would speak with them about their histories and experiences with literacy, and their current literacy practices. They then took the interview data and transformed them into narratives of the interviewee's experiences. Here, they focus on Harry, a World War II veteran who had relatively little formal schooling, but was an active reader. The story of Harry's literacy practices raises questions about the connection between school success and later work with reading and writing.

We first came in contact with Harry Graham when knocking on doors randomly as part of the door-to-door survey in Springside; he was immediately interested in what we were doing and was happy to be interviewed further. In order to build up a picture of him, we will begin with how he describes himself, and then move on to our descriptions of him and his literacy history.

As we did not want to impose our own descriptions of him, right at the end of the research we asked him for a description of himself. He was reluctant to write anything down; nevertheless he was happy to talk and the interviewer wrote it down as he spoke; every so often he was read back what had been written and then he would add more detail. This description is given in his pen-sketch in Aside 1; all the words are his words. When asked how he would describe himself physically, Harry was at a loss for a while and then he said, *I'd be lost in a crowd of three. Nondescript.*

Another way of getting an idea of Harry is to listen to him talking about reading and writing. Selecting from the hours of interviews with him, the quotes in Asides 2–6 are illustrative of some of the things Harry said about himself and his literacy. Two further ways of visualising Harry and his life are provided firstly by a short description of him taken from background notes, and then by an extract from diary notes of a visit to his house. Sarah described him as follows: *Harry is neat and dapper and has sailor's blue eyes. Despite poor physical health there is something agile and youthful about him . . . He's an alert thoughtful man . . . sociable and lively.* The diary notes come from a visit when he has been left a transcript of a previous interview, and the notes include a general description of his living room:

Room: dark red raised tufted carpet. Glass coffee table with copy of the Daily Mirror. A settee with wooden arms against the wall opposite the front door; fireplace to left as

---

Aside 1 Harry's pen-sketch

I'm sixty-six . . . How would I describe myself . . . I don't know really. I like to be liked and so I do everything to encourage people to like me. I help people and do things like that. My personality is I can't be serious about anything. Happy-go-lucky me. I can't be serious. Like to look on happy side of everything.

I haven't altered anything since my wife died. She died two years ago. I've never altered. She used to play pop at me about helping people . . . putting myself out. She used to say, 'bloody fool' and I still do that now. I always do anything on an impulse me. It just comes in my mind and I do it irrespective of what the cost entails. That's me. I don't hold any grudges against anybody.

The thing I enjoy doing most is being in company . . . men's company. I like men's company for the talk and I'm always out of place when there's women about.

One of the loves of my life is I love children. The house is full of them when school comes out. I like me kids, aye . . . all round they come in here . . . do what they like. They know more about me house than what I do. I'm invited to all the birthday parties. I never go but I get a piece of birthday cake. Daft really but I enjoy owt like that. It keeps you young having kids about. Everyone of them knows that I'm twenty-one. Ask any kid around here. They all call me by my first name, Harry. I hate being called Uncle or anything like that.

---

enter. Alcove between fireplace and far wall, contains modern stereo music centre. Collection of records and tapes: war songs. Next to music centre, shelves with Harry's files, notebooks and a black pottery sports car. Colour photos of kids. TV.

Harry had used the pens as asked [using specific colours for different changes] *and appeared to have understood and enjoyed adding to the transcript. His initial reaction to working on the script was, in his actual words: 'I tell you what, it sounds queer if you type it as you talk . . . And there's some things that I just couldn't alter it if I tried. It's right and that's it . . . I mean, it's me, isn't it?'*

His daughter had laughed when she read the script and remarked, 'It sounds just like you, Dad'. Harry was surprised by the way he speaks on the transcript but not bothered. He said he had kept reading and rereading the transcript, 'must have looked at them a thousand times'.

HARRY'S LITERACY HISTORY AND LITERACY LIFE

So far we have given Harry's description of himself and have heard him talking briefly about his literacy. We now turn to our making sense of his life. He has lived in Lancaster all his life. His father was a machinist at Williamsons, a local factory, and his mother worked in the canteen there. They were short of money and his memory of holidays was of going to the beach at Morecambe for the day, walking there and back (a distance of six miles), and loving it. He recalls both his parents reading a daily paper which his father used to bring home from work. This would have been in the 1930s. Harry remembers waiting expectantly, so that he could read the daily cartoon strip. He also recalls swapping comics with other children in the neighbourhood, and his parents buying him an annual every Christmas. Apart from these, he remembers no other books in the home.

5   He attended a local infants school and junior school. He recalls writing on a slate and remembers the transition to exercise books (Aside 2). As the anecdote about the Grammar School (Aside 3) indicates, he passed the examination but his parents could not afford the cost of the books and uniform for him to go there. (The school, the examination and the uniform all still exist.) He went instead to Lune Street school which at that time was a *through school,* combining both primary and secondary age pupils. While at school he worked part time as an errand boy for a local butcher and left school at the age of fourteen to work there full time.

He had around fourteen jobs from then until the age of seventeen when he entered the Royal Navy as an ordinary seaman. He remained in the navy until the end of the Second World War, when he joined the fire service in Lancaster. He moved up through the ranks of the fire service and stayed there until he retired. He has lived in several parts of Lancaster and moved to Springside to be near his daughter; he explains how *she was bottom in everything,* left school at sixteen and

---

Aside 2 Writing on a slate

Oh! Well I can't understand it. The length of time they do at school now and all this new stuff that they teach them. And all the modern aids they have. I mean my teeth are still sat on edge now when I think about it. When I were writing on a slate with one of them things. And ee . . . and it still makes my mouth water, writing on a slate.

Aside 3 My education was nil

My education was nil actually. I did pass the exam for the Grammar School when I was ten years old but as my mother said, 'I can't afford to buy you the cap, never mind the uniform and books', so the opportunity was missed, I must have had the potential though. And I know I can put things into sentences and start new paragraphs in the proper places. But it's the ramblings in between instead of getting down to the nitty gritty. Somebody that was educated would probably say in two sentences what it would take me two pages.

went on to *the college of knowledge*, the College of Further Education, where she took a two-year course in hairdressing. She owned a local hairdresser's, which she sold recently in order to go to college to train to be a nurse. She has two children, one of whom has just left the girls' Grammar School and is also taking a nursing course. Harry's son, who lives a mile away across town, went to the boys' Grammar School and on to university, although he left before completing a degree, and is a nurse at the Infirmary. He comments that there have been nurses from his family at the hospital ever since it was built a century ago. His wife died a few years ago and Harry lives alone, maintaining a network of friends and relations in the city.

After the first contact, he was visited at his house and interviewed several times over a period of a few months. As well as the interviews and visits to his home. Harry also collected his junk mail for a week for us. He seems to have quite a regular routinised life. He goes to the local library at least once a week, and Sarah also went there with him. We also interviewed him with an old friend, Ted. Harry lives alone but he has regular contact with other members of his family. His sister-in-law does his shopping, and his son who lives nearby helps him in other ways.

Aside 4 Learning at work

I'm not illiterate. But I think it's a . . . something you've got to be trained at really. I always remember my fire service training. When I was doing the hotels and boarding houses. We had to do these fire precautions. Had to go round all the hotels and boarding houses from here to Barrow and issue a paper to them telling them what requirements were needed you see. I knew what they wanted but it was putting it into these words. So I went through all the old files and got . . . and I made a play on words. I put my words into their . . . my requirements into their words you see. Until I got it off where I could do it from memory. You know, like I could just do it parrot fashion and . . . But it was a struggle.

Aside 5 Reading in the library

Oh well, I like to live in the past. I'm very interested in things that happened years ago . . . I'll go and say 'Can I have the Guardian for 1940?' And they bring you the big book, you see [referring to the local newspaper upstairs in the Reference room at the library]. *You've got all the Guardians there for twelve month. And I just . . . I'm away. And I'll stop there till I've read it all. I spend many a happy hour up there. And seen my own name many a time* [laughing]. *That brought back memories. I live in the past. I never look to the future, me.*

We gradually built up a picture of his life and the role of literacy in it. There are many examples in the transcripts of Harry using different literacies. For a retired person who might be seen as leading a fairly quiet local life he reports a wide range of different literate activities. He has a keen interest in local history and keeps magazines and newspapers associated with this; he spends time reading about this in the library, often taking notes from books. Connected with this he has books, photos and records to do with family history, and says that he and his wife traced his family back to the 1600s, looking up names in church record books and going round cemeteries. He reads a lot, usually about the war and is *never without a book.* Every night he reads in bed for an hour before going to sleep. He only reads *authentic war books,* meaning factual books, and never fiction. He borrows books from the library, going there every Thursday morning, and also buys second-hand books and swaps with friends. Despite not seeing himself as *a writer,* he sometimes writes letters and has written a story for a magazine about his war experiences; during the period we were studying his literacy practices he started writing his life history. Sometimes he refers to writing as *a struggle,* feeling he lacks the necessary training, although at other times he is more positive about it. He always writes letters out in rough first, he is concerned about *proper English,* and sometimes he tears up letters he has written rather then send them.

He uses literacy to keep up with current affairs and local issues. He reads a national daily paper sitting on the settee after breakfast *first thing in the morning, cup of tea and read the paper.* On Fridays he reads the weekly local paper, cutting out and keeping some things for reference. He also reads the local free newspaper which is delivered to the door, church newsletters and the residents' association newsletter, as well as watching television and listening to local radio. Literacy has other roles in his everyday life: his sister does much of his shopping and he keeps money-saving coupons for her to use; reading and writing have a role in organising his finances and paying bills; he has used medical reference books to check on his health, and his son's train timetables to plan holidays; he keeps a diary for future appointments and birthdays; and he takes phone messages for his son who does not have a phone. He helps neighbours with some aspects of literacy, such as helping them with their tax forms, and in turn is helped by others, for example when his son helped him write a job reference for a former colleague.

10   This kind of help can be seen as part of a complex system of support and reciprocity extending over many years. Within the family, Harry recalls that he began supporting his son's literacy development when he was little. His son would sit on his knee and pick out words from Harry's newspaper, for example: *what we used to do was give him a pen and tell him 'Ring all the "thes" or the "ands"'. That's how he got started, sat down with newspaper.* When his son went to grammar school, he began studying subjects such as Latin which Harry couldn't help him with. So Harry then supported him through finding others *in the circle* who could help him. His wife used to read the children stories, and his son sometimes helped his daughter with her maths. Now Harry's grandchildren often do their homework in his house; neighbours' children often come round and he has sometimes helped them with their homework.

Aside 6 Helping others with writing

Oh aye. I've been asked. People come across, 'Will you make me tax form out for me?' And they've fetched all the papers and I've managed the tax forms for them, you know. Things like that.

On reflection I think this was because I was an officer in the Fire Brigade—people must have thought I was an academic, but I got my rank with hard work in studying for the exams, the last and hardest one was when I was fifty-two years old. Well I must be. And I must look the part. I've had people come round for what-do-you-call-its . . . to get a job. References. I've had people come round for references. And I gave them a reference. I gave one lad a reference. He was a fireman and he wanted a job. And he came round to me 'cos I used to be his Officer and asked me for a reference. And I give him one you see. And my lad came round . . . I always take a copy. And my lad come round, who's very well educated and he started laughing at it. I said, 'What's to do?' He said, 'That's no good'. He said, 'You don't do things like that'. And he wrote a proper one out you see. So that I got in my car right away and I took it round to this fellow and I said, 'Give us that one back and have this'.

It was rambling, you see. Instead of getting down to nitty gritty. Oh no, I didn't feel bad about it. No, because what did they expect of me anyway? Well I said, I wrote down what I felt about him and it was all true. So what more do they want. And yet, my lad laughed at it. Well, I read his and he actually said as much in a few words you see. That's what annoyed me. I wish I could do that.

One particular literacy event which is a regular part of his life is that Harry and Ted meet each week on a Wednesday morning to read through and discuss the local newspaper. They sit in the front room of one of their houses, drinking tea and discussing local politics and people they know, *generally putting the world to rights*, as Ted puts it. Sometimes they compose letters to the paper; they plan them together, then Ted writes them out and sends them off. These are *critical contentious letters* aiming to *expand people's opinions a wee bit*. If these letters are accepted by the newspaper, they are published on the letters page of the paper as unsigned anonymous letters coming from *A local resident* or *A taxpayer*. This is a type of letter which is common in local newspapers. These weekly meetings, then, represent a fairly complex literacy event, involving several stages and a range of technologies.

Other current activities he mentions involving literacy include shopping, paying bills, leaving messages, health care, holidays and entertainment. In these activities the networks operate in both directions and are part of broader social patterns of reciprocity. People help Harry and in the same way people have approached Harry for help, with tax forms and other forms. At the working men's club men discuss the war, and sometimes exchange and discuss books and magazines on the subject. This would be part of other networks of support at the club, so, for example, Harry has a friend who mends his car. There are also examples of support at work; when he was in the fire service, a colleague helped him to revise for exams, teaching him the idea of how there is a formula for passing exams, a way of answering questions. Harry used to accompany his wife to graveyards and the library in their search for information about her ancestry. Harry's sister-in-law helps Harry with his shopping sometimes. She takes tokens he has collected for money off various items. She also sometimes walks his dog. When his wife was alive, she and her sister used to shop together.

Having given an overview of Harry's literacy practices, we now turn to making sense of them, looking for patterns and meanings within Harry's practices. In later chapters we will be looking for patterns across different members of the community, and putting them in the explanatory framework of a broader social context. Beginning with making sense of Harry's practices, we will explore them through three themes which appeared prominent in his data.

RULING PASSIONS

The starting-point for understanding Harry and his contemporary practices is the war, the Second World War which he experienced as a young man over fifty years ago. We've called this his ruling passion. He often turned the conversation round to the war; many of his stories were about the war and his interests were linked to it. When we went to interview people *we* wanted to find out about reading, writing and literacy practices. Unfortunately, it seemed, the people we interviewed often wanted to talk about something else; each person had a ruling passion, something *they* wanted to talk about and share with us. We talked to them about literacy, it seemed, and they talked to us about their lives. Often this appeared to have no relation to reading and writing, and we were tempted to say, 'No, don't talk about that: tell us about where you keep your books; tell us if you use the library'. In fact as the interviews continued, we found that when people told us their stories, they ended up telling us much more about literacy.

15   Examples of Harry's literacy practices which have been given already have links with his ruling passion. He has been reading *authentic war stories*—the phrase recurs—ever since the war finished, joining a number of different libraries in his search for more and more new books on the subject. He discusses and exchanges war books with friends. They are his main reading interest; they have titles like *In Danger's Hour, The Longest Battle, The War at Sea, The British Sailor, Fly for Your Life.*

Harry has also given us interesting information about literacy activities during the war. He kept a diary, although it was confiscated since, for security reasons, service personnel were not allowed to write diaries in wartime. He described the pleasure he got from receiving local newspapers, parcels of pens and paper, and letters from friends and relatives when he was at sea. Letters were sent and arrived in monthly batches. All mail was checked and parts cut out with razor blades. The post took three months to come and the waiting was *unbearable.* He has talked about the letters he wrote home, often written standing while on watch. He found it difficult to write, knowing it would be read by an outsider. Sailors were not allowed to say where they were or what the weather was like; Harry described the coded messages he sent to his mother to describe his location: the first letter of each paragraph spelled out the place where he was. He never told anyone about this and he was never discovered.

In talking about the war Harry speaks of *pumping adrenaline* and the comradeship amongst the men serving. He seems to feel real nostalgia for some aspects of war, but he is also haunted by memories of horror. When he went round the library with Sarah, he pulled a particular book off the shelf and turned to diagrams of a battle he had been involved in; he explained the details to her. (See Aside 7.)

Recently, his ruling passion has also motivated Harry to write, in several different ways. He has been trying to make contact with another serviceman who served on the same ship. He has been pursuing this by writing letters to *The Soldier* magazine and a veterans' association magazine. Harry took great care over writing the first letter. It was important to him; he was scared of adopting the wrong tone or failing to communicate what he wanted to say. He rewrote it

---

Aside 7 Diary notes: Harry in the library

We walked past the computer—'Ever used that?' 'No call to'—and on round the corner to the history section. A small sign at the top of the shelves read WAR STORIES. 'This is where I come . . . nowhere else.' Not wanting to inhibit his search for books I started to browse a bit, half watching him. He has very swift movements. He pulled books out, glanced at the covers, put them back. This went on for about five minutes. Then he pulled one out and started to leaf through it; he appeared to be looking at pictures in it—diagrams and photographs. He replaced it. I pulled out a Laurens van der Post. He came over. 'That's a good author', he said. I was surprised. I didn't imagine he'd like someone like that but I didn't comment. 'Mind, it's not a patch on the real stuff—too much writing in it' (it was a slim book) '. . . the author not the people, if you know what I mean.' 'Description?' I asked. 'Yeah, description, that's it. I like the words people said . . . out of their mouths . . . not all this word play, or florification [sic]. There's a lot glorify it.' He was staring at the shelves and pounced on a book. 'I'm in this one.' He flicked through it and found a diagram—some sea battle—lots of lines and little ships. He pointed to one, 'That was me. I was in on that.' I looked at the diagram. I saw a flat line drawing which evoked nothing in me. 'Makes me tingle looking at it,' he said. This is an extreme example of a literacy event which was both shared—we were both looking at a diagram in a book—and, at least at the time, interpreted so differently by the two of us, it could not possibly be called a shared literacy experience.

several times. He has started a correspondence with one old shipmate who wrote an article in one of the magazines.

He also wrote a story for *Landing Craft* magazine. He was invited to do this after attending a meeting of the veterans' association which brings out the magazine. It took him *an hour to write it out, and then about an hour to go through it crossing things out and putting things back in again.* A friend across the road typed it out and he sent it off. It was his first time in print. Part of this article is shown in Aside 8 to give an idea of his style of writing.

20   During our research Harry began to write his own *authentic war story*. When we first talked to him he said he did not enjoy writing at all, but a year later he was surprised to discover that he actually got a great deal of pleasure from writing. He started this partly because of the landing craft article and also has been encouraged by his son and other people. He is enjoying this kind of writing: *it brings back memories and it's one of the pleasures of my life.* When writing about the war he questions what style he should use: should he keep his story fairly light and amusing for the reader—*there's plenty of humour in war*—or should he describe the darker side and the dirty side of things as well? Would this shock or disturb people? In many ways he needs to make sense of everything that happened. He writes it out by hand and his son will type it for him and will *flower it up a bit . . . not the actual thoughts of the words but flower it up a bit . . . like the dawn broke. It was cloudy, rainy, anything like that, you see.*

The first way of understanding Harry's literacy practices, then, is to locate them in the war, his ruling passion and something not immediately connected with literacy. A second way is to examine how Harry talks about reading and writing, the frames he puts upon it. There are two theories of Harry's which seem to structure his view of literacy; they are the way in which he uses the dimension educated–uneducated and his attitude to reality and fantasy.

EDUCATED AND UNEDUCATED

When we asked people about their home and community literacy practices, they often replied in terms of education, providing memories of their own education or details of their children's education. Talking about education was the easiest way into talking about literacy for them and it was often a frame they used to make sense of our research. This was true of Harry. A theme which kept recurring in Harry's transcripts was the distinction between *educated* and *uneducated*. He frequently uses the two words when referring to people, as in Asides 3, 6 and 9. Getting a place at the Grammar School, but not being able to afford to go, has been a lifelong disappointment to him. It has also affected his working life. He recounts that when he was in the navy, he was denied access on to a training course because he didn't have *the education*. He also describes how this has affected his work opportunities, particularly speed of promotion in the fire service.

Harry appears to view the world as being divided between educated people and uneducated people. It seems to be his yardstick for talking about people, including himself. He often talks of his own lack of education, and suggests that the occasional difficulties he has with writing tasks are due to this. He left school

---

Aside 8 Saga of the Landing Ship

LST 304 PARTY MONKEY DRAFT

It was late May 1944, I was rotting in Chatham Barracks again, having just been 'paid off' a destroyer, which we had just given to the Russians. Ginger Leonards and I were old hands, no one could put one over on us. We were not green, falling in for morning parades was not for us. Too many rotten jobs were handed out, plus there was a big enough workforce, without our help. About 15,000 ratings milling about nowhere to sling ones mick, long queues for meals, no money, no prospects.

I had a shovel, Ginger had a brush which we hid every night. Each morning we collected our tools and strolled around the Barracks, brushing here, shovelling there whenever anyone of rank appeared. It was a monotonous life. One morning sat in our usual chairs, the 30 seater heads, a P/O came in, heard us dripping and said 'How would you lads like a good draft'. Don't read on if you know whats coming. 'We are opening a new shore base in Grimsby and there is 7 days leave with it'. It gets worse doesn't it. 'What have we to do to get on it?' 'Just knock on the back window of the Drafting Office and ask for 'Party Monkey Draft' hurry there are only two places left'. 10 seconds later we handed in our station cards, we were in, couldn't believe our luck. 'Listen to the pipes' the wren said. Sure enough the next day Monkey draft fell in on North Road. The Chiefy shouts 'When I call your name, I will give you a number. Fall in on the rating holding the board with that number'. Ginger and I both got 304. Hand in your kitbags and hammocks, steaming bags only. Boarding the train in the barracks it puffed its way with many stops until eventually it stopped in Pompy Barracks. What an odd way to get to Grimsby. We fell in—we fell out—fell in again until finally we boarded a ferry which delivered us to a thing called LST 304. What a let down. What had we 'volunteered' for?

Party Monkey Draft turned out to be an RN Medical Party headed by Surgeon Lt. CDR French, 3 Sur.Lts, 12 sick berth attendants, 20 seamen with a P/O in charge. When the ship unloaded on the beach it was turned in to a hospital ship run by the above, it had none of the fineries of a proper hospital ship, in fact none at all, but it served its purposes . . .

---

at fourteen. In contrast, Harry talks of others who are educated, in particular his son who gives him support with some writing: there is the example in Aside 6 of the son helping Harry re-write a reference for someone; also typing up and *flowering up* Harry's Second World War story.

Harry contrasts himself with his son who is *educated*. His son went to the Grammar School, and on to university. He dropped out of university. Harry has mixed feelings about *the educated*. He respects his son's literacy skills, which he appears to see as being superior to his own. His son can write concisely and during

---

Aside 9 Quotes on education by Harry

- *Good heavens I must have been illiterate when I left school.*
- *And I went in front of the Officer who dealt with all these things and his first question was, 'Where was you educated?' I told him the Marsh School and Dallas Road Elementary School. He said, 'I'm sorry but you haven't got the education for this job.'*
- *And so I'd no education.*
- *Well don't you think that's a lack of education in the first place?*
- *I've exactly the same feelings but lack of education. I can't express myself in words like Ted can. I can't even write letters where I can express myself.*
- *I get my son to write it out 'cos he was educated and I wasn't.*
- *But he's well educated and he can put in two words what it would take me a sheet of paper. I know what I want to say but I can't put it in words. And that's with my opinions as well. I have strong opinions on a lot of things but I just can't express them right.*
- *I was Secretary of that* [the club] *for a few years. And I used to have to write and write. Write the minutes out and I'd come home and I'd write them all out. And then I had to put notices on the board and notices everywhere. And it's very trying when you don't want to make any mistakes. I'd try and put it into the proper English. Except my education doesn't go that far.*
- *And in the Fire Brigade when it come to hydraulics and all these formulas, it were foreign to me but I had to learn them. And I studied for hours and hours over them. Trying to catch up on education which I never had. Especially on arithmetic and hydraulics and . . .*
- Helping children with homework: *Oh yes. But it got . . . it was embarrassing really. 'Cos they were far and away ahead of me. Because my education was nil really.*
- *And accept me as you find me, that's it. That's how it should be. It's been a problem all my life. This education business. They come out with things now even at bloomin' junior school. And I never did them at senior school.*
- *Because my education wasn't all that good. In fact, it was blooming awful.*
- *Then me son who has a lot better education than me can type it out and put it into better . . .*
- On the point of the research: *Is it to do with education? Right from start to the finish, getting people from different walks of life to see how they've fared in education.*

---

nursing training wrote a case study on a patient which has now become part of a training manual. His son is very good at exams. Harry has no doubt that his son could pass the exams in the fire service with ease, exams Harry struggled over; but without any knowledge of the actual practicalities of the job. This is something

which annoys Harry. He sees a clear distinction between practical expertise and educational or academic expertise.

25   He talks more than once about how educated people are people who are good
at exams, good at paperwork, but how those skills are not necessarily the most
important in working life. Harry comes across as practical, quick-witted and
calm. Those things are important in the fire service. Any educated person might
be able to revise for fire service exams and pass them, but that would not mean
they would necessarily be any good at the job.

So, although he feels uneducated and although he still feels a sense of injustice
about not having had the passport of a grammar school education to help him in
his working life, he does not actually seem to aspire to being an *educated person*
or to feel any great respect for those who are. Harry identifies strongly with
working people who do practical jobs, and dirty jobs. He has spent his working
life in dangerous, dirty and stressful situations. Cutting bodies out of mangled
vehicles in motorway accidents, and continually risking life to save others, or
pulling corpses from burning buildings, is perhaps the least enviable of all jobs.
Fire-fighters keep a low profile. Harry is modest, and quite unselfpitying, but he
is very aware that practical expertise is undervalued in society. When he is talking about people from the university there is a respect for them but it is always
tinged with some sort of but: there are things that they can't do.

Harry's views on how people learn also derive from this division. The skills
which were vital for his job were not skills which anyone could learn from books.
He thinks apprenticeship is the best form of training and contrasts this with
book learning: *Books can't teach you anything . . . nothing like that . . . it's daft. I've
told my son he could pass the exams on the fire service with no problem. He's great
at book learning . . . he'd come out top. But he wouldn't be able to do the job 'cos it's
nothing to do with book learning.* He also criticises the lectures he had to attend
on training courses, where he kept his *eyes open with match sticks,* and he has
never enjoyed giving talks at meetings.

Harry says that he *must have been illiterate when I left school . . . I had the potential . . . but I never got any further with it.* At one point in the navy he was refused a particular job because he was told he didn't have the education for it. It
was in the fire service that he studied hard to catch up on *the education which I
never had.* There was an entrance test and exams for promotion. He studied hard
for these. Part of the job was to read and keep up with technical bulletins, in-
forming others of incidents and industrial changes. Information about new
chemical hazards, equipment, changed procedures was displayed on notice-
boards and they were expected to read these. As he was promoted there were
more literacy demands at work, including writing reports and providing statements as a witness to accidents.

He provides a good example of changing work practices leading to new literacy demands. From the early 1960s, new government legislation made fire authorities responsible for overseeing fire safety and carrying out inspections of
businesses. The Fire Brigade in every town had to go round offices and shops,
checking fire precautions and issuing certificates. Later on it included hotels and

boarding houses and it took three years to certify all the buildings in the area: *And every one you went to, it was miles and miles of paper, written reports explaining why and how.* Harry and Ted described all this, and how as a result of the inspections attitudes to the Fire Brigade changed. Fire Officers were expected to impose and enforce an Act which they did not fully understand at first. They learned about it as they went along. This involved training centres being set up and officers going on courses; many of them were not interested in this, they had joined *to fight fires not to do office work.* On the courses they were taught about the new acts; how to inspect premises; and how to communicate with the public. They were not taught how to actually write the reports. Harry recounts how he learnt by reading and copying from old reports filed in the fire station: *you took out the bits that was relevant to yours and you wrote that in. And then after a few weeks you started developing your own . . . your own little way of doing it. It was a play on words really. You can write a sentence out ten different ways with different words but all meaning the same.* He chuckled when he thought about how other people would now be using his old reports as models and copying out bits of them.

30   Harry and Ted were also active in various committees in the Fire Brigade and in the local working men's club. This involved a range of literacy practices. When asked about minute-taking, Ted reported *and we strictly observed the rules of permitted procedure which are standard, you know. And we drew up agendas and appointed officials annually. And they were all like conducted, by and large, on standard committee procedure and rules.* The procedures were all handed down from the past. All the committees kept to the same old rules whether or not they were relevant to today. Harry was secretary for a while; he had to write minutes and put up notices. He found all this very difficult, wrote them all out at home, trying *to put it into proper English.*

Despite his feeling on being uneducated, it is clear that Harry participated in a wide range of complex literacy practices both in his work life and in his community life. It is also clear that he learned them as an adult and picked them up informally. This first theme, then, is an attitude to education which reflects early childhood experiences, and which structures how he sees the world today, how he deals with people and how he feels about literacy.

FICTION, TRUTH AND REALITY

This theme emerged slowly. For Harry the only stories worth telling or reading are *authentic*, real-life stories. He seems to look down on novels. His wife used to read a lot of novels and also stories to the children. He didn't understand what she saw in the stories. Harry appears to feel a clear distinction between reading factual books and reading fiction—one is educational, the other almost a waste of time. Interestingly, Harry received praise at school for his imaginative stories. It was fine as a child, but not as an adult. He accepts that a child reading a novel might be learning something from it, but there is an edge to what he says which somehow implies that some other activity might be preferable. Also, it is fine to have his own imagination, but he does not want anyone else's. This view is also apparent in his television viewing. He'll watch documentaries or quiz programmes but not

Aside 10 Imagination and reading

HARRY: *Well I've got a book upstairs . . . The Longest Battle . . . The War at Sea '39–'45. Which obviously impressed me because it's fact. And because I was there at the time, it's interesting . . . And that's the only books I read is factual.*

INTERVIEWER: *You don't read novels?*

HARRY: *Oh no. I can't be interested. No. Other people's imagination. I'd sooner read the real thing . . . I don't really like reading tripe. But then again if they* [children] *read a novel, they're learning something from it, aren't they?*

INTERVIEWER: *Do you think novels are tripe?*

HARRY: *Oh yes, aye. It's somebody's imagination. I couldn't read anybody else's imagination. I'd sooner read the real authentic thing, you see. As it happened.*

> *. . . Oh aye. We used to have compositions . . . and I always had to go and read mine out because I had the best imagination in class.*

INTERVIEWER: [laughing] *Well this is rather strange isn't it?*

HARRY: *Aye. It is, yes.*

INTERVIEWER: *So, why do you feel so little respect for imagination then? If you were good at it.*

HARRY: *Well my imagination . . . I mean it's all right to me but I wouldn't want to read anybody else's . . . I remember as a kid I had a very vivid imagination. I could write compositions about anything that . . . just all made up. Never anything true to life.*

INTERVIEWER: *What do you think changed that? Just leaving school?*

HARRY: *Probably, aye. I don't know really. You could go into a lot of blarney about the war really. When you go in as a boy and come out as a man. It certainly makes a man of you. And that's where imagination's worse thing ever.*

INTERVIEWER: *Do you think it's dishonest?*

HARRY: *Oh aye. And it's bad for you anyway. You can imagine all sorts of things. And it never happens. There's nowt as good as true life, is there?*

> *It's a queer attitude I've got really. I can't go along with anybody else's imaginations. I don't mind my own* [laughs].

INTERVIEWER: *Quite a few . . . particularly men I've spoken to have said that.*

HARRY: *Yeah, aye. I suppose men are a lot different to women. Women fantasise a lot.*

> *. . . Oh if it's a novel of somebody's own imagination, I won't even look at it. No, I could make my own story up better.*

INTERVIEWER: *So is that what it is? That you feel that really you could do better?*

HARRY: *Oh yeah, aye. In fact the people at work said they'd like me . . . to put down my life story, you see. Because I've had a right good life you know, and all that. And I wish I had the ability to do it.*

soap operas or plays. When questioned, Harry suggested imagination was a dangerous thing—*the last thing you want in wartime.* He also talked of not believing in dreams and fantasies: *they get you nowhere.* Harry was not the only man we interviewed to express a preference for reality and a hostility to fiction. . . .

When we returned Harry's transcript to him in the collaborative ethnography phase of the research, he was pleased with it and read and re-read the script. As the diary quote at the beginning of the chapter makes clear, he was pleased with the way it sounded and at ease with his own voice.

The life story that Harry is now writing is for himself and for other seamen like him (See Aside 8). It is important to him that he writes in his own voice, a voice other men like him can relate to. He is a compulsive reader of *authentic* war stories, but has no interest in reading books by officers. Harry feels his own reading has given him a good sense of how to approach this writing, but he lacks confidence in some aspects of the project. He feels confident about the structure of the story, the technical information, the language of seamen and writing dialogue. His memory of the war is very vivid. But he feels he needs to include more literary passages, with descriptive language to convey atmosphere and weather, to conjure up storms with. This links up with the educated–uneducated theme where he is going to pass his writing on to his *educated* son to *flower-up* for him. There is no sense of this being a failing or an intrusion on his son's part. It seems to be a collaborative venture which is agreeable to them both. It is the point at which the educated and the uneducated meet on mutual ground and share literacy skills.

35   There is a connection between this theme and his ruling passion. Harry's passionate interest in the war fifty years later seems in part to be a search for the truth. This is not so much a political truth but a need to rediscover, or recreate the real experiences of servicemen like him.

He is using literacy to make sense of his own life. He is doing this through both his reading and his writing; his reading about the war is to make sense of his experiences, his writing makes sense of his experiences and communicates them to other people. The writing also validates the experiences and provides a voice for *ordinary people.*

≋ Critical Reflections

1. Reflecting on his own literacies, Harry draws a sharp distinction between educated and uneducated literacy practices and individuals. How do you define an educated person? An uneducated person? What literacy practices do you associate with education, and what not? Why do you think you have drawn the definitions that you have?

2. In their interview with Harry, Barton and Hamilton asked him to think about his daily literacy practices—the things he reads (from mail to newspapers to books) and writes (from lists to letters). Spend one day keeping a log of your

own literacy practices and reflect on it. In your log, what did you find that is surprising? What did you expect to find?

3. Barton and Hamilton refer to a "complex system of support and reciprocity" that surrounds Harry's reading and writing practices. What do you see as involved in that system? What exchanges does Harry make, and how do they affect his literacies?

4. The concepts of educated and uneducated are very important in Harry's reflection on his literacies. How do you understand his definition of each, and what in the reading supports your definitions?

⩶ MAKING CONNECTIONS

1. Using the definition of vernacular and dominant literacies from the other Barton and Hamilton reading included here ("Literacy Practices," p. 60), which of your own literacy practices do you find to be vernacular, which dominant, and why do you define them as you have?

2. In Aside 5.7 in this chapter, the author refers to an incident when she and Harry interpreted a literacy event—in this case, both looking at a diagram of a battle in which Harry participated—very differently. In "Literacy Practices," Barton and Hamilton suggest that shared interpretations are central to shared literacies. Applying this concept to "Fierce Intimacies," do you think that Cedric participated in the literacies shared by some of the other students at Brown? Why or why not?

3. In "What High School Is," Theodore Sizer outlines a system of education and discusses what he sees as its purpose. Would such a system produce a student whom Harry would define as "educated," or would it produce a different kind of student? Why?

LORENE CARY

From BLACK ICE

This chapter is excerpted from Lorene Cary's book, *Black Ice*. In it, Cary writes about her experiences as one of the first African-American students, and among the first female students, at the formerly all-male St. Paul's, an elite college preparatory school in New Hampshire. Cary entered St. Paul's in the fall of 1972, only a year after the school had become co-educational. From her middle-class background in Philadelphia, Cary decided that at St. Paul's, she would "turn it out"—compete and succeed among the predominantly wealthy white students there.

Cary graduated from St. Paul's in 1974 and went on to the University of Pennsylvania, where she earned a B.A. and an M.A. She also received an additional M.A. from the University of Sussex in England. She has worked as a writer for *Time* magazine and as an editor for *T.V. Guide* and *Newsweek*. She has published two additional books and currently teaches writing at the University of Pennsylvania.

Early in my first term at St. Paul's I began to dream old dreams. They were childhood dreams that I had thought I'd done with, like bed-wetting. In one dream, I was encircled by bears, friendly, round-faced teddies as big as I. The bears were animated, sepia-colored versions of pen-and-ink drawings in one of my books. In the dream I was a child again, joyfully naked. The bears held paws and danced around me in a circle. We sang together. They protected and adored me. Then—as I knew would happen, the foreknowledge lending betrayal to their song—they began to leer and sneer. Their eyes shone with malice. They closed in about me. I was naked, and their teeth gleamed sharp and white against the sepia.

I ran from them, ducking under their interlocked paws, pricking my skin on hairs as sharp as the pen that had drawn them. I ran and ran and ran to the edge of a precipice and awakened just as they were about to catch me.

The first time I dreamt this dream at St. Paul's, I expected to wake up on Addison Street in West Philadelphia. But there were no city noises to comfort me, and no headlights sweeping like searchlights across the blinds.

I dreamt that I was watching my own funeral. I was a small, grayish corpse in a short coffin. From the back of the church I could see the tips of my feet and my folded hands above the polished mahogany. I observed the mourning with self-absorbed satisfaction.

5   In another dream, I was walking on the sidewalk on Addison Street toward my friend Siboney to ask if she wanted to play. Under my feet the sidewalk shimmered with broken glass. Then the shimmering became movement. The cement squares began to shift. They had been shifting, in fact, from the beginning of time. The solidity had been an illusion. So, too, had been the unbroken surface. Holes yawned between the squares, small ones, then bigger and bigger. They emitted radiant heat and the sounds of souls in despair. An anthropomorphic sea of magma howled and gurgled fire. I had to walk. I had to walk the walk, but at every step, the holes swirled around. If I made one wrong step, I would tumble into hell.

I did not talk about my nightmare vision in religion class, but I thought about it. I did not speak to the girls in my room about the bears, but I thought of them, too, while I laughed and listened for betrayal. The bears warned me to beware of slipping into friendship.

Girls came and went in my room. I liked it that way. I wanted the company—and the prosperous appearance of company. They taught me about tollhouse cookies; Switzerland; the names of automobiles, shampoos, rock groups, Connecticut cities; casual shoes and outdoor-equipment catalogues. I learned that other girls, too, tired during sports, that their calf muscles, like mine, screamed out pain when they walked down the stairs. I learned about brands of tampons. I learned that these girls thought their hair dirty when they did not wash it daily.

"I hear what you're saying, but I just don't see it. I'm looking at your hair, but I don't see grease."

"Oh, my God, it's, like, hanging down in clumps!" One girl pulled a few strands from her scalp to display the offending sheen. "Look."

10   I learned that their romanticized lusts sounded like mine felt, as did their ambivalent homesickness, and their guarded, girlish competitiveness.

As they came to sit and stay, however, differences emerged between us. Taken together, these girls seemed more certain than I that they deserved our good fortune. They were sorry for people who were poorer than they, but they did not feel guilty to think of the resources we were sucking up—forests, meadows and ponds, the erudition of well-educated teachers, water for roaring showers, heat that blew out of opened windows everywhere, food not eaten but mixed together for disgusting fun after lunch. They took it as their due. It was boot-camp preparation for America's leaders, which we were told we would one day be. They gave no indication that they worried that others, smarter or more worthy, might, at that very moment, be giving up hope of getting what we had.

I did not, however, tell the girls what I was thinking. We did not talk about how differently we saw the world. Indeed my black and their white heritage was not a starting point for our relationship, but rather was the outer boundary. I could not cross it, because there sprang up a hard wall of denial impervious to my inexperienced and insecure assault. "Well, as far as I'm concerned," one girl after another would say, "it doesn't matter to me if somebody's white or black or green or purple. I mean people are just people."

The motion, having been made, would invariably be seconded.

"Really. I mean, it's the person that counts."

15   Having castigated whites' widespread inability to see individuals for the skin in which they were wrapped, I could hardly argue with "it's the person that counts." I didn't know why they always chose green and purple to dramatize their indifference, but my ethnicity seemed diminished when the talk turned to Muppets. It was like they were taking something from me.

"I'm not purple." What else could you say?

"The truth is," somebody said, "I . . . this is *so* silly . . . I'm really embarrassed, but, it's like, there *are* some things you, God, you just feel ashamed to admit that you think about this stuff, but I always kind of wondered if, like, black guys and white guys were, like, different . . ."

They shrieked with laughter. Sitting on the afghan my mother had crocheted for me in the school colors of red and white, their rusty-dusty feet all over my good afghan, they laughed and had themselves a ball.

"Now, see, that's why people don't want to say anything," one girl said. "Look, you're getting all mad."

20   "I'm not mad."

"You look it."

"I'm not mad. I don't even know about any differences between white guys and black guys," I said deliberately avoiding the word boys. (Black manhood seemed at stake. Everything seemed at stake.) Then I added as archly as possible: "I don't mess around with white boys."

The party broke up soon after. I sat still, the better to control my righteous anger. It always came down to this, I thought, the old song of the South. I wanted something more meaningful. I wanted it to mean something that I had come four hundred miles from home, and sat day after day with them in Chapel, in class. I wanted it to mean something that after Martin Luther King's and Malcolm X's assassinations, we kids sweated together in sports, are together at Seated Meal, studied and talked together at night. It couldn't be just that I was to become like them or hang onto what I'd been. It couldn't be that lonely and pointless.

I looked across the quad to Jimmy's window, and waved. He was not in his room, but the mere sight of his lighted window brought me back to my purpose. It was not to run my ass ragged trying to wrench some honesty out of this most disingenuous of God's people. I had come to St. Paul's to turn it out. How had I lost sight of the simple fact?

25 In a few days "inside" grades for the Fall Term caught me by surprise. I had barely settled in. During reports the Rector said that interim grades were merely to give us an idea of our progress. Students called them "warning" grades. Groupmasters handed them to each student in the evening.

I churned with anticipation all day. At one moment it seemed to me that I'd been doing brilliantly. I was understanding St. Fuster's musical Spanish, speaking glibly in religion about "systems of belief," hiding from Mr. Buxton the crush I was developing, trooping good-naturedly through the inanity of trigonometry, drawing and redrawing the folds of a draped cloth in art.

One wrong answer, however, would change my perspective completely. Sure, I was understanding St. Fuster better, but my essays were grammatical disasters. In religion, I skittered over the surface of the language, never quite knowing what I meant to say until the moment I opened my mouth. I only *thought* Mr. Buxton hadn't noticed my crush. I had fallen asleep during eighth-period trig. In art class, my colors were timid; my perspective was off.

Mr. Hawley handed me the thin piece of paper on which the computer in the Schoolhouse basement had recorded my warning grades. On my sheet were five grades, two Honors and three High Passes. What I saw when I looked at my warning grades were two Bs and three Cs. The school had made it quite clear in the catalog and elsewhere that St. Paul's grades were not letter-grade equivalents. They'd told us that High Honors were rare as A-pluses, and that Honors meant just that. No matter. I saw average. I saw failure. And what I saw on that paper, Mr. Hawley saw in my face.

"There are several things about these warning grades you should keep in mind," he said. "The first is that although they may look like real grades and feel like real grades, they are not real grades.

30   "OK. Now, how accurate an indicator are these? Well, I'm sure that in some of your courses, there hasn't been enough work assigned and graded for teachers to evaluate. And in that case, many teachers feel safer grading on the low side, just so that no one gets a false sense of security. So, it is possible that you might be doing better than these grades, and it is extremely unlikely that you'd be doing any worse."

He told me that High Passes were not the end of the world. "The other thing that I doubt you are giving yourself credit for," he said, "is that you've just come in, as a new Fifth Former—not many people come in the Fifth Form, as you've noticed, and there's a reason why, many reasons—and you've just come straight from your old hometown high. Some of these other students have had a different preparation. I am certain that you'll catch on fast. Look, you have caught on fast. I've got old girls in this house who'd kill for those grades. But the fact is, I don't see how you can expect much more of yourself right now."

Mr. Hawley told me that he'd seen students take a year or two to adjust to St. Paul's, not just public-school students, but kids from fancy day schools.

"I've only got two years," I said.

"You're doing great."

35   When girls on my hall asked about my grades, I joked: "It's like when the Ghost of Christmas Yet To Come points to the gravestone," I said. "All I want to know is: Is this what will be or what may be?"

"Oh, you'll do fine."

I wondered if anyone here had ever expected me to do better than this. White faces of the adults flashed in my head, smiling, encouraging, tilted to one side, asking if I'd like to talk, extending their welcome. "If you need anything . . ." Early on they'd told me that I'd do fine. I felt betrayed, first by them, then by my own naiveté. HPs were probably what they'd meant by fine—for black scholarship kids. Maybe that's what they'd been saying all along, only I hadn't heard it.

No sooner had the furor of warning grades subsided than the excitement of Parents' Day began. A few parents appeared on the last Friday afternoon in October, and by Saturday morning they were everywhere, cars clogging the roads, adult voices filling the Schoolhouse, where they waited in long lines for ten-minute talks with our teachers.

Parents who had no money or no time did not come, but mine did. And so did my grandparents. They surrounded me as we walked slowly along the paths. Seeing them made me know how much I'd missed them. I guided them through the days' activities as if marching through a dream.

40   In the evening, they came to the show we'd prepared for them. I sang in the chorus, and they saw me sing. I showed them my books and my papers. I walked them to each of my favorite places along the paths and pointed out where gardeners had been working all week to spruce up the grounds. My father remembered that dorm proctors at Lincoln University had handed out fresh new blankets on anniversary weekends, just before festivities, and then collected them again when parents went home. We laughed about that. But St. Paul's was no

Lincoln, they kept saying, that tiny black college in rural Pennsylvania where milk from the nearby cows had tasted of onion grass in the spring.

I recalled the photographs of my father and his classmates, young black men with shiny hair, baring their legs and hamming it up for the camera; the photo of my father and mother, who had married the Saturday before my father graduated. They stood under a huge old tree, grinning broadly, my mother in her pedal-pusher pants, her body curving like an S against his, her arm waving in the air. Every time one of us mentioned Lincoln—and we did, again and again, because it was the only college we knew well—I thought of those photographs. As often as I saw the image in my mind, I heard snatches of what had been their old favorite song:

> . . . *Our day will come*
>
> *And we'll have ev'rything,*
>
> *We'll share the joy*
>
> *Falling in love can bring.*
>
> *No one can tell me that I'm too young to know*
>
> *I love you so,*
>
> *And you love me . . .*
>
> *Our day wi-ill come.*

I could not stop thinking of them like that, their arms entwined like the branches of a mulberry, certain that they would do together what their parents had been unable to do. "We decided we were *not* going to end up divorced. We just decided it," they always said. I'd wondered how they could have been so sure. "Our dreams have magic because we'll always stay/In love this way/Our day will come."

Lincoln looked green in the pictures, and, as if it were not full enough with their promise, and the promise of so many young men, black Greeks, black gods ready to march out into the world and grab it for their own, it was also home to the prepubescent Julian Bond "just running around the campus like any other little faculty kid," and, he, of course, was now in government.

My mother lit a cigarette in my room, and my father made a face. I could not take my eyes off the pack. My mother had changed brands. So absorbed had I been with my own changes, that I had not expected any from them, and my mother least of all. It was a small thing, the brand of cigarettes, but it occurred to me for the first time that in leaving home, I gave up the right to know the details of their daily life. Things might be the same when I got back for the next vacation, or they might not. I had no way of knowing, because I wasn't there.

45   Whatever I had planned to tell them—about how I did not feel like myself here, how I was worried that the recruiters expected little more than survival from us, how I was beginning to doubt that they could *see* excellence in us, because it might pop out through thick lips and eyes or walk on flat feet or sit on big, bodacious behinds—I kept to myself. I showed off my familiarity with my new school. Why, I was fitting in fine. My teachers said so. My new friends said so—Hey, girls, come meet my folks. . . .

Soon they had to leave. Because it was more convenient. St. Paul's School did not switch to Standard Time until Sunday night when the parents were gone. My family was amused by the custom; I was not. "It's just like St. Paul's. It's practically a metaphor," I said ("metaphor" having become one of my favorite new words), "for the arrogance of this place. Isn't that the most arrogant thing you've ever seen, just changing *time!*"

"Well, honey," said my grandmother, "it's just for a little while. It's not as if they were going to keep it that way."

"When you think about it, it's an arbitrary change anyway," my father said. "And now that we need to save energy, who knows whether they might just change it some more to take better advantage of the daylight."

Everyone smiled mildly at me as if I were being unreasonable. I let the subject drop.

50   I fell asleep that night listening to the country sounds that replaced the parents' festive noise. In the branches, dead limbs creaked like old doors. Every hour until midnight the Chapel tower's metallic throat pealed out the wrong time, sharp and bright and sure.

November set in cold and damp. The work of the school chugged along: *I think I can, I think I can, I think I can.* The chipper refrain from childhood came chugging through my mind as I ran through the rain between classes. I did not have a raincoat that fall. *I think I can I think I can I think I can.* I slogged around the muddy field and hurled myself through wind sprints. Browner mud, grayer skies, blacker water. The wind penetrated the fiber of my clothing. The sun did not. But the engine of the school chugged on. Work and more work, with no way to get out. People and more people, with no way to get away from them, the same people day after day, becoming more familiar, their walks, their accents, their quirks and behavior. They said the same things, cracked the same jokes. So did I. I bored myself. We bored each other. Our teasing grew less witty and meaner.

It was in November that my soccer team played one of the boys' club teams. Our coach urged us to play aggressively. The ball flew up and down the field. I cursed its every reversal, knowing that I'd have to turn around and run back down the same field I'd just run up. Back and forth and back and forth, meaninglessly, mercilessly. The ball zinged, and I ran parallel to it, out on the edge of the field, in wing position, just like I didn't have any better sense. The drudgery was punctuated now and then by panic when a ball popped toward me. "Close up the hole! Close up the hole! Take it down. You're free, you're free!" and then I'd see the expanse of field between me and the goal, and I'd know that I could not tag along, but would have to run fast, faster than the mob coming at me. I wheezed and ran and wheezed. I opened my mouth wide, but I felt as if I were sucking air through a straw.

I think I can I think I can I think I can. Up jumped the good little girl inside, ever hopeful, she who believed that all she needed was one more win. Up she jumped as if this were a fifth-grade penmanship contest, the tie-breaker in a spelling bee, an audition for *Annie Get Your Gun:* "Anything you can do I can do better, I can do anything better than you." I knew this little girl. She looked like the freckled six-year-old in my mother's wallet. She felt like Pollyanna.

The ball came at me. The crazy little girl inside tore after it. Girls who had beaten me in wind sprints were unable to catch me. My arms pumped up and down as I ran. They helped push me forward. Maybe this was it, I thought, maybe. I almost cried with gratitude. Asthma came to clamp round my chest, but this time I was not afraid of suffocating. I huffed puffs of steam into the cold air.

55 I didn't see the little guy who came to steal the ball. I didn't see him at all until he was right in front of me like a sudden insult. I was stunned. The ball was mine. The goal was in sight. I could see the goal tender's fear, his awkward alarm. I loved how he called out to his fullbacks—as if they could stop me. But who was this little guy who would not be moved?

He put out his foot to snag the ball. He got it, and pulled it just to the side of me. I scooped the ball back with the inside of my foot, and knew I had to move it again, but could not, because he was there, the little guy again, his cleat coming, slender and tenacious. Then I charged. There was screaming around us, coming closer. I had to have the ball. I had to drive it in. I didn't realize I had fallen until the impact of the hard ground went up through my hip and reverberated inside my head. The ball rolled away. The whistle blew, and they stopped the game for us. His face contorted to hold back his tears. Clouds drifted overhead, wispy and beautiful.

I saw him a couple days later. He swung himself gingerly between his crutches as if his armpits were sore. He smiled bravely at me.

"I'm sorry," I said to him, trying to feel more intensely the throbbing in the purplish lump that had appeared on the side of my own leg.

"That's all right," he said, shrugging his shoulders above the crutches. "You couldn't help it. Are you all right?"

60 "Sure. Got a bruise or two." I felt like a brutish distortion of those big, black women I so admired, like Sojourner Truth as the actresses portrayed her: "Ah kin push a plow as far as a man—*And ain't I a voman?!*"

I worked harder the rest of the term than I had ever known I could work. I looked up more vocabulary words and wrote papers and practiced grammar. I worked and reworked trigonometry equations. I took to paraphrasing an old nun I'd once seen in a movie. She croaks at the girl whom the Virgin Mary has visited: "I have read the words of our Lord God until my eyes burned like the very fires of hell. Why should God choose *you?*"

No longer convinced of the special brilliance I had once expected to discover in myself, no longer certain that my blackness gave me precocious wisdom, or that I could outslick these folks, I held onto that crazy old nun. They might be smarter than I or better prepared or more athletic. They might know the rules better, whatever the unspoken rules were for leaping to the top of this world and staying there. But I could work. I could read until my eyes burned like the very fires of hell! I could outwork them all. (Ain't I a voman?) Will, it seemed to me, was the only quality I had in greater abundance than my fellows, and I would will myself to work.

Examinations were the test of my resolve. During exams there were no more classes and no more sports, only studying, and for big stakes—exams were worth large fractions of our final grades. I felt the rush of pure competition. Studying distracted me from other people, thoughts, worries.

At the appointed hour we walked to the gymnasium, where folding tables and chairs were arranged in rows on white mats that muffled the noise of our footsteps. Blue books were stacked, fresh and clean, on the front desks. Teachers handed out their questions and smiled encouragement. Our religion exam asked one question in its final section: "Who is Jesus?"

65   I was unprepared for the question—and for the gusher of feelings it released. Suddenly it mattered to me that in His name the red-bearded men, missionaries, soldiers, capitalists, adventurists all, clambered over the earth as if it were a woman's body; that in Jesus' name they triumphed and we suffered, and in Jesus' name, too—for Christ's sake—we both claimed justice, oh, and looked for the faith to unite:

> Join hands, then, brothers of the faith
>
> Whate'er your race may be!
>
> Who serves my Father as a son
>
> Is surely kin to me.

(We sang it in chapel, John Oxenham's words—he had a name—set to the generic "Negro melody" in the hymnal.)

It mattered to me to get it right about Him: the lamb-shepherd-bridegroom-buffoon, the Way and the Light, the dreamy boy on the calendars tacked onto the wall over my great-grandmother's side of the bed. It mattered, though I could not write it, and there was no place for it, that she criticized and judged, that she told us, with reference to the color of the man we should marry: Don't darken your bread. It mattered that when she died she took with her any hope of her approval, so long withheld, but so close that at times we nearly had it. She'd snatched it back into the grave with her like a setting sun pulling the last streaks of light from the sky.

The blue-eyed boy over the bed, talking to the elders at the temple, holding His hands out to the children: Only He would love those unworthy of love. He was the bridegroom, the resurrection, and the light. I wanted so to believe, to make what Tillich called "the leap of faith." I imagined myself jumping at a brick wall, naked, bruised, leaping at a garden beyond. My head filled with noise and pictures, scraps of music from Hollywood Bible epics, the remembered tastes of the papery African Methodist Episcopal wafer and grape juice, and the comfort of sucking my own fleshy thumb at night. *Take, eat.* God only knows what I actually wrote.

By the time the exams were collected, I arose, stiff and tremulous. I had no idea how I would face studying for the next, or sitting to write it, letting loose in my head so much noise and chaos in the quiet, orderly gym.

But I did. We all did, again and again until it was over.

70   Just three months after my parents had delivered me to St. Paul's I was on my way home again. Fumiko came with me. On the bus to the station, I buzzed with

exhaustion and anticipation. One student in the back of the bus pulled out a joint; a couple of others passed bottles in brown paper bags.

"Have some?"

As we drove through the Merrimack River valley, I thought of the winos' street-corner toast:

If wine was a river and I was a duck

I'd dive to the bottom and never come up,

But since wine ain't no river, and I ain't no duck,

I'ma drink this wine 'til I'm fucked up.

"No, thanks," I said. I used an off-handed voice and lit a cigarette to show my cool. My mother would have killed me had I arrived with liquor on my breath. I could smell it even as Fumiko and I dozed.

I thought and then dreamt about the wet necks of bottles everywhere, and about a glamorous adulthood, when I would drink, not out of a bottle, but from thin glasses clinking ice cubes. I loved ice. I thought about a girl at school who made piña coladas, and in a blender, no less, before Seated Meal—the very drink my grandmother and her friends sipped ("Oh, no, my dear, just one for me; these things sneak up on you!") at their club dinners. I thought about my other grandmother, who drank until cheap Scotch released the rage within her and the insatiable hunger: for more life, more beauty, more men, more food, more love, more money, more luck. I thought of her asleep on the toilet and awake the next morning, the smell of Scotch excreting from the fine pores of her velvety skin, of her toothless shame and the guilty, secretive search for her teeth. I thought of her soprano voice, that was cracked and pitted now by alcohol and tobacco. How could you have a voice like that and destroy it? I wondered. How could you live with yourself?

75   When I could bear my own homecoming thoughts no longer, I turned to Fumiko. We made excited eyes and talk together. She was an excellent traveling companion and, when we arrived home, a perfect houseguest. Fumiko's exquisite Japanese manners delighted my family. She brought gifts: pink-and-white-faced dolls with embroidered kimonos and silky black hair. My mother installed them in the china closet where they still reign. After a trans-Pacific phone call, her parents shipped us a five-gallon keg of Japan's best soy sauce.

Whenever my family seemed in danger of confusing Fumiko and her dolls, I warned them pedantically: they were not to make geisha-girl cracks; they were not to treat her as if she did not speak English; they were not to pull out their five facts about Japan for her confirmation and agreement.

In fact, my mother recognized without any help from me that Fumiko was a teenager, mischievous, full of hormones, and in need of maternal guidance. When Fumiko announced that she had given our telephone number to a Philly-born boy she'd met at another prep school, my mother set strict visitation rules.

"If that child thinks that I'm letting her waltz out of this house with some Puerto Rican from North Philly, she'd better think again."

"Oh, Mom, he's not 'some Puerto Rican,'" I said archly. (More and more often, I found myself mortified by my family's lack of Third World unity.) "He's a guy who goes to a prep school . . . just like we do."

80 "I don't know him. I promised that girl's parents that I would be a mother to her just like I'm a mother to my own children. I tell you what: I would not want anyone to let my child go off in some strange city with some strange man they'd never even met. That is *not* my idea of looking out for a young girl, and despite what you all may think about yourselves and your independence, the fact is that you are still children, and I *am* still mother.

"And besides," she continued, taking another tack, no doubt because of some scrap of resistance in my face, "let me tell you one thing. Some of the weirdest people I know are educated people. Why? I don't know. But the fact that he's a preppie doesn't mean a damn thing to me. I am not impressed by education. He could be even crazier than he would have been had he stayed home in North Philly!"

So Fumiko's admirer came to visit on a weekday afternoon (not evening). The trip took an hour and a half on public transportation. ("I am *not* using up my gas and my day to chauffeur some boy. If he can't find his way, with that education he's getting, well, shame on him.") When he arrived, my mother made a face to indicate that he was bigger than she'd expected. He had a bigger bush, and a hat that he made the mistake of leaving on in our house. Something else was wrong, too.

My mother and I went into the kitchen to leave them alone together. We closed the door. "I'm sorry," my mother said after a minute. "I can't take this any longer."

"Oh, Mama, please," I whispered. "It's just for a little while. My Lord, you've only given them an hour or two. How much could a little funk hurt in one hour?"

85 "A little funk? Is that what they're teaching you? You don't smell like that. Not yet at least. God knows that child doesn't smell at all."

"Japanese don't smell."

"That's the goofiest thing you've said yet. I know *he* smells, though, and I can't have it. I just cannot have it."

"What are you going to do?"

My mother looked at me scornfully and mounted the staircase. I was aware that I was placing the tender feelings of this big, funky dude ahead of my mother's sovereignty in her own house. I spent a few idle moments wishing that they had gone to the movies as they'd wanted. I had promised to chaperone. Then I spent a few more moments cursing my mother's need to lord it over us that this was her house. Her house. I had thought St. Paul's would have freed me of all that, but instead, I was back here getting double doses, just so I wouldn't forget under the subversive tutelage of those people, people who obviously had no control over their own children. Mom had several complaints about what those people were doing to me: they had me eating too fast, dumping pepper on my food as if she hadn't already seasoned it just right, neglecting to wash my hands frequently enough, forgetting to mind my tongue. By the time I had done thinking and sighing, my mother returned from upstairs.

90 She stood on the landing. "Now I want to do a little something," she announced to the pair on the brown brocade couch, worn shiny in patches.

"What is it?" Fumiko asked, prettily biting her consonants.

"Close your eyes, everybody!" Mama's voice was falsely bright.

I knew that tone. I watched her with suspicious dread from the kitchen. Then I saw them close their eyes, and my mother pulled from behind her back an aerosol can of deodorant.

"Keep them closed!" she sang.

95   She sprayed all around them, making sure to get some mist on the big, odoriferous interloper. Then she opened the window behind them a crack to let in the winter air.

"Just a funny little family custom," she said to Fumiko as she floated back into the kitchen. "There," she said to me. "All done! Just like a needle at the doctor's."

I visited Karen and Ruthie. They asked how St. Paul's was, and whether or not I liked it. I wanted to answer them honestly. I wanted them to know how my life had changed so that we could sit down in the dim light of Karen's living room and talk about it. But I did not have enough words or time to make them see it and feel it with me, and besides, nobody, not even my best friends, cared as much about St. Paul's as its students. Nobody else lived there. They lived, as we Paulies joked, in the real world.

Fumiko told them in her halting English that St. Paul's was "very hard." I agreed, and once they laughed, I broke into the monologue that I repeated, with variations according to the audience, for years: "First of all, you've got to understand that the teachers are all a little screwy. You've got to be to stay in a place like that for twenty years. These are the people who decided to opt out of real life at some point, and they are set loose on us twenty-four hours a day.

"OK? You got the picture? There is no escape from these people. They are out to improve you: how you read, how you write, how you run, how you look, what you say at the dinner table, how you *think*. You see what I mean by no escape? Meanwhile, back at the dorm, the white kids are blasting the hardest hard rock you've ever heard . . . ."

100   Later, I figured, when I understood the school better, then I could talk to them seriously about it. For now, I wanted to make them laugh. I wanted to entertain. I didn't dare risk being boring or snobbish or cry-babyish about my new school. I didn't want to lose them.

"Now you tell me about everybody at Yeadon. How was the new majorette squad this season? Did Mr. Cenatempo let you do flaming batons this year?"

Each time we began a new subject, I needed them to fill me in on facts, and I had to fill Fumiko in. I didn't know what they'd just read in English, or who had sung the solos in this year's *Messiah*, or what prank Bob Bailey had pulled in science lab. Too much exposition weighed down our conversation. We couldn't anticipate each other anymore or jump back and forth between subjects until we landed in intimate territory. I was with my friends, but I could not get the full pleasure of them. I wanted to weep with frustration.

Two nights before we returned to school, I stayed up by myself drinking my mother's Christmas liqueur late into the night. I decided to level with myself. My new friends and I knew each other's daily routines, but we had no history—and no future, I thought, when we all went back to our real lives. But back in real life, Karen and Ruthie and I, once past the memories, had to work hard just to keep talking. At my own house I felt as if I were fighting for a new position in the family order, while Mama pretended not to notice and Dad maybe didn't notice for real. Everywhere I went I felt out of place. The fact was that I had left home in September gleeful and smug. I took it as divine justice that now I felt as if I no longer belonged anywhere.

CRITICAL REFLECTIONS

1. Early in this chapter, Lorene Cary describes her frustration with white girls at St. Paul's, remembering that she had come to the school to "turn it out." How would you describe the tension that she experiences between socializing and "turning it out"?

2. Cary complains to her parents at Parents' Weekend that St. Paul's decision to switch to Standard Time until after the weekend (and after the rest of the country) was a metaphor for the school. What do you think this metaphor symbolizes to her?

3. Cary vows that she would "turn it out" at St. Paul's. Do you think she succeeds in doing so in this chapter? Why or why not? What are the costs and benefits of "turning it out," or not doing so, as you see them?

4. Describe what you think is happening in the relationship between Cary and her family and friends when she and her friend Fumiko return to Philadelphia at the holiday break during their first year at St. Paul's. She writes that she "took it as divine justice that now I felt as if I no longer belonged anywhere"—why?

MAKING CONNECTIONS

1. Consider the conversation between Lorene Cary and her family with the one between the speaker and her brother in "Self-Portrait with Politics." What are the similarities and differences between these families' positions on education as they are represented in the selections here?

2. In "Literacy Practices," David Barton and Mary Hamilton outline a basic definition for, and what they believe to be the relevance of, literacy practices. What literacy practices do you see represented in Lorene's experiences at St. Paul's in this chapter?

3. Like "I Just Wanna Be Average" and "Fierce Intimacies," *Black Ice* is also in part a narrative about Lorene Cary's literacy development. What literacies do you think she is developing at St. Paul's? How are they similar to and/or different from the ones developed by the main characters in "Average" and "Intimacies"?

4. In "Engaged Pedagogy," bell hooks writes that while in college she became "estranged from her education." Do you think Cary experiences a similar phenomena? Why or why not?

MARK EDMUNDSON

ON THE USES OF A LIBERAL EDUCATION: I. AS LITE ENTERTAINMENT FOR BORED COLLEGE STUDENTS

When this article appeared in *Harper's* magazine in 1997, it was paired with Earl Shorris's article, "On the Uses of a Liberal Education: II. As a Weapon in the Hands of the Restless Poor" (pages 187–201). A liberal education is one designed to help students become well-rounded thinkers with a thorough understanding of the liberal arts, which are academic subjects (like history, literature, philosophy, and mathematics) that are not necessarily tied to any particular trade or skill. Organized as they were, the two "On the Uses of a Liberal Education" articles presented two very different ideas about the purpose and definition of a liberal education and the audience for whom such an education was intended. Edmundson is a Professor of English at the University of Virginia.

Today is evaluation day in my Freud class, and everything has changed. The class meets twice a week, late in the afternoon, and the clientele, about fifty undergraduates, tends to drag in and slump, looking disconsolate and a little lost, waiting for a jump start. To get the discussion moving, they usually require a joke, an anecdote, an off-the-wall question—When you were a kid, were your Halloween getups ego costumes, id costumes, or superego costumes? That sort of thing. But today, as soon as I flourish the forms, a buzz rises in the room. Today they write their assessments of the course, their assessments of *me,* and they are without a doubt wide-awake. "What is your evaluation of the instructor?" asks question number eight, entreating them to circle a number between five (excellent) and one (poor). Whatever interpretive subtlety they've acquired during the term is now out the window. Edmundson: one to five, stand and shoot.

And they do. As I retreat through the door—I never stay around for this phase of the ritual—I look over my shoulder and see them toiling away like the devil's auditors. They're pitched into high writing gear, even the ones who struggle to squeeze out their journal entries word by word, stoked on a procedure they have by now supremely mastered. They're playing the informed consumer, letting the provider know where he's come through and where he's not quite up to snuff.

But why am I so distressed, bolting like a refugee out of my own classroom, where I usually hold easy sway? Chances are the evaluations will be much like what they've been in the past—they'll be just fine. It's likely that I'll be commended for being "interesting" (and I am commended, many times over), that I'll be cited for my relaxed and tolerant ways (that happens, too), that my sense of humor and capacity to connect the arcana of the subject matter with current culture will come in for some praise (yup). I've been hassled this term, finishing a manuscript, and so haven't given their journals the attention I should have, and for that I'm called—quite civilly, though—to account. Overall, I get off pretty well.

Yet I have to admit that I do not much like the image of myself that emerges from these forms, the image of knowledgeable, humorous detachment and bland tolerance. I do not like the forms themselves, with their number ratings, reminiscent of the sheets circulated after the TV pilot has just played to its sample audience in Burbank. Most of all I dislike the attitude of calm consumer expertise that pervades the responses. I'm disturbed by the serene belief that my function—and, more important, Freud's, or Shakespeare's, or Blake's—is to divert, entertain, and interest. Observes one respondent, not at all unrepresentative: "Edmundson has done a fantastic job of presenting this difficult, important & controversial material in an enjoyable and approachable way."

5   Thanks but no thanks. I don't teach to amuse, to divert, or even, for that matter, to be merely interesting. When someone says she "enjoyed" the course—and that word crops up again and again in my evaluations—somewhere at the edge of my immediate complacency I feel encroaching self-dislike. That is not at all what I had in mind. The off-the-wall questions and the sidebar jokes are meant as lead-ins to stronger stuff—in the case of the Freud course, to a complexly tragic view of life. But the affability and the one-liners often seem to be all that land with the students; their journals and evaluations leave me little doubt.

I want some of them to say that they've been changed by the course. I want them to measure themselves against what they've read. It's said that some time ago a Columbia University instructor used to issue a harsh two-part question. One: What book did you most dislike in the course? Two: What intellectual or characterological flaws in you does that dislike point to? The hand that framed that question was surely heavy. But at least it compels one to see intellectual work as a confrontation between two people, student and author, where the stakes matter. Those Columbia students were being asked to relate the quality of an *encounter*, not rate the action as though it had unfolded on the big screen.

Why are my students describing the Oedipus complex and the death drive as being interesting and enjoyable to contemplate? And why am I coming across as an urbane, mildly ironic, endlessly affable guide to this intellectual territory, operating without intensity, generous, funny, and loose?

Because that's what works. On evaluation day, I reap the rewards of my partial compliance with the culture of my students and, too, with the culture of the university as it now operates. It's a culture that's gotten little exploration. Current critics tend to think that liberal-arts education is in crisis because universities have been invaded by professors with peculiar ideas: deconstruction, Lacanianism, feminism, queer theory. They believe that genius and tradition are out and that P.C., multiculturalism, and identity politics are in because of an invasion by tribes of tenured radicals, the late millennial equivalents of the Visigoth hordes that cracked Rome's walls.

But mulling over my evaluations and then trying to take a hard, extended look at campus life both here at the University of Virginia and around the country eventually led me to some different conclusions. To me, liberal-arts education is as ineffective as it is now not chiefly because there are a lot of strange theories in the air. (Used well, those theories *can* be illuminating.) Rather, it's that university culture, like American culture writ large, is, to put it crudely, ever more devoted to consumption and entertainment, to the using and using up of goods and images. For someone growing up in America now, there are few available alternatives to the cool consumer worldview. My students didn't ask for that view, much less create it, but they bring a consumer weltanschauung to school, where it exerts a powerful, and largely unacknowledged, influence. If we want to understand current universities, with their multiple woes, we might try leaving the realms of expert debate and fine ideas and turning to the classrooms and campuses, where a new kind of weather is gathering.

10   From time to time I bump into a colleague in the corridor and we have what I've come to think of as a Joon Lee fest. Joon Lee is one of the best students I've taught. He's endlessly curious, has read a small library's worth, seen every movie, and knows all about showbiz and entertainment. For a class of mine he wrote an essay using Nietzsche's Apollo and Dionysus to analyze the pop group The Supremes. A trite, cultural-studies bonbon? Not at all. He said striking things about conceptions of race in America and about how they shape our ideas of beauty. When I talk with one of his other teachers, we run on about the general splendors of his work and presence. But what inevitably follows a JL fest is a mournful reprise about the divide that separates him and a few other remarkable students from their contemporaries. It's not that some aren't nearly as bright— in terms of intellectual ability, my students are all that I could ask for. Instead, it's that Joon Lee has decided to follow his interests and let them make him into a singular and rather eccentric man; in his charming way, he doesn't mind being at odds with most anyone.

It's his capacity for enthusiasm that sets Joon apart from what I've come to think of as the reigning generational style. Whether the students are sorority/fraternity types, grunge aficionados, piercer/tattooers, black or white, rich or middle class (alas, I teach almost no students from truly poor backgrounds), they are, nearly across the board, very, very self-contained. On good days they display a light, appealing glow; on bad days, shuffling disgruntlement. But there's little fire, little passion to be found.

This point came home to me a few weeks ago when I was wandering across the university grounds. There, beneath a classically cast portico, were two students, male and female, having a rip-roaring argument. They were incensed, bellowing at each other, headstrong, confident, and wild. It struck me how rarely I see this kind of full-out feeling in students anymore. Strong emotional display is forbidden. When conflicts arise, it's generally understood that one of the parties will say something sarcastically propitiating ("whatever" often does it) and slouch away.

How did my students reach this peculiar state in which all passion seems to be spent? I think that many of them have imbibed their sense of self from consumer culture in general and from the tube in particular. They're the progeny of 100 cable channels and omnipresent Blockbuster outlets. TV, Marshall McLuhan famously said, is a cool medium. Those who play best on it are low-key and nonassertive; they blend in. Enthusiasm, à la Joon Lee, quickly looks absurd. The form of character that's most appealing on TV is calmly self-interested though never greedy, attuned to the conventions, and ironic. Judicious timing is preferred to sudden self-assertion. The TV medium is inhospitable to inspiration, improvisation, failures, slipups. All must run perfectly.

Naturally, a cool youth culture is a marketing bonanza for producers of the right products, who do all they can to enlarge that culture and keep it grinding. The Internet, TV, and magazines now teem with what I call persona ads, ads for Nikes and Reeboks and Jeeps and Blazers that don't so much endorse the capacities of the product per se as show you what sort of person you will be once you've acquired it. The Jeep ad that features hip, outdoorsy kids whipping a Frisbee from mountaintop to mountaintop isn't so much about what Jeeps can do as it is about the kind of people who own them. Buy a Jeep and be one with them. The ad is of little consequence in itself, but expand its message exponentially and you have the central thrust of current consumer culture—buy in order to be.

15   Most of my students seem desperate to blend in, to look right, not to make a spectacle of themselves. (Do I have to tell you that those two students having the argument under the portico turned out to be acting in a role-playing game?) The specter of the uncool creates a subtle tyranny. It's apparently an easy standard to subscribe to, this Letterman-like, Tarantino-like cool, but once committed to it, you discover that matters are rather different. You're inhibited, except on ordained occasions, from showing emotion, stifled from trying to achieve anything original. You're made to feel that even the slightest departure from the reigning code will get you genially ostracized. This is a culture tensely committed to a laid-back norm.

Am I coming off like something of a crank here? Maybe. Oscar Wilde, who is almost never wrong, suggested that it is perilous to promiscuously contradict people who are much younger than yourself. Point taken. But one of the lessons that consumer hype tries to insinuate is that we must never rebel against the new, never even question it. If it's new—a new need, a new product, a new show, a new style, a new generation—it must be good. So maybe, even at the risk of winning the withered, brown laurels of crankdom, it pays to resist new-ness-worship and cast a colder eye.

Praise for my students? I have some of that too. What my students are, at their best, is decent. They are potent believers in equality. They help out at the soup kitchen and volunteer to tutor poor kids to get a stripe on their résumés, sure. But they also want other people to have a fair shot. And in their commitment to fairness they are discerning; there you see them at their intellectual best. If I were on trial and innocent, I'd want them on the jury.

What they will not generally do, though, is indict the current system. They won't talk about how the exigencies of capitalism lead to a reserve army of the unemployed and nearly inevitable misery. That would be getting too loud, too brash. For the pervading view is the cool consumer perspective, where passion and strong admiration are forbidden. "To stand in awe of nothing, Numicus, is perhaps the one and only thing that can make a man happy and keep him so," says Horace in the *Epistles,* and I fear that his lines ought to hang as a motto over the university in this era of high consumer capitalism.

It's easy to mount one's high horse and blame the students for this state of af-fairs. But they didn't create the present culture of consumption. (It was largely my own generation, that of the Sixties, that let the counterculture search for pleasure devolve into a quest for commodities.) And they weren't the ones re-sponsible, when they were six and seven and eight years old, for unplugging the TV set from time to time or for hauling off and kicking a hole through it. It's my generation of parents who sheltered these students, kept them away from the hard knocks of everyday life, making them cautious and overfragile, who de-manded that their teachers, from grade school on, flatter them endlessly so that the kids are shocked if their college profs don't reflexively suck up to them.

20   Of course, the current generational style isn't simply derived from culture and environment. It's also about dollars. Students worry that taking too many chances with their educations will sabotage their future prospects. They're aware of the fact that a drop that looks more and more like one wall of the Grand Canyon separates the top economic tenth from the rest of the population. There's a sentiment currently abroad that if you step aside for a moment, to write, to travel, to fall too hard in love, you might lose position permanently. We may be on a conveyor belt, but it's worse down there on the filth-strewn floor. So don't sound off, don't blow your chance.

But wait. I teach at the famously conservative University of Virginia. Can I ex-tend my view from Charlottesville to encompass the whole country, a whole gen-eration of college students? I can only say that I hear comparable stories about classroom life from colleagues everywhere in America. When I visit other schools to lecture, I see a similar scene unfolding. There are, of course, terrific students everywhere. And they're all the better for the way they've had to strive against the existing conformity. At some of the small liberal-arts colleges, the tradition of strong engagement persists. But overall, the students strike me as being sweet and sad, hovering in a nearly suspended animation.

Too often now the pedagogical challenge is to make a lot from a little. Teaching Wordsworth's "Tintern Abbey," you ask for comments. No one responds. So you call on Stephen. Stephen: "The sound, this poem really flows." You: "Stephen seems interested in the music of the poem. We might extend his comment to ask if the poem's music coheres with its argument. Are they consistent? Or is there an emotional pain submerged here that's contrary to the poem's appealing melody?" All right, it's not usually that bad. But close. One friend describes it as rebound teaching: they proffer a weightless comment, you hit it back for all you're worth, then it comes dribbling out again. Occasionally a professor will try to explain away this intellectual timidity by describing the students as perpetrators of postmodern irony, a highly sophisticated mode. Everything's a slick counterfeit, a simulacrum, so by no means should any phenomenon be taken seriously. But the students don't have the urbane, Oscar Wilde-type demeanor that should go with this view. Oscar was cheerful, funny, confident, strange. (Wilde, mortally ill, living in a Paris flophouse: "My wallpaper and I are fighting a duel to the death. One or the other of us has to go.") This generation's style is considerate, easy to please, and a touch depressed.

Granted, you might say, the kids come to school immersed in a consumer mentality—they're good Americans, after all—but then the university and the professors do everything in their power to fight that dreary mind-set in the interest of higher ideals, right? So it should be. But let us look at what is actually coming to pass.

Over the past few years, the physical layout of my university has been changing. To put it a little indecorously, the place is looking more and more like a retirement spread for the young. Our funds go to construction, into new dorms, into renovating the student union. We have a new aquatics center and ever-improving gyms, stocked with StairMasters and Nautilus machines. Engraved on the wall in the gleaming aquatics building is a line by our founder, Thomas Jefferson, declaring that everyone ought to get about two hours' exercise a day. Clearly even the author of the Declaration of Independence endorses the turning of his university into a sports-and-fitness emporium.

25   But such improvements shouldn't be surprising. Universities need to attract the best (that is, the smartest *and* the richest) students in order to survive in an ever more competitive market. Schools want kids whose parents can pay the full freight, not the ones who need scholarships or want to bargain down the tuition costs. If the marketing surveys say that the kids require sports centers, then, trustees willing, they shall have them. In fact, as I began looking around, I came to see that more and more of what's going on in the university is customer driven. The consumer pressures that beset me on evaluation day are only a part of an overall trend.

From the start, the contemporary university's relationship with students has a solicitous, nearly servile tone. As soon as someone enters his junior year in high school, and especially if he's living in a prosperous zip code, the informational material—the advertising—comes flooding in. Pictures, testimonials, videocassettes, and CD-ROMs (some bidden, some not) arrive at the door from colleges across the country, all trying to capture the student and his tuition cash. The freshman-to-be sees photos of well-appointed dorm rooms; of elaborate phys-ed facilities; of fine dining rooms; of expertly kept sports fields; of orchestras and drama troupes; of students working alone (no overbearing grown-ups in range), peering with high seriousness into computers and microscopes; or of students arrayed outdoors in attractive conversational garlands.

Occasionally—but only occasionally, for we usually photograph rather badly; in appearance we tend at best to be styleless—there's a professor teaching a class. (The college catalogues I received, by my request only, in the late Sixties were austere affairs full of professors' credentials and course descriptions; it was clear on whose terms the enterprise was going to unfold.) A college financial officer recently put matters to me in concise, if slightly melodramatic, terms: "Colleges don't have admissions offices anymore, they have marketing departments." Is it surprising that someone who has been approached with photos and tapes, bells and whistles, might come in thinking that the Freud and Shakespeare she had signed up to study were also going to be agreeable treats?

How did we reach this point? In part the answer is a matter of demographics and (surprise) of money. Aided by the G.I. bill, the college-going population in America dramatically increased after the Second World War. Then came the baby boomers, and to accommodate them, schools continued to grow. Universities expand easily enough, but with tenure locking faculty in for lifetime jobs, and with the general reluctance of administrators to eliminate their own slots, it's not easy for a university to contract. So after the baby boomers had passed through—like a fat meal digested by a boa constrictor—the colleges turned to energetic promotional strategies to fill the empty chairs. And suddenly college became a buyer's market. What students and their parents wanted had to be taken more and more into account. That usually meant creating more comfortable, less challenging environments, places where almost no one failed, everything was enjoyable, and everyone was nice.

Just as universities must compete with one another for students, so must the individual departments. At a time of rank economic anxiety, the English and history majors have to contend for students against the more success-insuring branches, such as the sciences and the commerce school. In 1968, more than 21 percent of all the bachelor's degrees conferred in America were in the humanities; by 1993, that number had fallen to about 13 percent. The humanities now must struggle to attract students, many of whose parents devoutly wish they would study something else.

30   One of the ways we've tried to stay attractive is by loosening up. We grade much more softly than our colleagues in science. In English, we don't give many Ds, or Cs for that matter. (The rigors of Chem 101 create almost as many English majors per year as do the splendors of Shakespeare.) A professor at Stanford recently explained grade inflation in the humanities by observing that the undergraduates were getting smarter every year; the higher grades simply recorded how much better they were than their predecessors. Sure.

Along with softening the grades, many humanities departments have relaxed major requirements. There are some good reasons for introducing more choice into curricula and requiring fewer standard courses. But the move, like many others in the university now, jibes with a tendency to serve—and not challenge—the students. Students can also float in and out of classes during the first two weeks of each term without making any commitment. The common name for this time span—shopping period—speaks volumes about the consumer mentality that's now in play. Usually, too, the kids can drop courses up until the last month with only an innocuous "W" on their transcripts. Does a course look too challenging? No problem. Take it pass-fail. A happy consumer is, by definition, one with multiple options, one who can always have what he wants. And since a course is something the students and their parents have bought and paid for, why can't they do with it pretty much as they please?

A sure result of the university's widening elective leeway is to give students more power over their teachers. Those who don't like you can simply avoid you. If the clientele dislikes you en masse, you can be left without students, period. My first term teaching I walked into my introduction to poetry course and found it inhabited by one student, the gloriously named Bambi Lynn Dean. Bambi and I chatted amiably awhile, but for all that she and the pleasure of her name could offer, I was fast on the way to meltdown. It was all a mistake, luckily, a problem with the scheduling book. Everyone was waiting for me next door. But in a dozen years of teaching I haven't forgotten that feeling of being ignominiously marooned. For it happens to others, and not always because of scheduling glitches. I've seen older colleagues go through hot embarrassment at not having enough students sign up for their courses: they graded too hard, demanded too much, had beliefs too far out of keeping with the existing disposition. It takes only a few such instances to draw other members of the professoriat further into line.

And if what's called tenure reform—which generally just means the abolition of tenure—is broadly enacted, professors will be yet more vulnerable to the whims of their customer-students. Teach what pulls the kids in, or walk. What about entire departments that don't deliver? If the kids say no to Latin and Greek, is it time to dissolve classics? Such questions are being entertained more and more seriously by university administrators.

How does one prosper with the present clientele? Many of the most successful professors now are the ones who have "decentered" their classrooms. There's a new emphasis on group projects and on computer-generated exchanges among the students. What they seem to want most is to talk to one another. A classroom now is frequently an "environment," a place highly conducive to the exchange of existing ideas, the students' ideas. Listening to one another, students sometimes change their opinions. But what they generally can't do is acquire a new vocabulary, a new perspective, that will cast issues in a fresh light.

35   The Socratic method—the animated, sometimes impolite give-and-take between student and teacher—seems too jagged for current sensibilities. Students frequently come to my office to tell me how intimidated they feel in class; the thought of being embarrassed in front of the group fills them with dread. I remember a student telling me how humiliating it was to be corrected by the teacher, by me. So I asked the logical question: "Should I let a major factual error go by so as to save discomfort?" The student—a good student, smart and earnest—said that was a tough question. He'd need to think about it.

Disturbing? Sure. But I wonder, are we really getting students ready for Socratic exchange with professors when we push them off into vast lecture rooms, two and three hundred to a class, sometimes face them with only grad students until their third year, and signal in our myriad professorial ways that we often have much better things to do than sit in our offices and talk with them? How bad will the student-faculty ratios have to become, how teeming the lecture courses, before we hear students righteously complaining, as they did thirty years ago, about the impersonality of their schools, about their decline into knowledge factories? "This is a firm," said Mario Savio at Berkeley during the Free Speech protests of the Sixties, "and if the Board of Regents are the board of directors, . . . then . . . the faculty are a bunch of employees and we're the raw material. But we're a bunch of raw material that don't mean . . . to be made into any product."

Teachers who really do confront students, who provide significant challenges to what they believe, can be very successful, granted. But sometimes such professors generate more than a little trouble for themselves. A controversial teacher can send students hurrying to the deans and the counselors, claiming to have been offended. ("Offensive" is the preferred term of repugnance today, just as "enjoyable" is the summit of praise.) Colleges have brought in hordes of counselors and deans to make sure that everything is smooth, serene, unflustered, that everyone has a good time. To the counselor, to the dean, and to the university legal squad, that which is normal, healthy, and prudent is best.

An air of caution and deference is everywhere. When my students come to talk with me in my office, they often exhibit a Franciscan humility. "Do you have a moment?" "I know you're busy. I won't take up much of your time." Their presences tend to be very light; they almost never change the temperature of the room. The dress is nondescript: clothes are in earth tones; shoes are practical-cross-trainers, hiking boots, work shoes, Dr. Martens, with now and then a stylish pair of raised-sole boots on one of the young women. Many, male and female both, peep from beneath the bills of monogrammed baseball caps. Quite a few wear sports, or even corporate, logos, sometimes on one piece of clothing but occasionally (and disconcertingly) on more. The walk is slow; speech is careful, sweet, a bit weary, and without strong inflection. (After the first lively week of the term, most seem far in debt to sleep.) They are almost unfailingly polite. They don't want to offend me; I could hurt them, savage their grades.

Naturally, there are exceptions, kids I chat animatedly with, who offer a joke, or go on about this or that new CD (almost never a book, no). But most of the traffic is genially sleepwalking. I have to admit that I'm a touch wary, too. I tend to hold back. An unguarded remark, a joke that's taken to be off-color, or simply an uncomprehended comment can lead to difficulties. I keep it literal. They scare me a little, these kind and melancholy students, who themselves seem rather frightened of their own lives.

40   Before they arrive, we ply the students with luscious ads, guaranteeing them a cross between summer camp and lotusland. When they get here, flattery and nonstop entertainment are available, if that's what they want. And when they leave? How do we send our students out into the world? More and more, our ad-

ministrators call the booking agents and line up one or another celebrity to usher the graduates into the millennium. This past spring, Kermit the Frog won himself an honorary degree at Southampton College on Long Island; Bruce Willis and Yogi Berra took credentials away at Montclair State; Arnold Schwarzenegger scored at the University of Wisconsin-Superior. At Wellesley, Oprah Winfrey gave the commencement address. (Wellesley—one of the most rigorous academic colleges in the nation.) At the University of Vermont, Whoopi Goldberg laid down the word. But why should a worthy administrator contract the likes of Susan Sontag, Christopher Hitchens, or Robert Hughes—someone who might actually say something, something disturbing, something "offensive"—when he can get what the parents and kids apparently want and what the newspapers will softly commend—more lite entertainment, more TV?

Is it a surprise, then, that this generation of students—steeped in consumer culture before going off to school, treated as potent customers by the university well before their date of arrival, then pandered to from day one until the morning of the final kiss-off from Kermit or one of his kin—are inclined to see the books they read as a string of entertainments to be placidly enjoyed or languidly cast down? Given the way universities are now administered (which is more and more to say, given the way that they are currently marketed), is it a shock that the kids don't come to school hot to learn, unable to bear their own ignorance? For some measure of self-dislike, or self-discontent—which is much different than simple depression—seems to me to be a prerequisite for getting an education that matters. My students, alas, usually lack the confidence to acknowledge what would be their most precious asset for learning: their ignorance.

Not long ago, I asked my Freud class a question that, however hoary, never fails to solicit intriguing responses: Who are your heroes? Whom do you admire? After one remarkable answer, featuring T. S. Eliot as hero, a series of generic replies rolled in, one gray wave after the next: my father, my best friend, a doctor who lives in our town, my high school history teacher. Virtually all the heroes were people my students had known personally, people who had done something local, specific, and practical, and had done it for them. They were good people, unselfish people, these heroes, but most of all they were people who had delivered the goods.

My students' answers didn't exhibit any philosophical resistance to the idea of greatness. It's not that they had been primed by their professors with complex arguments to combat genius. For the truth is that these students don't need debunking theories. Long before college, skepticism became their habitual mode. They are the progeny of Bart Simpson and David Letterman, and the hyper-cool ethos of the box. It's inane to say that theorizing professors have created them, as many conservative critics like to do. Rather, they have substantially created a university environment in which facile skepticism can thrive without being substantially contested.

Skeptical approaches have potential value. If you have no all-encompassing religious faith, no faith in historical destiny, the future of the West, or anything comparably grand, you need to acquire your vision of the world somewhere. If it's from literature, then the various visions literature offers have to be inquired into skeptically. Surely it matters that women are denigrated in Milton and in Pope, that some novelistic voices assume an overbearing godlike authority, that the poor are, in this or that writer, inevitably cast as clowns. You can't buy all of literature wholesale if it's going to help draw your patterns of belief.

45   But demystifying theories are now overused, applied mechanically. It's all logocentrism, patriarchy, ideology. And in this the student environment—laidback, skeptical, knowing—is, I believe, central. Full-out debunking is what plays with this clientele. Some have been doing it nearly as long as, if more crudely than, their deconstructionist teachers. In the context of the contemporary university, and cool consumer culture, a useful intellectual skepticism has become exaggerated into a fundamentalist caricature of itself. The teachers have buckled to their students' views.

At its best, multiculturalism can be attractive as well-deployed theory. What could be more valuable than encountering the best work of far-flung cultures and becoming a citizen of the world? But in the current consumer environment, where flattery plays so well, the urge to encounter the other can devolve into the urge to find others who embody and celebrate the right ethnic origins. So we put aside the African novelist Chinua Achebe's abrasive, troubling *Things Fall Apart* and gravitate toward hymns on Africa, cradle of all civilizations.

What about the phenomenon called political correctness? Raising the standard of civility and tolerance in the university has been—who can deny it?—a very good thing. Yet this admirable impulse has expanded to the point where one is enjoined to speak well—and only well—of women, blacks, gays, the disabled, in fact of virtually everyone. And we can owe this expansion in many ways to the student culture. Students now do not wish to be criticized, not in any form. (The culture of consumption never criticizes them, at least not overtly.) In the current university, the movement for urbane tolerance has devolved into an imperative against critical reaction, turning much of the intellectual life into a dreary Sargasso Sea. At a certain point, professors stopped being usefully sensitive and became more like careful retailers who have it as a cardinal point of doctrine never to piss the customers off.

To some professors, the solution lies in the movement called cultural studies. What students need, they believe, is to form a critical perspective on pop culture. It's a fine idea, no doubt. Students should be able to run a critical commentary against the stream of consumer stimulations in which they're immersed. But cultural-studies programs rarely work, because no matter what you propose by way of analysis, things tend to bolt downhill toward an uncritical discussion of students' tastes, into what they like and don't like. If you want to do a Frankfurt School-style analysis of Braveheart, you can be pretty sure that by mid-class Adorno and Horkheimer will be consigned to the junk heap of history and you'll be collectively weighing the charms of Mel Gibson. One sometimes wonders if cultural studies hasn't prospered because, under the guise of serious intellectual analysis, it gives the customers what they most want—easy pleasure, more TV. Cultural studies becomes nothing better than what its detractors claim it is— Madonna studies—when students kick loose from the critical perspective and groove to the product, and that, in my experience teaching film and pop culture, happens plenty.

On the issue of genius, as on multiculturalism and political correctness, we professors of the humanities have, I think, also failed to press back against our students' consumer tastes. Here we tend to nurse a pair of—to put it charitably—disparate views. In one mode, we're inclined to a programmatic debunking criticism. We call the concept of genius into question. But in our professional lives per se, we aren't usually disposed against the idea of distinguished achievement. We argue animatedly about the caliber of potential colleagues. We support a star system, in which some professors are far better paid, teach less, and under better conditions than the rest. In our own profession, we are creating a system that is the mirror image of the one we're dismantling in the curriculum. Ask a professor what she thinks of the work of Stephen Greenblatt, a leading critic of Shakespeare, and you'll hear it for an hour. Ask her what her views are on Shakespeare's genius and she's likely to begin questioning the term along with the whole "discourse of evaluation." This dual sensibility may be intellectually incoherent. But in its awareness of what plays with students, it's conducive to good classroom evaluations and, in its awareness of where and how the professional bread is buttered, to self-advancement as well.

50   My overall point is this: It's not that a leftwing professorial coup has taken over the university. It's that at American universities, leftliberal politics have collided with the ethos of consumerism. The consumer ethos is winning.

Then how do those who at least occasionally promote genius and high literary ideals look to current students? How do we appear, those of us who take teaching to be something of a performance art and who imagine that if you give yourself over completely to your subject you'll be rewarded with insight beyond what you individually command?

I'm reminded of an old piece of newsreel footage I saw once. The speaker (perhaps it was Lenin, maybe Trotsky) was haranguing a large crowd. He was expostulating, arm waving, carrying on. Whether it was flawed technology or the man himself, I'm not sure, but the orator looked like an intricate mechanical device that had sprung into fast-forward. To my students, who mistrust enthusiasm in every form, that's me when I start riffing about Freud or Blake. But more and more, as my evaluations showed, I've been replacing enthusiasm and intellectual animation with stand-up routines, keeping it all at arm's length, praising under the cover of irony.

It's too bad that the idea of genius has been denigrated so far, because it actually offers a live alternative to the demoralizing culture of hip in which most of my students are mired. By embracing the works and lives of extraordinary people, you can adapt new ideals to revise those that came courtesy of your parents, your neighborhood, your clan—or the tube. The aim of a good liberal-arts education was once, to adapt an observation by the scholar Walter Jackson Bate, to see that "we need not be the passive victims of what we deterministically call 'circumstances' (social, cultural, or reductively psychological-personal), but that by linking ourselves through what Keats calls an 'immortal free-masonry' with the great we can become freer—freer to be ourselves, to be what we most want and value."

But genius isn't just a personal standard; genius can also have political effect. To me, one of the best things about democratic thinking is the conviction that genius can spring up anywhere. Walt Whitman is born into the working class and thirty-six years later we have a poetic image of America that gives a passionate dimension to the legalistic brilliance of the Constitution. A democracy needs to constantly develop, and to do so it requires the most powerful visionary minds to interpret the present and to propose possible shapes for the future. By continuing to notice and praise genius, we create a culture in which the kind of poetic gamble that Whitman made—a gamble in which failure would have entailed rank humiliation, depression, maybe suicide—still takes place. By rebelling against established ways of seeing and saying things, genius helps us to apprehend how malleable the present is and how promising and fraught with danger is the future. If we teachers do not endorse genius and self-overcoming, can we be surprised when our students find their ideal images in TV's latest persona ads?

55   A world uninterested in genius is a despondent place, whose sad denizens drift from coffee bar to Prozac dispensary, unfired by ideals, by the glowing image of the self that one might become. As Northrop Frye says in a beautiful and now dramatically unfashionable sentence, "The artist who uses the same energy and genius that Homer and Isaiah had will find that he not only lives in the same palace of art as Homer and Isaiah, but lives in it at the same time." We ought not to deny the existence of such a place simply because we, or those we care for, find the demands it makes intimidating, the rent too high.

What happens if we keep trudging along this bleak course? What happens if our most intelligent students never learn to strive to overcome what they are? What if genius, and the imitation of genius, become silly, outmoded ideas? What you're likely to get are more and more one-dimensional men and women. These will be people who live for easy pleasures, for comfort and prosperity, who think of money first, then second, and third, who hug the status quo; people who believe in God as a sort of insurance policy (cover your bets); people who are never surprised. They will be people so pleased with themselves (when they're not in despair at the general pointlessness of their lives) that they cannot imagine humanity could do better. They'll think it their highest duty to clone themselves as frequently as possible. They'll claim to be happy, and they'll live a long time.

It is probably time now to offer a spate of inspiring solutions. Here ought to come a list of reforms, with due notations about a core curriculum and various requirements. What the traditionalists who offer such solutions miss is that no matter what our current students are given to read, many of them will simply translate it into melodrama, with flat characters and predictable morals. (The unabated capitalist culture that conservative critics so often endorse has put students in a position to do little else.) One can't simply wave a curricular wand and reverse acculturation.

Perhaps it would be a good idea to try firing the counselors and sending half the deans back into their classrooms, dismantling the football team and making the stadium into a playground for local kids, emptying the fraternities, and boarding up the student-activities office. Such measures would convey the message that American colleges are not northern outposts of Club Med. A willingness on the part of the faculty to defy student conviction and affront them occasionally—to be usefully offensive—also might not be a bad thing. We professors talk a lot about subversion, which generally means subverting the views of people who never hear us talk or read our work. But to subvert the views of our students, our customers, that would be something else again.

Ultimately, though, it is up to individuals—and individual students in particular—to make their own way against the current sludgy tide. There's still the library, still the museum, there's still the occasional teacher who lives to find things greater than herself to admire. There are still fellow students who have not been cowed. Universities are inefficient, cluttered, archaic places, with many unguarded corners where one can open a book or gaze out onto the larger world and construe it freely. Those who do as much, trusting themselves against the weight of current opinion, will have contributed something to bringing this sad dispensation to an end. As for myself, I'm canning my low-key one-liners; when the kids' TV-based tastes come to the fore, I'll aim and shoot. And when it's time to praise genius, I'll try to do it in the right style, full-out, with faith that finer artistic spirits (maybe not Homer and Isaiah quite, but close, close), still alive somewhere in the ether, will help me out when my invention flags, the students doze, or the dean mutters into the phone. I'm getting back to a more exuberant style; I'll be expostulating and arm waving straight into the millennium, yes I will.

CRITICAL REFLECTIONS

1. A liberal education has traditionally referred to one that engenders the development of the intellect, as opposed to one focused on the cultivation of particular skills. What do you see as the uses of a liberal education for you or for others? Why do you identify the purpose that you do?

2. How do you think Edmundson characterizes the students in his Freud class? What evidence in the reading suggests this portrayal to you?

3. Edmundson attributes part of what he interprets as the problems with contemporary students to consumer media culture, writing (among other things) that students are "the progeny of 100 cable channels and omnipresent Blockbuster outlets" (129). As someone either part of this generation, or attending school with members of this generation, what is your response to Edmundson's characterization?

4. What do you think Edmundson would define as the purpose of education? Do you think he would outline this purpose differently for his students than he would for himself? Why or why not?

5. Edmundson objects to the idea that his job is "to divert, entertain, and interest" in response to a comment on a student evaluation. How do you interpret his objection? What do you see as instructors' jobs in college courses?

6. In this article, Edmundson imagines a conversation with a student, "Stephen," about Wordworth's poem, "Tintern Abbey" (on pages 130–131). Based on

this brief passage, what do you think Edmundson might define as "important for the student to know" about this poem? Might there be alternatives to this kind of discussion that would elicit different kinds of responses (and engagement) from students?

≋ MAKING CONNECTIONS

1. A number of readings in this text—most notably Edmundson's, Gannon's, Suskind's, Rose's, Moffatt's, and Jordan's—focus on the group sometimes called traditional college students. Among these readings, students are portrayed in myriad ways. Which of these portrayals do you consider to be most antithetical to one another, and which most aligned with one another? Why do you make the connections (or disconnections) between them that you do?

2. How do you think Edmundson would react to the definitions of the purpose of college reflected in the collages constructed by Rutgers students in "What College is REALLY Like?" Why do you think he would respond as you say he would?

3. In "The Banking Model of Education," Paolo Freire describes an educational model that stems from students' interests and issues. How do you think Edmundson would respond to Freire's model? What about to Freire's interpretation of the banking model?

4. When this article was initially published, it was followed by Earl Shorris's article, "On the Uses of a Liberal Education: II." What do you think Edmundson and Shorris would identify as important aspects of a liberal education and students' roles in a liberal education? Would they agree? Disagree? Why?

ANDREA R. FISHMAN

BECOMING LITERATE: A
LESSON FROM THE AMISH

When she wrote this article, Andrea Fishman was a high school English teacher in Carlisle, Pennsylvania. (She now teaches at Westchester University.) For her Ph.D., Fishman took a leave from teaching high school to spend time with the Amish people of Pennsylvania and observe their literacy practices. Old Order Amish came to the United States in the early 1700s; many remain in the same communities where their ancestors have lived for generations—over 17,000 Amish live in Pennsylvania. The Amish believe that they should live apart from mainstream culture. They live in isolated communities, often in relatively rural areas. Amish homes have no electricity; Amish people do not drive cars and, instead, travel in covered carriages. By rejecting elements of contemporary culture, they believe that they can maintain their way of life.

One clear, frost-edged January Sunday night, two families gathered for supper and an evening's entertainment. One family—mine—consisted of a lawyer, a teacher, and their twelve-year-old son; the other family—the Fishers—consisted of Eli and Anna, a dairy farmer and his wife, and their five children, ranging in age from six to seventeen. After supper in the Fisher's large farm kitchen— warmed by a wood stove and redolent of the fragrances of chicken corn soup, homemade bread, and freshly baked apples—the table was cleared and an additional smaller one set up to accommodate games of Scrabble, double Dutch solitaire, and dominoes. As most of us began to play, adults and children randomly mixed, Eli Fisher, Sr., settled into his brown leather recliner with the newspaper, while six-year-old Eli, Jr., plopped on the corner of the couch nearest his father with a book.

Fifteen or twenty minutes later, I heard Eli, Sr., ask his son, "Where are your new books?" referring to a set of outgrown Walt Disney books we had brought for little Eli and his seven-year-old brother, Amos. Eli, Jr., pointed to a stack of brightly colored volumes on the floor, from which his father chose *Lambert, the Sheepish Lion.* As Eli, Jr., climbed onto the arm of the recliner and snuggled against his father, Eli, Sr., began reading the book out loud in a voice so commandingly dramatic that soon everyone was listening to the story, instead of playing their separate games. Broadly portraying the roles of both Lambert and his lioness mother and laughing heartily at the antics of the cub who preferred cavorting with the sheep to stalking with the lions, Eli held his enlarged audience throughout the rest of the story.

As most of us returned to our games when he finished reading, Eli, Sr., asked of anyone and everyone, "Where's the *Dairy?*" Daniel, the Fishers' teenage son, left his game and walked toward his father. "It's in here," he said, rummaging through the newspapers and magazines in the rack beside the couch until he found a thick newsletter called *Dairy World,* published by the Independent Buyers Association, to which Eli belonged.

Eli leafed through the publication, standing and walking toward the wood stove as he did. Leaning against the wall, he began reading aloud without preface. All conversation stopped as everyone once again attended to Eli's loudly expressive reading voice, which said:

> A farmer was driving his wagon down the road. On the back was a sign which read: "Experimental Vehicle. Runs on oats and hay. Do not step in exhaust."

Everyone laughed, including Eli, Sr., who then read the remaining jokes on the humor page to his attentive audience. All our games forgotten, we shared the best and the worst riddles and jokes we could remember until it was time for bed.

5   Occasions like this one occur in many homes and have recently attracted the interest of family literacy researchers (Heath; Taylor; Wells). The scene at the Fishers could have been the scene in any home where parents value reading and

writing and want their children to value them as well. It would not be surprising if Eli and Anna, like other literacy-oriented parents, read bedtime stories to their children, helped with their homework, and encouraged them to attain high school diplomas, if not college degrees. But Eli and Anna do none of these things: they read no bedtime stories, they are annoyed if their children bring schoolwork home, and they expect their children to go only as far in school as they did themselves, as far as the eighth grade.

So, although Eli and Anna appeared on that Sunday night to be ideal proliteracy parents, they may not be, according to commonly described standards, and one significant factor may account for their variations from the supposed ideal: Eli and Anna are not mainstream Americans but are Old Order Amish, raising their family according to Old Order tradition and belief. The Sunday night gathering I just described took place by the light of gas lamps in a house without radio, stereo, television, or any other electrical contrivance. Bedtime in that house is more often marked by singing or silence than by reading. Schoolwork rarely enters there because household, field, and barn chores matter more. And the Fisher children's studying is done in a one-room, eight-grade, Old Order school taught by an Old Order woman who attended the same kind of school herself. So while Eli, Jr., like his siblings, is learning the necessity and the value of literacy, what literacy means to him and the ways in which he learns it may differ in both obvious and subtle ways from what it means and how it's transmitted to many mainstream children, just as Eli's world differs from theirs, both obviously and subtly.

As suggested earlier, Eli, Jr., lives in a house replete with print, from the kitchen bulletin board to the built-in bookcases in the playroom to the table and magazine rack in the living room. There are children's classics and children's magazines. There are local newspapers, shoppers' guides, and other adult periodicals. And there are books of children's Bible stories, copies of the King James Version of the Bible, and other inspirational volumes, none of which mark the Fishers' home as notably different from that of many other Christian Americans.

Yet there are differences, easily overlooked by a casual observer but center to the life of the family and to their definition of literacy. One almost invisible difference is the sources of these materials. Eli and Anna attempt to carefully control the reading material that enters their home. Anna buys books primarily from a local Christian bookstore and from an Amish-operated dry goods store, both of which she trusts not to stock objectionable material. When she sees potentially interesting books in other places—in the drugstore, in the book or card shop, or at a yard sale—she uses the publisher's name as a guide to acceptable content. Relatives and friends close to the family also supply appropriate books both as gifts and as recommendations, which Anna trusts and often chooses to follow up.

Another, slightly more visible difference comes in the form of books and periodicals around the Fisher house that would not be found in many mainstream farm, or Christian homes. Along with the local newspaper in the rack beside the couch are issues of *Die Botschaft,* which describes itself as "A Weekly Newspaper Serving Old Order Amish Communities Everywhere." On the desk copy of *The*

Amish Directory, which alphabetically lists all the Amish living in Pennsylvania and Maryland by nuclear family groups, giving crucial addresses and other information, along with maps of the eighty-seven church districts included.

10   On top of the breakfront in the sitting area are copies of songbooks, all in German: some for children, some for adults, and one—the *Ausbund*—for everyone, for this is the church hymnal, a collection of hymns written by tortured and imprisoned sixteenth-century Anabaptists about their experiences and their faith. Kept with these songbooks is a German edition of the Bible and a copy of the *Martyrs Mirror,* an oversized, weighty tome full of graphic descriptions in English of the tortured deaths of early Anabaptists, each illustrated by a black and white woodcut print.

Despite what may seem to be the esoteric nature of these texts, none remain in their special places gathering dust, for all are used regularly, each reinforcing in a characteristic way the Amish definition of literacy and each facilitating the image Eli, Jr., has of himself as literate.

Because singing is central to Amish religious observance and expression, songbooks are used frequently by all members of the family. Because singing requires knowing what is in the text and because Amish singing, which is unaccompanied and highly stylized, requires knowing how to interpret the songs exactly as everyone else does, the songbooks represent a kind of reading particularly important to the community, a kind that must be mastered to be considered literate. Yet because singing may mean holding the text and following the words as they appear or it may mean holding the text and following the words from memory or from others' rendition, children of Eli's age and younger all participate, appearing and feeling as literate as anyone else.

Functioning similarly are the German Bible and the *Martyrs Mirror.* Though only the older Fishers read that Bible, they do so regularly and then share what they've read with their children. It is the older Fishers, too, who read the *Martyrs Mirror,* but that text Eli, Sr., usually reads aloud during family devotions, so that Anna and all the children, regardless of age, participate similarly through his oral presentations.

While it may seem easier to accept such variant definitions of reading in shared communal situations like these, the participation of Eli, Jr., was equally welcome and equally effective in shared individual reading. When individual oral reading was clearly text-bound, as it is during family devotions, Eli was always enabled to participate in ways similar to his brothers' and sisters', making him a reader like them. When all the Fishers took turns reading the Bible aloud, for example, someone would read Eli's verse aloud slowly, pausing every few words, so that he could repeat what was said and thereby take his turn in the rotation.

15   When the older children were assigned Bible verses or *Ausbund* hymn stanzas to memorize, Eli was assigned the same one as Amos, the sibling closest in age. Their assignment would be shorter and contain less complex vocabulary than the one the older children got, yet Amos and Eli would also practice their verse together, as the older children did, and would take their turns reciting, as the older children did, making Eli again able to participate along with everyone else.

Because oral reading as modeled by Eli, Sr., is often imitated by the others, Eli, Jr., always shared his books by telling what he saw or knew about them. No one ever told him that telling isn't the same as reading, even though they may look alike, so Eli always seemed like a reader to others and felt like a reader himself. When everyone else sat reading or playing reading-involved games in the living room after supper or on Sunday afternoons, Eli did the same, to no one's surprise, to everyone's delight, and with universal, though often tacit, welcome and approval. When the other children received books as birthday and Christmas presents, Eli received them too. And when he realized at age six that both of his brothers had magazine subscriptions of their own, Eli asked for and got one as well. Eli never saw his own reading as anything other than real; he did not see it as make-believe or bogus, and neither did anyone else. So, despite the fact that before he went to school Eli, Jr., could not read according to some definitions, he always could according to his family's and his own.

Just as all the Fishers read, so they all write, and just as Eli was enabled to define reading in a way that made him an Amish reader, so he could define writing in a way that made him an Amish writer. Letter writing has always been a primary family activity and one central to the Amish community. Anna writes weekly to *Die Botschaft*, acting as the scribe from her district. She, Eli, Sr., and sixteen-year-old Sarah all participate in circle letters, and the next three children all write with some regularity to cousins in other Amish settlements.

Yet, no matter who is writing to whom, their letters follow the same consistently modeled Amish format, beginning with "Greetings . . . ," moving to recent weather conditions, then to family and community news of note, and ending with a good-bye and often a philosophical or religious thought. I've never seen anyone in the community instructed to write this way, but in the Fisher family, letters received and even letters written are often read out loud, and though this oral sharing is done for informative rather than instructive purposes, it provides an implicit model for everyone to follow.

With all the other family members writing letters, reading them out loud and orally sharing those they have received, Eli, Jr., wanted to write and receive letters, too, and no one said he couldn't. When he was very young, he dictated his messages to Sarah and drew pictures to accompany what she wrote down for him. Then, even before he started school, Eli began copying the dictated messages Sarah recorded, so that the letters would be in his own hand, as the drawings were.

20   Other forms of writing also occur in the Fisher household for everyone to see and use. Greeting cards, grocery lists, bulletin board reminders, and bedtime notes from children to absent parents were all part of Eli's life to some extent and his preschool writing and drawing always adorned the refrigerator, along with the school papers of his brothers and sisters.

In addition, the Fishers played writing-involved games—including Scrabble and Boggle—in which everyone participated, as the family revised the rules to suit their cooperative social model and their definition of literacy. In any game at the

Fishers, the oldest person or persons playing may assist the younger ones. No question of fairness arises unless only some players go unaided. Older players, too, may receive help from other players or from onlookers. Score is always kept, and, while some moves are ruled illegal, age or aid received neither bars nor assures a winner. Eli, Jr., therefore, has always played these games as well as anyone else.

Obviously, Eli, Jr., learned a great deal about literacy from all these preschool experiences, but what he learned went far beyond academic readiness lessons. More important, Eli learned that literacy is a force in the world—his world—and it is a force that imparts power to all who wield it. He could see for himself that reading and writing enable people as old as his parents and as young as his siblings to fully participate in the world in which they live. In fact, it might have seemed to him that, to be an Amish man, one must read and write, and to be a Fisher, one must read and write as well.

So, even before the age of six, Eli began to recognize and acquire the power of literacy, using it to affiliate himself with the larger Amish world and to identify himself as Amish, a Fisher, a boy, and Eli Fisher, Jr. However, what enabled Eli to recognize all these ways of defining and asserting himself through literacy was neither direct instruction nor insistence from someone else. Rather, it was the ability that all children have long before they can read and write print text, the ability, as Friere puts it, "to read the world." "It is possible," Friere asserts, "to view objects and experiences as texts, words, and letters, and to see the growing awareness of the world as a kind of reading, through which the self learns and changes" (6). Eli, Jr., clearly illustrates this understanding of how children perceive and comprehend the seemingly invisible text of their lives. What he came to understand and accept this way were the definition and the role of print literacy as his society and culture both consciously and tacitly transmit them.

When Eli, Jr., began school, therefore, he was both academically and socially ready to begin. To smooth the transition from home to school, Eli's teacher—like most in Old Order schools—held a "preschool day" in the spring preceding his entry to first grade. On that day, Eli and Mary, the two prospective first-graders in Meadow Brook School, came to be initiated as "scholars." Verna, their teacher, had moved the two current first-graders to other seats, clearing the two desks immediately in front of hers for the newcomers; all that day Mary and Eli sat in the first-grade seats, had "classes," and did seatwork like all the other children. They seemed to know they were expected to follow the rules, to do what they saw others doing, to practice being "scholars," and Verna reinforced that notion, treating those two almost as she would anyone else.

25   To begin one lesson, for example, "Let's talk about bunnies," she instructed, nodding her head toward the two littlest children, indicating that they should stand beside her desk. She then showed them pictures of rabbits, with the word *bunnies* and the number depicted indicated in word and numeral on each picture. After going through the pictures, saying, "three bunnies," "four bunnies," and having the children repeat after her, Verna asked three questions and got three choral answers.

"Do bunnies like carrots?" she asked.

"Yes," the two children answered together.

"Do they like lettuce?"

"Yes."

"Do they sometimes get in Mother's garden?"

"Yes."

Were it not for some enthusiastic head nodding, Eli, Jr., and Mary could have been fully matriculated students.

When she was ready to assign seatwork, Verna gave the preschoolers pictures of bunnies to color and asked, "What do we do first? Color or write our names?"

"Write our names," the pair chorused, having practiced that skill earlier in the day.

"Yes, we always write our names first. Go back to your desk, write your name, then color the picture. Do nothing on the back of the paper." And the children did exactly that, doing "what we do" precisely "the way we do it."

30 Verna also conducted what she called a reading class for the two preschoolers, during which they sat, and she held an open picture book facing them. Talking about the pictures, Verna made simple statements identifying different aspects of and actions in the illustrations. After each statement Verna paused, and the children repeated exactly what she had said. The oral text accompanying the picture said:

Sally is eating chips and watching TV.

Sally has a red fish.

Sally has spilled the chips.

After "reading" the text this way, the children answered questions about it.

"What does Sally have?" Verna asked.

"A fish," they replied.

"What color is her fish?"

"Red."

"Did Sally spill the chips?"

"Yes."

"Did the cat eat the chips?"

"Yes."

While the content of this lesson seems incongruous, I know, its form and conduct fit the Meadow Brook model perfectly. Precise recall and yeses are all that the questions demand. Even the last question, while not covered in the "reading," requires recognition of only what happens in the picture.

What happened in Meadow Brook School that day—and what would happen in the eight school years to follow—reinforced, extended, and rarely contradicted what Eli already knew about literacy. Reading and writing at school allowed him to further affiliate and identify himself with and within his social group. While his teacher occasionally gave direct instructions, those instructions tended to be for activities never before seen or experienced; otherwise, Eli and Mary knew to follow the behavioral and attitudinal lead of the older children and to look to them for assistance and support, just as they looked to the teacher. In other words, reading the school world came as naturally to these children as reading the world anywhere else, and the message in both texts was emphatically the same.

Most important here, however, may be the remarkable substantive coherence that Meadow Brook School provided, a coherence that precluded any conflict over what, how, or even whether to read and write. Eli's experience as a Fisher had taught him that reading comes in many forms—secular and religious, silent and oral, individual and communal—and they all count. Through his at-home experience, Eli had also learned which other, more specific, less obvious abilities count as reading in his world. He had learned to value at least four significant abilities: (1) the ability to select and manage texts, to be able to find his mother's letter in *Die Botschaft* or to find a particular verse in the Bible; (2) the ability to empathize with people in texts and to discern the implicit lessons their experiences teach: to empathize with Lambert the lion, who taught the possibility of peaceful coexistence, and to empathize with the Anabaptist martyrs, who taught the rightness of dying for one's faith; (3) the ability to accurately recall what was read, to remember stories, riddles, and jokes or to memorize Bible and hymn verses; and (4) the ability to synthesize what is read in a single text with what is already known or to synthesize information across texts in Amish-appropriate ways.

When Eli got to school, he found a similar definition of reading in operation. He and Mary were helped to select and manage text. Their attention was directed toward what mattered in the text and away from what did not. They were helped to discover the single right answer to every question. They had only to recall information without interpreting or extending it in any significant way. And they were expected to empathize with the people in Verna's lunchtime oral reading without questioning or hypothesizing about what had happened or what would happen next.

35   Similarly, before Eli went to school, he knew what counted as writing in his world, just as he knew what counted as reading. He learned at home that being able to write means being able to encode, to copy, to follow format, to choose content, and to list. And, when he arrived at school, this same definition, these same abilities, were all that mattered there, too.

While the dimensions of reading and writing that count at Meadow Brook and elsewhere in Eli's life seem little different from those that count in mainstream situations—a terrifying fact, I would suggest—it is important to recognize that several mainstream-valued skills are completely absent from the Amish world as I've experienced it. Critical reading—individual analysis and interpretation—of the sort considered particularly important by most people who are mainstream-educated or mainstream educators is not valued by the Amish because of its potentially divisive, counterproductive power.

Literary appreciation, too, is both irrelevant and absent because the study of text-as-object is moot. How a writer enables a reader to empathize with his characters doesn't matter; only the ability to empathize matters. Text, whether biblical or secular, is perceived not as an object but as a force acting in the world, and it is the impact of that force that counts.

When it comes to writing, the existing Amish definition also differs in what is absent, rather than what is present. While grammar, spelling, and punctuation do count for the Old Order, they do so only to the extent that word order, words, and punctuation must allow readers to read—that is, to recognize and make sense of their reading. If a reader readily understands the intention of an adjective used as an adverb, a singular verb following a plural noun, a sentence fragment, or a compound verb containing a misplaced comma, the Amish do not see these as errors warranting attention, despite the fact that an outside reader may.

Equally irrelevant in Old Order schools is the third-person formal essay—the ominous five-paragraph theme—so prevalent in mainstream classrooms. Amish children never learn to write this kind of composition, not because they are not college-bound but because the third-person-singular point of view assumed by an individual writer is foreign to this first-person-plural society; thesis statements, topic sentences, and concepts like coherence, unity, and emphasis are similarly alien.

40   One final distinction separates the Amish definition of literacy from that of many mainstream definitions: the absence of originality as a desirable feature. Not only do community constraints limit the number of appropriate topics and forms an Amish writer may use, but original approaches to or applications of those topics and forms is implicitly discouraged by the similarity of models and assignments and by the absence of fiction as an appropriate personal genre. All aspects of community life reward uniformity; while writing provides an outlet for individual expression and identification, singular creativity stays within community norms.

For Eli Fisher, Jr., then, the definition of literacy he learned at home was consistent with the one he found at school, though it differed in several important ways from those of most MLA members, for example. Yet for Eli, as for Friere, "deciphering the word flowed naturally from reading the immediate world" (7). From reading his world, this six-year-old derived a complete implicit definition that told him what literacy is and whether literacy matters. I can't help but wonder, however, what would have happened had Eli gone to school and been told, explicitly or through more powerful behaviors, that he really didn't know what counted as reading and writing, that his reading and writing were not real but other unknown or alien varieties were. What would have happened had his quiet imitative behavior made him invisible in the classroom or, worse yet, made his teacher assume that he was withdrawn, problematic, or less than bright? What if his work were devalued because it was obviously copied or just unoriginal? What if he had been called on to perform individually in front of the class, to stand up and stand out? Or what if he had been asked to discuss private issues in public? Or to evaluate what he read?

Had any of these things happened, I suspect that Eli would have had to make some difficult choices that would have amounted to choosing between what he had learned and learned to value at home and what he seemed expected to learn at school. To conform to his teacher's demands and values, he would have had to devalue or disavow those of his parents—a demand that public schools seem to make frequently of children from cultural or socioeconomic groups differing from those of their teachers or their schools, a demand that seems unfair, un-called for, and unnecessary, not to mention counterproductive and destructive.

Eli Fisher's experience suggests, therefore, that those of us who deal with children unlike ourselves need to see our classrooms and our students differently from the way we may have seen them in the past. We need to realize that students, even first-graders, have been reading the world—if not the word—for at least five, six, or seven years; they come to school not devoid of knowledge and values but with a clear sense of what their world demands and requires, including what, whether, and how to read and write, though their understandings may differ significantly from our own. We need to realize that our role may not be to prepare our students to enter mainstream society but, rather, to help them see what mainstream society offers and what it takes away, what they may gain by as-similating and what they may lose in that process. Through understanding their worlds, their definitions of literacy, and their dilemmas, not only will we better help them make important literacy-related decisions, but we will better help ourselves to do the same.

Works Cited

Freire, Paulo. "The Importance of the Act of Reading." *Journal of Education* Winter 1983: 5–10.

Heath, Shirley Brice. *Ways with Words: Language, Life, and Work in Communities and Classrooms.* Cambridge: Cambridge UP, 1983.

Taylor, Denny. *Family Literacy.* Portsmouth: Heinemann, 1983.

Wells, Gordon. *The Meaning Makers.* Portsmouth: Heinemann, 1986.

▓▓ Critical Reflections

1. Describing the ways that she believes Eli, Jr., understands literacy in his Amish home, Andrea Fishman writes:

   Obviously, Eli, Jr., learned a great deal about literacy from all these preschool experiences, but what he learned went far beyond academic readiness lessons. More important, Eli learned that literacy is a force in the world—his world—and it is a force that imparts power to all who wield it (145).

What kind of power do you think literacy wielded in the Fisher's house, and what in the reading helps you to define the kinds of power that you have?

2. What do you see Eli, Jr., and the other Fisher children learning in their educations at the Old Order School? How is what he learns similar or different from what you have learned in your schooling?

3. Fishman asks, then answers, a question about what would have happened to Eli, Jr., had he gone to a mainstream school with the literacy background he developed in his Old Order education. Do you agree with Fishman's prediction about this imagined transition? Why or why not? Support your response with evidence from the reading and from your own experiences.

▰▰ MAKING CONNECTIONS

1. Consider the Fisher children's school experiences through the idea of the banking model in Freire's chapter. Do you think that this schooling is an example of a banking model education, or does the schooling here reflect an approach not captured in Freire's analysis?

2. Running through the excerpts from Lorene Cary's *Black Ice* are implications about the values that were embedded in Cary's education at St. Paul's School. What values do you find perpetuated through the Fishers' educations? How similar or different are they from the values that you find perpetuated in Cary's experience at St. Paul's?

3. Consider Fishman's hypothetic transition for Eli, Jr., from an Old Order to a mainstream classroom. Then, consider the transitions made by others who moved from a familiar to an unfamiliar school, like Mike Rose or Cedric Jennings. Would you define their experiences in that transition as Fishman imagines Eli, Jr.'s, would have been had he made the same move? Are there intersections between their very different experiences, or are they too disparate?

JUNE JORDAN

NOBODY MEAN MORE TO ME THAN YOU[1] AND THE FUTURE LIFE OF WILLIE JORDAN

Before her death in 2002, June Jordan had published 26 books and countless articles and poems. Most recently, she was a Professor of African-American Studies at the University of California-Berkeley; however, she believed that learning should extend far beyond the classroom. At Berkeley, she created and directed the Poetry for the People Project, which worked with communities to learn about and create poetry that represented issues important to them. Like the project, this essay demonstrates Jordan's commitment to language as a tool for social advocacy and social change.

Black English is not exactly a linguistic buffalo; as children, most of the thirty-five million Afro-Americans living here depend on this language for our discovery of the world. But then we approach our maturity inside a larger social body that will not support our efforts to become anything other than the clones of those who are neither our mothers nor our fathers. We begin to grow up in a house where every true mirror shows us the face of somebody who does not belong there, whose walk and whose talk will never look or sound "right," because that house was meant to shelter a family that is alien and hostile to us. As we learn our way around this environment, either we hide our original word habits, or we completely surrender our own voice, hoping to please those who will never respect anyone different from themselves: Black English is not exactly a linguistic buffalo, but we should understand its status as an endangered species, as a perishing, irreplaceable system of community intelligence, or we should expect its extinction, and, along with that, the extinguishing of much that constitutes our own proud, and singular identity.

What we casually call "English," less and less defers to England and its "gentlemen." "English" is no longer a specific matter of geography or an element of class privilege; more than thirty-three countries use this tool as a means of "intranational communication."[2] Countries as disparate as Zimbabwe and Malaysia, or Israel and Uganda, use it as their non-native currency of convenience. Obviously, this tool, this "English," cannot function inside thirty-three discrete societies on the basis of rules and values absolutely determined somewhere else, in a thirty-fourth other country, for example.

In addition to that staggering congeries of non-native users of English, there are five countries, or 333,746,000 people, for whom this thing called "English" serves as a native tongue.[3] Approximately 10% of these native speakers of "English" are Afro-American citizens of the U.S.A. I cite these numbers and varieties of human beings dependent on "English" in order, quickly, to suggèst how strange and how tenuous is any concept of "Standard English." Obviously, numerous forms of English now operate inside a natural, an uncontrollable, continuum of development. I would suppose "the standard" for English in Malaysia is not the same as "the standard" in Zimbabwe. I know that standard forms of English for Black people in this country do not copy that of whites. And, in fact, the structural differences between these two kinds of English have intensified, becoming more Black, or less white, despite the expected homogenizing effects of television[4] and other mass media.

Nonetheless, white standards of English persist, supreme and unquestioned, in these United States. Despite our multi-lingual population, and despite the deepening Black and white cleavage within that conglomerate, white standards control our official and popular judgements of verbal proficiency and correct, or incorrect, language skills, including speech. In contrast to India, where at least fourteen languages co-exist as legitimate Indian languages, in contrast to Nicaragua, where all citizens are legally entitled to formal school instruction in their regional or tribal languages, compulsory education in America compels ac-comodation to exclusively white forms of "English." White English, in America, is "Standard English."

5   This story begins two years ago. I was teaching a new course, "In Search of the Invisible Black Woman," and my rather large class seemed evenly divided be-tween young Black women and men. Five or six white students also sat in atten-dance. With unexpected speed and enthusiasm we had moved through historical narratives of the 19th century to literature by and about Black women, in the 20th. I had assigned the first forty pages of Alice Walker's *The Color Purple*, and I came, eagerly, to class that morning:

"So!" I exclaimed, aloud. "What did you think? How did you like it?"

The students studied their hands, or the floor. There was no response. The tense, resistant feeling in the room fairly astounded me.

At last, one student, a young woman still not meeting my eyes, muttered something in my direction:

"What did you say?" I prompted her.

10   "Why she have them talk so funny. It don't sound right."

"You mean the language?"

Another student lifted his head: "It don't look right, neither. I couldn't hardly read it."

At this, several students dumped on the book. Just about unanimously, their criticisms targeted the language. I listened to what they wanted to say and silently marvelled at the similarities between their casual speech patterns and Alice Walker's written version of Black English.

But I decided against pointing to these identical traits of syntax; I wanted not to make them self-conscious about their own spoken language—not while they clearly felt it was "wrong." Instead I decided to swallow my astonishment. Here was a negative Black reaction to a prize winning accomplishment of Black litera-ture that white readers across the country had selected as a best seller. Black re-jection was aimed at the one irreducibly Black element of Walker's work: the lan-guage—Celie's Black English. I wrote the opening lines of *The Color Purple* on the blackboard and asked the students to help me translate these sentences into Standard English:

You better not never tell nobody but God. It'd kill your mammy.

Dear God,

I am fourteen years old. I have always been a good girl. Maybe you can give me a sign letting me know what is happening to me.

Last spring after Little Lucious come I heard them fussing. He was pulling on her arm. She say it too soon, Fonso. I aint well. Finally he leave her alone. A week go by, he pulling on her arm again. She say, Naw, I ain't gonna. Can't you see I'm already half dead, an all of the children.[5]

Our process of translation exploded with hilarity and even hysterical, shocked laughter: The Black writer, Alice Walker, knew what she was doing! If rudimentary criteria for good fiction includes the manipulation of language so that the syntax and diction of sentences will tell you the identity of speakers, the probable age and sex and class of speakers, and even the locale—urban/rural/southern/western—then Walker had written, perfectly. This is the translation into Standard English that our class produced:

Absolutely, one should never confide in anybody besides God. Your secrets could prove devastating to your mother.

Dear God,

I am fourteen years old. I have always been good. But now, could you help me to understand what is happening to me?

Last spring, after my little brother, Lucious, was born, I heard my parents fighting. My father kept pulling at my mother's arm. But she told him, "It's too soon for sex, Alfonso. I am still not feeling well." Finally, my father left her alone. A week went by, and then he began bothering my mother, again: Pulling her arm. She told him, "No, I won't! Can't you see I'm already exhausted from all of these children?"

15   (Our favorite line was "It's too soon for sex, Alphonso.")
Once we could stop laughing, once we could stop our exponentially wild improvisations on the theme of Translated Black English, the students pushed me to explain their own negative first reactions to their spoken language on the printed page. I thought it was probably akin to the shock of seeing yourself in a photograph for the first time. Most of the students had never before seen a written facsimile of the way they talk. None of the students had ever learned how to read and write their own verbal system of communication: Black English. Alternatively, this fact began to baffle or else bemuse and then infuriate my students. Why not? Was it too late? Could they learn how to do it, now? And, ultimately, the final test question, the one testing my sincerity: Could I teach them? Because I had never taught anyone Black English and, as far as I knew, no one, anywhere in the United States, had ever offered such a course, the best I could say was "I'll try."
He looked like a wrestler.
He sat dead center in the packed room and, every time our eyes met, he quickly nodded his head as though anxious to reassure, and encourage, me.
Short, with strikingly broad shoulders and long arms, he spoke with a surprisingly high, soft voice that matched the soft bright movement of his eyes. His name was Willie Jordan. He would have seemed even more unlikely in the context of Contemporary Women's Poetry, except that ten or twelve other Black men were taking the course, as well. Still, Willie was conspicuous. His extreme

fitness, the muscular density of his presence underscored the riveted, gentle attention that he gave to anything anyone said. Generally, he did not join the loud and rowdy dialogue flying back and forth, but there could be no doubt about his interest in our discussions. And, when he stood to present an argument he'd prepared, overnight, that nervous smile of his vanished and an irregular stammering replaced it, as he spoke with visceral sincerity, word by word.

20   That was how I met Willie Jordan. It was in between "In Search of the Invisible Black Women" and "The Art of Black English." I was waiting for Departmental approval and I supposed that Willie might be, so to speak, killing time until he, too, could study Black English. But Willie really did want to explore Contemporary Women's poetry and, to that end, volunteered for extra research and never missed a class.

Towards the end of that semester, Willie approached me for an independent study project on South Africa. It would commence the next semester. I thought Willie's writing needed the kind of improvement only intense practice will yield. I knew his intelligence was outstanding. But he'd wholeheartedly opted for "Standard English" at a rather late age, and the results were stilted and frequently polysyllabic, simply for the sake of having more syllables. Willie's unnatural formality of language seemed to me consistent with the formality of his research into South African apartheid. As he projected his studies, he would have little time, indeed, for newspapers. Instead, more than 90% of his research would mean saturation in strictly historical, if not archival, material. I was certainly interested. It would be tricky to guide him into a more confident and spontaneous relationship both with language and apartheid. It was going to be wonderful to see what happened when he could catch up with himself, entirely, and talk back to the world.

September, 1984: Breezy fall weather and much excitment! My class, "The Art of Black English," was full to the limit of the fire laws. And, in Independent Study, Willie Jordan showed up, weekly, fifteen minutes early for each of our sessions. I was pretty happy to be teaching, altogether!

I remember an early class when a young brother, replete with his ever present pork-pie hat, raised his hand and then told us that most of what he'd heard was "all right" except it was "too clean." "The brothers on the street," he continued, "they mix it up more. Like 'fuck' and 'motherfuck.' Or like 'shit.'" He waited. I waited. Then all of us laughed a good while, and we got into a brawl about "correct" and "realistic" Black English that led to Rule 1.

Rule 1: *Black English is about a whole lot more than mothafuckin.*

25   As a criterion, we decided, "realistic" could take you anywhere you want to go. Artful places. Angry places. Eloquent and sweetalkin places. Polemical places. Church. And the local Bar & Grill. We were checking out a language, not a mood or a scene or one guy's forgettable mouthing off.

It was hard. For most of the students, learning Black English required a fall-back to patterns and rhythms of speech that many of their parents had beaten out of them. I mean *beaten.* And, in a majority of cases, correct Black English could be achieved only by striving for *incorrect* Standard English, something they were still pushing at, quite uncertainly. This state of affairs led to Rule 2.

Rule 2: *If it's wrong in Standard English it's probably right in Black English, or, at least, you're hot.*

It was hard. Roommates and family members ridiculed their studies, or remained incredulous, "You *studying* that shit? At school?" But we were beginning to feel the companionship of pioneers. And we decided that we needed another rule that would establish each one of us as equally important to our success. This was Rule 3.

Rule 3: *If it don't sound like something that come out somebody mouth then it don't sound right. If it don't sound right then it ain't hardly right. Period.*

30   This rule produced two weeks of compositions in which the students agonizingly tried to spell the sound of the Black English sentence they wanted to convey. But Black English is, preeminently, an oral/spoken means of communication. *And spelling don't talk.* So we needed Rule 4.

Rule 4: *Forget about the spelling. Let the syntax carry you.*

Once we arrived at Rule 4 we started to fly because syntax, the structure of an idea, leads you to the world view of the speaker and reveals her values. The syntax of a sentence equals the structure of your consciousness. If we insisted that the language of Black English adheres to a distinctive Black syntax, then we were postulating a profound difference between white and Black people, *per se.* Was it a difference to prize or to obliterate?

There are three qualities of Black English—the presence of life, voice, and clarity—that testify to a distinctive Black value system that we became excited about and self-consciously tried to maintain.

1. Black English has been produced by a pre-technocratic, if not anti-technological, culture. More, our culture has been constantly threatened by annihilation or, at least, the swallowed blurring of assimilation. Therefore, our language is a system constructed by people constantly needing to insist that we exist, that we are present. Our language devolves from a culture that abhors all abstraction, or anything tending to obscure or delete the fact of the human being who is here and now/the truth of the person who is speaking or listening. Consequently, *there is no passive voice construction possible in Black English.* For example, you cannot say, "Black English is being eliminated." You must say, instead, "White people eliminating Black English." The assumption of the presence of life governs all of Black English. Therefore, overwhelmingly, *all action takes place in the language of the present indicative.* And every sentence assumes the living and active participation of at least two human beings, the speaker and the listener.

35   2. A primary consequence of the person-centered values of Black English is the delivery of voice. If you speak or write Black English, your ideas will necessarily possess that otherwise elusive attribute, *voice.*

3. One main benefit following from the person-centered values of Black English is that of *clarity.* If your idea, your sentence, assumes the presence of at least two living and active people, you will make it understandable because the motivation behind every sentence is the wish to say something real to somebody real.

As the weeks piled up, translation from Standard English into Black English or vice versa occupied a hefty part of our course work.

Standard English (hereafter S.E.): "In considering the idea of studying Black English those questioned suggested—"

(What's the subject? Where's the person? Is anybody alive in there, in that idea?)

Black English (hereafter B.E.): "I been asking people what you think about somebody studying Black English and they answer me like this:"

But there were interesting limits. You cannot "translate" instances of Standard English preoccupied with abstraction or with nothing/nobody evidently alive, into Black English. That would warp the language into uses antithetical to the guiding perspective of its community of users. Rather you must first change those Standard English sentences, themselves, into ideas consistent with the person-centered assumptions of Black English.

GUIDELINES FOR BLACK ENGLISH

1. Minimal number of words for every idea: This is the source for the aphoristic and/or poetic force of the language; eliminate every possible word.

2. Clarity: If the sentence is not clear it's not Black English.

3. Eliminate use of the verb *to be* whenever possible. This leads to the deployment of more descriptive and therefore, more precise verbs.

4. Use *be* or *been* only when you want to describe a chronic, ongoing state of things.
   He *be* at the office, by 9. (He is always at the office by 9.)
   He *been* with her since forever.

5. Zero copula: Always eliminate the verb *to be* whenever it would combine with another verb, in Standard English.
   S.E.: She is going out with him.
   B.E.: She going out with him.

6. Eliminate *do* as in:
   S.E.: What do you think? What do you want?
   B.E.: What you think? What you want?
   Rules number 3, 4, 5, and 6 provide for the use of the minimal number of verbs per idea and, therefore, greater accuracy in the choice of verb.

7. In general, if you wish to say something really positive, try to formulate the idea using emphatic negative structure.
   S.E.: He's fabulous.
   B.E.: He bad.

8. Use double or triple negatives for dramatic emphasis.
   S.E.: Tina Turner sings out of this world.
   B.E.: Ain nobody sing like Tina.

9. Never use the *-ed* suffix to indicate the past tense of a verb.
   S.E.: She closed the door.
   B.E.: She close the door. Or, she have close the door.

10. Regardless of intentional verb time, only use the third person singular, present indicative, for use of the verb *to have,* as an auxiliary.
    S.E.: He had his wallet then he lost it.
    B.E.: He have him wallet then he lose it.
    S.E.: He had seen that movie.
    B.E.: We seen that movie. Or, we have see that movie.

11. Observe a minimal inflection of verbs. Particularly, never change from the first person singular forms to the third person singular.
    S.E. Present Tense Forms: He goes to the store.
    B.E.: He go to the store.
    S.E.: Past Tense Forms: He went to the store.
    B.E.: He go to the store. Or, he gone to the store. Or, he been to the store.

12. The possessive case scarcely ever appears in Black English. Never use an apostrophe ('s) construction. If you wander into a possessive case component of an idea, then keep logically consistent: *ours, his, theirs, mines.* But, most likely, if you bump into such a component, you have wandered outside the underlying world-view of Black English.
    S.E.: He will take their car tomorrow.
    B.E.: He taking they car tomorrow.

13. Plurality: Logical consistency, continued: If the modifier indicates plurality then the noun remains in the singular case.
    S.E.: He ate twelve doughnuts.
    B.E.: He eat twelve doughnut.
    S.E.: She has many books.
    B.E.: She have many book.

14. Listen for, or invent, special Black English forms of the past tense, such as: "He losted it. That what she felted." If they are clear and readily understood, then use them.
    Do not hesitate to play with words, sometimes inventing them: e.g. "astropotomous" means huge like a hippo plus astronomical and, therefore, signifies real big.

15. In Black English, unless you keenly want to underscore the past tense nature of an action, stay in the present tense and rely on the overall context of your ideas for the conveyance of time and sequence.

16. Never use the suffix *-ly* form of an adverb in Black English.
    S.E.: The rain came down rather quickly.
    B.E.: The rain come down pretty quick.

17. Never use the indefinite article *an* in Black English.
    S.E.: He wanted to ride an elephant.
    B.E.: He want to ride him a elephant.

18. Invarient syntax: in correct Black English it is possible to formulate an imperative, an interogative, and a simple declarative idea with the same syntax:
    B.E.: You going to the store?

You going to the store.

You going to the store!

Where was Willie Jordan? We'd reached the mid-term of the semester. Students had formulated Black English guidelines, by consensus, and they were now writing with remarkable beauty, purpose, and enjoyment:

"I ain hardly speakin for everybody but myself so understan that."—Kim Parks

Samples from student writings:

40   "Janie have a great big ole hole inside her. Tea Cake the only thing that fit that hole . . .

"That pear tree beautiful to Janie, especial when bees fiddlin with the blossomin pear there growin large and lovely. But personal speakin, the love she get from starin at that tree ain the love what starin back at her in them relationship." (Monica Morris)

"Love is a big theme in, *They Eye Was Watching God*. Love show people new corners inside theyself. It pull out good stuff and stuff back bad stuff . . . Joe worship the doing uh his own hand and need other people to worship him too. But he ain't think about Janie that she a person and ought to live like anybody common do. Queen life not for Janie." (Monica Morris)

"In both life and writin, Black womens have varietous experience of love that be cold like a iceberg or fiery like a inferno. Passion got for the other partner involve, man or woman, seem as shallow, ankle-deep water or the most profoundest abyss." (Constance Evans)

"Family love another bond that ain't never break under no pressure." (Constance Evans)

45   "You know it really cold/When the friend you/Always get out the fire/Act like they don't know you/When you in the heat." (Constance Evans)

"Big classroom discussion bout love at this time. I never take no class where us have any long arguin for and against for two or three day. New to me and great. I find the class time talkin a million time more interestin than detail bout the book." (Kathy Esseks)

As these examples suggest, Black English no longer limited the students, in any way. In fact, one of them, Philip Garfield, would shortly "translate" a pivotal scene from Ibsen's *Doll House*, as his final term paper:

NORA: I didn't gived no shit. I thinked you a asshole back then, too, you make it so hard for me save mines husband life.

KROGSTAD: Girl, it clear you ain't any idea what you done. You done exact what I once done, and I losed my reputation over it.

NORA: You asks me believe you once act brave save you wife life?

KROGSTAD: Law care less why you done it.

NORA: Law must suck.

KROGSTAD: Suck or no, if I wants, judge screw you wid dis paper.

NORA: No way, man. (Philip Garfield)

But where was Willie? Compulsively punctual, and always thoroughly pre-pared with neatly typed compositions, he had disappeared. He failed to show up for our regularly scheduled conference, and I received neither a note nor a phone call of explanation. A whole week went by. I wondered if Willie had finally been captured by the extremely current happenings in South Africa: passage of a new constitution that did not enfranchise the Black majority, and militant Black South African reaction to that affront. I wondered if he'd been hurt, somewhere. I won-dered if the serious workload of weekly readings and writings had overwhelmed him and changed his mind about independent study. Where was Willie Jordan?

One week after the first conference that Willie missed, he called: "Hello, Professor Jordan? This is Willie. I'm sorry I wasn't there last week. But something has come up and I'm pretty upset. I'm sorry but I really can't deal right now."

50   I asked Willie to drop by my office and just let me see that he was okay. He agreed to do that. When I saw him I knew something hideous had happened. Something had hurt him and scared him to the marrow. He was all agitated and stammering and terse and incoherent. At last, his sadly jumbled account let me surmise, as follows: Brooklyn police had murdered his unarmed, twenty-five year old brother, Reggie Jordan. Neither Willie nor his elderly parents knew what to do about it. Nobody from the press was interested. His folks had no money. Police ran his family around and around, to no point. And Reggie was really dead. And Willie wanted to fight, but he felt helpless.

With Willie's permission I began to try to secure legal counsel for the Jordan family. Unfortunately Black victims of police violence are truly numerous while the resources available to prosecute their killers are truly scarce. A friend of mine at the Center for Constitutional Rights estimated that just the preparatory costs for bringing the cops into court normally approaches $180,000. Unless the exe-cution of Reggie Jordan became a major community cause for organizing, and protest, his murder would simply become a statistical item.

Again, with Willie's permission, I contacted every newspaper and media per-son I could think of. But the William Bastone feature article in *The Village Voice* was the only result from that canvassing.

Again, with Willie's permission, I presented the case to my class in Black English. We had talked about the politics of language. We had talked about love and sex and child abuse and and men and women. But the murder of Reggie Jordan broke like a hurricane across the room.

There are few "issues" as endemic to Black life as police violence. Most of the students knew and respected and liked Jordan. Many of them came from the very neighborhood where the murder had occurred. All of the students had known somebody close to them who had been killed by police, or had known frightening moments of gratuitous confrontation with the cops. They wanted to do everything at once to avenge death. Number One: They decided to com-pose personal statements of condolence to Willie Jordan and his family written in Black English. Number Two: They decided to compose individual messages to the police, in Black English. These should be prefaced by an explanatory paragraph composed by the entire group. Number Three: These individual messages, with their lead paragraph, should be sent to *Newsday*.

55   The morning after we agreed on these objectives, one of the young women students appeared with an unidentified visitor, who sat through the class, smiling in a peculiar, comfortable way.

Now we had to make more tactical decisions. Because we wanted the messages published, and because we thought it imperative that our outrage be known by the police, the tactical question was this: Should the opening, group paragraph be written in Black English or Standard English?

I have seldom been privy to a discussion with so much heart at the dead heat of it. I will never forget the eloquence, the sudden haltings of speech, the fierce struggle against tears, the furious throwaway, and useless explosions that this question elicited.

That one question contained several others, each of them extraordinarily painful to even contemplate. How best to serve the memory of Reggie Jordan? Should we use the language of the killers—Standard English—in order to make our ideas acceptable to those controlling the killers? But wouldn't what we had to say be rejected, summarily, if we said it in our own language, the language of the victim, Reggie Jordan? But if we sought to express ourselves by abandoning our language wouldn't that mean our suicide on top of Reggie's murder? But if we expressed ourselves in our own language wouldn't that be suicidal to the wish to communicate with those who, evidently, did not give a damn about us/Reggie/police violence in the Black community?

At the end of one of the longest, most difficult hours of my own life, the students voted, unanimously, to preface their individual messages with a paragraph composed in the language of Reggie Jordan. "*At least we don't give up nothing else. At least we stick to the truth: Be who we been. And stay all the way with Reggie.*"

60   It was heartbreaking to proceed, from that point. Everyone in the room realized that our decision in favor of Black English had doomed our writings, even as the distinctive reality of our Black lives always has doomed our efforts to "be who we been" in this country.

I went to the blackboard and took down this paragraph, dictated by the class: "... YOU COPS!

WE THE BROTHER AND SISTER OF WILLIE JORDAN, A FELLOW STONY BROOK STUDENT WHO THE BROTHER OF THE DEAD REGGIE JORDAN. REGGIE, LIKE MANY BROTHER AND SISTER, HE A VICTIM OF BRUTAL RACIST POLICE, OCTOBER 25, 1984. US APPALL, FED UP, BECAUSE THAT ANOTHER SENSELESS DEATH WHAT OCCUR IN OUR COMMUNITY. THIS WHAT WE FEEL, THIS, FROM OUR HEART, FOR WE AIN'T STAYIN' SILENT NO MORE:"

With the completion of this introduction, nobody said anything. I asked for comments. At this invitation, the unidentified visitor, a young Black man, ceaselessly smiling, raised his hand. He was, it so happens, a rookie cop. He had just joined the force in September and, he said, he thought he should clarify a few things. So he came forward and sprawled easily into a posture of barroom, or fireside, nostalgia:

65   "See," Officer Charles enlightened us, "Most times when you out on the street and something come down you do one of two things. Over-react or under-react. Now, if you under-react then you can get yourself kilt. And if you over-react then maybe you kill somebody. Fortunately it's about nine times out of ten and you will over-react. So the brother got kilt. And I'm sorry about that, believe me. But what you have to understand is what kilt him: Over-reaction. That's all. Now you talk about Black people and white police but see, now, I'm cop myself. And (big smile) I'm Black. And just a couple months ago I was on the other side. But see it's the same for me. You a cop, you the ultimate authority: the Ultimate Authority. And you on the street, most of the time you can only do one of two things: over-react or under-react. That's all it is with the brother: Over-reaction. Didn't have nothing to do with race."

That morning Officer Charles had the good fortune to escape without being boiled alive. But barely. And I remember the pride of his smile when I read about the fate of Black policemen and other collaborators, in South Africa. I remember him, and I remember the shock and palpable feeling of shame that filled the room. It was as though that foolish, and deadly, young man had just relieved himself of his foolish, and deadly, explanation, face to face with the grief of Reggie Jordan's father and Reggie Jordan's mother. Class ended quietly. I copied the paragraph from the blackboard, collected the individual messages and left to type them up.

Newsday rejected the piece.

The Village Voice could not find room in their "Letters" section to print the individual messages from the students to the police.

None of the tv news reporters picked up the story.

70   Nobody raised $180,000 to prosecute the murder of Reggie Jordan.

Reggie Jordan is really dead.

I asked Willie Jordan to write an essay pulling together everything important to him from that semester. He was still deeply beside himself with frustration and amazement and loss. This is what he wrote, un-edited, and in its entirety:

"Throughout the course of this semester I have been researching the effects of oppression and exploitation along racial lines in South Africa and its neighboring countries. I have become aware of South African police brutalization of native Africans beyond the extent of the law, even though the laws themselves are catalyst affliction upon Black men, women and children. Many Africans die each year as a result of the deliberate use of police force to protect the white power structure.

"Social control agents in South Africa, such as policemen, are also used to force compliance among citizens through both overt and covert tactics. It is not uncommon to find bold-faced coercion and cold-blooded killings of Blacks by South African police for undetermined and/or inadequate reasons. Perhaps the truth is that the only reasons for this heinous treatment of Blacks rests in racial differences. We should also understand that what is conveyed through the media is not always accurate and may sometimes be construed as the tip of the iceberg at best.

75 "I recently received a painful reminder that racism, poverty, and the abuse of power are global problems which are by no means unique to South Africa. On October 25, 1984 at approximately 3:00 p.m. my brother, Mr. Reginald Jordan, was shot and killed by two New York City policemen from the 75th precinct in the East New York section of Brooklyn. His life ended at the age of twenty-five. Even up to this current point in time the Police Department has failed to provide my family, which consists of five brothers, eight sisters, and two parents, with a plausible reason for Reggie's death. Out of the many stories that were given to my family by the Police Department, not one of them seems to hold water. In fact, I honestly believe that the Police Department's assessment of my brother's murder is nothing short of ABSOLUTE BULLSHIT, and thus far no evidence had been produced to alter perception of the situation.

"Furthermore, I believe that one of three cases may have occurred in this incident. First, Reggie's death may have been the desired outcome of the police officer's action, in which case the killing was premeditated. Or, it was a case of mistaken identity, which clarifies the fact that the two officers who killed my brother and their commanding parties are all grossly incompetent. Or, both of the above cases are correct, i.e., Reggie's murderers intended to kill him and the Police Department behaved insubordinately.

"Part of the argument of the officers who shot Reggie was that he had attacked one of them and took his gun. This was their major claim. They also said that only one of them had actually shot Reggie. The facts, however, speak for themselves. According to the Death Certificate and autopsy report, Reggie was shot eight times from point-blank range. The Doctor who performed the autopsy told me himself that two bullets entered the side of my brother's head; four bullets were sprayed into his back, and two bullets struck him in the back of his legs. It is obvious that unnecessary force was used by the police and that it is extremely difficult to shoot someone in his back when he is attacking or approaching you.

"After experiencing a situation like this and researching South Africa I believe that to a large degree, justice may only exist as rhetoric. I find it difficult to talk of true justice when the oppression of my people both at home and abroad attests to the fact that inequality and injustice are serious problems whereby Blacks and Third World people are perpetually short-changed by society. Something has to be done about the way in which this world is set up. Although it is a difficult task, we do have the power to make a change."

—Willie J. Jordan Jr.
EGL 487, Section 58, November 14, 1984
It is my privilege to dedicate this book to the future life of Willie J. Jordan Jr.
August 8, 1985

ENDNOTES

1. Black English aphorism crafted by Monica Morris, a Junior at S.U.N.Y. at Stony Brook, October, 1984.

2. *English is Spreading, But What Is English.* A presentation by Professor S.N. Sridahr, Dept. of Linguistics, S.U.N.Y. at Stonybrook, April 9, 1985: Dean's Conversation Among the Disciplines.

3. Ibid.

4. *New York Times,* March 15, 1985, Section One, p 14: Report on study by Linguistics at the University of Pennsylvania.

5. Alice Walker, *The Color Purple,* p. 11, Harcourt Brace, N.Y.

≡≈ CRITICAL REFLECTIONS

1. June Jordan's argument here echoes one made by linguists, that Black English (like other dialects of English) is a central force of intelligence in the African-American community. Focus on a community to which you belong that has its own special language. What is that language? Why do you use it in that community, and not elsewhere?

2. What do you think Jordan means when she argues that "white English, in America, is Standard English"? Do you agree with her? Why or why not?

3. How do you think Jordan and her students define literacy in their class, "The Art of Black English"? How is this definition connected to their community? Whose interests does it serve and not serve?

4. One of the rules of Black English, according to Jordan and her students, is that actions are always attributed to someone—there is no passive voice. Chose one page from another reading from this text. Where do you find passive and active voices, and how do these uses of voice affect you as a reader?

5. In the middle section of this reading, Jordan lists the rules that she and her students developed for Black English as a result of their study of that dialect. Develop a similar set of guidelines for a dialect used in a specific community of which you are a part—perhaps the community you considered above, or another. What are the rules there?

6. This reading is about the value of using Black English for Jordan and her students, especially Willie, but Jordan used primarily standardized English to write it. Why do you think she made this decision?

≡≈ MAKING CONNECTIONS

1. Construct a dialogue about college between Willie Jordan and one of the players from "The Last Shot." What would they discuss, and how would they talk about it?

2. In "Literacy Among the Amish," Andrea Fishman describes a school where the definition of literacy is closely linked to the Old Order Amish community where the school is located. Jordan argues that Black English also reflects values of the African-American community, though she taught this class at the State University of New York (SUNY) at Stony Brook, a predominantly white institution located in a suburban area of New York City. Do you see Jordan's goals and those of the Old Order Amish as analogous? Different? How and why?

3. Create a test using a dialect of English that you use with your friends. For the test, write a brief passage using the dialect, then write questions about the passage in the same dialect. Administer it to others who don't use that dialect and analyze the results, both of your work to create the test and of their performance on it. What do you think accounts for their results? What do those who took the test think accounts for the results?

ROBERT LOUTHAN

HEAVY MACHINERY

Robert Louthan, this poem's author, has written several books of poetry. This poem is included in *Working Classics: Poems on Industrial Life*. Like other poems in that collection, it offers a contrast between poetry and work; it offers to readers the opportunity to consider the distinctions between those concepts.

> What is poetry for? To tell the man
> who has just driven home
> too fast from his job at the factory
> that what he wants is out of this world,
> 5   that the descending sun and materializing moon
> weren't installed in his windshield but beyond it,
> that his eyes can't fly, that their fluttering lids
> are certainly wings but atrophied,
> and a steering wheel is the only orbit
> 10   he'll ever own? Oh yes. But it should also
> give him something consoling to say to the guys
> tomorrow at break: no matter how delicate the stars may look
> the cosmos is heavy machinery, and much harder to operate
> than the kind they work and curse.
> 15   And it should tell him the rest: the future
> features bedtime, and to go to sleep is to remove
> and unfold and let go
> of the mind, the levitating blanket.

CRITICAL REFLECTIONS

1. After reading this poem, how would you answer the question Louthan poses in the first line—what is poetry for? Why is it for what you say it is?

2. What do you see as the role of literacy and education for the speaker in this poem? What words in the poem indicate to you that this is the purpose?

3. Re-create this poem in different genres: a five-paragraph theme, a fictional story, and a memo to a boss. What would each say?

▄▄▄ MAKING CONNECTIONS

1. Reflecting on the role of literacy and education that you have identified for this poem, do you see it reflected in any of the other readings you have completed in this book? If you do, where do you, and what are the connections? If you do not, how is this reading different?

2. Study the photographs on page 359–370. Do any reflect the sentiments in this poem? Why or why not?

MIKE ROSE

"I JUST WANNA BE AVERAGE"

This chapter is excerpted from a longer book by Rose called *Lives on the Boundary*. In it, Rose begins by questioning the institutional mechanisms that classify students as underprepared (such as placing students into different tracks in K-12 schools or sorting college students into basic writing and first-year composition at the college level). He weaves in his own experiences as a student placed in the Voc[ational]-Ed[ucation] track as a starting place to question tracking mechanisms; in this chapter, he describes his experiences in Voc-Ed high school classes and his journey to the college prep track. In later chapters, Rose goes on to describe his experiences working as a teacher with students labeled "underprepared" or "less than able," showing through illustration and example how flawed these definitions can be. Rose is now a Professor in the School of Education at UCLA, where he has continued to study the ways that people learn and the factors that affect learning.

Between 1880 and 1920, well over four million Southern Italian peasants immigrated to America. Their poverty was extreme and hopeless—twelve hours of farm labor would get you one lira, about twenty cents—so increasing numbers of desperate people booked passage for the United States, the country where, the steamship companies claimed, prosperity was a way of life. My father left Naples before the turn of the century; my mother came with her mother from Calabria in 1921. They met in Altoona, Pennsylvania at the lunch counter of Tom and Joe's, a steamy diner with twangy-voiced waitresses and graveyard stew.

For my mother, life in America was not what the promoters had told her father it would be. She grew up very poor. She slept with her parents and brothers and sisters in one room. She had to quit school in the seventh grade to care for her sickly younger brothers. When her father lost his leg in a railroad accident, she began working in a garment factory where women sat crowded at their stations, solitary as penitents in a cloister. She stayed there until her marriage. My father had found a freer route. He was closemouthed about his past, but I know that he had been a salesman, a tailor, and a gambler; he knew people in the mob and had, my uncles whisper, done time in Chicago. He went through a year or two of Italian elementary school and could write a few words—those necessary to scribble measurements for a suit—and over the years developed a quiet urbanity, a persistence, and a slowly debilitating arteriosclerosis.

When my father proposed to my mother, he decided to open a spaghetti house, a venture that lasted through the war and my early years. The restaurant collapsed in bankruptcy in 1951 when Altoona's major industry, the Pennsylvania Railroad, had to shut down its shops. My parents managed to salvage seven hundred dollars and, on the advice of the family doctor, headed to California, where the winters would be mild and where I, their seven-year-old son, would have the possibility of a brighter future.

At first we lived in a seedy hotel on Spring Street in downtown Los Angeles, but my mother soon found an ad in the *Times* for cheap property on the south side of town. My parents contacted a woman named Mrs. Jolly, used my mother's engagement ring as a down payment, and moved to 9116 South Vermont Avenue, a house about one and one-half miles northwest of Watts. The neighborhood was poor, and it was in transition. Some old white folks had lived there for decades and were retired. Younger black families were moving up from Watts and settling by working-class white families newly arrived from the South and the Midwest. Immigrant Mexican families were coming in from Baja. Any such demographic mix is potentially volatile, and as the fifties wore on, the neighborhood would be marked by outbursts of violence.

5   I have many particular memories of this time, but in general these early years seem a peculiar mix of physical warmth and barrenness: a gnarled lemon tree, thin rugs, a dirt alley, concrete in the sun. My uncles visited a few times, and we went to the beach or to orange groves. The return home, however, left the waves and spray, the thick leaves and split pulp far in the distance. I was aware of my parents watching their money and got the sense from their conversations that things could quickly take a turn for the worse. I started taping pennies to the bottom of a shelf in the kitchen.

My father's health was bad, and he had few readily marketable skills. Poker and pinochle brought in a little money, and he tried out an idea that had worked in Altoona during the war: He started a "suit club." The few customers he could scare up would pay two dollars a week on a tailor-made suit. He would take the measurements and send them to a shop back East and hope for the best. My mother took a job at a café in downtown Los Angeles, a split shift 9:00 to 12:00 and 5:00 to 9:00, but her tips were totaling sixty cents a day, so she quit for a night shift at Coffee Dan's. This got her to the bus stop at one in the morning, waiting on the same street where drunks were urinating and hookers were catching the last of the bar crowd. She made friends with a Filipino cook who would scare off the advances of old men aflame with the closeness of taxi dancers. In a couple of years, Coffee Dan's would award her a day job at the counter. Once every few weeks my father and I would take a bus downtown and visit with her, sitting at stools by the window, watching the animated but silent mix of faces beyond the glass.

My father had moved to California with faint hopes about health and a belief in his child's future, drawn by that far edge of America where the sun descends into green water. What he found was a city that was warm, verdant, vast, and indifferent as a starlet in a sports car. Altoona receded quickly, and my parents must have felt isolated and deceived. They had fallen into the abyss of paradise— two more poor settlers trying to make a go of it in the City of the Angels.

Let me tell you about our house. If you entered the front door and turned right you'd see a small living room with a couch along the east wall and one along the west wall—one couch was purple, the other tan, both bought used and both well worn. A television set was placed at the end of the purple couch, right at arm level. An old Philco radio sat next to the TV, its speaker covered with gold lamé. There was a small coffee table in the center of the room on which sat a murky fishbowl occupied by two listless guppies. If, on entering, you turned left you would see a green Formica dinner table with four chairs, a cedar chest given as a wedding present to my mother by her mother, a painted statue of the Blessed Virgin Mary, and a black trunk. I also had a plastic chaise longue between the door and the table. I would lie on this and watch television.

A short hallway leading to the bathroom opened on one side to the kitchen and, on the other, to the bedroom. The bedroom had two beds, one for me and one for my parents, a bureau with a mirror, and a chest of drawers on which we piled old shirt boxes and stacks of folded clothes. The kitchen held a refrigerator and a stove, small older models that we got when our earlier (and newer) models were repossessed by two silent men. There was one white wooden chair in the corner beneath wall cabinets. You could walk in and through a tiny pantry to the backyard and to four one-room rentals. My father got most of our furniture from a secondhand store on the next block; he would tend the store two or three hours a day as payment on our account.

10　　As I remember it, the house was pretty dark. My mother kept the blinds in the bedroom drawn—there were no curtains there—and the venetian blinds in the living room were, often as not, left closed. The walls were bare except for a faded picture of Jesus and a calendar from the *Altoona Mirror*. Some paper carnations bent out of a white vase on the television. There was a window on the north side of the kitchen that had no blinds or curtains, so the sink got good light. My father would methodically roll up his sleeves and show me how to prepare a sweet potato or avocado seed so it would sprout. We kept a row of them on the sill above the sink, their shoots and vines rising and curling in the morning sun.

The house was on a piece of land that rose about four feet up from heavily trafficked Vermont Avenue. The yard sloped down to the street, and three steps and a short walkway led up the middle of the grass to our front door. There was a similar house immediately to the south of us. Next to it was Carmen's Barber Shop. Carmen was a short, quiet Italian who, rumor had it, had committed his first wife to the crazy house to get her money. In the afternoons, Carmen could be found in the lot behind his shop playing solitary catch, flinging a tennis ball high into the air and running under it. One day the police arrested Carmen on charges of child molesting. He was released but became furtive and suspicious. I never saw him in the lot again. Next to Carmen's was a junk store where, one summer, I made a little money polishing brass and rewiring old lamps. Then came a dilapidated real estate office, a Mexican restaurant, an empty lot, and an appliance store owned by the father of Keith Grateful, the streetwise, chubby boy who would become my best friend.

Right to the north of us was a record shop, a barber shop presided over by old Mr. Graff, Walt's Malts, a shoe repair shop with a big Cat's Paw decal in the window, a third barber shop, and a brake shop. It's as I write this that I realize for the first time that three gray men could have had a go at your hair before you left our street.

Behind our house was an unpaved alley that passed, just to the north, a power plant the length of a city block. Massive coils atop the building hissed and cracked through the day, but the doors never opened. I used to think it was abandoned— feeding itself on its own wild arcs—until one sweltering afternoon a man was electrocuted on the roof. The air was thick and still as two firemen—the only men present—brought down a charred and limp body without saying a word.

The north and south traffic on Vermont was separated by tracks for the old yellow trolley cars, long since defunct. Across the street was a huge garage, a tiny hot dog stand run by a myopic and reclusive man named Freddie, and my dreamland, the Vermont Bowl. Distant and distorted behind thick lenses, Freddie's eyes never met yours; he would look down when he took your order and give you your change with a mumble. Freddie slept on a cot in the back of his grill and died there one night, leaving tens of thousands of dollars stuffed in the mattress.

15   My father would buy me a chili dog at Freddie's, and then we would walk over to the bowling alley where Dad would sit at the lunch counter and drink coffee while I had a great time with pinball machines, electric shooting galleries, and an ill-kept dispenser of cheese corn. There was a small, dark bar abutting the lanes, and it called to me. I would devise reasons to walk through it: "'Scuse me, is the bathroom in here?" or "Anyone see my dad?" though I can never remember my father having a drink. It was dark and people were drinking and I figured all sorts of mysterious things were being whispered. Next to the Vermont Bowl was a large vacant lot overgrown with foxtails and dotted with car parts, bottles, and rotting cardboard. One day Keith heard that the police had found a human head in the brush. After that we explored the lot periodically, coming home with stickers all the way up to our waists. But we didn't find a thing. Not even a kneecap.

When I wasn't with Keith or in school, I would spend most of my day with my father or with the men who were renting the one-room apartments behind our house. Dad and I whiled away the hours in the bowling alley, watching TV, or planting a vegetable garden that never seemed to take. When he was still mobile, he would walk the four blocks down to St. Regina's Grammar School to take me home to my favorite lunch of boiled wieners and chocolate milk. There I'd sit, dunking my hot dog in a jar of mayonnaise and drinking my milk while Sheriff John tuned up the calliope music on his "Lunch Brigade." Though he never complained to me, I could sense that my father's health was failing, and I began devising child's ways to make him better. We had a box of rolled cotton in the bathroom, and I would go in and peel off a long strip and tape it around my jaw. Then I'd rummage through the closet, find a sweater of my father's, put on one of his hats—and sneak around to the back door. I'd knock loudly and wait. It would take him a while to get there. Finally, he'd open the door, look down, and quietly say, "Yes, Michael?" I was disappointed. Every time. Somehow I thought I could fool him. And, I guess, if he had been fooled, I would have succeeded in redefining things: I would have been the old one, he much younger, more agile, with strength in his legs.

The men who lived in the back were either retired or didn't work that much, so one of them was usually around. They proved to be, over the years, an unusual set of companions for a young boy. Ed Gionotti was the youngest of the lot, a handsome man whose wife had run off and who spoke softly and never smiled. Bud Hall and Lee McGuire were two out-of-work plumbers who lived in adjacent units and who weekly drank themselves silly, proclaiming in front of God and everyone their undying friendship or their unequivocal hatred. Old Cheech was a lame Italian who used to hobble along grabbing his testicles and rolling his eyes while he talked about the women he claimed to have on a string. There was Lester, the toothless cabbie, who several times made overtures to me and who, when he moved, left behind a drawer full of syringes and burnt spoons. Mr. Smith was a rambunctious retiree who lost his nose to an untended skin cancer. And there was Mr. Berryman, a sweet and gentle man who eventually left for a retirement hotel only to be burned alive in an electrical fire.

Except for Keith, there were no children on my block and only one or two on the immediate side streets. Most of the people I saw day to day were over fifty. People in their twenties and thirties working in the shoe shop or the garages didn't say a lot; their work and much of what they were working for drained their spirits. There were gang members who sauntered up from Hoover Avenue, three blocks to the east, and occasionally I would get shoved around, but they had little interest in me either as member or victim. I was a skinny, bespectacled kid and had neither the coloring nor the style of dress or carriage that marked me as a rival. On the whole, the days were quiet, lazy, lonely. The heat shimmering over the asphalt had no snap to it; time drifted by. I would lie on the couch at night and listen to the music from the record store or from Walt's Malts. It was new and quick paced, exciting, a little dangerous (the church had condemned Buddy Knox's "Party Doll"), and I heard in it a deep rhythmic need to be made whole with love, or marked as special, or released in some rebellious way. Even the songs about lost love—and there were plenty of them—lifted me right out of my socks with their melodious longing:

Came the dawn,

and my heart and her love and the night

were gone.

But I know I'll never forget

her kiss in the moonlight Oooo . . .

such a kiss Oooo Oooo such a night . . .

In the midst of the heat and slow time the music brought the promise of its origins, a promise of deliverance, a promise that, if only for a moment, life could be stirring and dreamy.

But the anger and frustration of South Vermont could prove too strong for music's illusion; then it was violence that provided deliverance of a different order. One night I watched as a guy sprinted from Walt's to toss something on our lawn. The police were right behind, and a cop tackled him, smashing his face into the sidewalk. I ducked out to find the packet: a dozen glassine bags of heroin. Another night, one August midnight, an argument outside the record store ended with a man being shot to death. And the occasional gang forays brought with them some fated kid who would fumble his moves and catch a knife.

20   It's popular these days to claim you grew up on the streets. Men tell violent tales and romanticize the lessons violence brings. But, though it was occasionally violent, it wasn't the violence in South L.A. that marked me, for sometimes you can shake that ugliness off. What finally affected me was subtler, but more pervasive: I cannot recall a young person who was crazy in love or lost in work or one old person who was passionate about a cause or an idea. I'm not talking about an absence of energy—the street toughs and, for that fact, old Cheech had energy. And I'm not talking about an absence of decency, for my father was a thoughtful man. The people I grew up with were retired from jobs that rub away the heart or were working hard at jobs to keep their lives from caving in or were anchorless and in between jobs and spouses or were diving headlong into a barren tomorrow: junkies, alcoholics, and mean kids walking along Vermont looking to throw a punch. I developed a picture of human existence that rendered it short and brutish or sad and aimless or long and quiet with rewards like afternoon naps, the evening newspaper, walks around the block, occasional letters from children in other states. When, years later, I was introduced to humanistic psychologists like Abraham Maslow and Carl Rogers, with their visions of self-actualization, or even Freud with his sober dictum about love and work, it all sounded like a glorious fairy tale, a magical account of a world full of possibility, full of hope and empowerment. Sindbad and Cinderella couldn't have been more fanciful.

Some people who manage to write their way out of the working class describe the classroom as an oasis of possibility. It became their intellectual playground, their competitive arena. Given the richness of my memories of this time, it's funny how scant are my recollections of school. I remember the red brick building of St. Regina's itself, and the topography of the playground: the swings and basketball courts and peeling benches. There are images of a few students: Erwin Petschaur, a muscular German boy with a strong accent; Dave Sanchez, who was good in math; and Sheila Wilkes, everyone's curly-haired heartthrob. And there are two nuns: Sister Monica, the third-grade teacher with beautiful hands for whom I carried a candle and who, to my dismay, had wedded herself to Christ; and Sister Beatrice, a woman truly crazed, who would sweep into class, eyes wide, to tell us about the Apocalypse.

All the hours in class tend to blend into one long, vague stretch of time. What I remember best, strangely enough, are the two things I couldn't understand and over the years grew to hate: grammar lessons and mathematics. I would sit there watching a teacher draw her long horizontal line and her short, oblique lines and break up sentences and put adjectives here and adverbs there and just not get it, couldn't see the reason for it, turned off to it. I would hide by slumping down in my seat and page through my reader, carried along by the flow of sentences in a story. She would test us, and I would dread that, for I always got Cs and Ds. Mathematics was a bit different. For whatever reasons, I didn't learn early math very well, so when it came time for more complicated operations, I couldn't keep up and started daydreaming to avoid my inadequacy. This was a strategy I would rely on as I grew older. I fell further and further behind. A memory: The teacher is faceless and seems very far away. The voice is faint and is discussing an equation written on the board. It is raining, and I am watching the streams of water form patterns on the windows.

I realize now how consistently I defended myself against the lessons I couldn't understand and the people and events of South L.A. that were too strange to view head-on. I got very good at watching a blackboard with minimum awareness. And I drifted more and more into a variety of protective fantasies. I was lucky in that although my parents didn't read or write very much and had no more than a few books around the house, they never debunked my pursuits. And when they could, they bought me what I needed to spin my web.

One early Christmas they got me a small chemistry set. My father brought home an old card table from the secondhand store, and on that table I spread out my test tubes, my beaker, my Erlenmeyer flask, and my gas-generating apparatus. The set came equipped with chemicals, minerals, and various treated papers—all in little square bottles. You could send away to someplace in Maryland for more, and I did, saving pennies and nickels to get the substances that were too exotic for my set, the Junior Chemcraft: Congo red paper, azurite, glycerine, chrome alum, cochineal—this from female insects!—tartaric acid, chameleon paper, logwood. I would sit before my laboratory and play for hours. My father rested on the purple couch in front of me watching wrestling or *Gunsmoke* while I measured powders or heated crystals or blew into solutions that my breath would turn red or pink. I was taken by the blends of names and by the colors that swirled through the beaker. My equations were visual and phonetic. I would hold a flask up to the hall light, imagining the veils of a million atoms dancing. Sulfur and alcohol hung in the air. I wanted to shake down the house.

25   One day my mother came home from Coffee Dan's with an awful story. The teenage brother of one of her waitress friends was in the hospital. He had been fooling around with explosives in his garage "where his mother couldn't see him," and something happened, and "he blew away part of his throat. For God's sake, be careful," my mother said. "Remember poor Ada's brother." Wow! I thought. How neat! Why couldn't my experiments be that dangerous? I really lost heart when I realized that you could probably eat the chemicals spread across my table.

I knew what I had to do. I saved my money for a week and then walked with firm resolve past Walt's Malts, past the brake shop, across Ninetieth Street, and into Palazolla's market. I bought a little bottle of Alka-Seltzer and ran home. I chipped up the wafers and mixed them into a jar of white crystals. When my mother came home, dog tired, and sat down on the edge of the couch to tell me and Dad about her day, I gravely poured my concoction into a beaker of water, cried something about the unexpected, and ran out from behind my table. The beaker foamed ominously. My father swore in Italian. The second time I tried it, I got something milder—in English. And by my third near-miss with death, my parents were calling my behavior cute. Cute! Who wanted cute? I wanted to toy with the disaster that befell Ada Pendleton's brother. I wanted all those wonderful colors to collide in ways that could blow your voice box right off.

But I was limited by the real. The best I could do was create a toxic antacid. I loved my chemistry set—its glassware and its intriguing labels—but it wouldn't allow me to do the things I wanted to do. St. Regina's had an all-purpose room, one wall of which was lined with old books—and one of those shelves held a row of plastic-covered space novels. The sheen of their covers was gone, and their futuristic portraits were dotted with erasures and grease spots like a meteor shower of the everyday. I remember the rockets best. Long cylinders outfitted at the base with three slick fins, tapering at the other end to a perfect conical point, ready to pierce out of the stratosphere and into my imagination: X-fifteens and Mach 1, the dark side of the moon, the Red Planet, Jupiter's Great Red Spot, Saturn's rings—and beyond the solar system to swirling wisps of galaxies, to stardust.

I would check out my books two at a time and take them home to curl up with a blanket on my chaise longue, reading, sometimes, through the weekend, my back aching, my thoughts lost between galaxies. I became the hero of a thousand adventures, all with intricate plots and the triumph of good over evil, all many dimensions removed from the dim walls of the living room. We were given time to draw in school, so, before long, all this worked itself onto paper. The stories I was reading were reshaping themselves into pictures. My father got me some butcher paper from Palazolla's, and I continued to draw at home. My collected works rendered the Horsehead Nebula, goofy space cruisers, robots, and Saturn. Each had its crayon, a particular waxy pencil with mood and meaning: rust and burnt sienna for Mars, yellow for the Sun, lime and rose for Saturn's rings, and bright red for the Jovian spot. I had a little sharpener to keep the points just right. I didn't write any stories; I just read and drew. I wouldn't care much about writing until late in high school.

The summer before the sixth grade, I got a couple of jobs. The first was at a pet store a block or so away from my house. Since I was still small, I could maneuver around in breeder cages, scraping the heaps of parakeet crap from the tin floor, cleaning the water troughs and seed trays. It was pretty awful. I would go home after work and fill the tub and soak until all the fleas and bird mites came floating to the surface, little Xs in their multiple eyes. When I heard about a job selling strawberries door-to-door, I jumped at it. I went to work for a white-haired Chicano named Frank. He would carry four or five kids and dozens of crates of strawberries in his ramshackle truck up and down the avenues of the better neighborhoods: houses with mowed lawns and petunia beds. We'd work all day for seventy-five cents, Frank dropping pairs of us off with two crates each, then picking us up at preassigned corners. We spent lots of time together, bouncing around on the truck bed redolent with strawberries or sitting on a corner, cold, listening for the sputter of Frank's muffler. I started telling the other kids about my books, and soon it was my job to fill up that time with stories.

30   Reading opened up the world. There I was, a skinny bookworm drawing the attention of street kids who, in any other circumstances, would have had me for breakfast. Like an epic tale-teller, I developed the stories as I went along, relying on a flexible plot line and a repository of heroic events. I had a great time. I sketched out trajectories with my finger on Frank's dusty truck bed. And I stretched out each story's climax, creating cliffhangers like the ones I saw in the Saturday serials. These stories created for me a temporary community.

It was around this time that fiction started leading me circuitously to a child's version of science. In addition to the space novels, St. Regina's library also had half a dozen books on astronomy—*The Golden Book of the Planets* and stuff like that—so I checked out a few of them. I liked what I read and wheedled enough change out of my father to enable me to take the bus to the public library. I discovered star maps, maps of lunar seas, charts upon charts of the solar system and the planetary moons: Rhea, Europa, Callisto, Miranda, Io. I didn't know that most of these moons were named for women—I didn't know classical mythology—but I would say their names to myself as though they had a woman's power to protect: Europa, Miranda, Io . . . The distances between stars fascinated me, as did the sizes of the big telescopes. I sent away for catalogs. Then prices fascinated me too. I wanted to drape my arm over a thousand-dollar scope and hear its motor drive whirr. I conjured a twelve-year-old's life of the astronomer: sitting up all night with potato chips and the stars, tracking the sky for supernovas, humming "Earth Angel" with the Penguins. What was my mother to do but save her tips and buy me a telescope?!

It was a little reflecting job, and I solemnly used to carry it out to the front of the house on warm summer nights, to find Venus or Alpha Centauri or trace the stars in Orion or lock onto the moon. I would lay out my star maps on the concrete, more for their magic than anything else, for I had trouble figuring them out. I was no geometer of the constellations; I was their balladeer. Those nights were very peaceful. I was far enough away from the front door and up enough from the sidewalk to make it seem as if I rested on a mound of dark silence, a mountain in Arizona, perhaps, watching the sky alive with points of light. Poor Freddie, toothless Lester whispering promises about making me feel good, the flat days, the gang fights—all this receded, for it was now me, the star child, lost in an eyepiece focused on a reflecting mirror that cradled, in its center, a shimmering moon.

The loneliness in Los Angeles fosters strange arrangements. Lou Minton was a wiry man with gaunt, chiseled features and prematurely gray hair, combed straight back. He had gone to college in the South for a year or two and kicked around the country for many more before settling in L.A. He lived in a small downtown apartment with a single window and met my mother at the counter of Coffee Dan's. He had been alone too long and eventually came to our house and became part of the family. Lou repaired washing machines, and he had a car, and he would take me to the vast, echoing library just west of Pershing Square and to the Museum of Science and Industry in Exposition Park. He bought me astronomy books, taught me how to use tools, and helped me build model airplanes from balsa wood and rice paper. As my father's health got worse, Lou took care of him.

My rhapsodic and prescientific astronomy carried me into my teens, consumed me right up till high school, losing out finally, and only, to the siren call of pubescence—that endocrine hoodoo that transmogrifies nice boys into gawky flesh fiends. My mother used to bring home *Confidential* magazine, a peep-show rag specializing in the sins of the stars, and it beckoned me mercilessly: Jayne Mansfield's cleavage, Gina Lollobrigida's eyes, innuendos about deviant sexuality, ads for Frederick's of Hollywood—spiked heels, lacy brassieres, the epiphany of silk panties on a mannequin's hips. Along with Phil Everly, I was through with counting the stars above.

35   Budding manhood. Only adults talk about adolescence budding. Kids have no choice but to talk in extremes; they're being wrenched and buffeted, rabbit-punched from inside by systemic thugs. Nothing sweet and pastoral here. Kids become ridiculous and touching at one and the same time: passionate about the trivial, fixed before the mirror, yet traversing one of the most important rites of passage in their lives—liminal people, silly and profoundly human. Given my own expertise, I fantasized about concocting the fail-safe aphrodisiac that would bring Marianne Bilpusch, the cloakroom monitor, rushing into my arms or about commanding a squadron of bosomy, linguistically mysterious astronauts like Zsa Zsa Gabor. My parents used to say that their son would have the best education they could afford. Maybe I would be a doctor. There was a public school in our neighborhood and several Catholic schools to the west. They had heard that quality schooling meant private, Catholic schooling, so they somehow got the money together to send me to Our Lady of Mercy, fifteen or so miles southwest of Ninety-first and Vermont. So much for my fantasies. Most Catholic secondary schools then were separated by gender.

It took two buses to get to Our Lady of Mercy. The first started deep in South Los Angeles and caught me at midpoint. The second drifted through neighborhoods with trees, parks, big lawns, and lots of flowers. The rides were long but were livened up by a group of South L.A. veterans whose parents also thought that Hope had set up shop in the west end of the county. There was Christy Biggars, who, at sixteen, was dealing and was, according to rumor, a pimp as well. There were Bill Cobb and Johnny Gonzales, grease-pencil artists extraordinaire, who left Nembutal-enhanced swirls of "Cobb" and "Johnny" on the corrugated walls of the bus. And then there was Tyrrell Wilson. Tyrrell was the coolest kid I knew. He ran the dozens like a metric halfback, laid down a rap that outrhymed and outpointed Cobb, whose rap was good but not great—the curse of a moderately soulful kid trapped in white skin. But it was Cobb who would sneak a radio onto the bus, and thus underwrote his patter with Little Richard, Fats Domino, Chuck Berry, the Coasters, and Ernie K. Doe's mother-in-law, an awful woman who was "sent from down below." And so it was that Christy and Cobb and Johnny G. and Tyrrell and I and assorted others picked up along the way passed our days in the back of the bus, a funny mix brought together by geography and parental desire.

Entrance to school brings with it forms and releases and assessments. Mercy relied on a series of tests, mostly the Stanford-Binet, for placement, and somehow the results of my tests got confused with those of another student named Rose. The other Rose apparently didn't do very well, for I was placed in the vocational track, a euphemism for the bottom level. Neither I nor my parents realized what this meant. We had no sense that Business Math, Typing, and English-Level D were dead ends. The current spate of reports on the schools criticizes parents for not involving themselves in the education of their children. But how would someone like Tommy Rose, with his two years of Italian schooling, know what to ask? And what sort of pressure could an exhausted waitress apply? The error went undetected, and I remained in the vocational track for two years. What a place.

My homeroom was supervised by Brother Dill, a troubled and unstable man who also taught freshman English. When his class drifted away from him, which was often, his voice would rise in paranoid accusations, and occasionally he would lose control and shake or smack us. I hadn't been there two months when one of his brisk, face-turning slaps had my glasses sliding down the aisle. Physical education was also pretty harsh. Our teacher was a stubby ex-lineman who had played old-time pro ball in the Midwest. He routinely had us grabbing our ankles to receive his stinging paddle across our butts. He did that, he said, to make men of us. "Rose," he bellowed on our first encounter; me standing geeky in line in my baggy shorts. "'Rose'? What the hell kind of name is that?"

"Italian, sir," I squeaked.

40   "Italian! Ho. Rose, do you know the sound a bag of shit makes when it hits the wall?"

"No, sir."

"Wop!"

Sophomore English was taught by Mr. Mitropetros. He was a large, bejeweled man who managed the parking lot at the Shrine Auditorium. He would crow and preen and list for us the stars he'd brushed against. We'd ask questions and glance knowingly and snicker, and all that fueled the poor guy to brag some more. Parking cars was his night job. He had little training in English, so his lesson plan for his day work had us reading the district's required text, Julius Caesar, aloud for the semester. We'd finish the play way before the twenty weeks was up, so he'd have us switch parts again and again and start again: Dave Snyder, the fastest guy at Mercy, muscling through Caesar to the breathless squeals of Calpurnia, as interpreted by Steve Fusco, a surfer who owned the school's most envied paneled wagon. Week ten and Dave and Steve would take on new roles, as would we all, and render a water-logged Cassius and a Brutus that are beyond my powers of description.

Spanish I—taken in the second year—fell into the hands of a new recruit. Mr. Montez was a tiny man, slight, five foot six at the most, soft-spoken and delicate. Spanish was a particularly rowdy class, and Mr. Montez was as prepared for it as a doily maker at a hammer throw. He would tap his pencil to a room in which Steve Fusco was propelling spitballs from his heavy lips, in which Mike Dweetz was taunting Billy Hawk, a half-Indian, half-Spanish, reed-thin, quietly explosive boy. The vocational track at Our Lady of Mercy mixed kids traveling in from South L.A. with South Bay surfers and a few Slavs and Chicanos from the harbors of San Pedro. This was a dangerous miscellany: surfers and hodads and South-Central blacks all ablaze to the metronomic tapping of Hector Montez's pencil.

45   One day Billy lost it. Out of the corner of my eye I saw him strike out with his right arm and catch Dweetz across the neck. Quick as a spasm, Dweetz was out of his seat, scattering desks, cracking Billy on the side of the head, right behind the eye. Snyder and Fusco and others broke it up, but the room felt hot and close and naked. Mr. Montez's tenuous authority was finally ripped to shreds, and I think everyone felt a little strange about that. The charade was over, and when it came down to it, I don't think any of the kids really wanted it to end this way. They had pushed and pushed and bullied their way into a freedom that both scared and embarrassed them.

Students will float to the mark you set. I and the others in the vocational classes were bobbing in pretty shallow water. Vocational education has aimed at increasing the economic opportunities of students who do not do well in our schools. Some serious programs succeed in doing that, and through exceptional teachers—like Mr. Gross in Horace's Compromise—students learn to develop hypotheses and troubleshoot, reason through a problem, and communicate effectively—the true job skills. The vocational track, however, is most often a place for those who are just not making it, a dumping ground for the disaffected. There were a few teachers who worked hard at education; young Brother Slattery, for example, combined a stern voice with weekly quizzes to try to pass along to us a skeletal outline of world history. But mostly the teachers had no idea of how to engage the imaginations of us kids who were scuttling along at the bottom of the pond.

And the teachers would have needed some inventiveness, for none of us was groomed for the classroom. It wasn't just that I didn't know things—didn't know how to simplify algebraic fractions, couldn't identify different kinds of clauses, bungled Spanish translations—but that I had developed various faulty and inadequate ways of doing algebra and making sense of Spanish. Worse yet, the years of defensive tuning out in elementary school had given me a way to escape quickly while seeming at least half alert. During my time in Voc. Ed., I developed further into a mediocre student and a somnambulant problem solver, and that affected the subjects I did have the wherewithal to handle: I detested Shakespeare; I got bored with history. My attention flitted here and there. I fooled around in class and read my books indifferently—the intellectual equivalent of playing with your food. I did what I had to do to get by, and I did it with half a mind.

But I did learn things about people and eventually came into my own socially. I liked the guys in Voc. Ed. Growing up where I did, I understood and admired physical prowess, and there was an abundance of muscle here. There was Dave Snyder, a sprinter and halfback of true quality. Dave's ability and his quick wit gave him a natural appeal, and he was welcome in any clique, though he always kept a little independent. He enjoyed acting the fool and could care less about studies, but he possessed a certain maturity and never caused the faculty much trouble. It was a testament to his independence that he included me among his friends—I eventually went out for track, but I was no jock. Owing to the Latin alphabet and a dearth of *R*s and *S*s, Snyder sat behind Rose, and we started exchanging one-liners and became friends.

There was Ted Richard, a much-touted Little League pitcher. He was chunky and had a baby face and came to Our Lady of Mercy as a seasoned street fighter. Ted was quick to laugh and he had a loud, jolly laugh, but when he got angry he'd smile a little smile, the kind that simply raises the corner of the mouth a quarter of an inch. For those who knew, it was an eerie signal. Those who didn't found themselves in big trouble, for Ted was very quick. He loved to carry on what we would come to call philosophical discussions: What is courage? Does God exist? He also loved words, enjoyed picking up big ones like *salubrious* and equivocal and using them in our conversations—laughing at himself as the word hit a chuckhole rolling off his tongue. Ted didn't do all that well in school—baseball and parties and testing the courage he'd speculated about took up his time. His textbooks were *Argosy* and *Field and Stream,* whatever newspapers he'd find on the bus stop—from *the Daily Worker* to pornography—conversations with uncles or hobos or businessmen he'd meet in a coffee shop, *The Old Man and the Sea.* With hindsight, I can see that Ted was developing into one of those rough-hewn intellectuals whose sources are a mix of the learned and the apocryphal, whose discussions are both assured and sad.

50   And then there was Ken Harvey. Ken was good-looking in a puffy way and had a full and oily ducktail and was a car enthusiast . . . a hodad. One day in religion class, he said the sentence that turned out to be one of the most memorable of the hundreds of thousands I heard in those Voc. Ed. years. We were talking

about the parable of the talents, about achievement, working hard, doing the best you can do, blah-blah-blah, when the teacher called on the restive Ken Harvey for an opinion. Ken thought about it, but just for a second, and said (with studied, minimal affect), "I just wanna be average." That woke me up. Average?! Who wants to be average? Then the athletes chimed in with the clichés that make you want to laryngectomize them, and the exchange became a platitudinous melee. At the time, I thought Ken's assertion was stupid, and I wrote him off. But his sentence has stayed with me all these years, and I think I am finally coming to understand it.

Ken Harvey was gasping for air. School can be a tremendously disorienting place. No matter how bad the school, you're going to encounter notions that don't fit with the assumptions and beliefs that you grew up with—maybe you'll hear these dissonant notions from teachers, maybe from the other students, and maybe you'll read them. You'll also be thrown in with all kinds of kids from all kinds of backgrounds, and that can be unsettling—this is especially true in places of rich ethnic and linguistic mix, like the L.A. basin. You'll see a handful of students far excel you in courses that sound exotic and that are only in the curriculum of the elite: French, physics, trigonometry. And all this is happening while you're trying to shape an identity, your body is changing, and your emotions are running wild. If you're a working-class kid in the vocational track, the options you'll have to deal with this will be constrained in certain ways: You're defined by your school as "slow"; you're placed in a curriculum that isn't designed to liberate you but to occupy you, or, if you're lucky, train you, though the training is for work the society does not esteem; other students are picking up the cues from your school and your curriculum and interacting with you in particular ways. If you're a kid like Ted Richard, you turn your back on all this and let your mind roam where it may. But youngsters like Ted are rare. What Ken and so many others do is protect themselves from such suffocating madness by taking on with a vengeance the identity implied in the vocational track. Reject the confusion and frustration by openly defining yourself as the Common Joe. Champion the average. Rely on your own good sense. Fuck this bullshit. Bullshit, of course, is everything you—and the others—fear is beyond you: books, essays, tests, academic scrambling, complexity, scientific reasoning, philosophical inquiry.

The tragedy is that you have to twist the knife in your own gray matter to make this defense work. You'll have to shut down, have to reject intellectual stimuli or diffuse them with sarcasm, have to cultivate stupidity, have to convert boredom from a malady into a way of confronting the world. Keep your vocabulary simple, act stoned when you're not or act more stoned than you are, flaunt ignorance, materialize your dreams. It is a powerful and effective defense—it neutralizes the insult and the frustration of being a vocational kid and, when perfected, it drives teachers up the wall, a delightful secondary effect. But like all strong magic, it exacts a price.

My own deliverance from the Voc. Ed. world began with sophomore biology. Every student, college prep to vocational, had to take biology, and unlike the other courses, the same person taught all sections. When teaching the vocational group, Brother Clint probably slowed down a bit or omitted a little of the fundamental biochemistry, but he used the same book and more or less the same syllabus across the board. If one class got tough, he could get tougher. He was young and powerful and very handsome, and looks and physical strength were high currency. No one gave him any trouble.

I was pretty bad at the dissecting table, but the lectures and the textbook were interesting: plastic overlays that, with each turned page, peeled away skin, then veins and muscle, then organs, down to the very bones that Brother Clint, pointer in hand, would tap out on our hanging skeleton. Dave Snyder was in big trouble, for the study of life—versus the living of it—was sticking in his craw. We worked out a code for our multiple-choice exams. He'd poke me in the back: once for the answer under *A,* twice for *B,* and so on; and when he'd hit the right one, I'd look up to the ceiling as though I were lost in thought. Poke: cytoplasm. Poke, poke: methane. Poke, poke, poke: William Harvey. Poke, poke, poke, poke: islets of Langerhans. This didn't work out perfectly, but Dave passed the course, and I mastered the dreamy look of a guy on a record jacket. And something else happened. Brother Clint puzzled over this Voc. Ed. kid who was racking up 98s and 99s on his tests. He checked the school's records and discovered the error. He recommended that I begin my junior year in the College Prep program. According to all I've read since, such a shift, as one report put it, is virtually impossible. Kids at that level rarely cross tracks. The telling thing is how chancy both my placement into and exit from Voc. Ed. was; neither I nor my parents had anything to do with it. I lived in one world during spring semester, and when I came back to school in the fall, I was living in another.

55   Switching to College Prep was a mixed blessing. I was an erratic student. I was undisciplined. And I hadn't caught onto the rules of the game: Why work hard in a class that didn't grab my fancy? I was also hopelessly behind in math. Chemistry was hard; toying with my chemistry set years before hadn't prepared me for the chemist's equations. Fortunately, the priest who taught both chemistry and second-year algebra was also the school's athletic director. Membership on the track team covered me; I knew I wouldn't get lower than a *C.* U.S. history was taught pretty well, and I did okay. But civics was taken over by a football coach who had trouble reading the textbook aloud—and reading aloud was the centerpiece of his pedagogy. College Prep at Mercy was certainly an improvement over the vocational program—at least it carried some status—but the social science curriculum was weak, and the mathematics and physical sciences were simply beyond me. I had a miserable quantitative background and ended up copying some assignments and finessing the rest as best I could. Let me try to explain how it feels to see again and again material you should once have learned but didn't.

You are given a problem. It requires you to simplify algebraic fractions or to multiply expressions containing square roots. You know this is pretty basic material because you've seen it for years. Once a teacher took some time with you, and you learned how to carry out these operations. Simple versions, anyway. But that was a year or two or more in the past, and these are more complex versions, and now you're not sure. And this, you keep telling yourself, is ninth- or even eighth-grade stuff.

Next it's a word problem. This is also old hat. The basic elements are as familiar as story characters: trains speeding so many miles per hour or shadows of buildings angling so many degrees. Maybe you know enough, have sat through enough explanations, to be able to begin setting up the problem: "If one train is going this fast . . ." or "This shadow is really one line of a triangle . . . ." Then: "Let's see . . ." "How did Jones do this?" "Hmmmm." "No." "No, that won't work." Your attention wavers. You wonder about other things: a football game, a dance, that cute new checker at the market. You try to focus on the problem again. You scribble on paper for a while, but the tension wins out and your attention flits elsewhere. You crumple the paper and begin daydreaming to ease the frustration.

The particulars will vary, but in essence this is what a number of students go through, especially those in so-called remedial classes. They open their textbooks and see once again the familiar and impenetrable formulas and diagrams and terms that have stumped them for years. There is no excitement here. *No* excitement. Regardless of what the teacher says, this is not a new challenge. There is, rather, embarrassment and frustration and, not surprisingly, some anger in being reminded once again of longstanding inadequacies. No wonder so many students finally attribute their difficulties to something inborn, organic: "That part of my brain just doesn't work." Given the troubling histories many of these students have, it's miraculous that any of them can lift the shroud of hopelessness sufficiently to make deliverance from these classes possible.

Through this entire period, my father's health was deteriorating with cruel momentum. His arteriosclerosis progressed to the point where a simple nick on his shin wouldn't heal. Eventually it ulcerated and widened. Lou Minton would come by daily to change the dressing. We tried renting an oscillating bed—which we placed in the front room—to force blood through the constricted arteries in my father's legs. The bed hummed through the night, moving in place to ward off the inevitable. The ulcer continued to spread, and the doctors finally had to amputate. My grandfather had lost his leg in a stockyard accident. Now my father too was crippled. His convalescence was slow but steady, and the doctors placed him in the Santa Monica Rehabilitation Center, a sun-bleached building that opened out onto the warm spray of the Pacific. The place gave him some strength and some color and some training in walking with an artificial leg. He did pretty well for a year or so until he slipped and broke his hip. He was confined to a wheelchair after that, and the confinement contributed to the diminishing of his body and spirit.

60   I am holding a picture of him. He is sitting in his wheelchair and smiling at the camera. The smile appears forced, unsteady, seems to quaver, though it is frozen in silver nitrate. He is in his mid-sixties and looks eighty. Late in my junior year, he had a stroke and never came out of the resulting coma. After that, I would see him only in dreams, and to this day that is how I join him. Sometimes the dreams are sad and grisly and primal: my father lying in a bed soaked with his suppuration, holding me, rocking me. But sometimes the dreams bring him back to me healthy: him talking to me on an empty street, or buying some pic-

tures to decorate our old house, or transformed somehow into someone strong and adept with tools and the physical.

Jack MacFarland couldn't have come into my life at a better time. My father was dead, and I had logged up too many years of scholastic indifference. Mr. MacFarland had a master's degree from Columbia and decided, at twenty-six, to find a little school and teach his heart out. He never took any credentialing courses, couldn't bear to, he said, so he had to find employment in a private system. He ended up at Our Lady of Mercy teaching five sections of senior English. He was a beatnik who was born too late. His teeth were stained, he tucked his sorry tie in between the third and fourth buttons of his shirt, and his pants were chronically wrinkled. At first, we couldn't believe this guy, thought he slept in his car. But within no time, he had us so startled with work that we didn't much worry about where he slept or if he slept at all. We wrote three or four essays a month. We read a book every two to three weeks, starting with the *Iliad* and ending up with Hemingway. He gave us a quiz on the reading every other day. He brought a prep school curriculum to Mercy High.

MacFarland's lectures were crafted, and as he delivered them he would pace the room jiggling a piece of chalk in his cupped hand, using it to scribble on the board the names of all the writers and philosophers and plays and novels he was weaving into his discussion. He asked questions often, raised everything from Zeno's paradox to the repeated last line of Frost's "Stopping by Woods on a Snowy Evening." He slowly and carefully built up our knowledge of Western intellectual history—with facts, with connections, with speculations. We learned about Greek philosophy, about Dante, the Elizabethan world view, the Age of Reason, existentialism. He analyzed poems with us, had us reading sections from John Ciardi's *How Does a Poem Mean?*, making a potentially difficult book accessible with his own explanations. We gave oral reports on poems Ciardi didn't cover. We imitated the styles of Conrad, Hemingway, and *Time* magazine. We wrote and talked, wrote and talked. The man immersed us in language.

Even MacFarland's barbs were literary. If Jim Fitzsimmons, hung over and irritable, tried to smart-ass him, he'd rejoin with a flourish that would spark the indomitable Skip Madison—who'd lost his front teeth in a hapless tackle—to flick his tongue through the gap and opine, "good chop," drawing out the single "o" in stinging indictment. Jack MacFarland, this tobacco-stained intellectual, brandished linguistic weapons of a kind I hadn't encountered before. Here was this *egghead*, for God's sake, keeping some pretty difficult people in line. And from what I heard, Mike Dweetz and Steve Fusco and all the notorious Voc. Ed. crowd settled down as well when MacFarland took the podium. Though a lot of guys groused in the schoolyard, it just seemed that giving trouble to this particular teacher was a silly thing to do. Tomfoolery, not to mention assault, had no place in the world he was trying to create for us, and instinctively everyone knew that. If nothing else, we all recognized MacFarland's considerable intelligence and respected the hours he put into his work. It came to this: The troublemaker would look foolish rather than daring. Even Jim Fitzsimmons was reading *On the Road* and turning his incipient alcoholism to literary ends.

There were some lives that were already beyond Jack MacFarland's ministrations, but mine was not. I started reading again as I hadn't since elementary school. I would go into our gloomy little bedroom or sit at the dinner table while, on the television, Danny McShane was paralyzing Mr. Moto with the atomic drop, and work slowly back through *Heart of Darkness,* trying to catch the words in Conrad's sentences. I certainly was not MacFarland's best student; most of the other guys in College Prep, even my fellow slackers, had better backgrounds than I did. But I worked very hard, for MacFarland had hooked me. He tapped my old interest in reading and creating stories. He gave me a way to feel special by using my mind. And he provided a role model that wasn't shaped on physical prowess alone, and something inside me that I wasn't quite aware of responded to that. Jack MacFarland established a literacy club, to borrow a phrase of Frank Smith's, and invited me—invited all of us—to join.

65   There's been a good deal of research and speculation suggesting that the acknowledgment of school performance with extrinsic rewards—smiling faces, stars, numbers, grades—diminishes the intrinsic satisfaction children experience by engaging in reading or writing or problem solving. While it's certainly true that we've created an educational system that encourages our best and brightest to become cynical grade collectors and, in general, have developed an obsession with evaluation and assessment, I must tell you that venal though it may have been, I loved getting good grades from MacFarland. I now know how subjective grades can be, but then they came tucked in the back of essays like bits of scientific data, some sort of spectroscopic readout that said, objectively and publicly, that I had made something of value. I suppose I'd been mediocre for too long and enjoyed a public redefinition. And I suppose the workings of my mind, such as they were, had been private for too long. My linguistic play moved into the world; like the intergalactic stories I told years before on Frank's berry-splattered truck bed, these papers with their circled, red B-pluses and A-minuses linked my mind to something outside it. I carried them around like a club emblem.

One day in the December of my senior year, Mr. MacFarland asked me where I was going to go to college. I hadn't thought much about it. Many of the students I teach today spent their last year in high school with a physics text in one hand and the Stanford catalog in the other, but I wasn't even aware of what "entrance requirements" were. My folks would say that they wanted me to go to college and be a doctor, but I don't know how seriously I ever took that; it seemed a sweet thing to say, a bit of supportive family chatter, like telling a gangly daughter she's graceful. The reality of higher education wasn't in my scheme of things: No one in the family had gone to college; only two of my uncles had completed high school. I figured I'd get a night job and go to the local junior college because I knew that Snyder and Company were going there to play ball. But I hadn't even prepared for that. When I finally said, "I don't know," MacFarland looked down at me—I was seated in his office—and said, "Listen, you can write."

My grades stank. I had A's in biology and a handful of B's in a few English and social science classes. All the rest were C's—or worse. MacFarland said I would do well in his class and laid down the law about doing well in the others. Still, the record for my first three years wouldn't have been acceptable to any four-year school. To nobody's surprise, I was turned down flat by USC and UCLA. But Jack MacFarland was on the case. He had received his bachelor's degree from Loyola University, so he made calls to old professors and talked to somebody in admissions and wrote me a strong letter. Loyola finally accepted me as a probationary student. I would be on trial for the first year, and if I did okay, I would be granted regular status. MacFarland also intervened to get me a loan, for I could never have afforded a private college without it. Four more years of religion classes and four more years of boys at one school, girls at another. But at least I was going to college. Amazing.

In my last semester of high school, I elected a special English course fashioned by Mr. MacFarland, and it was through this elective that there arouse at Mercy a fledgling literati. Art Mitz, the editor of the school newspaper and a very smart guy, was the kingpin. He was joined by me and by Mark Dever, a quiet boy who wrote beautifully and who would die before he was forty. MacFarland occasionally invited us to his apartment, and those visits became the high point of our apprenticeship: We'd clamp on our training wheels and drive to his salon.

He lived in a cramped and cluttered place near the airport, tucked away in the kind of building that architectural critic Reyner Banham calls a *dingbat*. Books were all over: stacked, piled, tossed, and crated, underlined and dog eared, well worn and new. Cigarette ashes crusted with coffee in saucers or spilled over the sides of motel ashtrays. The little bedroom had, along two of its walls, bricks and boards loaded with notes, magazines, and oversized books. The kitchen joined the living room, and there was a stack of German newspapers under the sink. I had never seen anything like it: a great flophouse of language furnished by City Lights and Café le Metro. I read every title. I flipped through paperbacks and scanned jackets and memorized names: Gogol, *Finnegans Wake,* Djuna Barnes, Jackson Pollock, *A Coney Island of the Mind,* F. O. Matthiessen's *American Renaissance,* all sorts of Freud, *Troubled Sleep,* Man Ray, *The Education of Henry Adams,* Richard Wright, *Film as Art,* William Butler Yeats, Marguerite Duras, *Redburn, A Season in Hell, Kapital.* On the cover of Alain-Fournier's *The Wanderer* was an Edward Gorey drawing of a young man on a road winding into dark trees. By the hotplate sat a strange Kafka novel called *Amerika,* in which an adolescent hero crosses the Atlantic to find the Nature Theater of Oklahoma. Art and Mark would be talking about a movie or the school newspaper, and I would be consuming my English teacher's library. It was heady stuff. I felt like a Pop Warner athlete on steroids.

70   Art, Mark, and I would buy stogies and triangulate from MacFarland's apartment to the Cinema, which now shows X-rated films but was then L.A.'s premiere art theater, and then to the musty Cherokee Bookstore in Hollywood to hobnob with beatnik homosexuals—smoking, drinking bourbon and coffee, and trying out awkward phrases we'd gleaned from our mentor's bookshelves. I was happy and precocious and a little scared as well, for Hollywood Boulevard

was thick with a kind of decadence that was foreign to the South Side. After the Cherokee, we would head back to the security of MacFarland's apartment, slaphappy with hipness.

Let me be the first to admit that there was a good deal of adolescent passion in this embrace of the avant-garde: self-absorption, sexually charged pedantry, an elevation of the odd and abandoned. Still it was a time during which I absorbed an awful lot of information: long lists of titles, images from expressionist paintings, new wave shibboleths, snippets of philosophy, and names that read like Steve Fusco's misspellings—Goethe, Nietzsche, Kierkegaard. Now this is hardly the stuff of deep understanding. But it was an introduction, a phrase book, a Baedeker to a vocabulary of ideas, and it felt good at the time to know all these words. With hindsight I realize how layered and important that knowledge was.

It enabled me to do things in the world. I could browse bohemian bookstores in far-off, mysterious Hollywood; I could go to the Cinema and see events through the lenses of European directors; and, most of all, I could share an evening, talk that talk, with Jack MacFarland, the man I most admired at the time. Knowledge was becoming a bonding agent. Within a year or two, the persona of the disaffected hipster would prove too cynical, too alienated to last. But for a time it was new and exciting: It provided a critical perspective on society, and it allowed me to act as though I were living beyond the limiting boundaries of South Vermont.

⩵ CRITICAL REFLECTIONS

1. In the beginning of this chapter, Mike Rose provides a thorough description of his childhood home and neighborhood. Why do you think he includes this?

2. What do you see as the purpose of school at St. Regina's and Our Lady of Mercy? What evidence from this chapter leads you to identify the purpose that you have?

3. Rose writes in this chapter that "Students will float to the mark you set. I and the others in the vocation classes were bobbing in pretty shallow water." What do you think he means by this statement? How do you think the mark gets set?

4. What do you think Ken Harvey meant when he announced in class, "I just wanna be average."

5. What do you see as the role played by MacFarland in Rose's education?

⩵ MAKING CONNECTIONS

1. Throughout this chapter, Rose hints at (but doesn't often directly address) what he sees as the potential of education and literacy. First, summarize how you think Rose understands this. Then, consider Rose's position against Booker T. Washington's. What similarities and differences do you find among their positions?

2. Consider Rose's educational experience at St. Regina's and Our Lady of Mercy against the provisions of the No Child Left Behind Act (found on the World Wide Web at www.ed.gov/offices/OESE/esea/). How do you think these schools would fare? What remedies might the Bush administration prescribe, and what do you think their effects would be?

MICHAEL RYAN

THE DITCH

This poem is included in a collection called *Working Classics: Poems on Industrial Life.* (Several other poems included here are from the same collection.) Like many poems, it provides a white-hot, intensive glimpse into a moment, rather than trying to cover a long period of time with a great many words. The author of this poem, Michael Ryan, has won numerous awards for his poetry, and has also written books about poetry. Ryan now teaches poetry and creative writing at the University of California-Irvine.

In the ditch, half-ton sections of cast-iron molds
hand-greased at the seams with pale petroleum waste
and screw-clamped into five-hundred-gallon cylinders
drummed with rubber-headed sledges inside and out
5   to settle tight the wet concrete
that, dried and caulked, became Monarch Septic Tanks;
and, across the ditch, my high school football coach,
Don Compo, spunky pug of a man,
bronze and bald, all biceps and pecs,
10   raging at some "attitude" of mine
he snipped from our argument about Vietnam—
I mean *raging*, scarlet, veins bulging from his neck,
he looked like a hard-on stalking back and forth—
but I had started college, this was a summer job,
15   I no longer had to take his self-righteous, hectoring shit,
so I was chuckling merrily, saying he was ludicrous,
and he was calling me "College Man Ryan"
and with his steel-toed workboot kicking dirt
that clattered against the molds and puffed up between us.

20   It's probably not like this anymore, but every coach
in my hometown was a lunatic. Each had different quirks
we mimicked, beloved bromides whose parodies we intoned,
but they all conducted practice like bootcamp,
the same tirades and abuse, no matter the sport,
25   the next game the next battle in a neverending war.
Ex-paratroopers and -frogmen, at least three

finally-convicted child molesters, genuine sadists
fixated on the Commie menace and our American softness
that was personally bringing the country to the brink of collapse—
30   in this company, Don Compo didn't even seem crazy.
He had never touched any of us;
his violence was verbal, which we were used to,
having gotten it from our fathers
and given it back to our brothers and to one another
35   since we had been old enough to button our own pants.

Any minute—no guessing what might spring it—
he could be butting your face-mask and barking up your nostrils,
but generally he favored an unruffled, moralistic carping
in which I, happy to spot phoniness,
40   saw pride and bitterness masquerading as teaching.
In the locker-room, I'd sit where I could roll my eyeballs
as he droned, but, across the ditch,
he wasn't lecturing, but fuming, flaring
as I had never seen in four years of football,
45   and it scared and thrilled me to defy him and mock him
when he couldn't make me handwash jockstraps after practice
or do pushups on my fingertips in a mud puddle.

But it was myself I was taunting. I could see my retorts
snowballing toward his threat to leap the ditch
50   and beat me to a puddle of piss ("you craphead,
you wiseass"), and my unspading a shovel from a dirt pile
and grasping its balance deliberately down the handle
and inviting him to try it.
Had he come I would have hit him.
55   There's no question about that.
For a moment, it ripped through our bewilderment,
which then closed over again
like the ocean
if a cast-iron mold were dropped in.
60   I was fired when the boss broke the tableau.
"The rest of you," he said, "have work to do,"
and, grabbing a hammer and chisel, Don Compo
mounted the mold between us in the ditch
and with one short punch split it down the seam.

▬▬ CRITICAL REFLECTIONS

1. The ditch is a central metaphor in this poem. What do you think it is meant to stand for?

2. What do you think this poem is about?

3. Translate Ryan's portrait of Don Compo into a narrative about him. What was he like? How does the language that Ryan uses in the poem communicate this likeness to you?

4. What role does education play in this poem for Ryan?

5. Re-create this poem in different genres: a five-paragraph theme, a fictional story, and a memo to a boss. What would each say?

⋙ MAKING CONNECTIONS

1. Don Compo refers to "College Man Ryan" in this poem. What parallels do you see between Compo's characterization and that of Mike Rose, one of the characters from "The Last Shot," or Cedric Jennings?

2. Reflect on the role of education that you have identified in this poem. Do you find similar roles in other readings included here?

EARL SHORRIS

ON THE USES OF A LIBERAL EDUCATION: II. AS A WEAPON IN THE HANDS OF THE RESTLESS POOR

This article, published in *Harper's* magazine in 1997, was paired with Mark Edmundson's "On the Uses of a Liberal Education: I. As Lite Entertainment for Bored College Students" (pages 126–139). A liberal education is one designed to help students become well-rounded thinkers with a thorough understanding of the liberal arts, which are academic subjects (like history, literature, philosophy, and mathematics) that are not necessarily tied to any particular trade or skill. Organized as they were, the two "On the Uses of a Liberal Education" articles presented two very different ideas about the purpose and definition of a liberal education and the audience for whom such an education was intended. The Clemente Course that Shorris describes here is still operating, now in over 17 locations in the United States and abroad.

Next month I will publish a book about poverty in America, but not the book I intended. The world took me by surprise—not once, but again and again. The poor themselves led me in directions I could not have imagined, especially the one that came out of a conversation in a maximum-security prison for women that is set, incongruously, in a lush Westchester suburb fifty miles north of New York City.

I had been working on the book for about three years when I went to the Bedford Hills Correctional Facility for the first time. The staff and inmates had developed a program to deal with family violence, and I wanted to see how their ideas fit with what I had learned about poverty.

Numerous forces—hunger, isolation, illness, landlords, police, abuse, neighbors, drugs, criminals, and racism, among many others—exert themselves on the poor at all times and enclose them, making up a "surround of force" from which, it seems, they cannot escape. I had come to understand that this was what kept the poor from being political and that the absence of politics in their lives was what kept them poor. I don't mean "political" in the sense of voting in an election but in the way Thucydides used the word: to mean activity with other people at every level, from the family to the neighborhood to the broader community to the city-state.

By the time I got to Bedford Hills, I had listened to more than six hundred people, some of them over the course of two or three years. Although my method is that of the bricoleur, the tinkerer who assembles a thesis of the bric-a-brac he finds in the world, I did not think there would be any more surprises. But I had not counted on what Viniece Walker was to say.

5   It is considered bad form in prison to speak of a person's crime, and I will follow that precise etiquette here. I can tell you that Viniece Walker came to Bedford Hills when she was twenty years old, a high school dropout who read at the level of a college sophomore, a graduate of crackhouses, the streets of Harlem, and a long alliance with a brutal man. On the surface Viniece has remained as tough as she was on the street. She speaks bluntly, and even though she is HIV positive and the virus has progressed during her time in prison, she still swaggers as she walks down the long prison corridors. While in prison, Niecie, as she is known to her friends, completed her high school requirements and began to pursue a college degree (psychology is the only major offered at Bedford Hills, but Niecie also took a special interest in philosophy). She became a counselor to women with a history of family violence and a comforter to those with AIDS.

Only the deaths of other women cause her to stumble in the midst of her swaggering step, to spend days alone with the remorse that drives her to seek redemption. She goes through life as if she had been imagined by Dostoevsky, but even more complex than his fictions, alive, a person, a fair-skinned and freckled African-American woman, and in prison. It was she who responded to my sudden question, "Why do you think people are poor?"

We had never met before. The conversation around us focused on the abuse of women. Niecie's eyes were perfectly opaque-hostile, prison eyes. Her mouth was set in the beginning of a sneer.

"You got to begin with the children," she said, speaking rapidly, clipping out the street sounds as they came into her speech.

She paused long enough to let the change of direction take effect, then resumed the rapid, rhythmless speech. "You've got to teach the moral life of downtown to the children. And the way you do that, Earl, is by taking them downtown to plays, museums, concerts, lectures, where they can learn the moral life of downtown."

10   I smiled at her, misunderstanding, thinking I was indulging her. "And then they won't be poor anymore?"

She read every nuance of my response, and answered angrily, "And they won't be poor no more."

"What you mean is—"

"What I mean is what I said—a moral alternative to the street."

She didn't speak of jobs or money. In that, she was like the others I had listened to. No one had spoken of jobs or money. But how could the "moral life of downtown" lead anyone out from the surround of force? How could a museum push poverty away? Who can dress in statues or eat the past? And what of the political life? Had Niecie skipped a step or failed to take a step? The way out of poverty was politics, not the "moral life of downtown." But to enter the public world, to practice the political life, the poor had first to learn to reflect. That was what Niecie meant by the "moral life of downtown." She did not make the error of divorcing ethics from politics. Niecie had simply said, in a kind of shorthand, that no one could step out of the panicking circumstance of poverty directly into the public world.

15   Although she did not say so, I was sure that when she spoke of the "moral life of downtown" she meant something that had happened to her. With no job and no money, a prisoner, she had undergone a radical transformation. She had followed the same path that led to the invention of politics in ancient Greece. She had learned to reflect. In further conversation it became clear that when she spoke of "the moral life of downtown" she meant the humanities, the study of human constructs and concerns, which has been the source of reflection for the secular world since the Greeks first stepped back from nature to experience wonder at what they beheld. If the political life was the way out of poverty, the humanities provided an entrance to reflection and the political life. The poor did not need anyone to release them; an escape route existed. But to open this avenue to reflection and politics a major distinction between the preparation for the life of the rich and the life of the poor had to be eliminated.

Once Niecie had challenged me with her theory, the comforts of tinkering came to an end; I could no longer make an homage to the happenstance world and rest. To test Niecie's theory, students, faculty, and facilities were required. Quantitative measures would have to be developed; anecdotal information would also be useful. And the ethics of the experiment had to be considered: I resolved to do no harm. There was no need for the course to have a "sink or swim" character; it could aim to keep as many afloat as possible.

When the idea for an experimental course became clear in my mind, I discussed it with Dr. Jaime Inclan, director of the Roberto Clemente Family Guidance Center in lower Manhattan, a facility that provides counseling to poor people, mainly Latinos, in their own language and in their own community. Dr. Inclan offered the center's conference room for a classroom. We would put three metal tables end to end to approximate the boat-shaped tables used in discussion sections at the University of Chicago of the Hutchins era,[1] which I used as a model for the course. A card table in the back of the room would hold a coffeemaker and a few cookies. The setting was not elegant, but it would do. And the front wall was covered by a floor-to-ceiling blackboard.

Now the course lacked only students and teachers. With no funds and a budget that grew every time a new idea for the course crossed my mind, I would have to ask the faculty to donate its time and effort. Moreover, when Hutchins said, "The best education for the best is the best education for us all," he meant it: he insisted that full professors teach discussion sections in the college. If the Clemente Course in the Humanities was to follow the same pattern, it would require a faculty with the knowledge and prestige that students might encounter in their first year at Harvard, Yale, Princeton, or Chicago.

I turned first to the novelist Charles Simmons. He had been assistant editor of *The New York Times Book Review* and had taught at Columbia University. He volunteered to teach poetry, beginning with simple poems, Housman, and ending with Latin poetry. Grace Glueck, who writes art news and criticism for the *New York Times*, planned a course that began with cave paintings and ended in the late twentieth century. Timothy Koranda, who did his graduate work at MIT, had published journal articles on mathematical logic, but he had been away from his field for some years and looked forward to getting back to it. I planned to teach the American history course through documents, beginning with the Magna Carta, moving on to the second of Locke's Two Treatises of Government, the Declaration of Independence, and so on through the documents of the Civil War. I would also teach the political philosophy class.

20   Since I was a naïf in this endeavor, it did not immediately occur to me that recruiting students would present a problem. I didn't know how many I needed. All I had were criteria for selection:

Age: 18–35.

Household income: Less than 150 percent of the Census Bureau's Official Poverty Threshold (though this was to change slightly).

Educational level: Ability to read a tabloid newspaper.

Educational goals: An expression of intent to complete the course.

Dr. Inclan arranged a meeting of community activists who could help recruit students. Lynette Lauretig of The Door, a program that provides medical and educational services to adolescents, and Angel Roman of the Grand Street Settlement, which offers work and training and GED programs, were both willing to give us

---

[1]Under the guidance of Robert Maynard Hutchins (1929–1951), the University of Chicago required year-long courses in the humanities, social sciences, and natural sciences for the Bachelor of Arts degree. Hutchins developed the curriculum with the help of Mortimer Adler, among others; the Hutchins courses later influenced Adler's Great Books program.

access to prospective students. They also pointed out some practical considerations. The course had to provide bus and subway tokens, because fares ranged between three and six dollars per class per student, and the students could not afford sixty or even thirty dollars a month for transportation. We also had to offer dinner or a snack, because the classes were to be held from 6:00 to 7:30 P.M.

The first recruiting session came only a few days later. Nancy Mamis-King, associate executive director of the Neighborhood Youth & Family Services program in the South Bronx, had identified some Clemente Course candidates and had assembled about twenty of her clients and their supervisors in a circle of chairs in a conference room. Everyone in the room was black or Latino, with the exception of one social worker and me.

After I explained the idea of the course, the white social worker was the first to ask a question: "Are you going to teach African history?"

"No. We'll be teaching a section on American history, based on documents, as I said. We want to teach the ideas of history so that—"

"You have to teach African history."

25 "This is America, so we'll teach American history. If we were in Africa, I would teach African history, and if we were in China, I would teach Chinese history."

"You're indoctrinating people in Western culture."

I tried to get beyond her. "We'll study African art," I said, "as it affects art in America. We'll study American history and literature; you can't do that without studying African-American culture, because culturally all Americans are black as well as white, Native American, Asian, and so on." It was no use; not one of them applied for admission to the course.

A few days later Lynette Lauretig arranged a meeting with some of her staff at The Door. We disagreed about the course. They thought it should be taught at a much lower level. Although I could not change their views, they agreed to assemble a group of Door members who might be interested in the humanities.

On an early evening that same week, about twenty prospective students were scheduled to meet in a classroom at The Door. Most of them came late. Those who arrived first slumped in their chairs, staring at the floor or greeting me with sullen glances. A few ate candy or what appeared to be the remnants of a meal. The students were mostly black and Latino, one was Asian, and five were white; two of the whites were immigrants who had severe problems with English. When I introduced myself, several of the students would not shake my hand, two or three refused even to look at me, one girl giggled, and the last person to volunteer his name, a young man dressed in a Tommy Hilfiger sweatshirt and wearing a cap turned sideways, drawled, "Henry Jones, but they call me Sleepy, because I got these sleepy eyes—"

30 "In our class, we'll call you Mr. Jones."

He smiled and slid down in his chair so that his back was parallel to the floor.

Before I finished attempting to shake hands with the prospective students, a waiflike Asian girl with her mouth half-full of cake said, "Can we get on with it? I'm bored."

I liked the group immediately.

Having failed in the South Bronx, I resolved to approach these prospective students differently. "You've been cheated," I said. "Rich people learn the humanities; you didn't. The humanities are a foundation for getting along in the world, for thinking, for learning to reflect on the world instead of just reacting to whatever force is turned against you. I think the humanities are one of the ways to become political, and I don't mean political in the sense of voting in an election but in the broad sense." I told them Thucydides' definition of politics.

35   "Rich people know politics in that sense. They know how to negotiate instead of using force. They know how to use politics to get along, to get power. It doesn't mean that rich people are good and poor people are bad. It simply means that rich people know a more effective method for living in this society.

"Do all rich people, or people who are in the middle, know the humanities? Not a chance. But some do. And it helps. It helps to live better and enjoy life more. Will the humanities make you rich? Yes. Absolutely. But not in terms of money. In terms of life.

"Rich people learn the humanities in private schools and expensive universities. And that's one of the ways in which they learn the political life. I think that is the real difference between the haves and have-nots in this country. If you want real power, legitimate power, the kind that comes from the people and belongs to the people, you must understand politics. The humanities will help.

"Here's how it works: We'll pay your subway fare; take care of your children, if you have them; give you a snack or a sandwich; provide you with books and any other materials you need. But we'll make you think harder, use your mind more fully, than you ever have before. You'll have to read and think about the same kinds of ideas you would encounter in a first-year course at Harvard or Yale or Oxford.

"You'll have to come to class in the snow and the rain and the cold and the dark. No one will coddle you, no one will slow down for you. There will be tests to take, papers to write. And I can't promise you anything but a certificate of completion at the end of the course. I'll be talking to colleges about giving credit for the course, but I can't promise anything. If you come to the Clemente Course, you must do it because you want to study the humanities, because you want a certain kind of life, a richness of mind and spirit. That's all I offer you: philosophy, poetry, art history, logic, rhetoric, and American history.

40   "Your teachers will all be people of accomplishment in their fields," I said, and I spoke a little about each teacher. "That's the course. October through May, with a two-week break at Christmas. It is generally accepted in America that the liberal arts and the humanities in particular belong to the elites. I think you're the elites."

The young Asian woman said, "What are you getting out of this?"

"This is a demonstration project. I'm writing a book. This will be proof, I hope, of my idea about the humanities. Whether it succeeds or fails will be up to the teachers and you."

All but one of the prospective students applied for admission to the course.

I repeated the new presentation at the Grand Street Settlement and at other places around the city. There were about fifty candidates for the thirty positions in the course. Personal interviews began in early September.

45   Meanwhile, almost all of my attempts to raise money had failed. Only the novelist Starling Lawrence, who is also editor in chief of W. W. Norton, which had contracted to publish the book; the publishing house itself; and a small, private family foundation supported the experiment. We were far short of our budgeted expenses, but my wife, Sylvia, and I agreed that the cost was still very low, and we decided to go ahead.

Of the fifty prospective students who showed up at the Clemente Center for personal interviews, a few were too rich (a postal supervisor's son, a fellow who claimed his father owned a factory in Nigeria that employed sixty people) and more than a few could not read. Two home-care workers from Local 1199 could not arrange their hours to enable them to take the course. Some of the applicants were too young: a thirteen-year-old and two who had just turned sixteen.

Lucia Medina, a woman with five children who told me that she often answered the door at the single-room occupancy hotel where she lived with a butcher knife in her hand, was the oldest person accepted into the course. Carmen Quinones, a recovering addict who had spent time in prison, was the next eldest. Both were in their early thirties.

The interviews went on for days.

Abel Lomas[2] shared an apartment and worked part-time wrapping packages at Macy's. His father had abandoned the family when Abel was born. His mother was murdered by his stepfather when Abel was thirteen. With no one to turn to and no place to stay, he lived on the streets, first in Florida, then back in New York City. He used the tiny stipend from his mother's Social Security to keep himself alive.

50   After the recruiting session at The Door, I drove up Sixth Avenue from Canal Street with Abel, and we talked about ethics. He had a street tough's delivery, spitting out his ideas in crudely formed sentences of four, five, eight words, strings of blunt declarations, with never a dependent clause to qualify his thoughts. He did not clear his throat with badinage, as timidity teaches us to do, nor did he waste his breath with tact.

"What do you think about drugs?" he asked, the strangely breathless delivery further coarsened by his Dominican accent. "My cousin is a dealer."

"I've seen a lot of people hurt by drugs."

"Your family has nothing to eat. You sell drugs. What's worse? Let your family starve or sell drugs?"

"Starvation and drug addiction are both bad, aren't they?"

55   "Yes," he said, not "yeah" or "uh-huh" but a precise, almost formal "yes."

"So it's a question of the worse of two evils? How shall we decide?"

The question came up near Thirty-fourth Street, where Sixth Avenue remains hellishly traffic-jammed well into the night. Horns honked, people flooded into the street against the light. Buses and trucks and taxicabs threatened their way from one lane to the next where the overcrowded avenue crosses the equally

---

[2]Not his real name.

crowded Broadway. As we passed Herald Square and made our way north again, I said, "There are a couple of ways to look at it. One comes from Immanuel Kant, who said that you should not do anything unless you want it to become a universal law; that is, unless you think it's what everybody should do. So Kant wouldn't agree to selling drugs or letting your family starve."

Again he answered with a formal "Yes."

"There's another way to look at it, which is to ask what is the greatest good for the greatest number: in this case, keeping your family from starvation or keeping tens, perhaps hundreds of people from losing their lives to drugs. So which is the greatest good for the greatest number?"

60   "That's what I think," he said.

"What?"

"You shouldn't sell drugs. You can always get food to eat. Welfare. Something."

"You're a Kantian."

"Yes."

65   "You know who Kant is?"

"I think so."

We had arrived at Seventy-seventh Street, where he got out of the car to catch the subway before I turned east. As he opened the car door and the light came on, the almost military neatness of him struck me. He had the newly cropped hair of a cadet. His clothes were clean, without a wrinkle. He was an orphan, a street kid, an immaculate urchin. Within a few weeks he would be nineteen years old, the Social Security payments would end, and he would have to move into a shelter.

Some of those who came for interviews were too poor. I did not think that was possible when we began, and I would like not to believe it now, but it was true. There is a point at which the level of forces that surround the poor can become insurmountable, when there is no time or energy left to be anything but poor. Most often I could not recruit such people for the course; when I did, they soon dropped out.

Over the days of interviewing, a class slowly assembled. I could not then imagine who would last the year and who would not. One young woman submitted a neatly typed essay that said, "I was homeless once, then I lived for some time in a shelter. Right now, I have got my own space granted by the Partnership for the Homeless. Right now, I am living alone, with very limited means. Financially I am overwhelmed by debts. I cannot afford all the food I need . . ."

70   A brother and sister, refugees from Tashkent, lived with their parents in the farthest reaches of Queens, far beyond the end of the subway line. They had no money, and they had been refused admission by every school to which they had applied. I had not intended to accept immigrants or people who had difficulty with the English language, but I took them into the class.

I also took four who had been in prison, three who were homeless, three who were pregnant, one who lived in a drugged dream-state in which she was abused, and one whom I had known for a long time and who was dying of AIDS. As I listened to them, I wondered how the course would affect them. They had no public life, no place; they lived within the surround of force, moving as fast as they could, driven by necessity, without a moment to reflect. Why should they care about fourteenth-century Italian painting or truth tables or the death of Socrates?

Between the end of recruiting and the orientation session that would open the course, I made a visit to Bedford Hills to talk with Niecie Walker. It was hot, and the drive up from the city had been unpleasant. I didn't yet know Niecie very well. She didn't trust me, and I didn't know what to make of her. While we talked, she held a huge white pill in her hand. "For AIDS," she said.

"Are you sick?"

"My T-cell count is down. But that's neither here nor there. Tell me about the course, Earl. What are you going to teach?"

75   "Moral philosophy."

"And what does that include?"

She had turned the visit into an interrogation. I didn't mind. At the end of the conversation I would be going out into "the free world"; if she wanted our meeting to be an interrogation, I was not about to argue. I said, "We'll begin with Plato: the *Apology,* a little of the *Crito,* a few pages of the *Phaedo* so that they'll know what happened to Socrates. Then we'll read Aristotle's *Nicomachean Ethics.* I also want them to read Thucydides, particularly *Pericles' Funeral Oration* in order to make the connection between ethics and politics, to lead them in the direction I hope the course will take them. Then we'll end with Antigone, but read as moral and political philosophy as well as drama."

"There's something missing," she said, leaning back in her chair, taking on an air of superiority.

The drive had been long, the day was hot, the air in the room was dead and damp. "Oh, yeah," I said, "and what's that?"

80   "Plato's *Allegory of the Cave.* How can you teach philosophy to poor people without the *Allegory of the Cave*? The ghetto is the cave.

Education is the light. Poor people can understand that."

At the beginning of the orientation at the Clemente Center a week later, each teacher spoke for a minute or two. Dr. Inclan and his research assistant, Patricia Vargas, administered the questionnaire he had devised to measure, as best he could, the role of force and the amount of reflection in the lives of the students. I explained that each class was going to be videotaped as another way of documenting the project. Then I gave out the first assignment: "In preparation for our next meeting, I would like you to read a brief selection from Plato's Republic: the Allegory of the Cave."

I tried to guess how many students would return for the first class. I hoped for twenty, expected fifteen, and feared ten. Sylvia, who had agreed to share the administrative tasks of the course, and I prepared coffee and cookies for twenty-five. We had a plastic container filled with subway tokens. Thanks to Starling Lawrence, we had thirty copies of Bernard Knox's *Norton Book of Classical Literature,* which contained all of the texts for the philosophy section except the *Republic* and the *Nicomachean Ethics.*

At six o'clock there were only ten students seated around the long table, but by six-fifteen the number had doubled, and a few minutes later two more straggled in out of the dusk. I had written a time line on the blackboard, showing them the temporal progress of thinking—from the role of myth in Neolithic societies to *The Gilgamesh Epic* and forward to the Old Testament, Confucius, the Greeks, the New Testament, the Koran, the Epic of SonJara, and ending with Nahuatl and Maya poems, which took us up to the contact between Europe and America, where the history course began. The time line served as context and geography as well as history: no race, no major culture was ignored. "Let's agree," I told them, "that we are all human, whatever our origins. And now let's go into Plato's cave."

85   I told them that there would be no lectures in the philosophy section of the course; we would use the Socratic method, which is called maieutic dialogue. "'Maieutic' comes from the Greek word for midwifery. I'll take the role of midwife in our dialogue. Now, what do I mean by that? What does a midwife do?"

It was the beginning of a love affair, the first moment of their infatuation with Socrates. Later, Abel Lomas would characterize that moment in his no-nonsense fashion, saying that it was the first time anyone had ever paid attention to their opinions.

Grace Glueck began the art history class in a darkened room lit with slides of the Lascaux caves and next turned the students' attention to Egypt, arranging for them to visit the Metropolitan Museum of Art to see the Temple of Dendur and the Egyptian Galleries. They arrived at the museum on a Friday evening. Darlene Codd brought her two-year-old son. Pearl Lau was late, as usual. One of the students, who had told me how much he was looking forward to the museum visit, didn't show up, which surprised me. Later I learned that he had been arrested for jumping a turnstile in a subway station on his way to the museum and was being held in a prison cell under the Brooklyn criminal courthouse. In the Temple of Dendur, Samantha Smoot asked questions of Felicia Blum, a museum lecturer. Samantha was the student who had burst out with the news, in one of the first sessions of the course, that people in her neighborhood believed it "wasn't no use goin' to school, because the white man wouldn't let you up no matter what." But in a hall where the statuary was of half-human, half-animal female figures, it was Samantha who asked what the glyphs meant, encouraging Felicia Blum to read them aloud, to translate them into English. Toward the end of the evening, Grace led the students out of the halls of antiquities into the Rockefeller Wing, where she told them of the connections of culture and art in Mali, Benin, and the Pacific Islands. When the students had collected their coats and stood together near the entrance to the museum, preparing to leave, Samantha stood apart, a tall, slim young woman, dressed in a deerstalker cap and a dark blue peacoat. She made an exaggerated farewell wave at us and returned to Egypt—her ancient mirror.

Charles Simmons began the poetry class with poems as puzzles and laughs. His plan was to surprise the class, and he did. At first he read the poems aloud to them, interrupting himself with footnotes to bring them along. He showed them poems of love and of seduction, and satiric commentaries on those poems by later poets. "Let us read," the students demanded, but Charles refused. He tantalized them with the opportunity to read poems aloud. A tug-of-war began between him and the students, and the standoff was ended not by Charles directly but by Hector Anderson. When Charles asked if anyone in the class wrote poetry, Hector raised his hand.

"Can you recite one of your poems for us?" Charles said.

90   Until that moment, Hector had never volunteered a comment, though he had spoken well and intelligently when asked. He preferred to slouch in his chair, dressed in full camouflage gear, wearing a nylon stocking over his hair and eating slices of fresh cantaloupe or honeydew melon.

In response to Charles's question, Hector slid up to a sitting position. "If you turn that camera off," he said. "I don't want anybody using my lyrics." When he was sure the red light of the video camera was off, Hector stood and recited verse after verse of a poem that belonged somewhere in the triangle formed by Ginsberg's Howl, the Book of Lamentations, and hip-hop. When Charles and the students finished applauding, they asked Hector to say the poem again, and he did. Later Charles told me, "That kid is the real thing." Hector's discomfort with Sylvia and me turned to ease. He came to our house for a small Christmas party and at other times. We talked on the telephone about a scholarship program and about what steps he should take next in his education. I came to know his parents. As a student, he began quietly, almost secretly, to surpass many of his classmates.

Timothy Koranda was the most professorial of the professors. He arrived precisely on time, wearing a hat of many styles—part fedora, part Borsalino, part Stetson, and at least one-half World War I campaign hat. He taught logic during class hours, filling the blackboard from floor to ceiling, wall to wall, drawing the intersections of sets here and truth tables there and a great square of oppositions in the middle of it all. After class, he walked with students to the subway, chatting about Zen or logic or Heisenberg.

On one of the coldest nights of the winter, he introduced the students to logic problems stated in ordinary language that they could solve by reducing the phrases to symbols. He passed out copies of a problem, two pages long, then wrote out some of the key phrases on the blackboard. "Take this home with you," he said, "and at our next meeting we shall see who has solved it. I shall also attempt to find the answer."

By the time he finished writing out the key phrases, however, David Iskhakov raised his hand. Although they listened attentively, neither David nor his sister Susana spoke often in class. She was shy, and he was embarrassed at his inability to speak perfect English.

95   "May I go to blackboard?" David said. "And will see if I have found correct answer to zis problem."

Together Tim and David erased the blackboard, then David began covering it with signs and symbols. "If first man is earning this money, and second man is closer to this town . . . ," he said, carefully laying out the conditions. After five minutes or so, he said, "And the answer is: B will get first to Cleveland!"

Samantha Smoot shouted, "That's not the answer. The mistake you made is in the first part there, where it says who earns more money."

Tim folded his arms across his chest, happy. "I shall let you all take the problem home," he said.

When Sylvia and I left the Clemente Center that night, a knot of students was gathered outside, huddled against the wind. Snow had begun to fall, a slippery powder on the gray ice that covered all but a narrow space down the center of the sidewalk. Samantha and David stood in the middle of the group, still arguing over the answer to the problem. I leaned in for a moment to catch the character of the argument. It was even more polite than it had been in the classroom, because now they governed themselves.

100   One Saturday morning in January, David Howell telephoned me at home. "Mr. Shores," he said, Anglicizing my name, as many of the students did.

"Mr. Howell," I responded, recognizing his voice.

"How you doin', Mr. Shores?"

"I'm fine. How are you?"

"I had a little problem at work." Uh-oh, I thought, bad news was coming. David is a big man, generally good-humored but with a quick temper. According to his mother, he had a history of violent behavior. In the classroom he had been one of the best students, a steady man, twenty-four years old, who always did the reading assignments and who often made interesting connections between the humanities and daily life. "What happened?"

105   "Mr. Shores, there's a woman at my job, she said some things to me and I said some things to her. And she told my supervisor I had said things to her, and he called me in about it. She's forty years old and she don't have no social life, and I have a good social life, and she's jealous of me."

"And then what happened?" The tone of his voice and the timing of the call did not portend good news.

"Mr. Shores, she made me so mad, I wanted to smack her up against the wall. I tried to talk to some friends to calm myself down a little, but nobody was around."

"And what did you do?" I asked, fearing this was his one telephone call from the city jail. "Mr. Shores, I asked myself, 'What would Socrates do?'"

David Howell had reasoned that his coworker's envy was not his problem after all, and he had dropped his rage.

110   One evening, in the American history section, I was telling the students about Gordon Wood's ideas in *The Radicalism of the American Revolution*. We were talking about the revolt by some intellectuals against classical learning at the turn of the eighteenth century, including Benjamin Franklin's late-life change of heart, when Henry Jones raised his hand.

"If the Founders loved the humanities so much, how come they treated the natives so badly?"

I didn't know how to answer this question. There were confounding explanations to offer about changing attitudes toward Native Americans, vaguely useful references to views of Rousseau and James Fenimore Cooper. For a moment I wondered if I should tell them about Heidegger's Nazi past. Then I saw Abel Lomas's raised hand at the far end of the table. "Mr. Lomas," I said.

Abel said, "That's what Aristotle means by incontinence, when you know what's morally right but you don't do it, because you're overcome by your passions."

The other students nodded. They were all inheritors of wounds caused by the incontinence of educated men; now they had an ally in Aristotle, who had given them a way to analyze the actions of their antagonists.

115   Those who appreciate ancient history understand the radical character of the humanities. They know that politics did not begin in a perfect world but in a so-

ciety even more flawed than ours: one that embraced slavery, denied the rights of women, practiced a form of homosexuality that verged on pedophilia, and endured the intrigues and corruption of its leaders. The genius of that society originated in man's re-creation of himself through the recognition of his humanness as expressed in art, literature, rhetoric, philosophy, and the unique notion of freedom. At that moment, the isolation of the private life ended and politics began.

The winners in the game of modern society, and even those whose fortune falls in the middle, have other means to power: they are included at birth. They know this. And they know exactly what to do to protect their place in the economic and social hierarchy. As Allan Bloom, author of the nationally best-selling tract in defense of elitism, *The Closing of the American Mind,* put it, they direct the study of the humanities exclusively at those young people who "have been raised in comfort and with the expectation of ever increasing comfort."

In the last meeting before graduation, the Clemente students answered the same set of questions they'd answered at orientation. Between October and May, students had fallen to AIDS, pregnancy, job opportunities, pernicious anemia, clinical depression, a schizophrenic child, and other forces, but of the thirty students admitted to the course, sixteen had completed it, and fourteen had earned credit from Bard College. Dr. Inclan found that the students' self-esteem and their abilities to divine and solve problems had significantly increased; their use of verbal aggression as a tactic for resolving conflicts had significantly decreased. And they all had notably more appreciation for the concepts of benevolence, spirituality, universalism, and collectivism.

It cost about $2,000 for a student to attend the Clemente Course. Compared with unemployment, welfare, or prison, the humanities are a bargain. But coming into possession of the faculty of reflection and the skills of politics leads to a choice for the poor—and whatever they choose, they will be dangerous: they may use politics to get along in a society based on the game, to escape from the surround of force into a gentler life, to behave as citizens, and nothing more; or they may choose to oppose the game itself. No one can predict the effect of politics, although we all would like to think that wisdom goes our way. That is why the poor are so often mobilized and so rarely politicized. The possibility that they will adopt a moral view other than that of their mentors can never be discounted.

And who wants to run that risk?

120   On the night of the first Clemente Course graduation, the students and their families filled the eighty-five chairs we crammed into the conference room where classes had been held. Robert Martin, associate dean of Bard College, read the graduates' names. David Dinkins, the former mayor of New York City, handed out the diplomas. There were speeches and presentations. The students gave me a plaque on which they had misspelled my name. I offered a few words about each student, congratulated them, and said finally, "This is what I wish for you: May you never be more active than when you are doing nothing . . ." I saw their smiles of recognition at the words of Cato, which I had written on the blackboard early in the course. They could recall again too the moment when we had come to the denouement of Aristotle's brilliantly constructed thriller, the *Nicomachean Ethics*—the idea that in the contemplative life man was most like

God. One or two, perhaps more of the students, closed their eyes. In the momentary stillness of the room it was possible to think.

The Clemente Course in the Humanities ended a second year in June 1997. Twenty-eight new students had enrolled; fourteen graduated. Another version of the course will begin this fall in Yucatan, Mexico, using classical Maya literature in Maya.

On May 14, 1997, Viniece Walker came up for parole for the second time. She had served more than ten years of her sentence, and she had been the best of prisoners. In a version of the Clemente Course held at the prison, she had been my teaching assistant. After a brief hearing, her request for parole was denied. She will serve two more years before the parole board will reconsider her case.

A year after graduation, ten of the first sixteen Clemente Course graduates were attending four-year colleges or going to nursing school; four of them had received full scholarships to Bard College. The other graduates were attending community college or working full-time. Except for one: she had been fired from her job in a fast-food restaurant for trying to start a union.

▰▰ CRITICAL REFLECTIONS

1. One of the central themes of this article is what kind of knowledge people need to have a voice in the dominant culture, who gets to amass that knowledge, and how it is amassed. What kind of knowledge do *you* think people need for this voice? Who has it, and how do they get it?

2. Viniece Walker tells Shorris that she thinks people won't be poor when they can learn "the moral life of downtown." What do you think she means by this? Based on an analysis of the curriculum used for the Clemente Course, what are the ideas that you think Shorris sees as central for participating in "the moral life of downtown"?

3. What do you think Shorris sees as the purpose of education?

4. When he talks to prospective students, Shorris tells them that "Rich people learn the humanities in private schools and expensive universities. And that's one of the ways in which they learn the political life. If you want real power, legitimate power . . . you must understand politics. The humanities will help" (192). Do you agree with Shorris's statements about who learns humanities and why the humanities are important? Why or why not?

▰▰ MAKING CONNECTIONS

1. In "How They've Fared in Education," Harry Graham makes a sharp distinction between educated and uneducated people and practices. Here, Viniece Walker identifies a line between people who do and do not participate in "the moral life of downtown." Do you think participation in that life, or being considered educated, makes a difference? Why or why not?

2. While talking about the Clemente Course with students, Shorris tells them that "It is generally accepted in America that the liberal arts and the humanities in particular belong to the elites." How do you think the students that Edmundson writes about would respond to this idea?

3. Responding to a comment from one of the basketball players featured in "The Last Shot" (on pages 240–265), author Darcy Frey writes that while writing the article, "I have tried to ignore our racial differences in an attempt at some broader understanding. Stephon's [the player's] comment may be his way of telling me that understanding begins with race." In the discussion of Shorris' conversations with (and about) students, and in the Clemente curriculum, do you think Shorris is mindful of this idea? Why or why not?

RON SUSKIND

FIERCE INTIMACIES

"Fierce Intimacies" is one chapter from *Wall Street Journal* reporter Ron Suskind's book, *A Hope in the Unseen.* For the book, Suskind chronicled the first-year experience of Cedric Jennings. Brown first encountered Cedric Jennings when writing a story about students who attended under-funded, challenged high schools but wished to attain academic success. Suskind became so interested in Cedric's experiences that he decided to follow him from his school, located in an economically impoverished area in Washington, D.C., to Brown University, an Ivy League university in Providence, Rhode Island. Cedric's high school and his neighborhood were predominantly African-American. When Cedric arrived at Brown he not only encountered academic challenges unlike any he had before, but he also found himself immersed in a culture where it seemed everyone else shared common knowledge and interests about which Cedric knew very little. In this chapter, Cedric is experiencing tension with his roommate, Ron, and trying to work out friendships with Zayd, a Caucasian student whom Cedric feels understands elements of his culture, and Chaniqua, an African-American student who had a very different experience before coming to Brown. At the same time, Cedric is trying to understand how and where he can fit into the world of academics and intellectual activity at Brown.

The freckled blonde girl sitting to Cedric's right in History of Education—8:30 A.M. to 9:50, M, W—is leading the class . . . in sleep. It's a mere ten minutes into this morning's lecture, the last in September, and she's already gone, chin buried in her collar, head bobbing gently.

Public sleeping has a way of spreading across a lecture hall. Someone hears soft, steady breathing from a neighboring desk and soon offers an accompaniment, which is why eyelids are drooping at desks near the blonde in what soon will become an informal sleep study.

Professor Tom James, a sort of opaque, soft-spoken man in his early forties, is no match for the lack of natural light and the humming ventilation system in this basement classroom. Still, he pushes forward gamely—there's a lot of ground to cover in this survey course—and by 8:55 he's tying social characteristics of late-eighteenth-century American progressives to the emergence of public educational institutions, schools that carried, he asserts, "an evangelical fervor in what they saw as the serious business of educating youngsters, especially the hoards of immigrants."

Cedric looks over at the sleepers and shakes his head. "How can they sleep?" he murmurs under his breath. "They must already know this stuff." He turns back to his notebook and scribbles "immigrant."

5   "How many of you have been to Ellis Island?" James asks, drawing ten hands out of the thirty attendees, a high ratio among the conscious. Ellis Island is not a core concept in Southeast Washington (it is, in fact, the sort of white people's history often passed over in favor of Afrocentric studies), and Cedric has never heard the reference. He jots the word "Ellis" on his pad. It floats on a white sea, without context.

"What happened to that evangelical fervor?" James asks the class. "Have we lost it along the way?"

On Cedric's left is his unit-mate Maura McLarty, a red-haired Irish girl bred in the strong public schools of Andover, Massachusetts, daughter of an administrative judge. Already on her third page of precise notes, she listens intently as a talkative student in the first row parries with James on the "evangelical fervor" question. The religious metaphors, meanwhile, prompt Cedric to put down his pencil on a thin half-page of scribbles and daydream of Scripture Cathedral.

One month into this new world of higher education, Cedric Jennings's chin is barely above the waterline. So many class discussions are full of references he doesn't understand—he often feels like a foreigner, like one of those Asian kids he sees in the math lab who can barely speak English but integrate fractions at blinding speed. By now, he understands that Maura *knows* what to write on her pad and the sleepers *will* be able to skim the required readings, all of them guided by some mysterious encoded knowledge of history, economics, and education, of culture and social events, that they picked up in school or at home or God knows where.

Class is dismissed, and Cedric nods a farewell to Maura and moves quickly for the door, happy to be alone as he walks across campus to Spanish, a class that offers a brief respite. There, at least, everyone stumbles along on the same uncertain footing of *cómo estás* and *bastante biens* and he doesn't feel as conspicuous or obtuse or ill prepared as he does in education class . . . and almost everywhere else he goes at Brown.

10   The day is sunny and splendid. Blazing yellow and red leaves that draw peepers to this part of New England are crunching under his Nikes. The thing he loves most, he decides, is walking between classes, a time he can feel purposeful, like he's on his way somewhere.

After Spanish, he affords himself an indulgence. Dr. Korb sends him $200 on the 15th of each month for miscellaneous costs and spending money. The money tends to go fast, but today he still has a little left from the September check, and he decides to go out for lunch.

All it takes to eat well at Cafe Paragon on Thayer Street, where the eavesdropping is superb, is $10. Every stratum of the Brown society is represented here—from godlike tenured don to midlevel administrators, assistant and associate profs, grad students and lowly undergraduates. The atmospherics are mixed just right. The music is Euro-funk, edgy but quiet enough to allow for easy conversation at the closely packed mahogany tables. The waitresses are a carefully selected sampling of the university's comeliest females in all-black outfits, the skin-snug tank tops provided by management. Here, gentleman profs can drink musty Warsteiner Ale or Italian Perini Beer (both $3.25) to wash down a thoroughly adequate burger ($2.50). For undergraduates, meanwhile, the Paragon is a just affordable luxury of theoretical adulthood and an escape from Food Service cold cuts—though, usually, freshmen get carded.

On this sunny, unseasonably warm Wednesday in late September, the place is jammed. Of the many issues to discuss, affirmative action is proving the ideal back-to-school subject. Stoking long-standing disputes on the subject, there is news of late, starting with July's decision by the California Board of Regents to end preferential admissions based on race and this fall's demonstrations at the University of California at Berkeley and elsewhere by minority students.

At Brown, like most top private institutions, affirmative action is offered to "less qualified" and "underrepresented" minority students. Yet, like at its peer institutions, Brown's bold initiative doesn't go much beyond the offer of admission. Once they arrive, affirmative action kids are generally left to sink or swim academically. Brown offers plenty of counseling and tutoring to struggling students, but, as any academic dean will tell you, it's up to the students to seek it out, something that a drowning minority student will avoid at all costs, fearing it will trumpet a second-class status that he or she may fear classmates have suspected from the first. Not surprisingly, dropout rates among minorities, particularly those of lower income, tend to be higher than the rest.

15   On all sides of this carefully parsed, middle-ground policy are encampments of passionately intense discussion. At the cafe today are several exchanges on the subject. Cedric, settling at a table inside, orders a ginger ale and trains his ears to a table immediately to his right. Two professors, both white, are leaning in close over a pair of Anchor Steams.

"Are we doing a service to young people to boost them above their academic level and then not offer the services they need?" asks the squat one with flying gray hair. "Because, who really can? Who can offer that sort of enrichment? You can hardly blame the university. It would take years, and money, and a whole different educational track to bring some affirmative action students to a level where they could compete. There's no choice but laissez-faire, sink or swim. They should be going to middle-rung universities. There's no right, as far as I see, to go to an Ivy League institution. If they work hard, their kids can come here. Hell, it's what everyone else had to do."

As his burger arrives, Cedric listens and pretends to read the *Brown Daily Herald,* the student newspaper. Eventually, the professors are drowned out by loud conversation at the table on his other side. It's all Cedric can do not to respond. Their words make him think of Leon Trilling and what he said. He imagines telling them about his long journey, that his struggle has built in him a kind of strength—a conviction about his ability to overcome obstacles—that other kids don't have. But of course that strength is hard to measure, and lately he's become uncertain if it will be enough to get him where he needs to be.

The loud people pay their check and leave. The professors, meanwhile, have moved on to the companion controversy about hiring minority faculty members. "It's a mockery," the other professor, a tall, distinguished-looking guy, spits, ticking off the names of a few minority professors around campus. "A lot of them are good teachers, sure. But they're unpublished, not respected, not scholars. What do they bring? Their passionate, oh-so personal 'perspective.' Nothing special about that. Jesus, everyone's got one of those."

Faculty club interlocutions over "publish or perish" or how affirmative action exacerbates the conflict between the magnetic lecturers and the dogged scholars are not on Cedric's radar. He manages to be dismissive, digging into his burger, his $2.50 indulgence.

20 A few minutes later, he emerges from the restaurant and passes a clutch of wrought-iron tables on the sidewalk, favored spots in the warm sun. He spots Stephan Wheelock, his Richard Wright instructor, twenty-four and black and bursting with passionate personal perspective. Stephan is eating a barbecued chicken sandwich with a friend, a thirty-something white guy who's visiting Providence. Cedric waves and offers a cursory hello as he passes.

Stephan nods back a greeting and then continues talking excitedly with the friend as Cedric waits for the light to change before crossing the street. "At least, you know, Brown is a socially conscious place. But, you see, it has been a huge transition for me coming here, being brought here under the guise of equality," says Stephan, graduate of Tougaloo College in Mississippi, a black school not far from Oxford where his father is a preacher and his mother a librarian. "I am constantly having to play catch-up with guys who've spent the past five years speaking three languages, visiting Europe, and reading all the right books. Here, at Brown, they say, 'Don't worry, you're all equal, starting on the same footing. Ready, set, go!' They just don't get it. Where I come from, people don't go to France to study. A trip to France is a big deal. I haven't been reading all the right books since I was twelve and then have some Rhodes Scholar Daddy tell me the rest. I didn't have that kind of access, access that could empower me."

Throughout the day, the overheard conversations at lunch echo in Cedric's head. More than the specifics, he recalls the intensity of the dialogues. At this point, affirmative action is the last thing he wants to hear or think about. During dinner and studying that evening, he finds himself responding to the professors under his breath: So, he got in. If he fails, he fails; if he makes it, he makes it. Why does everyone have to draw conclusions about an entire race from that, or take sides. He wanted a chance; he got one.

The next day, Cedric awakens with renewed ardor, a determination to compete on an even footing, to meet Brown's academic rigors head-on. After lunch, he strides into his Richard Wright class. Stephan Wheelock smiles at him— "Helloooo, Cedric," he says theatrically—and Cedric offers a grim nod.

He is counting on this class about the familiar novels of Richard Wright— some of the few books he's previously read—to help teach him the thinking and writing skills he so desperately needs.

25   Up to now, it has not been happening. One short paper—an ungraded one-page autobiographical essay he wrote in class on the first day—came back last week with few comments. With all sixteen students, about half of whom are black or Hispanic, now settled around the seminar table or at desks lining the walls, Wheelock goes over a few "scheduling changes," cutting assignments off the syllabus, like he did last class and the one before, lightening the class's requirements. Then he starts the discussion with an overview of Richard Wright's signature 1940 novel, *Native Son*, which the class is supposed to have read by now.

Cedric, sitting against the wall, opens his copy of the book. He knows it cold. He watches Wheelock—light-skinned, with stylishly thin bifocals on the end of a small, thin nose—going through a brief synopsis of the plot. The book's central character, Bigger Thomas, is a laborer whose days of poverty and brutishness and frustration lead to the killing of a white woman. After discussing the basic plot for fifteen minutes, Wheelock advances his literary deconstruction by mentioning the novel's oft-noted companion essay—"How 'Bigger' Was Born"—in which Wright tells at length about the creation of his main character, about the five "Biggers" he's known since his childhood.

"Why did Wright decide to put this essay at the back of the book?" Wheelock asks portentously, as most of the class begins flipping through its 1993 edition of the book. "Back in 1940, Wright made a literary decision as to where to put it. Clearly, he put it at the end for a reason."

A half-hour of discourse is launched. Cedric looks around the room. There are plenty of black faces. It may not be calculus—his love—but he really knows this book. If he doesn't raise his hand now, then when? His arm shoots up. "All right, yes, Cedric?" Stephan says, delighted.

"Umm, I think Wright wanted you to figure things out for yourself, so you wouldn't be thinking about all these larger forces, like racial repression and violence right off," Cedric says. "He had to put the explanatory essay in the back . . . otherwise you'd sort of know the answer before you asked the question."

30   Stephan nods agreement and other students follow up. Cedric exhales. That wasn't so hard. The discussion winds along another few minutes until Brandon, another black in the class, raises his hand. He seems confused.

"Professor Wheelock," he says. "I have an earlier edition of the book and, well, the essay, 'How Bigger Was Born,' is in the front rather than the back. It runs, you know, before you get into the actual novel."

There's silence. Air seems to escape from the room. Everyone instantly sees the mishap, which reduces half an hour of vigorous discussion to a waste of breath. Some shake their head, disbelieving, trying not to laugh.

A dazed Wheelock nods once, wordless. His mind seems to race, looking to grab anything to halt the freefall.

"Well, okay . . ." he says finally, trying to recover. "So, the question, then, would be why did the powers that be in the publishing world decide to put the essay in the book's back, you know, in the edition most of you got?"

35   The frantic rebound gets little response, and in a moment he begins shuffling assignment sheets in front of his chair.

"Let's see," he says, forcing a smile. "What do you say we get out a little early today?"

Cedric, sitting at a desk against the wall, looks across a roomful of slackened jaws and stunned gazes—white, black, Hispanic, and Asian—and puts his head in his hands.

In room 216 of East Andrews Hall, being alone in the room means the automatic granting of "music control." As agreed upon and enacted on the last day of September, if the other roommate comes in, he has to wait, silently and without complaints—no matter how long it takes—for control of the music to be ceded. Music control is ceded only when the controlling roommate leaves the room. The roommate left behind then immediately assumes control. If one roommate leaves, then returns to find other roommate playing his own music, too bad. Simple enough?

Rob is sitting on his bed. Cedric, on his.

40   "Agreed," says Cedric, curtly.

"Okay, agreed," says Rob, and the two say nothing more that night. They just sit there in the silence. Since neither of them had "music control" at the time of the agreement, the only way it could be granted was for one to leave. So that night, no one moves and no music is played.

It has not been a good first month for Cedric Jennings and Rob Burton. First, there was the issue of cleanliness, born of a cultural collision between one boy who grew up in casual comfort with a cleaning lady twice a week and the other who spent his life scrubbing dishes and toilets to stave off squalor. Cedric has always been fastidious about his person. Though his room on V Street, his one private place, was often a mess, he always has been neatly dressed and exhaustively scrubbed in public. Now, nothing is private. Just like his person, his room is constantly on display; he might as well be wearing it. The message sent from Rob is the opposite. Rob's impulse—getting stronger as he feels less and less inclined to give in to Cedric—is not to care about how messy the room is. He doesn't mind the disarray, why should anyone else? Because his coolness and self-confidence is subterranean, springing from beneath his casual demeanor, it's important that surface issues, like how clean you keep your room, are afterthoughts.

Meanwhile, if Cedric focuses on what he considers Rob's faults—his messiness, and, now, his taste in music—he doesn't have to think about how Rob is a popular kid, at ease, easygoing, and reasonably good looking with his ice-blue eyes. He also tests well; comes from a strong, loving, *Leave It to Beaver* family, and can be sort of funny in the arch, smug, iconoclastic way college kids need to be.

People are constantly coming by the room seeking Rob—to go out drinking with him at the Underground, Brown's on-campus club, where beer is served; to go to this party or that; to stroll over to the Gate, the favorite campus eatery just a few feet from the dorm, for a late snack; or just to visit, because he makes them feel comfortable.

45   Cedric knows *he* makes them feel uncomfortable. And he is fast on his way to becoming a hermit—or so he thinks one night when he's alone with coveted music control and answers several knocks on the door, like Rob's social secretary.

Cedric is not malicious. Deep down, he sort of likes Rob. He's just up to his eyeballs in confusion and fear of failure and loneliness—and he feels worse when he sees the fun everyone else seems to be having.

Clearly, some East Andrews residents are spending serious time and energy having fun. They're doing all the things that college freshmen have been doing, under various guises and with various aids, since the first tenderfoot left home for Harvard in 1636.

Despite Brown's self-consciousness about each student's individuality, the four preferred pastimes are the same here as they are at most every other college: drink beer, smoke pot, dance to deafening music until you drop, and, on the rare occasion, get naked with some other warm body.

Possibly the best explanation why Cedric Jennings is in Brown's class of 1999 is that he managed to steer clear of the buffet table of adolescent experimentation, believing—rightly, it turns out—that in his neighborhood most of those dishes were poisoned. This was an extraordinary feat, considering how peer pressure at Ballou was backed up by violence and the almost irresistible urge for teenagers to salve deep despair with sex, drugs, and music.

50   Cedric knows all this, just as he knows his resistance was made possible, back when, by Barbara's fierce code, Pastor Long's admonitions against all such licentiousness, and the constant reminders of Cedric Gilliam's[1] broken journey, testifying to what can happen when someone without hope of personal betterment discovers drinking and drugs. But, eventually, something else took root. Cedric, needing to justify his monkish routine night after night, developed a genuine belief that sacrifice, hard work, and extremely clean living would lead to rewards, including a scholarship to a top college.

But now that he's made it, the guideposts are gone and all around him smart kids are getting high, getting drunk, and screwing. Even the real smart ones, kids who can eat Cedric's lunch in almost any subject.

Sitting alone on his bed one Saturday night, there's a knock on the door and a few kids from down the hall crowd in, rosy with anticipation of a night of some drinking, an off-campus party one of them has heard about, and then, who knows, maybe some late-night pizza.

"Hey Cedric, come on," one of them says.

"Naaaaaw," says Cedric, declining nicely, trying to show he appreciates their asking. "I just don't do that kind of stuff." And everyone nods meaningfully, though Cedric can tell they don't really understand. In a moment, they're gone.

55   Just as well, he thinks, half meaning it. Self-denial and a strict code of dos and don'ts are, at this point, knitted into his very being. "It's who I am," he says to himself, over and over. "I can't change now." He gathers up his laundry and spends the next two hours in the first-floor laundry room, flipping through an issue of *Billboard* he's already read—a Saturday night with the spin cycle, just

---

[1]Cedric Jenning's father.

like the last two, hoping someone from his unit will happen by and then hoping they won't. Back upstairs about midnight, his clothes folded and the dorm empty, he fusses with his CDs, playing and replaying beloved tracks, singing the songs with perfect inflection. One of his favorites comes on. He begins a dance, one step, then slides and spins. But, twirling around, his reflection is framed in the closed window—a young black man dancing alone in his room—and he feels like a fool.

Two days later, on Monday night, October 1, he can't take the solitude anymore and ventures out into the hall. People passing in and out of rooms are, invariably, friendly. He imagines that they view the quiet, tallish black student as an oddity, a curiosity. Whoever gets to know him first, really know him, will have stories to tell and the rapt attention of others. So Cedric, sensing this diffident fascination, smiles at all comers but offers few openings.

At the end of the hall, a door is open and both roommates seem to be hanging out. It's John Frank and Zayd Dohrn's room—two guys with many options. If the social life of this unit were a tennis tournament, John and Zayd would be the number one seeded doubles team.

John was born to thrive here. He's Jewish and conventionally handsome with brown hair and green-blue eyes—bright, affable, and engaging. Beneath that and a three-day growth, he's also shrewd and sophisticated. Among the thirty-three kids on the second and third floors of East Andrews, he's off to the fastest start, already a member of the Brown Derbys, the widely known Brown a cappella group whose mixture of song and shtick draws big crowds. He's also probably the first to get laid, groveling with a unit-mate after one of the first weekend's parties.

"Hey, it's Cedric," John says, genuinely surprised, ushering him in. "Entrez!"

60   Cedric wanders around, taking in the room. John's side is a disaster, even messier than Rob's lair, with clothes piled so high and wide that the bed looks like a plateau on top of a lush fiber mountain. "My Gaaawwd," Cedric says.

"Just got done cleaning," says John, his standard line.

The other side of the room is as neat as Cedric's—a few books stacked in one corner of a spotless desk next to a bottle of hand cream, a few avant-garde posters, several pairs of stylish shoes and boots perfectly aligned on the closet floor. Reclining on a bed with tight hospital corners is Zayd Dohrn.

"Yo, C," he says. "'Bout time you dropped by."

"Oh, hey Zayd," says Cedric, who has had a few brief hallway encounters with the tall blond. But his attention is elsewhere, at what must be the largest CD tower in the unit. It's John's three-hundred-CD monstrosity of spinning shelves, a tower that the two roommates share, standing like a lighthouse above the mess. Cedric is drawn to it, amazed.

65   "That's quite a CD collection. Wow," Cedric says. "Just look at it."

"They're mostly John's CDs," says Zayd.

"But the ones Cedric's admiring are yours," says John.

Cedric spots plenty of familiar music. Hip-hop artists, rappers, soul, rhythm and blues. "You got 'Ready to Die,' by Biggie Smalls? I mean, you know, a white guy with this stuff?"

"Yeah," says Zayd, "I think he's great."

70   For the first time, Cedric's stark notions about white America are blurred. He looks at Zayd, back at some other titles, and then at Zayd again. Yup, still white.

Then it's like there's no one else around and the two of them are just talking, real easy and natural, about hip-hop artists they like and lyrics that really hit home. Zayd is not only informed and interested, he actually defers to Cedric's knowledge.

"You know, Biggie is married to Faith," Cedric says, mentioning the female R&B artist Faith Evans and plucking one of her CDs off the tower.

"What? Really?" says Zayd.

"Yeah," says Cedric, offering up some choice morsels. "They sometimes refer to each other in the music. Oh, it's a whole thing."

75   "For real?" says Zayd, adding a touch of street to his voice.

And Cedric grins, "Fo' reeeeeal."

Later that night, lying in bed, Cedric is still sort of smiling to himself. If he is a hopeful kid by nature, it may be because in his darkest moments some glimmer of light has often appeared. He's not certain—not yet—but he thinks he may have found his first friend at Brown.

In the darkness, he tried to think back across the previous few weeks to any brief encounters he's had with this Zayd—from Chicago, Cedric thinks—trying to fill the outline with some more color.

One moment comes into focus. It was the very first week of school, when everything was loose and open, before cliques started forming. He was standing in the hallway with Kim Sherman, the artistic girl from Tennessee, and Zayd. They were right near the door of Mimi Yang, the senior psychology major who is the unit's peer counselor, looking at an envelope taped to her door that was over-flowing with condoms and latex gloves, a sort of low-rent safe sex dispenser.

80   "What's that glove for?" Cedric asked.

"It's for fisting," Kim said, and told him how homosexuals sometimes use their fist for anal sex and that it can transmit the HIV virus.

"Yeah, right, fisting," said Zayd. And then to Cedric, "You never heard of fisting?"

"Naw. Gaaawd. It's gross. I mean, it's worse than oral sex," said Cedric, ventur-ing to the limits of his sexual knowledge.

"What's wrong with giving a woman oral sex?" asked Zayd.

85   Kim added, "Listen, Cedric, just about every guy tries that."

"Not where I'm from. Black guys don't do that, except crack heads or some-thing. Why would you want to be down there?"

Kim giggled and looked over at Zayd, whom she kind of likes.

"Oral sex is my forte," he said, as Cedric stared at him, astonished by his can-dor. Zayd shrugged. "Hey, I'll try anything."

Yes, Cedric remembers it all clearly. What kind of person lives by such a credo? This college sure is one strange place, Cedric laughs to himself. Zayd? What kind of a name is *Zayd*?

90   Chiniqua Milligan rushes into the reading room of Brown's sprawling mod-ernist Rockefeller Library, searching for a familiar face. Across a carrier deck of

linoleum, she spots the group of boys chuckling at a table tucked between the towering periodical racks. She speed walks across the room. "Sorry I'm late— can't believe all you are still here," she says, huffing.

The male quartet from Wheelock's class—Cedric, two other black students, and a student from Japan—is delighted. Cedric jumps up, "'Bout time you made it," he says, smiling, and helps her with her chair as the other boys look her up and down, real quick.

It's the first meeting of the Richard Wright study group. Tonight's task is to plan a class discussion on *Native Son*—a discussion this group will lead next class—but little was accomplished by the guys in the hour before Chiniqua's arrival.

Once she settles into her chair at the reading room table, work commences quickly. Questions are listed, and one of the black guys says he'll type them up and print out copies. In a few minutes, everyone is dispersed.

Outside the library, on one of the first cool evenings of autumn, Chiniqua and Cedric begin the long walk back to the dorm. As the only two black freshmen in Unit 15, it's no surprise that they've managed to size each other up pretty well over the past month.

95   Cedric, who has been looking futilely since he arrived for someone fitting his profile, sometimes jokes—when he and Chiniqua bump into each other and no one else is around—that she's a "ghetto girl in disguise." She laughs politely at this. But Chiniqua Milligan is actually more of a paradigm of what's possible in urban education when commitment is matched with real money. Her father is a bus driver, and her mother is a teacher's aide. Chiniqua and her sister were raised in an apartment in a black working-class neighborhood of upper Manhattan called Inwood, forty blocks north of Harlem. As a studious sixth grader, Chiniqua was pulled out of line and offered a stunning gift. She entered Prep for Prep, a much hailed Manhattan-based program that identifies promising black and Hispanic sixth graders from the New York City public schools. It offers them tutoring on one weeknight and on Saturdays and then places them into the city's top private schools as seventh graders. Cedric has already bumped into a few Prep for Preppers at Brown and is certain he'll meet more. He's heard they're all over this campus.

For them, Brown doesn't have to offer affirmative action. It's already been handled, long ago. Chiniqua, who scored an 1100 on her SATs, received years of counseling—both academic and social—to assist with the collision of cultures she ingested each day crossing fifty blocks of Manhattan.

She rose through the exclusive Columbia Prep, a cocoon for the children of Wall Street chieftains and assorted celebrities, including Woody and Mia, Robert DeNiro, and Bill Cosby. She beat out nearly everyone, graduating third in her class. At Brown, she's thriving in a tough pre-med program and manages a heavy schedule of classes.

The O.J. Simpson acquittal was yesterday afternoon, and the university is embroiled in racial discussion, though not *between* the races. It's all intramural, as it is throughout much of the country, with whites moaning to whites as they feel the bite—in many cases for the first time—of being clobbered in what escalated into a racial contest. And many blacks, so accustomed to being routed by whites, feel a swell of jumbled, out-of-context pride.

Chiniqua feels some of that pride and senses that Cedric must, too. Out of all the kids in the unit, however, they can discuss such sensitive racial sensations only with each other. "So what'd'jou think?" Cedric asks. "Him getting off. You think he's innocent?"

100   "All I know is that it's over and a lot of people I spent the last couple hours with are crazy angry—though they won't say nothing around me."

Tonight was Brown's traditional response to the divisive national or campus issues: a mandatory "outreach" meeting held in all the freshman dorms. Chiniqua tells him that's why she was late to the library.

"Oh yeah, the race outreach," Cedric says sheepishly. "I just didn't go. I just decided I wasn't."

"Well, I went," she says with a how-could-you look. "I was the ONLY one there."

"Was it bad?"

105   "No, just like always. All of them just talking. No one says anything. Everything's fine, everything's good. He's acquitted, so what. It's nothing special. . . . We is all saints here, anyway.

"Only about half the unit showed up, even though it was supposed to be mandatory," she continues, moving easily between black-speak and flawless diction in her usual speedy canter. "Some other people were there, some facilitators, and we did these exercises. They asked us questions, like, when we were kids, were our dolls of many colors, or all one, you know in terms of their skin tone. And you stand up if yours was a certain kind of doll . . . people didn't know what to do."

They walk for a while in silence. Cedric looks over at her, catching a glimpse of the side of her face, with its high cheekbones and large, dark eyes. She's compact, about five-foot-six, with a lean figure that's adorned artfully in a short leather skirt and turtleneck, wide belt, and midcalf boots. She knows he's looking and likes it, looking forward at nothing and looking good.

"Oh yeah," she says, remembering one other thing. "I told the facilitators I had to leave early, that I had this other meeting. They were so deflated. It was like the whole thing was going to collapse with no black person to look at." She laughs lightly at this, reconciled over years to often being the lone black in any room.

Chiniqua is sophisticated—for better or worse—in ways that she knows Cedric is not. Close contact with whites is no novelty for her. She's been a passing friend and fierce competitor of white kids for years. She knows some are nice, some are not—just like blacks—and they're no more gifted or graced. It was she, after all, who wrecked the grading curves in high school. White kids? There's a lot about her that they can never, ever understand and not much hope of any breakthroughs anytime soon.

110   Like a lot of black and Hispanic kids who come here from integrated settings, she finds herself already drifting toward her designated racial enclave. Much like the assimilated Jewish kids drawn to orthodox Sabbath services at Hillel House, Brown offers Chiniqua—who was reluctant to attend militant black rallies in Harlem or troll clubs on 125th Street—a sterling opportunity to reestablish her

racial bona fides and validate her blackness. Safely inside these gates, she can now pick up a dose of black culture pasteurized by ambition, whether it's a tweedy, just tenured black professor talking about radicalism at a coffee clatch or fellow black achievers partying hard this week because next week is already blocked out for studying.

In the past two weekends, she's been going over to dorm room parties at Harambee House, Brown's lone black dorm, and has tried to lure Cedric over. They've definitely become friends. He's a little awkward, she thinks, but kind of nice and not bad looking. It could develop into more. But he's hard to size up. A few weeks ago, he said something about having spent his whole life with blacks and wanting to see if there's a place for him among nonblacks.

"So you coming with me this weekend to Harambee?" Chiniqua asks, managing to make it sound casual. "Just people hanging around, you know, like us. . . . It must get mighty lonely just being by yourself so much."

"No, it's okay," Cedric says as they get off the elevator at the second floor—he breaking away toward his room; she, toward hers. "I'll be fine. Really, I will."

She knows he's lying, so she makes sure the invitation is left standing.

115   "Well, maybe some other time."

Cedric takes the other path a few nights later, when he ventures out of his lair and finds himself a racial stranger in many rooms. Mostly they're dorm rooms on the second floor of Andrews, where freshmen, here like elsewhere, spend an unfathomable number of hours sitting on their beds—heads against the wall or propped pillows—semistudying or not, listening to music, catching a little TV, sending off e-mail messages while flipping through yesterday's student newspaper and talking about "you know, nothing," which means everything. Just plain being is pretty damn interesting in these first few months of stay-up-as-late-as-you-want independence.

John and Zayd's room, with the unit's top CD collection, is a favored place to hang, and there's often a crowd inside. When Zayd's there, Cedric feels comfortable dropping by, so he frequently takes a route that passes by the room on his way in and out of the dorm after dinner.

One evening in mid-October he sees Zayd combing his short, dirty-blond hair in the mirror near his open door. They've seen each other a few times in the past couple of weeks, walking back from classes in the late afternoon or catching a midnight slice of pizza at the Gate.

"Hey, it's been a couple of days. What's up?" asks Zayd, and soon the two are sitting on Zayd's bed, some Boyz II Men on the CD, and Cedric is filling the room with his talk.

120   For Cedric, each encounter with Zayd is an opportunity. As a trustworthy white peer—Cedric's first—Zayd is a sounding board for questions and comments that Cedric has harbored for years, notions about white America that reverberate endlessly in the echo chamber of Southeast.

"So, do you think the cops framed O.J.?" Cedric says, prodding.

Zayd, who by inclination and rearing is sympathetic toward the so-called oppressed, nods along but is reserved. "Do cops frame black suspects? Absolutely, all the time. Did they frame O.J.? I think there's just too much evidence to fabricate. I think, though, that O.J. was helped by all the black guys who've been framed for all the years."

Cedric nods at this judicious response and wants to know Zayd's thoughts on other black martyrs. Midway through his list, John wanders in. By then, Cedric has made it to Marion Barry, whom he says "was completely framed by white cops." John jumps in with the standard white counterresponse, "Look, he did it. Right? He was smoking the crack in the room with the girl. Doesn't matter if he was targeted or not."

"But, like, that's the point," says Cedric. "He was a suspect from the first day he became mayor, 'cause he's black. A black is a suspect, no matter who he is. And eventually they got him."

125 Zayd nods at this. "Yeah, definitely, blacks are racial suspects and that skews the equation."

Around they go, hashing it out in this freshly painted, drywalled holding pen, with its little mirror and sink, where kids hashed things out last year and will again next year and the year after. It's just that this year an exotic bird is among them, an authentic ghetto kid who, for whatever reason, made it through the urban inferno without donning an armor. Cedric can take his off. Once he finally starts talking, he's open and transparent.

He's a draw. The room usually fills when Cedric is around and, soon, Ira Volker is here, along with Florian Keil, his soft-spoken German roommate whose father runs a Boston arm of the Goethe Institute, the German government's cultural ministry abroad.

Neither says too much. But as they listen to Cedric's speech—his black urban expressions, sometimes wrapped around an inappropriate infinitive verb or dropped suffix—a little street creeps into all their voices, part accommodation, part unconscious imitation. Cedric, whose ear is sensitive to such inflections, is not sure if he should be flattered or offended.

Without offering much about himself, Cedric senses their ardor to make him part of the group. His blackness and his standoffishness, his unwillingness to party with them, seems to make everyone worry that there's an unspoken racial subtext: that he doesn't like them because they're white or something. Cedric knows everyone will feel better once he shows that he likes everyone else, proving that goodwill at Brown crosses racial lines. This bothers Cedric, and yet the desire to make himself belong actually intensifies as word spreads of the disputes with Rob. Well-intentioned fellow unit members try to intervene. A few nights after the racial discussions in Zayd's room, Zeina Mobassaleh gets Cedric alone in his room and makes a plea for reconciliation. "Cedric, why don't you and Rob just talk it out. Rob is really a nice guy. The problem is communication."

130 "Zeina, look, he and I are just so different, and us being across the room from each other, there's gonna be bad stuff," Cedric responds, shutting off her efforts.

Cedric doesn't want to get into the nuances of the conflict, but the situation is clearly souring with each day. His fatigue from acting as Rob's social secretary causes some mishaps, albeit unintentional. One night he forgets to pass on a phone message and Rob is understandably upset about it. Cedric, knowing he screwed up, manages to apologize.

Then it happens again. Someone called about not being able to meet Rob for a chemistry study session. Cedric took the message but then forgot to pass it on. A few hours later, while Cedric is reading his education textbook in the lounge, Rob storms in. He stood outside the chemistry building for an hour, waiting for his study partner. Eventually, he got the guy on the phone and felt like an idiot.

"You didn't give me the message, and it screwed up my whole night. I was standing out there for an hour," says Rob, barely suppressing a shout. "I mean, are you doing it on purpose?!"

"No, look, I was wrong," Cedric says, regretful. "Really, I'm sorry."

135 But Rob keeps going. He points his finger at Cedric and glares, hard-eyed. "Don't let it happen again." He stomps out of the lounge and back to the room.

Maybe Rob would have said the same thing had his roommate been white or Asian or Hispanic. But Cedric can't be sure of that. He sees condescension. He sees effrontery. He sees things that blacks see and maybe whites don't. A second later, he's rushing back to the room on Rob's heels.

The two of them square off in the middle of their room. "Don't you talk to me like I'm a child or something," Cedric shouts. "Talking to me like I'm less than you, like you have no respect for me. You don't know me, so don't speak to me like that."

"You don't know me, either," counters Rob, not practiced at confrontation the way Cedric is. "Listen, you're seeing things that aren't there."

"All I know is that if you talk to me that way again, I'm gonna fuck you up. I'll kick your ass."

140 "Just try it!" Rob shouts back, right up in Cedric's face, clearly knowing the proper response to that one. "Just fucking try it!" This time Cedric, who hasn't punched anyone since eighth grade, storms out of the room.

Roaming the halls, he searches for someone to talk to about the confrontation. Rob, it seems, is a friend of nearly everyone on the hall. Cedric knocks on Chiniqua's door. No answer. She's been visiting friends at Harambee a lot lately.

He runs down the hall. Zayd understands the dynamics of the unit, and he's not close to Rob. Zayd will understand. But while Cedric—pounding Zayd's locked door—has few cards in his hand, Zayd has many. Standing there, Cedric tries to figure out where Zayd might be. He could be visiting Bear Beinfeld, a popular sophomore who is Zayd's childhood friend and offers easy access to a more diverse, nonfreshman world. He could be visiting one of many women, lots of them in upper classes, that he already knows. He might be meeting a professor on Thayer Street. No way to find him; he could be anywhere.

Deflated, Cedric writes a note on Zayd's message pad with the grease pencil. "Zayd, Need to talk, quick,—Cedric. It's IMPORTANT. YOU CAN COME BY LATE!" Then he flees from the dorm, walking for hours around the dark campus, feeling like a fugitive and wondering what it would be like if he just dropped out and went home.

* * *

Cedric Jennings stares at his midterm paper in Calculus and finishes off a third box of Golden Grahams for lunch at Vernon Wooley Dining Hall, called the VeeDub. The grade is a 94. He looks up. Chiniqua and her roommate, Maura, are sitting across from him. He shows them the paper. They're effusive in their praise.

145 But it doesn't cheer him. He's told Chiniqua, at least, that this is just one level above beginner math and that he shot low out of fear.

Still, when she smiles at him, he smiles back. The two girls pile plates and glasses on their trays to go, and he pours another box of Golden Grahams. It's a cereal he ate a lot of at home, sometimes when there wasn't much else to eat. In the last couple of days, since midterms ended, he's been eating a lot of it.

"Cedric, how many bowls you gonna eat?" Chiniqua says.

"As many as it takes," he says, trying to make her laugh.

"Takes for what?" she says, rising with her tray. And then she bends in close to whisper, "You should eat some real food."

150 A frenzy of studying for mid-October's midterms gave Cedric a break from the fixating strife with Rob. Everyone, Rob included, had other things to worry about. Cedric, nonetheless, did most of his studying in Rockefeller Library to avoid his roommate. Not that he had that much studying. Calculus was a walk in the park, and his only other midterm test was in Spanish.

He didn't need to worry about bumping into Rob in room 216. His room-mate is all but living on the third floor, dividing evenings among rooms of various friends.

Cedric—with sound strategic instincts from a lifetime of confrontation—forces himself not to retreat from the group of white guys so he can't be characterized for everyone by Rob. He tries to stick with the group and shake off his confusion at their strange habits. For one, the white guys are more physical and affectionate toward one another than he's used to seeing among the black kids from high school, who were so wrapped up with burnishing their hard exteriors. Black kids from his school and neighborhood might have hung together endlessly but rarely showed the sort of self-deprecating, carefree vulnerability that's common here. He's not sure how to react. No one here is boastful. They all make fun of themselves—and each other—though their underlying confidence never seems jilted. It's the precise opposite of what has passed for normal his whole life, one spent around those whose underlying self-confidence was easily punctured.

One weekday night in Zayd and John's room, seven or eight kids, including Ira and Florian from across the hall, start teasing each other in a way that Cedric can't abide.

It's homosexual banter. Black guys just don't do it.

155 As the white boys start in, Cedric feels his gut tighten. "Come on, bend over and let me fill your gas tank," one says to another, and everyone starts to crack up. "Come on. You know you want it."

Cedric's not laughing. He can't. He becomes noticeably grim. They don't understand.

So they treat him just like he wants, deep down: just like another guy. Under those rules, anyone who shows uneasiness becomes the focal point. Comfort here is practically a moral concept. Visible discomfort, on an issue like this, brings a *Lord of the Flies* response: haze it out of him.

"Hey, Cedric," says Ira. "Bend over, and I'll fill your gas tank."

Cedric gets flushed.

160   "Come on, Cedric," says John, a sort of natural class president among the group. "It's okay. I'll bend over and you can fill up mine." Guffaws go around. Even Zayd can't resist the riptide.

Cedric jumps up from Zayd's bed. "I don't like that kind of talkin'," he says, loud and firm but still under control. He doesn't know what else to say. He looks down, pushes out the door, and races back to his empty room.

His door stays locked. Hours pass. At midnight, he has to go to the bathroom and ventures out, cracking the door first to see if anyone is in the hall. And then he sees it. On his grease pad is a neatly written message that anyone could walk by and read.

"Hey Cedric, Meet us later tonight in private and we all can have some real fun. Love, Ira and John."

Cedric blows up. In a second, he's pounding on Ira's door, and then they're nose to nose in the doorway. "Don't be leaving that mess on my door so I have to wipe it off."

165   "I didn't write anything," Ira counters. "I don't know what you're talking about."

"You're just doing this to annoy me, Ira! To get me going!"

A crowd is gathering in the hallway.

"Look, I do what I want to do. And I'll do what I want to do to you." Ira bellows. "So get out of my room."

Everything's in the open now, a spectator sport, a free feed.

170   "You can't just accuse Ira of doing it unless you know he did," says Corry—Cedric's Marcia Brady—out in the hall from a neighboring room. "You don't know it was Ira."

"I know it's him," Cedric rants. "He's done stuff like that before. Don't tell me. He's always saying stuff like that."

Zayd tries to diffuse it. "Everybody's not against you," he says, keeping his voice quiet and even. "You think that, but it's not true."

Cedric halts. He looks across the corridor, now filled with mostly white peers and a few of color. All eyes are on him. They know about Rob. And now this. Everyone just stares. All he wants is to get back to his room and never come out.

John, at Zayd's side, ends it. "Jesus, Cedric. You ignore people just to get attention, and then you get the attention and you don't want it."

175   Cedric looks, dazed, at John. His ringing ears are shutting off everything. How the hell did he end up here? While everyone stares, he walks back to his room and softly closes the door.

A few days later, Zayd is sitting on the moist grass of Brown's main green, on an oddly warm, short-sleeve October day, talking to his buddy, Bear, about Cedric.

"Other kids wonder why I'm his friend, what I see in him," he says, his smoothly muscled bare arms wrapped around peaks of bony knees. "And it's strange. We're like opposites. We're so different in so many ways, but I just find him so interesting."

More than any other student in the unit, Zayd has the luxury of autonomy. While John masters the fierce intimacies of a freshman dorm, Zayd seems to stand above the fray. He's considered a touch aloof, in part because he won't simply offer the full, instant disclosure that is common currency among college freshmen.

People, including Cedric, don't know much about him. The few things they do know are intriguing. Zayd starred at the Laboratory School of Chicago, a progressive private school run by the University of Chicago, and took some courses at the university. He went to Northwestern University film school two summers ago, when he was just sixteen, and has written a play called *Phallacy*, which he calls "a sexual farce."

180   One other thing is known about Zayd. He's a slender, wide-shouldered six-foot-two, with carefully cropped, pushed-back hair, high cheekbones under blue eyes, and the perfect proportion of eyebrows to slender nose that is the hallmark of male models. This, combined with his mysteriousness, causes some substantial sexual frisson among the women in the unit and his various classes—energy he casually harnesses in frequent, though usually short-lived, sexual liaisons.

But the most important quality that draws people to him is invisible. Zayd is the embodiment of an ethos that, more than anything, defines merit around this campus and many elite institutions like it: constant, fearless, rigorous experimentation—both social and intellectual. The more daring, the better. By that measure, Zayd is muscle bound.

Zayd Osceola Ayers Dohrn emerges from a reactor core of such headlong thinking: the elegant Chicago brownstone of two fiftyish college professors on the city's integrated and edgy south side, just a few blocks from the University of Chicago. Writers, artists, and savants of America's progressive vanguard have, for years, passed through his living room, pollinating him and his two brothers.

His prime directive, as he mentioned in Cedric's presence that first week of school, is "I'll try anything."

Which is why Zayd, among all the broad-thinking kids in this right-minded university, is the only one with the daring to knock on Cedric's door, which has been mostly locked—locking out the world—for a week since the much discussed hallway detonation. Zayd gets no answer and writes a provocative note: "C—Came by, heard music inside. I guess we're not friends anymore or something. Zayd."

185   He passes by again as October nears an end. It's now two weeks into what seems like Cedric's permanent hibernation, and Zayd wonders if it may end with a transfer application and a bare mattress. The doorknob clicks open. Zayd walks in, talking casually about some new album by Tupac Shakur, the controversial and glamorous rapper, talking like nothing ever happened. Cedric, parched with solitude, can't resist the company. To be sure, it's a strange, wild CD Tupac just released.

"You know, Tupac's uncle was this guy, Zayd Shakur, a radical black activist who was killed by the cops in the early '60s," Zayd continues. "That's who I'm named after. My mom and dad knew him—or, I guess they knew some Black Panthers who knew him."

"For real?" Cedric asks.

In a few days, parents will be coming for parents weekend, and the two of them talk about that for a while, sitting on Cedric's bed. Cedric says he doesn't know whether his mom will make it. It's a long way, and she doesn't have a lot of cash. Zayd nods, knowing not to ask too much, and says, "It's going to be very weird having all those parents around."

He pauses. "Remember my mom came by a few weeks ago—she might want to come by to say hi," he ventures, "if that's all right."

190   "That'd be fine, no big deal," Cedric answers easily, clearly relieved to be edging out of exile. Then they walk down to the corner to Sam Goody's to buy a CD, figuring they could share it.

≈ CRITICAL REFLECTIONS

1. The subject of affirmative action runs throughout "Fierce Intimacies"—in Cedric's experiences, the conversations he overhears at Cafe Paragon, and in Stephan Wheelock's class. Based on your reading of this chapter, as well as other experiences you may have had, how would you define equal opportunity in education—for students and for others?

2. This chapter is part of what might be considered a literacy narrative, that is, a story about a main character's experiences through a literacy development experience. Traditionally, these narratives have cast the main character's journey as a difficult, but ultimately positive and successful one. Based on your reading of "Fierce Intimacies," do you think that Cedric's journey has been successful thus far? Do you predict that it will be? Support your response with specific evidence from the chapter.

3. What do you think Cedric would define as the primary purposes of schooling (both inside and outside of his Brown classes) based on your reading of this chapter?

≈ MAKING CONNECTIONS

1. Working with the same idea of the literacy narrative described above, consider "Fierce Intimacies" against the excerpt from Frederick Douglass's book, a classic literacy narrative. Do you find that the ideas about literacy development in these excerpts parallel one another? Are there significant differences between them? Note that you might find that Douglass's chapter more directly addresses questions about literacy, and thus will need to read between the lines of "Fierce Intimacies."

2. In "The Banking Model," Freire outlines two approaches to education and extrapolates from them ideas about how the world should work. Based on what you have read of Cedric's school experiences in this chapter, what lessons about the ways the world works do you think Cedric is learning at Brown?

3. Both Cedric Jennings and Lorene Cary were African-American students who entered predominantly white institutions for parts of their schooling. What elements of their experiences (as related in these chapters) do you find to be similar and dissimilar?

READINGS ABOUT LEARNING (IN AND OUT OF SCHOOL)

■ W.E.B. DuBois, "Of Mr. Booker T. Washington and Others"

■ Kate Daniels, "Self-Portrait with Politics"

■ Frederick Douglass, from *Narrative of the Life of Frederick Douglass, An American Slave*

■ Darcy Frey, "The Last Shot"

■ Stanley Kaplan, "My 54-Year Love Affair with the SAT"

■ Nicholas Lemann, "The President's Big Test"

■ Theresa McCarty, "Community and Classroom"

■ Michael Moffatt, "What College Is REALLY Like"

■ "Executive Summary of the No Child Left Behind Act of 2001"

■ "Wendy Darling," "What 'No Child Left Behind' Left Behind"

■ Gary Orfield and Johanna Wald, "Testing, Testing"

■ Peter Sacks, "Do No Harm: Stopping the Damage to American Schools"

■ James Traub, "The Test Mess"

■ Booker T. Washington, "The Atlanta Exposition Address"

W.E.B. DuBois

OF MR. BOOKER T. WASHINGTON AND OTHERS

This chapter is part of W.E.B. (William Edward Burghardt) DuBois's 1903 book, *The Souls of Black Folk.* In it, DuBois said he wanted to show readers "the strange meaning of being black here in the dawning of the Twentieth Century." The issue of race and the problems with what DuBois called "the veil"—racism—were at the center of DuBois's life.

DuBois was born in 1868 in Great Barrington, Massachusetts, where he excelled as a student. He attended Fisk University in Atlanta, the University of Berlin, and received his Ph.D. at Harvard University. After graduating he took a teaching job at a small college in Ohio, but left there after two years to accept a fellowship at the University of Pennsylvania to study an economically impoverished neighborhood in Philadelphia. That study sharpened DuBois's interest in the social and economic conditions that created and perpetuated racism and denigrated black people. After completing his study, DuBois accepted a position in sociology at Atlanta University, where he turned his attention to the study of social structures and race.

As DuBois was conducting his work, Booker T. Washington was developing and raising money to support his Tuskegee Institute (later Tuskegee University). DuBois and Washington strongly disagreed over the role that education should play for black people. Where Washington argued that education should help blacks assimilate into the dominant (white) culture, DuBois argued that the "talented tenth"—the most intelligent top ten percent of black people—should be educated to help others work to change the dominant culture. By 1909, DuBois decided to work outside of the academy to advance his position. He founded a newspaper, *The Crisis,* to publicize these views. He also worked with others to form the National Association for the Advancement of Colored People (NAACP), an organization devoted to abolishing racism and educating black and white people about race-related issues. At the same time, DuBois was becoming involved with the Pan-African movement of Marcus Garvey, who advocated a return to Africa for all black people.

Eventually, DuBois became disheartened with the NAACP because he believed the organization was not singularly devoted in its purpose to the advancement of black people. He returned to Atlanta University, but continued his involvement with Garvey. At the same time, DuBois was becoming increasingly discouraged by what he perceived as the U.S. government's censorship of ideas and continued implicit support for racism. In the 1950s, DuBois left the United States for Ghana, where he renounced his American citizenship and joined the Communist Party. DuBois died in Ghana at the age of 95 after having devoted his life's work to eradicating racism and working for a more just world.

From birth till death enslaved; in word, in deed, unmanned!

. . . .

Hereditary bondsmen! Know ye not

Who would be free themselves must strike the blow?

BYRON.

Easily the most striking thing in the history of the American Negro since 1876 is the ascendancy of Mr. Booker T. Washington. It began at the time when war memories and ideals were rapidly passing; a day of astonishing commercial development was dawning; a sense of doubt and hesitation overtook the freedmen's sons,—then it was that his leading began Mr. Washington came, with a simple definite programme, at the psychological moment when the nation was a little ashamed of having bestowed so much sentiment on Negroes, and was concentrating its energies on Dollars. His programme of industrial education, conciliation of the South, and submission and silence as to civil and political rights, was not wholly original; the Free Negroes from 1830 up to wartime had striven to build industrial schools, and the American Missionary Association had from the first taught various trades; and Price and others had sought a way of honorable alliance with the best of the Southerners. But Mr. Washington first indissolubly linked these things; he put enthusiasm, unlimited energy, and perfect faith into this programme, and changed it from a by-path into a veritable Way of Life. And the tale of the methods by which he did this is a fascinating study of human life.

It startled the nation to hear a Negro advocating such a programme after many decades of bitter complaint; it startled and won the applause of the South, it interested and won the admiration of the North; and after a confused murmur of protest, it silenced if it did not convert the Negroes themselves.

To gain the sympathy and cooperation of the various elements comprising the white South was Mr. Washington's first task; and this, at the time Tuskegee was founded, seemed, for a black man, well-nigh impossible. And yet ten years later it was done in the word spoken at Atlanta: "In all things purely social we can be as separate as the five fingers, and yet one as the hand in all things essential to mutual progress." This "Atlanta Compromise" is by all odds the most notable thing in Mr. Washington's career. The South interpreted it in different ways: the radicals received it as a complete surrender of the demand for civil and political equality; the conservatives, as a generously conceived working basis for mutual understanding. So both approved it, and to-day its author is certainly the most distinguished Southerner since Jefferson Davis, and the one with the largest personal following.

Next to this achievement comes Mr. Washington's work in gaining place and consideration in the North. Others less shrewd and tactful had formerly essayed to sit on these two stools and had fallen between them; but as Mr. Washington knew the heart of the South from birth and training, so by singular insight he intuitively grasped the spirit of the age which was dominating the North. And so thoroughly did he learn the speech and thought of triumphant commercialism, and the ideals of material prosperity, that the picture of a lone black boy poring over a French grammar amid the weeds and dirt of a neglected home soon seemed to him the acme of absurdities. One wonders what Socrates and St. Francis of Assisi would say to this.

5   And yet this very singleness of vision and thorough oneness with his age is a mark of the successful man. It is as though Nature must needs make men narrow in order to give them force. So Mr. Washington's cult has gained unquestioning followers, his work has wonderfully prospered, his friends are legion, and his enemies are confounded. To-day he stands as the one recognized spokesman of his ten million fellows, and one of the most notable figures in a nation of seventy millions. One hesitates, therefore, to criticise a life which, beginning with so little, has done so much. And yet the time is come when one may speak in all sincerity and utter courtesy of the mistakes and shortcomings of Mr. Washington's career, as well as of his triumphs, without being thought captious or envious, and without forgetting that it is easier to do ill than well in the world.

The criticism that has hitherto met Mr. Washington has not always been of this broad character. In the South especially has he had to walk warily to avoid the harshest judgments,—and naturally so, for he is dealing with the one subject of deepest sensitiveness to that section. Twice—once when at the Chicago celebration of the Spanish-American War he alluded to the color-prejudice that is "eating away the vitals of the South," and once when he dined with President Roosevelt—has the resulting Southern criticism been violent enough to threaten seriously his popularity. In the North the feeling has several times forced itself into words, that Mr. Washington's counsels of submission overlooked certain elements of true manhood, and that his educational programme was unnecessarily narrow. Usually, however, such criticism has not found open expression, although, too, the spiritual sons of the Abolitionists have not been prepared to acknowledge that the schools founded before Tuskegee, by men of broad ideals and self-sacrificing spirit, were wholly failures or worthy of ridicule. While, then, criticism has not failed to follow Mr. Washington, yet the prevailing public opinion of the land has been but too willing to deliver the solution of a wearisome problem into his hands, and say, "If that is all you and your race ask, take it."

Among his own people, however, Mr. Washington has encountered the strongest and most lasting opposition, amounting at times to bitterness, and even to-day continuing strong and insistent even though largely silenced in outward expression by the public opinion of the nation. Some of this opposition is, of course, mere envy; the disappointment of displaced demagogues and the spite of narrow minds. But aside from this, there is among educated and thoughtful colored men in all parts of the land a feeling of deep regret, sorrow, and apprehension at the wide currency and ascendancy which some of Mr. Washington's theories have gained. These same men admire his sincerity of purpose, and are willing to forgive much to honest endeavor which is doing something worth the doing. They cooperate with Mr. Washington as far as they conscientiously can; and, indeed, it is no ordinary tribute to this man's tact and power that, steering as he must between so many diverse interests and opinions, he so largely retains the respect of all.

But the hushing of the criticism of honest opponents is a dangerous thing. It leads some of the best of the critics to unfortunate silence and paralysis of effort, and others to burst into speech so passionately and intemperately as to lose listeners. Honest and earnest criticism from those whose interests are most nearly touched,—criticism of writers by readers, of government by those governed, of leaders by those led,—this is the soul of democracy and the safeguard of modern society. If the best of the American Negroes receive by outer pressure a leader whom they had not recognized before, manifestly there is here a certain palpable gain. Yet there is also irreparable loss,—a loss of that peculiarly valuable education which a group receives when by search and criticism it finds and commissions its own leaders. The way in which this is done is at once the most elementary and the nicest problem of social growth. History is but the record of such group-leadership; and yet how infinitely changeful is its type and character! And of all types and kinds, what can be more instructive than the leadership of a group within a group?—that curious double movement where real progress may be negative and actual advance be relative retrogression. All this is the social student's inspiration and despair.

Now in the past the American Negro has had instructive experience in the choosing of group leaders, founding thus a peculiar dynasty which in the light of present conditions is worth while studying. When sticks and stones and beasts form the sole environment of a people, their attitude is largely one of determined opposition to and conquest of natural forces. But when to earth and brute is added an environment of men and ideas, then the attitude of the imprisoned group may take three main forms,—a feeling of revolt and revenge; an attempt to adjust all thought and action to the will of the greater group; or, finally, a determined effort at self-realization and self-development despite environing opinion. The influence of all of these attitudes at various times can be traced in the history of the American Negro, and in the evolution of his successive leaders.

10   Before 1750, while the fire of African freedom still burned in the veins of the slaves, there was in all leadership or attempted leadership but the one motive of revolt and revenge,—typified in the terrible Maroons, the Danish blacks, and Cato of Stono, and veiling all the Americas in fear of insurrection. The liberalizing tendencies of the latter half of the eighteenth century brought, along with kindlier relations between black and white, thoughts of ultimate adjustment and assimilation. Such aspiration was especially voiced in the earnest songs of Phyllis, in the martyrdom of Attucks, the fighting of Salem and Poor, the intellectual accomplishments of Banneker and Derham, and the political demands of the Cuffes.

Stern financial and social stress after the war cooled much of the previous humanitarian ardor. The disappointment and impatience of the Negroes at the persistence of slavery and serfdom voiced itself in two movements. The slaves in the South, aroused undoubtedly by vague rumors of the Haytian revolt, made three fierce attempts at insurrection,—in 1800 under Gabriel in Virginia, in 1822 under Vesey in Carolina, and in 1831 again in Virginia under the terrible Nat Turner. In the Free States, on the other hand, a new and curious attempt at self-development was made. In Philadelphia and New York color-prescription led to a withdrawal of Negro communicants from white churches and the formation of a peculiar socio-religious institution among the Negroes known as the African Church,—an organization still living and controlling in its various branches over a million of men.

Walker's wild appeal against the trend of the times showed how the world was changing after the coming of the cotton-gin. By 1830 slavery seemed hopelessly fastened on the South, and the slaves thoroughly cowed into submission. The free Negroes of the North, inspired by the mulatto immigrants from the West Indies, began to change the basis of their demands; they recognized the slavery of slaves, but insisted that they themselves were freemen, and sought assimilation and amalgamation with the nation on the same terms with other men. Thus, Forten and Purvis of Philadelphia, Shad of Wilmington, Du Bois of New Haven, Barbadoes of Boston, and others, strove singly and together as men, they said, not as slaves; as "people of color," not as "Negroes." The trend of the times, however, refused them recognition save in individual and exceptional cases, considered them as one with all the despised blacks, and they soon found themselves striving to keep even the rights they formerly had of voting and working and moving as freemen. Schemes of migration and colonization arose among them; but these they refused to entertain, and they eventually turned to the Abolition movement as a final refuge.

Here, led by Remond, Nell, Wells-Brown, and Douglass, a new period of self-assertion and self-development dawned. To be sure, ultimate freedom and assimilation was the ideal before the leaders, but the assertion of the manhood rights of the Negro by himself was the main reliance, and John Brown's raid was the extreme of its logic. After the war and emancipation, the great form of Frederick Douglass, the greatest of American Negro leaders, still led the host. Self-assertion, especially in political lines, was the main programme, and behind Douglass came Elliot, Bruce, and Langston, and the Reconstruction politicians, and, less conspicuous but of greater social significance Alexander Crummell and Bishop Daniel Payne.

Then came the Revolution of 1876, the suppression of the Negro votes, the changing and shifting of ideals, and the seeking of new lights in the great night. Douglass, in his old age, still bravely stood for the ideals of his early manhood,—ultimate assimilation *through* self-assertion, and on no other terms. For a time Price arose as a new leader, destined, it seemed, not to give up, but to re-state the old ideals in a form less repugnant to the white South. But he passed away in his prime. Then came the new leader. Nearly all the former ones had become leaders by the silent suffrage of their fellows, had sought to lead their own people alone, and were usually, save Douglass, little known outside their race. But Booker T. Washington arose as essentially the leader not of one race but of two,—a compromiser between the South, the North, and the Negro. Naturally the Negroes resented, at first bitterly, signs of compromise which surrendered their civil and political rights, even though this was to be exchanged for larger chances of economic development. The rich and dominating North, however, was not only weary of the race problem, but was investing largely in Southern enterprises, and welcomed any method of peaceful cooperation. Thus, by national opinion, the Negroes began to recognize Mr. Washington's leadership; and the voice of criticism was hushed.

15   Mr. Washington represents in Negro thought the old attitude of adjustment and submission; but adjustment at such a peculiar time as to make his programme unique. This is an age of unusual economic development, and Mr. Washington's programme naturally takes an economic cast, becoming a gospel of Work and Money to such an extent as apparently almost completely to overshadow the higher aims of life. Moreover, this is an age when the more advanced races are coming in closer contact with the less developed races, and the race-feeling is therefore intensified; and Mr. Washington's programme practically accepts the alleged inferiority of the Negro races. Again, in our own land, the reaction from the sentiment of war time has given impetus to race-prejudice against Negroes, and Mr. Washington withdraws many of the high demands of Negroes as men and American citizens. In other periods of intensified prejudice all the Negro's tendency to self-assertion has been called forth; at this period a policy of submission is advocated. In the history of nearly all other races and peoples the doctrine preached at such crises has been that manly self-respect is worth more than lands and houses, and that a people who voluntarily surrender such respect, or cease striving for it, are not worth civilizing.

In answer to this, it has been claimed that the Negro can survive only through submission. Mr. Washington distinctly asks that black people give up, at least for the present, three things,—

First, political power,

Second, insistence on civil rights,

Third, higher education of Negro youth,—

and concentrate all their energies on industrial education, the accumulation of wealth, and the conciliation of the South. This policy has been courageously and insistently advocated for over fifteen years, and has been triumphant for perhaps ten years. As a result of this tender of the palm-branch, what has been the return? In these years there have occurred:

1. The disfranchisement of the Negro.
2. The legal creation of a distinct status of civil inferiority for the Negro.
3. The steady withdrawal of aid from institutions for the higher training of the Negro.

These movements are not, to be sure, direct results of Mr. Washington's teachings; but his propaganda has, without a shadow of doubt, helped their speedier accomplishment. The question then comes: Is it possible, and probable, that nine millions of men can make effective progress in economic lines if they are deprived of political rights, made a servile caste, and allowed only the most meagre chance for developing their exceptional men? If history and reason give any distinct answer to these questions, it is an emphatic *No*. And Mr. Washington thus faces the triple paradox of his career:

1. He is striving nobly to make Negro artisans business men and property-owners; but it is utterly impossible, under modern competitive methods, for workingmen and property-owners to defend their rights and exist without the right of suffrage.
2. He insists on thrift and self-respect, but at the same time counsels a silent submission to civic inferiority such as is bound to sap the manhood of any race in the long run.
3. He advocates common-school and industrial training, and depreciates institutions of higher learning; but neither the Negro common-schools, nor Tuskegee itself, could remain open a day were it not for teachers trained in Negro colleges, or trained by their graduates.

This triple paradox in Mr. Washington's position is the object of criticism by two classes of colored Americans. One class is spiritually descended from Toussaint the Savior, through Gabriel, Vesey, and Turner, and they represent the attitude of revolt and revenge; they hate the white South blindly and distrust the white race generally, and so far as they agree on definite action, think that the Negro's only hope lies in emigration beyond the borders of the United States. And yet, by the irony of fate, nothing has more effectually made this programme seem hopeless than the recent course of the United States toward weaker and darker peoples in the West Indies, Hawaii, and the Philippines,—for where in the world may we go and be safe from lying and brute force?

The other class of Negroes who cannot agree with Mr. Washington has hitherto said little aloud. They deprecate the sight of scattered counsels, of internal disagreement; and especially they dislike making their just criticism of a useful and earnest man an excuse for a general discharge of venom from small-minded opponents. Nevertheless, the questions involved are so fundamental and serious that it is difficult to see how men like the Grimkes, Kelly Miller, J. W. E. Bowen, and other representatives of this group, can much longer be silent. Such men feel in conscience bound to ask of this nation three things:

1. The right to vote.
2. Civic equality.
3. The education of youth according to ability.

They acknowledge Mr. Washington's invaluable service in counselling patience and courtesy in such demands; they do not ask that ignorant black men vote when ignorant whites are debarred, or that any reasonable restrictions in the suffrage should not be applied; they know that the low social level of the mass of the race is responsible for much discrimination against it, but they also know, and the nation knows, that relentless color-prejudice is more often a cause than a result of the Negro's degradation; they seek the abatement of this relic of barbarism, and not its systematic encouragement and pampering by all agencies of social power from the Associated Press to the Church of Christ. They advocate, with Mr. Washington, a broad system of Negro common schools supplemented by thorough industrial training; but they are surprised that a man of Mr. Washington's insight cannot see that no such educational system ever has rested or can rest on any other basis than that of the well-equipped college and university, and they insist that there is a demand for a few such institutions throughout the South to train the best of the Negro youth as teachers, professional men, and leaders.

20   This group of men honor Mr. Washington for his attitude of conciliation toward the white South; they accept the "Atlanta Compromise" in its broadest interpretation; they recognize, with him, many signs of promise, many men of high purpose and fair judgment, in this section; they know that no easy task has been laid upon a region already tottering under heavy burdens. But, nevertheless, they insist that the way to truth and right lies in straightforward honesty, not in indiscriminate flattery; in praising those of the South who do well and criticising uncompromisingly those who do ill; in taking advantage of the opportunities at hand and urging their fellows to do the same, but at the same time in remembering that only a firm adherence to their higher ideals and aspirations will ever keep those ideals within the realm of possibility. They do not expect that the free right to vote, to enjoy civic rights, and to be educated, will come in a moment; they do not expect to see the bias and prejudices of years disappear at the blast of a trumpet; but they are absolutely certain that the way for a people to gain their reasonable rights is not by voluntarily throwing them away and insisting that they do not want them; that the way for a people to gain respect is not by continually belittling and ridiculing themselves; that, on the contrary, Negroes must insist continually, in season and out of season, that voting is necessary to modern manhood, that color discrimination is barbarism, and that black boys need education as well as white boys.

In failing thus to state plainly and unequivocally the legitimate demands of their people, even at the cost of opposing an honored leader, the thinking classes of American Negroes would shirk a heavy responsibility,—a responsibility to themselves, a responsibility to the struggling masses, a responsibility to the darker races of men whose future depends so largely on this American experiment, but especially a responsibility to this nation,—this common Fatherland. It is wrong to encourage a man or a people in evil-doing; it is wrong to aid and abet a national crime simply because it is unpopular not to do so. The growing spirit of kindliness and reconciliation between the North and South after the frightful differences of a generation ago ought to be a source of deep congratulation to all, and especially to those whose mistreatment caused the war; but if that reconciliation is to be marked by the industrial slavery and civic death of those same black men, with permanent legislation into a position of inferiority, then those black men, if they are really men, are called upon by every consideration of patriotism and loyalty to oppose such a course by all civilized methods, even though such opposition involves disagreement with Mr. Booker T. Washington. We have no right to sit silently by while the inevitable seeds are sown for a harvest of disaster to our children, black and white.

First, it is the duty of black men to judge the South discriminatingly. The present generation of Southerners are not responsible for the past, and they should not be blindly hated or blamed for it. Furthermore, to no class is the indiscriminate endorsement of the recent course of the South toward Negroes more nauseating than to the best thought of the South. The South is not "solid"; it is a land in the ferment of social change, wherein forces of all kinds are fighting for supremacy; and to praise the ill the South is to-day perpetrating is just as wrong as to condemn the good. Discriminating and broad-minded criticism is what the South needs,—needs it for the sake of her own white sons and daughters, and for the insurance of robust, healthy mental and moral development.

To-day even the attitude of the Southern whites toward the blacks is not, as so many assume, in all cases the same; the ignorant Southerner hates the Negro, the workingmen fear his competition, the money-makers wish to use him as a laborer, some of the educated see a menace in his upward development, while others—usually the sons of the masters—wish to help him to rise. National opinion has enabled this last class to maintain the Negro common schools, and to protect the Negro partially in property, life, and limb. Through the pressure of the money-makers, the Negro is in danger of being reduced to semi-slavery, especially in the country districts; the workingmen, and those of the educated who fear the Negro, have united to disfranchise him, and some have urged his deportation; while the passions of the ignorant are easily aroused to lynch and abuse any black man. To praise this intricate whirl of thought and prejudice is nonsense; to inveigh indiscriminately against "the South" is unjust; but to use the same breath in praising Governor Aycock, exposing Senator Morgan, arguing with Mr. Thomas Nelson Page, and denouncing Senator Ben Tillman, is not only sane, but the imperative duty of thinking black men.

It would be unjust to Mr. Washington not to acknowledge that in several instances he has opposed movements in the South which were unjust to the Negro; he sent memorials to the Louisiana and Alabama constitutional conventions, he has spoken against lynching, and in other ways has openly or silently set his influence against sinister schemes and unfortunate happenings. Notwithstanding this, it is equally true to assert that on the whole the distinct impression left by Mr. Washington's propaganda is, first, that the South is justified in its present attitude toward the Negro because of the Negro's degradation; secondly, that the prime cause of the Negro's failure to rise more quickly is his wrong education in the past; and, thirdly, that his future rise depends primarily on his own efforts. Each of these propositions is a dangerous half-truth. The supplementary truths must never be lost sight of: first, slavery and race-prejudice are potent if not sufficient causes of the Negro's position; second, industrial and common-school training were necessarily slow in planting because they had to await the black teachers trained by higher institutions,—it being extremely doubtful if any essentially different development was possible, and certainly a Tuskegee was unthinkable before 1880; and, third, while it is a great truth to say that the Negro must strive and strive mightily to help himself, it is equally true that unless his striving be not simply seconded, but rather aroused and encouraged, by the initiative of the richer and wiser environing group, he cannot hope for great success.

25   In his failure to realize and impress this last point, Mr. Washington is especially to be criticised. His doctrine has tended to make the whites, North and South, shift the burden of the Negro problem to the Negro's shoulders and stand aside as critical and rather pessimistic spectators; when in fact the burden belongs to the nation, and the hands of none of us are clean if we bend not our energies to righting these great wrongs.

The South ought to be led, by candid and honest criticism, to assert her better self and do her full duty to the race she has cruelly wronged and is still wronging. The North—her co-partner in guilt—cannot salve her conscience by plastering it with gold. We cannot settle this problem by diplomacy and suaveness, by "policy" alone. If worse come to worst, can the moral fibre of this country survive the slow throttling and murder of nine millions of men?

The black men of America have a duty to perform, a duty stern and delicate,—a forward movement to oppose a part of the work of their greatest leader. So far as Mr. Washington preaches Thrift, Patience, and Industrial Training for the masses, we must hold up his hands and strive with him, rejoicing in his honors and glorying in the strength of this Joshua called of God and of man to lead the headless host. But so far as Mr. Washington apologizes for injustice, North or South, does not rightly value the privilege and duty of voting, belittles the emasculating effects of caste distinctions, and opposes the higher training and ambition of our brighter minds,—so far as he, the South, or the Nation, does this,—we must unceasingly and firmly oppose them. By every civilized and peaceful method we must strive for the rights which the world accords to men, clinging unwaveringly to those great words which the sons of the Fathers would fain forget: "We hold these truths to be self-evident: That all men are created equal; that they are endowed by their Creator with certain unalienable rights; that among these are life, liberty, and the pursuit of happiness."

▰▰ CRITICAL REFLECTIONS

1. How do you think DuBois would describe the "Way of Life" espoused by Washington?

2. What are the connections that you think DuBois sees between Washington's investment in commercial interests and the way he [Washington] positions Black people?

3. In this chapter, DuBois positions Washington amidst a long history of Latin American, African, Black, and African-American activism. Where do you think

DuBois sees Washington "fitting" there? Where do you see DuBois "fitting" in this legacy?

4. How do you summarize what DuBois describes as "the triple paradox of [Washington's] career"?

5. In this chapter, DuBois implicitly endorses a group calling for "the education of youth according to ability." Later in this book, Washington discusses the "Talented Tenth." Both are references to DuBois's belief that the top ten percent of Black people should be educated to become leaders for others in their culture. What do you think DuBois would have this Talented Tenth learn? What would they then advocate?

6. Reading this chapter, what do you think DuBois would define as the purpose of education?

⚞ MAKING CONNECTIONS

1. How do you think Washington would respond to DuBois's criticisms in this chapter? Why do you think Washington would take that position?

2. Consider DuBois's characterization of the purpose of education for Black people with one of the contemporary readings in this book, such as Shorris's, Edmundson's, or Frey's. Do you find evidence of his characterization there? If you do, where? If you don't, what purpose do you find?

KATE DANIELS

SELF-PORTRAIT WITH POLITICS

This poem, included in *Working Classics: Poems on Industrial Life,* offers insight into the tensions that can arise when some family members perceive others to be changing. Author Kate Daniels was the first in her family to attend college; she worked at various jobs—from dishwasher to clerical worker—as she attended college. Daniels finished college and graduate school. She now teaches poetry and continues to work as a poet and biographer of poets.

> At the dinner table, my brother says something
> Republican he knows I will hate.
> He has said it only for me, hoping
> I will rise to the argument as I usually do
> 5   so he can call me "communist"
> and accuse me of terrible things—not loving
> the family, hating the country, unsatisfied
> with my life. I feel my fingers tighten

on my fork and ask for more creamed potatoes
10 to give me time to think.

He's right: It's true I am not satisfied
with life. Each time I come home
my brother hates me more for the life
of the mind I have chosen to live.
15 He works in a factory and can never understand
why I am paid a salary for teaching poetry
just as I can never understand his factory job
where everyone loves or hates the boss like god.
He was so intelligent as a child
20 his teachers were scared of him.
He did everything well and fast
and then shot rubberbands at the girls' legs
and metal lunchboxes lined up neatly beneath the desks.
Since then, something happened I don't know about.
25 Now he drives a forklift every day.
He moves things in boxes from one place
to another place. I have never worked
in a factory and can only imagine
the tedium, the thousand escapes
30 the bright mind must make.

But tonight I will not fight again.
I just nod and swallow and in spite
of everything remember my brother as a child.
When I was six and he was five, I taught him everything
35 I learned in school each day while we waited for dinner.
I remember his face—smiling always,
the round, brown eyes, and how his lower lip
seemed always wet and ready to kiss.
I remember for a long time his goal in life
40 was to be a dog, how we were forced
to scratch his head, the pathetic sound
of his human bark. Now he glowers
and acts like a tyrant and cannot eat
and thinks I think
45 I am superior to him.

The others ignore him as they usually do:
My mother with her bristly hair.
My father just wanting to get back to the TV.
My husband rolling his eyes in a warning at me.

50　　It has taken a long time to get a politics
　　　I can live with in a world that gave me
　　　poetry and my brother an assembly line.
　　　I accept my brother for what he is
　　　and believe in the beauty of work
55　　but also know the reality of waste,
　　　the good minds ground down through circumstance
　　　and loss. I mourn the loss of all I think
　　　he could have been, and this is what he feels,
　　　I guess, and cannot face and hates me
60　　for reminding him of what is gone and wasted
　　　and won't come back.

　　　For once, it's too sad to know all this.
　　　So I give my brother back his responsibility
　　　or blandly blame it all on sociology,
65　　and imagine sadly how it could have been different,
　　　how it will be different for the son I'll bear.
　　　And how I hope in thirty years he'll touch
　　　his sister as they touched as children
　　　and let nothing come between the blood they share.

≈ CRITICAL REFLECTIONS

1. Rewrite the relationship in this poem between the speaker and her brother as a narrative. What are the central tensions in it?

2. The speaker in this poem says, "He's right: It's true I am not satisfied/with life." Based on reading the poem, why do you think she isn't satisfied? What in the poem helps you make this statement?

3. Why do you think the brother in this poem reacts to the speaker as he does? Why does the speaker react to her brother as she does? Where does education "fit" in the equation?

4. Re-create this poem in different genres: a 5-paragraph theme, a fictional story, and a memo to a boss. What would each say?

≈ MAKING CONNECTIONS

1. Imagine a conversation between the speaker in this poem or her brother and Cedric Jennings. Would they have anything to talk about? Why or why not?

2. Several readings here focus on educational systems and structures—Sizer's, Rose's, Freire's, and Fishman's are just a few. Which of these systems do you think the speaker and her brother would find most effective, and why?

FREDERICK DOUGLASS

FROM NARRATIVE OF THE LIFE OF FREDERICK DOUGLASS, AN AMERICAN SLAVE

Frederick Douglass was born into slavery around the year 1818. Douglass writes that that he "was probably between seven and eight years old" when he left the plantation where he was born and went to work in the home of Captain Thomas Auld, his master's brother, in Baltimore. There, as he explains in this chapter, he learned to read and write. He was later returned to the country, gaining his freedom only after he fled a Baltimore shipyard in 1838. Douglass became an internationally noted abolitionist and crusader for the rights of oppressed people. In addition to his work with the anti-slavery movement, he also was an active supporter of woman suffrage (the struggle to allow women to vote). A brilliant speaker and writer, Douglass published his own newspaper, *The North Star;* authored three autobiographies; served as an advisor to President Lincoln; and filled a number of other governmental posts, including Ambassador to Haiti in the administration of Rutherford B. Hayes. Douglass died in 1895.

I lived in Master Hugh's family about seven years. During this time, I succeeded in learning to read and write. In accomplishing this, I was compelled to resort to various stratagems. I had no regular teacher. My mistress, who had kindly commenced to instruct me, had, in compliance with the advice and direction of her husband, not only ceased to instruct, but had set her face against my being instructed by any one else. It is due, however, to my mistress to say of her, that she did not adopt this course of treatment immediately. She at first lacked the depravity indispensable to shutting me up in mental darkness. It was at least necessary for her to have some training in the exercise of irresponsible power, to make her equal to the task of treating me as though I were a brute.

My mistress was, as I have said, a kind and tender-hearted woman; and in the simplicity of her soul she commenced, when I first went to live with her, to treat me as she supposed one human being ought to treat another. In entering upon the duties of a slaveholder, she did not seem to perceive that I sustained to her the relation of a mere chattel, and that for her to treat me as a human being was not only wrong, but dangerously so. Slavery proved as injurious to her as it did to me. When I went there, she was a pious, warm, and tender-hearted woman. There was no sorrow or suffering for which she had not a tear. She had bread for the hungry, clothes for the naked, and comfort for every mourner that came within her reach. Slavery soon proved its ability to divest her of these heavenly qualities. Under its influence, the tender heart became stone, and the lamblike disposition gave way to one of tiger-like fierceness. The first step in her downward course was in her ceasing to instruct me. She now commenced to practise her husband's precepts. She finally became even more violent in her opposition than her husband himself. She was not satisfied with simply doing as well as he had commanded; she seemed anxious to do better. Nothing seemed to make her more angry than to see me with a newspaper. She seemed to think that here lay the danger. I have had her rush at me with a face made all up of fury, and snatch from me a newspaper, in a manner that fully revealed her apprehension. She was an apt woman; and a little experience soon demonstrated, to her satisfaction, that education and slavery were incompatible with each other.

From this time I was most narrowly watched. If I was in a separate room any considerable length of time, I was sure to be suspected of having a book, and was at once called to give an account of myself. All this, however, was too late. The first step had been taken. Mistress, in teaching me the alphabet, had given me the *inch,* and no precaution could prevent me from taking the *ell.*

The plan which I adopted, and the one by which I was most successful, was that of making friends of all the little white boys whom I met in the street. As many of these as I could, I converted into teachers. With their kindly aid, obtained at different times and in different places, I finally succeeded in learning to read. When I was sent of errands, I always took my book with me, and by going one part of my errand quickly, I found time to get a lesson before my return. I used also to carry bread with me, enough of which was always in the house, and to which I was always welcome; for I was much better off in this regard than many of the poor white children in our neighborhood. This bread I used to bestow upon the hungry little urchins, who, in return, would give me that more valuable bread of knowledge. I am strongly tempted to give the names of two or three of those little boys, as a testimonial of the gratitude and affection I bear them; but prudence forbids;—not that it would injure me, but it might embarrass them; for it is almost an unpardonable offence to teach slaves to read in this Christian country. It is enough to say of the dear little fellows, that they lived on Philpot Street, very near Durgin and Bailey's ship-yard. I used to talk this matter of slavery over with them. I would sometimes say to them, I wished I could be as free as they would be when they got to be men. "You will be free as soon as you are twenty-one, *but I am a slave for life!* Have not I as good a right to be free as you have?" These words used to trouble them; they would express for me the liveliest sympathy, and console me with the hope that something would occur by which I might be free.

5   I was now about twelve years old, and the thought of being *a slave for life* began to bear heavily upon my heart. Just about this time, I got hold of a book entitled "The Columbian Orator." Every opportunity I got, I used to read this book. Among much of other interesting matter, I found in it a dialogue between a master and his slave. The slave was represented as having run away from his master three times. The dialogue represented the conversation which took place between them, when the slave was retaken the third time. In this dialogue, the whole argument in behalf of slavery was brought forward by the master, all of which was disposed of by the slave. The slave was made to say some very smart as

well as impressive things in reply to his master—things which had the desired though unexpected effect; for the conversation resulted in the voluntary emancipation of the slave on the part of the master.

In the same book, I met with one of Sheridan's mighty speeches on and in behalf of Catholic emancipation. These were choice documents to me. I read them over and over again with unabated interest. They gave tongue to interesting thoughts of my own soul, which had frequently flashed through my mind, and died away for want of utterance. The moral which I gained from the dialogue was the power of truth over the conscience of even a slaveholder. What I got from Sheridan was a bold denunciation of slavery, and a powerful vindication of human rights. The reading of these documents enabled me to utter my thoughts, and to meet the arguments brought forward to sustain slavery; but while they relieved me of one difficulty, they brought on another even more painful than the one of which I was relieved. The more I read, the more I was led to abhor and detest my enslavers. I could regard them in no other light than a band of successful robbers, who had left their homes, and gone to Africa, and stolen us from our homes, and in a strange land reduced us to slavery. I loathed them as being the meanest as well as the most wicked of men. As I read and contemplated the subject, behold! that very discontentment which Master Hugh had predicted would follow my learning to read had already come, to torment and sting my soul to unutterable anguish. As I writhed under it, I would at times feel that learning to read had been a curse rather than a blessing. It had given me a view of my wretched condition, without the remedy. It opened my eyes to the horrible pit, but to no ladder upon which to get out. In moments of agony, I envied my fellow-slaves for their stupidity. I have often wished myself a beast. I preferred the condition of the meanest reptile to my own. Any thing, no matter what, to get rid of thinking! It was this everlasting thinking of my condition that tormented me. There was no getting rid of it. It was pressed upon me by every object within sight or hearing, animate or inanimate. The silver trump of freedom had roused my soul to eternal wakefulness. Freedom now appeared, to disappear no more forever. It was heard in every sound, and seen in every thing. It was ever present to torment me with a sense of my wretched condition. I saw nothing without seeing it, I heard nothing without hearing it, and felt nothing without feeling it. It looked from every star, it smiled in every calm, breathed in every wind, and moved in every storm.

I often found myself regretting my own existence, and wishing myself dead; and but for the hope of being free, I have no doubt but that I should have killed myself, or done something for which I should have been killed. While in this state of mind, I was eager to hear any one speak of slavery. I was a ready listener. Every little while, I could hear something about the abolitionists. It was some time before I found what the word meant. It was always used in such connections as to make it an interesting word to me. If a slave ran away and succeeded in getting clear, or if a slave killed his master, set fire to a barn, or did any thing very wrong in the mind of a slaveholder, it was spoken of as the fruit of *abolition*. Hearing the word in this connection very often, I set about learning what it meant. The dictionary afforded me little or no help. I found it was "the act of abolishing;" but then I did not know what was to be abolished. Here I was perplexed. I did not dare to ask any one about its meaning, for I was satisfied that it was something they wanted me to know very little about. After a patient waiting, I got one of our city papers, containing an account of the number of petitions from the north, praying for the abolition of slavery in the District of Columbia, and of the slave trade between the States. From this time I understood the words *abolition* and *abolitionist,* and always drew near when that word was spoken, expecting to hear something of importance to myself and fellow-slaves. The light broke in upon me by degrees. I went one day down on the wharf of Mr. Waters; and seeing two Irishmen unloading a scow of stone, I went, unasked, and helped them. When we had finished, one of them came to me and asked me if I were a slave. I told him I was. He asked, "Are ye a slave for life?" I told him that I was. The good Irishman seemed to be deeply affected by the statement. He said to the other that it was a pity so fine a little fellow as myself should be a slave for life. He said it was a shame to hold me. They both advised me to run away to the north; that I should find friends there, and that I should be free. I pretended not to be interested in what they said, and treated them as if I did not understand them; for I feared they might be treacherous. White men have been known to encourage slaves to escape, and then, to get the reward, catch them and return them to their masters. I was afraid that these seemingly good men might use me so; but I nevertheless remembered their advice, and from that time I resolved to run away. I looked forward to a time at which it would be safe for me to escape. I was too young to think of doing so immediately; besides, I wished to learn how to write, as I might have occasion to write my own pass. I consoled myself with the hope that I should one day find a good chance. Meanwhile, I would learn to write.

The idea as to how I might learn to write was suggested to me by being in Durgin and Bailey's ship-yard, and frequently seeing the ship carpenters, after hewing, and getting a piece of timber ready for use, write on the timber the name of that part of the ship for which it was intended. When a piece of timber was intended for the larboard side, it would be marked thus—"L." When a piece was for the starboard side, it would be marked thus—"S." A piece for the larboard side forward, would be marked thus—"L. F." When a piece was for starboard side forward, it would be marked thus—"S. F." For larboard aft, it would be marked thus—"L. A." For starboard aft, it would be marked thus—"S. A." I soon learned the names of these letters, and for what they were intended when placed upon a piece of timber in the ship-yard. I immediately commenced copying them, and in a short time was able to make the four letters named. After that, when I met with any boy who I knew could write, I would tell him I could write as well as he. The next word would be, "I don't believe you. Let me see you try it." I would then make the letters which I had been so fortunate as to learn, and ask him to beat that. In this way I got a good many lessons in writing, which it is quite possible I should never have gotten in any other way. During this time, my copy-book was the board fence, brick wall, and pavement; my pen and ink was a lump of chalk. With these, I learned mainly how to write. I then commenced and continued copying the Italics in *Webster's Spelling Book,* until I could make them all without looking on the book. By this time, my little Master Thomas had gone to school, and learned how to write, and had written over a number of copy-books. These had been brought home, and shown to some of our near neighbors, and then laid aside. My mistress used to go to class meeting at the Wilk Street meeting-house every Monday afternoon, and leave me to take care of the house. When left thus, I used to spend the time in writing in the spaces left in Master Thomas's copy-book, copying what he had written. I continued to do this until I could write a hand very similar to that of Master Thomas. Thus, after a long, tedious effort for years, I finally succeeded in learning how to write.

CRITICAL REFLECTIONS

1. This version of Frederick Douglass's *Narrative* was published 16 years before the beginning of the Civil War and 18 years before Abraham Lincoln issued the Emancipation Proclamation, which abolished slavery. Reflect on what you know about the Antebellum Period (that is, the period before the Civil War). Who do you think might have been the audience for Douglass's work? What purposes might he have wanted to achieve with it?

2. In this chapter, Douglass conveys some very specific purposes for his developing abilities to read and to write. What do you see as these purposes? What benefits did they provide for Douglass? Again considering Douglass's likely audience, what do you think he wanted the audience to learn from these purposes?

3. Readers sometimes look to Frederick Douglass' *Narrative* as an example of the liberatory possibilities of literacy education. What do you see as the purpose of education for Douglass? Do you find it to be liberatory, or something else entirely?

MAKING CONNECTIONS

1. Douglass, Booker T. Washington, and W.E.B. DuBois all outline what they see as the potential for literacy education for African-Americans in their pieces in this book. Do you see their visions as similar to one another? Different? How and why?

2. Consider Douglass's *Narrative* in light of other literacy narratives included here. Do you see Douglass's experiences as similar to or different from those of the students in Earl Shorris's Clemente course, Cedric's experience at Brown University, the experiences of the Fisher family, or others in this text? How and why?

3. In "The Banking Model," Paolo Freire outlines a model for education that he believes will be useful for disempowered citizens. Do you think that Douglass would have endorsed Freire's alternative to the banking model? Why or why not?

DARCY FREY

THE LAST SHOT

Freelance journalist Darcy Frey published "The Last Shot" in *Harper's* magazine in 1993 to wide acclaim. To write it, he spent over a year with the Lincoln High School basketball players who are the main focus of the article. The article attracted readers interested in the intersections among race, education, and athletics with its complex portrait of the roles of basketball and education in the players' lives. It also appealed to readers interested in basketball with its intimate portrayal of the complicated negotiations that the players had to make every day. The article won critical acclaim, including the prestigious National Magazine Award for Feature Writing in 1994. As Frey explains, he does not use the real name of one player in the article; of those whom he does name, only one, Stephon Marbury, has gone on to NBA success. Frey expanded this article into a book, also called *The Last Shot*. He is a contributing writer to *Harper's* and to the *New York Times Magazine*.

AUGUST 1991

Russell Thomas places his right sneaker one inch behind the three-point line, considers the basket with a level gaze, cocks his wrist to shoot, then suddenly looks around. Has he spotted me, watching from the corner of the playground? No, something else is up: he is lifting his nose to the wind like a spaniel, he is gauging air currents. He waits until the wind settles, bits of trash feathering lightly to the ground. Then he sends a twenty-five-foot jump shot arcing through the soft summer twilight. It drops without a sound through the dead center of the bare iron rim. So does the next one. So does the one after that. Alone in the gathering dusk, Russell works the perimeter against imaginary defenders, unspooling jump shots from all points. Few sights on Brooklyn playgrounds stir the hearts and minds of the coaches and scouts who recruit young men for college basketball teams quite like Russell's jumper; they have followed its graceful trajectory ever since he made varsity at Abraham Lincoln High School, in Coney Island, two years ago. But the shot is merely the final gesture, the public flourish of a private regimen that brings Russell to this court day and night. Avoiding pickup games, he gets down to work: an hour of three-point shooting, then wind sprints up the fourteen flights in his project stairwell, then back to the court, where (much to his friends' amusement) he shoots one-handers ten feet from the basket while sitting in a chair.

At this hour Russell usually has the court to himself; most of the other players won't come out until after dark, when the thick humid air begins to stir with night breezes and the court lights come on. But this evening is turning out to be a fine one—cool and foggy. The low, slanting sun sheds a feeble pink light over the silvery Atlantic a block away, and milky sheets of fog roll off the ocean and drift in tatters along the project walkways. The air smells of sewage and saltwater. At the far end of the court, where someone has torn a hole in the chicken-wire fence, other players climb through and begin warming up.

Like most of New York's impoverished and predominantly black neighborhoods, Coney Island does not exactly shower its youth with opportunity. In the early 1960s, urban renewal came to Coney Island in the form of a vast tract of housing projects, packed so densely along a twenty-block stretch that a new skyline rose suddenly behind the boardwalk and amusement park. The experiment of public housing, which has isolated the nation's urban poor from the hearts of their cities, may have failed here in even more spectacular fashion because of Coney Island's utter remoteness. In this neighborhood, on a peninsula at the southern tip of Brooklyn, there are almost no stores, no trees, no police; just block after block of gray cement projects—hulking, prison-like, and jutting straight into the sea.

Most summer nights an amorphous unease settles over Coney Island as apartments become too stifling to bear and the streets fall prey to the gangs and drug dealers. Options are limited: to the south is the stiff gray meringue of the Atlantic; to the north, more than ten miles away, are the Statue of Liberty and the glass-and-steel spires of Manhattan's financial district. Officially, Coney Island is considered a part of the endless phantasmagoria that is New York City. But on nights like these, as the dealers set up their drug marts in the streets and alleyways, and the sounds of sirens and gunfire keep pace with the darkening sky, it feels like the end of the world.

5   Yet even in Coney Island there are some uses to which a young man's talent, ambition, and desire to stay out of harm's way may be put: there is basketball. Hidden behind the projects are dozens of courts, and every night they fill with restless teenagers, there to remain for hours until exhaustion or the hoodlums take over. The high-school dropouts and the aging players who never made it to college usually show up for a physical game at a barren strip of courts by the water known as Chop Chop Land, where bruises and minutes played are accrued at a one-to-one ratio. The younger kids congregate for rowdy games at Run-and-Gun Land. The court there is short and the rims are low, so everyone can dunk, and the only pass ever made is the one inbounding the ball. At Run-and-Gun, players stay on the move for another reason: the court sits just below one of the most dreaded projects, where Coney Island's worst hoodlums sometimes pass a summer evening "getting hectic," as they say—tossing batteries and beer bottles onto the court from apartment windows fifteen stories above.

The neighborhood's best players—the ones, like Russell, with aspirations—practice a disciplined, team-driven style of basketball at this court by the O'Dwyer projects, which has been dubbed the Garden after the New York Knicks' arena. In a neighborhood ravaged by the commerce of drugs, the Garden offers a tenuous sanctuary. A few years ago, community activists petitioned the housing authority to install night lights. And the players themselves resurfaced the court and put up regulation-height rims that snap back after a player dunks. Russell may be the only kid at the Garden who practices his defensive footwork while holding a ten-pound brick in each hand, but no one here treats the game as child's play. Even the hoodlums decline to vandalize the Garden, because in Coney Island the possibility of transcendence through basketball is an article of faith.

Most evenings this summer I have come to the Garden to watch Russell and his friends play ball. The notion that basketball can liberate dedicated players like these from the grinding daily privations of the ghetto has become a cherished parable, advanced by television sportscasters, college basketball publicists, and sneaker companies proselytizing the work ethic and $120 high-tops. And that parable is conveyed directly to the players at the Garden by the dozens of college coaches who arrive in Coney Island each year with assurances that even if a National Basketball Association contract isn't in the cards, a player's talent and tenacity will at least reward him with a free college education, a decent job, and a one-way ticket out of the neighborhood. But how does this process actually unfold? And what forces stand in its way? How often is basketball's promise of a better life redeemed? It was questions like these that drew me to this court, between Mermaid and Surf avenues.

"Just do it, right?" I glance to my left and there is Corey Johnson, smiling mischievously, eyes alight. He nods toward the court—players stretching out, taking lay-ups—and it does, in fact, resemble a sneaker commercial. "Work hard, play hard, buy yourself a pair of Nikes, young man," Corey intones. Corey is a deft mimic and he does a superb white TV announcer. "They get you where you want to go, which is out of the ghet-to!" He laughs, we shake hands, and he takes up an observation post by my side.

Corey is Russell's best friend and one of Lincoln High's other star seniors. He, too, expects to play college ball. But he specializes in ironic detachment and normally shows up courtside with his Walkman merely to watch for girls beneath his handsome, hooded eyes. Tonight he is wearing a fresh white T-shirt, expertly ripped along the back and sleeves to reveal glimpses of his sculpted physique; denim shorts that reach to his knees; and a pair of orange sneakers that go splendidly with his lid—a tan baseball cap with orange piping, which he wears with the bill pointing skyward. From his headphones come the sounds of Color Me Badd, and Corey sings along: I—wanna—sex—you—up . . . He loops his fingers around the chicken-wire fence and says, "I tell you, Coney Island is like a disease. Of the mind. It makes you lazy. You relax too much. 'Cause all you ever see is other guys relaxing."

10   Although a pickup game has begun at the basket nearest us, Russell still commands the other. As the last light drains from the sky, he finishes with three-pointers and moves on to baby hooks: fifteen with the left hand, fifteen with the right; miss one and start all over again. Corey smiles at his friend's hair-shirt discipline. Russell, it is hoped, will play next year in the Big East, one of the nation's top college conferences, in which Seton Hall, St. John's, Georgetown, Syracuse,

and others compete. Russell is six feet three, 180 pounds, with a shaved head and a small goatee that seems to mean business. Last spring the Lincoln team, with Russell leading the way, won the New York City public-school championship in a rout at Madison Square Garden that was broadcast citywide on cable TV. But one can never predict what may happen to Russell, because, as Corey observes, "Russell is Russell." I can guess what this means: Russell lives in one of the neighborhood's toughest projects, and misfortune often seems to shadow him. Last year a fight between Russell and his girlfriend turned violent. Terrified that his college scholarship had just been replaced by a stiff prison term, Russell climbed to the top of one of Coney Island's highest buildings. It took almost half an hour of reasoned talk by his high-school coach and members of the Sixtieth Precinct to bring him back from the edge.[1]

Russell may be tightly wound, but no Coney Island player can avoid for long the agonizing pressures that might bring a teenager with his whole life ahead of him to the edge of a roof. Basketball newsletters and scouting reports are constantly scrutinizing the players, and practically every day some coach shows up— appraising, coaxing, negotiating, and, as often as not, making promises he never keeps. Getting that scholarship offer is every player's dream—in anticipation, no one steps outside in Coney Island without a Syracuse cap or a St. John's sweatshirt. But in reality only a handful of the neighborhood's players have ever made it to such top four-year programs; most have been turned back by one obstacle or another in high school. Others who have enrolled in college never saw their dream to completion. The list is grim: there was Eric "Spoon" Marbury, who played for the University of Georgia but never graduated, and ended up back in Coney Island working construction; his younger brother Norman "Jou-Jou" Marbury, who lost his scholarship to highly ranked Tennessee because of academic problems in high school; and now David "Chocolate" Harris, a talented player who never even graduated from high school. He dropped out of Lincoln after his freshman year and became a small-time drug dealer. Earlier this summer police found him in an abandoned lot, his hood pulled over his head and a bullet through his skull. He was seventeen. Some of the players warming up at the Garden have written on the tongues of their sneakers, CHOCOLATE: R.I.P.

The orange court lights have come on now, displacing the encroaching darkness. Two players on either end of the court climb the fence and sit atop the backboards, hanging nets—a sign that a serious game is about to begin. Suddenly a ferocious grinding noise fills the air. It gets louder and louder, and then a teenage kid riding a Big Wheel careers onto the court. He darts through the playground crowd, leaving a wake of pissed-off players, then hops off his ride and watches it slam into the fence. "Ah, yes, Stephon Marbury," Corey says dryly, "future of the neighborhood."

Stephon—Eric and Norman Marbury's kid brother—is barely fourteen, has yet to begin high school, but already his recruiting has begun. At least one college

---

[1]Some New York City newspapers withheld Russell's name when reporting this incident. In keeping with the practice of withholding the names of minors involved in suicide threats or attempts, *Harper's Magazine* has changed Russell's name and the name of his mother in this article. No other names have been altered.

coach is known to have sent him fawning letters in violation of National Collegiate Athletic Association rules; street agents, paid under the table by colleges to bring top players to their programs, have begun cultivating Stephon; and practically every high-school coach in the city is heaping him with free gear—sneakers, caps, bags—in an attempt to lure him to his school. At first glance, Stephon doesn't look like the future of anything: he's diminutive, barely five feet nine, with the rounded forehead and delicate features of an infant. He sports a stylish razor cut and a pierced ear, and the huge gold stud seems to tilt his tiny bald head off its axis. Caught somewhere between puberty and superstardom, he walks around with his sneakers untied, the ends of his belt drooping suggestively from his pants, and half a Snickers bar extruding from his mouth.

With Stephon here, Corey wanders onto the court. Russell, too, is persuaded to give up his solo regimen. Basketball, it is commonly said, is a game of pure instinct, but the five-on-five contest that begins here is something else. Corey and Stephon are cousins, and Russell is as good as family—the three of them have played together since they were in grade school. They seem to move as if the spontaneous, magical geometry of the game had all been rehearsed in advance. Stephon, the smallest by far, is doing tricks with the ball as though it were dangling from his hand by a string, then gunning it to his older teammates with a series of virtuoso nolook passes: behind-the-back passes, sidearm passes, shovel passes. Corey is lulling defenders with his sleepy eyes, then exploding to the basket, where he casually tosses the ball through the hoop. Russell is sinking twenty-footers as if they were six-inch putts.

15 The game has just begun when a crowd starts to form: sidelined players, three deep, waiting their turn. A prostitute trolling for clients. A drunk yelling maniacally, "I played with Jordan, I played with Jabbar. They ain't shit. And neither are you!" A buffed-out guy in a silk suit and alligator shoes arrives, swigging from a bottle of Courvoisier. An agent? A scout? The crowd gives him elbow room. A couple of teenage mothers with strollers come by; they get less elbow room.

Basketball is so inextricably woven into the fabric of Coney Island life that almost everyone here can recite a complete oral history of the neighborhood's players. People remember the exact scores of summer tournament games played at this court ten years ago, or describe in rapturous detail the perfect arc that Carlton "Silk" Owens put on his jumper before he was shot in the elbow in 1982. Dog-eared copies of a ten-year-old University of Georgia catalogue with a picture of Spoon Marbury playing with future NBA great Dominique Wilkins get passed around like samizdat.

Russell, Corey, and Stephon are the natural heirs to this vaunted tradition. But this is a complicated business: given the failures that have preceded them, the new crew is watched by the neighborhood with a certain skittishness, a growing reluctance to care too deeply. Yet Coney Island offers its residents little else on which to hang their pride. So the proceedings here take on a desperate, exalted quality, and by unspoken agreement the misfortunes of bygone players are chalked up to either a lack of will or plain bad luck—both of which make possible the continuance of hope. Silk didn't go pro, it is said, "because that was the year they cut the college draft from three rounds to two." Another player, the explanation goes, had that pro game, went to the hoop both ways, "but he was done in by a shyster agent."

Still, the suspicion lingers that something larger and less comprehensible may be at work. Ten years ago, the Long Island City projects in Queens produced New York's best players, but the drug industry and the collapse of that neighborhood into violence, broken families, and ever-greater poverty put an end to its dynasty. In recent years the torch has passed to Coney Island, which struggles to avoid a similar fate.

It's past midnight now, and the ambient glow of Manhattan's remote skyscrapers has turned the sky a metallic blue. Standing courtside, we can see only the darkened outlines of the projects, looming in every direction, and the shirtless players streaking back and forth, drenched in a pool of orange light. For Russell, Corey, and Stephon, the hard labor of winning their scholarships lies ahead; for now this game is enough. Corey, sprinting downcourt, calls out, "Homeboy! Homeboy!" Standing under his own basket, Stephon lets fly with a long, improbable pass that Corey somehow manages to catch and dunk in one balletic leap. The game is stopped on account of pandemonium: players and spectators are screaming and staggering around the court—knees buckling, heads held in astonishment. Even Mr. Courvoisier loses his cool. Stephon laughs and points to the rim, still shuddering fearfully from its run-in with Corey's fists. "Yo, cuz," he yells. "Make it bleed!" Then he raises his arms jubilantly and dances a little jig, rendered momentarily insane by the sheer giddy pleasure of playing this game to perfection.

SEPTEMBER

20 Abraham Lincoln High School is a massive yellow-brick building of ornate stonework and steel-gated windows a few blocks north of the boardwalk. As Coney Island has deteriorated, so has Lincoln High, though the school itself sits about a mile from the projects at the end of Ocean Parkway, a stately, tree-lined boulevard. Across the parkway are Brighton Beach and several other Jewish neighborhoods, but the kids from those areas are usually sent elsewhere for their education, as Lincoln has become, little by little, a ghetto school for the projects.

A malaise has set in at Lincoln, as it has at so many inner-city public schools. Students regularly walk in and out of class, sleep at their desks, throw projectiles through doorways at friends in the hail. In the teachers' cafeteria, conversation often reverts to pension plans and whether the 2,500 Lincoln kids are as bad as last year or worse. The first day I dropped by, there was much commotion because the locker of a student was found to contain a handgun. On my second visit, the weapon in question was a six-inch knife. After one student was sent to the hospital with a neck wound requiring forty stitches, even some of the most peaceable kids began carrying X-Acto knives for protection.

Spectators at games in the New York Public School Athletic League (PSAL) are often frisked at the door by guards with metal detectors. Still, incidents occur. In the middle of the 1982 semifinals, between Alexander Hamilton and Ben Franklin, an off-duty security guard chased a knife-wielding fan directly onto the court and put a gun to his head while the crowd and players ran screaming for the exits. And then there is that ritual of basketball in the urban public schools: the pregame passeggiata of the neighborhood's drug dealers. During warm-ups in certain gyms, the steel doors will swing open and slowly, conspicuously, daring the security guards to stop them, the dealers will make their entrance, signaling to friends in the bleachers while strolling around the court draped in leather, fur, and several pounds of gold.

Into this chaos walk the college coaches—pin-striped and paisley-tied, bearing four-color photos of sold-out college arenas and statistics on how many games their teams play on national television. Usually they precede their visits by dropping the players brief notes, like the one from a Fordham coach to a Lincoln player describing how one of the college's basketball stars became rich beyond his wildest dreams. "This could be you someday," the coach wrote. "See how Fordham can change your life?" The coach signed off with the salutation, "Health, Happine$$, and Hundred$."

Most of the coaches are leery of Corey right now; he spends too much time with girls and, despite his intelligence, his grades are among the worst on the team. Stephon is, as far as the NCAA rules are concerned, off-limits for the next three years. So they come to see Russell. In the first week of school, Wichita State, St. Bonaventure, and the University of Delaware have paid him visits. After school today he sits down with Rod Baker, the head coach at the University of California at Irvine.

25 "My apologies for not coming to see you before, but the fact is one of our players just dropped out and suddenly we need another guard." Coach Baker is a trim, handsome black man wearing a natty blue suit, tasseled loafers, and a gleaming gold NCAA ring. "And the first person we thought of was Russell Thomas. I'm not bull-shitting you. Frankly, I think you're an impact player, a franchise player. Five years from now, I wouldn't be surprised if people were saying, 'Remember when Russell Thomas came in and changed the fortunes of Cal-Irvine?'" Baker runs a finger down each side of his well-groomed mustache. Russell smiles uncertainly.

"Now let me tell you about California. Ever been there?" Russell shakes his head. "Well, you're gonna think you died and went to heaven. I'm serious. What is it today—seventy degrees? Nice and sunny? In California this is a shitty day in December. That's the God's truth. And the other thing about going to school on the West Coast . . . " Baker looks down, allows himself a moment to collect his thoughts, then looks up at Russell. "Everybody's got certain things they want to get away from in their past." How on earth does Baker know about Russell's incident on the roof? "In California, Russell, you can get away from that, from all the stuff that brings you down in Coney Island. At Cal-Irvine you can be whoever you really want to be."

After Coach Baker leaves, Russell and I walk out to the football field behind the school, a lovely, tree-lined expanse of green in an otherwise barren urban setting. It's one of those crystalline September afternoons, with fall in the air but the sun pulsing down on the aluminum bleachers where we sit with the last warmth of summer. (Weather like this may ruin a Californian's day, but in Brooklyn this is as good as it gets.) "I was impressed with Coach Baker. I felt he was definitely leveling with me," Russell declares. "But I'm going to wait and see. Hear what they all have to say. Then decide. Try not to be pressured. Just take it one day at a time." Russell's initial comments after a recruiting session often mimic the solemn coach-speak to which he is subjected every day. So many people—high-school and college coaches and free-lance street agents—want a piece of Russell and try to influence where he will sign that it often takes him a while to locate his own thoughts. "They say it's the second-biggest decision I gotta make in my life—after I pick my wife." He looks around the field, swatting imaginary flies. "But I'm doing good, I'm handling it." He locates some gum on the bottom rung of the bleachers, picks it free, rolls it between two fingers, and flips it onto the grass. "It's normal to be confused, right?" Now the elastic of his right sock receives his complete attention as he performs a series of micro-adjustments to get the folds just right. "That's only human, isn't it?" He takes one more look around and, finding nothing else to distract him, falls silent.

The recruiting circus has been a fact of life for Russell and his friends ever since they were in junior high. Directly across the street from Lincoln sits William Grady Tech—another powerhouse PSAL team—and the two schools compete zealously for the pool of talent coming out of the Coney Island projects. Lincoln players often refer to Grady as "the best team money can buy." Grady players claim that Lincoln tries to lure them away with sneakers and promises to "pass them along" in their classes. Coaches at both schools deny such allegations, but it is a fact that thirteen-year-old Coney Island athletes are encouraged to shop for high schools the way the seniors pick colleges—according to which school will give them the most playing time, the best chance to win a city title, and the exposure to get recruited to the next level.

The pressure of playing basketball in Coney Island affects Russell in mysterious ways. One time last year he snuck out the back door of the locker room to avoid a postgame team meeting, leaving everyone wondering whether he was angry at himself for his performance or angry at his teammates for not passing him the ball. Probably both. This year, knowing how much is at stake, Russell has struggled to change. He does this in small ways. Over the summer he told me he was planning a new image for himself. I waited to see what he meant. The first day of school he arrived wearing penny loafers, just like the coaches. The next day, building from the bottom up, he had added pleated pants. Then suspenders. A paisley tie. Finally he topped off the look with a pair of non-prescription wire-rimmed glasses—"because they make you look educated. You know, the professor look."

30   But today Russell seems agitated in the old way, restless with an emotion he can't identify. "You know, I used to say that I couldn't wait to be a senior," he says.

"But I got to worry about classes, the season, recruiting, the SATs. That's a lot of pressure." According to NCAA rules, students who want to play sports at a four-year, Division I school, those with the nation's top athletic programs, must enter college having maintained at least a 70 average in high school and having received a combined score of 700 on the math and verbal sections of the SATs—the last an insurmountable obstacle to many black players with poor educations and little experience taking standardized tests. Failing that, a player must earn a two-year degree at a junior college before moving on to a four-year school. Many Division I coaches, however, refuse to recruit junior-college players, considering them damaged goods. So players who don't go directly to a four-year school often never get to play top college ball or earn their bachelor's degrees.

The first time Russell took the SATs, he received a combined score somewhere in the mid-500s. (You receive 400 points for signing your name.) This year he gave up his lunch period to study, and lately he's been carrying around a set of vocabulary flash cards, which he pulls out whenever there isn't a basketball in his hands. By dint of tremendous effort, Russell had also brought his average up to 78—the highest on the team. These are extraordinary developments for someone whose scheduling over the years has been so bad that he had never, until recently, finished a book or learned the fundamentals of multiplication, even as he was being called upon to answer reading-comprehension and algebra questions on the SATs. "I used to think there were smart people and dumb people, but that's not true," Russell says forcefully. "Everybody's got the same brain. They say a human mind can know a thousand words—it's like a little computer! But you got to practice." He pauses. "But how come it's always the guys who don't study who get their 700s? Seems like the guys who work hard always get screwed. But oh, well."

From across the football field, the chants and cries of cheerleading practice travel toward us with perfect clarity. Russell shades his eyes with his hands and watches a tumble of cartwheels. "It's nice out here, isn't it? All the trees and everything? Out where I live there's nothing but total corruption and evilness, drugs and stolen cars. All my friends be getting arrested, shot at . . . " It is not too much to say that basketball saved Russell. In junior high he was trouble, sometimes leaving home for long stretches to hang out on the streets with his friends. But he was spotted playing ball in the parks by one of Lincoln's unofficial recruiters, who persuaded him to enroll. In high school he gained confidence and won the hearts of teachers who admired his efforts while growing increasingly appalled by what he had never been taught. Now after school, while certain of his classmates walk over to Brighton Beach to hold up pensioners at gunpoint, Russell goes straight home, takes his vitamins, does his push-ups, and combs through college-recruiting brochures until bedtime. His dream is not to become a pro, he tells me, but "to graduate college, start me a nice little family, and get me a nice little job as a registered nurse."

Russell has begun throwing his things into his gym bag: books, towel, basketball. Something still bothers him, though, and he keeps going back to it, like a tongue to a broken tooth. "You know, I look at all these players, like Silk and Jou-

Jou. They're way better than me, and look what happened to them: Jou-Jou lost his scholarship, Silk never graduated. This recruiting business, man, it's scary. But Coach Baker—for some reason he made me feel secure, like he'll take good care of me, like I'm part of the family." Russell, so effusive about other matters, almost never mentions his own family. All I know is that his father moved away when Russell was young, leaving his mother to raise him and his two younger sisters. I can't help wondering if it isn't doubly hard for Russell to resist all the high-powered coaches who recruit him because he has lived most of his life without a father.

Russell's new girlfriend, Terry, comes into view across the field. She waves to us and starts walking toward the bleachers. "Now that girl is smart!" Russell exclaims. "She got an 88 average!" A cloud has just shifted in Russell's mood and the sun has reappeared. "She got a nice family too. They even got their own house. One of these days I'm going to marry that girl." Russell started seeing Terry not long after the incident with his previous girlfriend. All of Russell's friends were thrilled to see him involved with someone so pretty and levelheaded; Terry's friends thought she was crazy. But she stuck by Russell and recently he announced to his teammates that he would wear a small blue ribbon—Terry's favorite color—on his uniform this season. This, too, was part of the new Russell.

35 Terry is still a good fifty yards away. Russell puts his hand on my arm confidentially. "You know what happened to me last year, with that business on the roof?" This is the first time he's mentioned it to me. "I really thought my career was shattered. But you know, I see now it was good for me. I been through certain things other teenagers haven't. I learnt that part of success is failure, having hard times smack you in the face, having to go without having." Still gripping my arm, Russell looks me in the eye and says, "I'm gonna get my 700 and go Division I. Trust me. You know why? I've come too far, worked too hard already."

This is what this whole basketball business is about, isn't it? By playing ball and playing by the rules, a kid like Russell is saved from the streets—saved too from that unshakable belief in his own insignificance—and set on a path that could change his life. Terry is almost upon us now. Russell licks his fingertips and cleans a smudge off the top of his loafer. Then he takes a precautionary whiff of each armpit and, finding the results tolerable, shakes my hand and runs off to meet his girl.

OCTOBER

"Come on, Russell—we're jetting!" Stephon places his hand against the back of Russell's bald head and flicks it hard to make the skin sting.

"Damn, Stephon, stop sweating me! Can't you see I'm talking to my girl?" When Russell gets upset, his voice jumps to a higher register. "Can't you see I'm talking to my girl?" Stephon mimics. Russell tries to ignore him. He whispers something in Terry's ear, gives her a kiss, then slings his book bag over his shoulder and marches toward the locker room. The last class bell has rung, disgorging hundreds of students into the Lincoln corridors. Stephon lingers in the crowd and leans in close to Terry. "You know, when Russell goes to college, I'm next in line."

Terry is almost as tall as Stephon, and for an instant I think she's going to hit him. But she says, "You got some mouth," and walks away.

40   Stephon does not suffer from the usual array of adolescent insecurities, but why should he? As a freshman, he arrived at Lincoln already a legend, and his performance later today, during the season's first official practice, will do nothing to lower his profile. Hopes for this year's team are running so high that everyone gathers in the gym to see for himself: students, teachers, other coaches, and a reporter for *Newsday* who will cover the team all season.

And the players do not disappoint. All of them have improved since I saw them in August. Russell, once a stationary jump shooter, is shooting off the dribble, driving with authority to the hoop. For years, Russell had gotten a rap for "playing white"—taking a lay-up when he could have dunked. "No one thinks I can dunk 'cause I never dunked in public," he told me over the summer. "But between you and me, I dunk in the park all the time—when no one's looking." I was tempted to ask if this was a riddle (is a dunk really a dunk if no one is around to see it?), but Russell wasn't smiling. "I'm going to dunk this year. Trust me." And he does. At practice, Russell drives the lane and goes straight over Corey for an emphatic jam. The whole place erupts—guys are chanting his name, yelling, "He flushed it good!" Russell, ignoring the cheers, walks over to me and grips my shoulder. "See, it's all part of the plan," he says. "Just like the shoes." Now what the hell does that mean?

As for Corey, he seems to have added an extra cylinder for the coming season. At six feet one, Corey is so fast he doesn't even bother to fake; he just wastes his man on the first step and springs into the air as if coming off a trampoline. "Do the 360!" someone yells from the bleachers and Corey obliges, performing a gyrating dunk. "Statue of Liberty!" comes the next request, and Corey takes off near the foul line, soars toward the basket, and then—legs split, arm extended, ball held high like a torch—throws down a thunderous, backboard-rattling jam. Corey knows how to work a crowd, sometimes too well. Last year, in one of the season's crucial games, Corey was all alone under the basket, tried a fancy lay-up, and blew it. The coaches rose to their feet, howling in rage. Corey jogged downcourt shrugging, palms turned toward the ceiling. "Relax, guys," he said, nonchalance itself. "It's just basketball."

And then there is Stephon. He is making his debut as a high-school player today, but he takes the court as he always does—ever confident, leaning forward onto the balls of his feet in happy anticipation, arms jangling at his sides. "Mission day," he announces with a clap. "Time to get busy." Within moments he is making quick work of his competition, stunning the crowded, noisy gym into a reverential silence. Here he is, out by the three-point line. He does a stutter step to freeze the defense, then drives the lane. En route, he encounters the team's six-foot-seven center in midair, so he changes direction, shifts the ball from right hand to left, and sinks a reverse lay-up. I hear one of the coaches mutter, "Holy shi—," not even finishing the thought because here Stephon is again, off to the left. He drives, sees too many bodies in the paint, and pulls up for a jumper. He is way out of position, his lithe body still floating toward the basket, so he calculates his velocity, takes a little something off the ball, and banks it gently off the glass.

45 "Jesus, this kid's the real thing! Do you realize Stephon could keep us in TV tournaments for the next four years?" Bobby Hartstein, head coach of the Lincoln team, sounds overjoyed—and vastly relieved. Lincoln has had great players before, but never a virtual child prodigy like Stephon. All summer long, Coach Hartstein held his breath as other schools tried to lure his incoming star with promises of a starting position and a guaranteed supply of his favorite sneakers. One Brooklyn coach presented Stephon with a new uniform and treated him and his father to a series of extravagant dinners. A coach in the Bronx was rumored to have offered cash up front. But Lincoln had the edge. Stephon's three older brothers—Eric, Donnie, and Norman—had all starred at the school. And to close the sale, Hartstein made Stephon an extraordinary offer: the forty-two-year-old coach promised the fourteen-year-old player that he'd turn down any college coaching offer to personally shepherd Stephon through high school.

After practice the players all tumble down the school's front steps. Stephon walks up to me and says, "Take me to Mickey D's. I'm hungry. I could eat three Big Macs. You got any cash?" I've already agreed to drive Russell and Corey home, so I tell Stephon to hop in. "This is your ride?" Stephon stares slack-jawed at my ten-year-old Toyota. "When I get to college, I'm gonna get me a white Nissan Sentra—that shit is milk!"

"Just get in the damn car," Russell says. In the last few weeks, some schools that had recruited Russell aggressively in September have backed off, and Russell is taking it hard. No sooner had Russell made up his mind to sign with Cal-Irvine than Coach Baker called to say they were no longer interested—the guard they thought was leaving decided to come back. Meanwhile, other schools seem convinced that Russell won't ever pass his SATs. (Coaches somehow learn of Russell's test scores before he's even had time to show them to his mother.) With every school that courts and then abandons him, Russell goes through the full cycle of infatuation, falling in love, rejection, and recuperation; each time he survives with a little less of the spirit to forge on with the school year. Stephon wants the front seat of my car, but Russell says gruffly, "Six foot three gets the front. Five foot nine goes in back." Corey wisely stays out of it. He puts his Walkman on, pops the hatch, and climbs in the far back, draping his legs over the bumper.

Autumn is arriving quickly this year. For weeks now the sky has been a study in gray, and the trees along Ocean Parkway are already bare. On the drive to McDonald's we splash through piles of fallen leaves. "If you crash and I get injured, Coach is gonna kill you," Stephon advises me. Then he announces, to no one in particular, "When I go to college, I'm going to Syracuse or Georgia Tech."

"How come?" I ask.

50 "Because at Syracuse you play in front of 32,820 people every home game— it's crazy-loud in there," he says, meaning the Syracuse Carrier Dome. "And because Georgia Tech knows how to treat its point guards." Stephon is no doubt thinking of Kenny Anderson—the player he is most often compared with—who left Georgia Tech after his sophomore year to sign a five-season, $14.5 million contract with the NBA's New Jersey Nets. Anderson's salary is a figure Stephon knows as precisely as the seating capacity of the Carrier Dome.

Driving along, we pass beneath the elevated tracks over Stillwell Avenue, where four of New York City's subway lines come to an end. The Coney Island peninsula begins here; beyond the tracks are the projects. Few store owners will risk doing business out there, and the McDonald's near Stillwell is the last outpost of junk food before the streets plunge into the shadow of the high rises. We order our food to go and pile back into my car. Stephon, hungrily consuming his first burger, wedges himself between the two front seats in order to speak directly into his friend's ear. "So, Russell. What are they offering you?" Russell snatches his head away and stares out the window. "You mean you're just gonna sign?" Stephon goes on. "And then when you get to campus and see all them players driving those nice white Nissan Sentras, what are you gonna say to yourself? 'Oh well, I guess they got them from their mothers'?"

We ride along in hostile silence. As we drive down Mermaid Avenue toward the projects, the trees, shops, and pedestrians become scarcer, block by block. During the urban-renewal years, the city knocked down storefronts all along this stretch, but it abandoned much of its commercial-redevelopment plan after moving tenants into the projects. Now the only signs of life along some blocks are the drunks leaning against the plywood of boarded-up buildings and the mangy dogs scavenging vacant lots.

Russell says, "By the way, Stephon, the NCAA does not allow players to get cars."

"Ha! You think the NCAA gives a fuck about cars?" Stephon, still with his head next to Russell's, gives a shrill little laugh. "Why do you think the best players go where they go? 'Cause the schools promise to take care of them and their families. They say the magic word: money."

55   It's no secret where Stephon gets his head for business. Last summer, while I was watching Stephon play ball, his father, Donald Marbury, approached me. "You the guy writing about Lincoln?" he asked. "And you haven't even interviewed Mr. Lincoln himself?" We shook hands, and when I told him how much I wanted to speak to him, a sly smile crossed his creased and handsome face. "Well in that case I expect there will be some gratuities for me and my family." I must have looked surprised because Mr. Marbury snapped angrily, "Oh come on now! If it weren't for me and my boys, Lincoln wouldn't even be worth writing about!"

The Marbury story is a good one, though it may never be written to the father's liking. After starring at Lincoln, Eric went on to play for the University of Georgia, but he failed to graduate before his scholarship ran out and was now back in Coney Island. Donnie, the second son, displayed even greater promise, but he didn't have a 70 average in high school and had to do time at two junior colleges. After two years, he moved on to Texas A&M, where he led the Southwest Conference in scoring. But he too never graduated and was passed over in the college draft; now he's out in Utah, at another college, trying to finish his degree. Then came Norman. If ever Coney Island had produced pro material, it was he. The first public-school player in New York ever to be named all-city three years in a row, Norman was a dazzler—fast, strong, with a deadly outside shot and the ability, on drives to the basket, to take on the largest foes. He had his pick of top programs and eventually signed with Tennessee, which had assured him that if he chose their school, he could still attend for free even if he didn't make 700; he would simply have to sit out his freshman season, as the NCAA rules require. But in the summer of 1990, just weeks before he was set to leave for Knoxville, he came up 40 points short of 700 on his final SAT attempt. Tennessee broke its promise and withdrew its offer. Norman, Coney Island's finest product to date, packed his bags for a junior college in Florida. (He now plays for a Salt Lake City junior college.)

For years Donald Marbury had watched his boys fall short. Now he was down to his last—and most talented—son. "You want information, I expect that you will have the money to pay for it," he said to me last summer. I told him that wasn't possible and he shrugged dismissively. "I'm not like all them other Coney Island guys—too stupid to know the value of what they're sitting on." He tapped his brow. "This is a business—ain't nothing but. And if I don't receive satisfaction, I will take my business somewhere else."

Among the coaches who are now recruiting Stephon, it is said, as one did recently, that Donald Marbury "just won't stop dining out on his son's talent." As for Stephon, the coaches complain that he's a player always looking to "get over," to take advantage of any situation. But how should they act? The entire basketball establishment has been trying to buy Stephon for years: summer-league teams pay his way to tournaments around the country (last summer found him in Arizona); street agents take Stephon into the Nets' locker room for chats with the pros; basketball camps give him wardrobes full of free gear; and coaches are constantly laying on hands and giving him awkward little hugs, hoping to win his affection.

And the Marbury family knows only too well, from witnessing the fates of Eric, Donnie, and Norman, how abruptly the coaches will withdraw their largess. So the Marbury policy, as Stephon explains it to Russell in my car, has become quite simple: "If you don't ask, you don't get. Like if I wasn't getting my burn"— his playing time—"here at Lincoln? I'd be up and out with quickness."

60   By the time I reach the tag end of the peninsula, where Corey, Russell, and Stephon live, everyone has finished his burgers and fries, and I swing by their buildings to drop them off. It's not yet 6:00 P.M., but the drug dealers are already out. Russell spots a kid he used to play with at the Garden loping down the street with a rangy gait and his Georgetown cap on backward. "Look at him. Just doing the same ol' same ol'. Shoot 'em up. Bang bang." Dealers and players make up the principal social groups among young men in Coney Island, although there's cross-pollination, with washed-up players joining the gangs and dealers disrupting games to show off their playground moves. One major difference, however, is that the dealers own white Nissan Sentras whereas players like Stephon just talk about them.

Russell, Corey, and Stephon have never been involved with the gangs, but that leaves them broke most of the time, with few options for making money besides hawking sodas on the boardwalk during the summer. It's hard work, lugging a case of Cokes from the nearest supermarket a mile away, then selling them one by one in the blazing heat. For their trouble, they usually get a summons from the police. Later on those summer evenings, when the athletes start their work-outs, the dealers often gather at the sidelines to jeer. "They ain't doing nothing with their lives, so they don't want you to be doing nothing either," Russell explains. He climbs out of my car with a pile of SAT review books under his arm. "Man, I hate Coney Island. After I get to college, I'm never coming back. Until then, boys"—he gives us a weary salute—"I'm staying inside."

I drive down the block to drop off Stephon and Corey. They live on the fourth and fifth floors of the same building, directly over the Garden. After leaning into the window to slap my hand, Stephon starts walking with that King Marbury stride toward his building. I watch as he swaggers across the deserted play-ground, trailing his hand along the jungle gym. All the guys drinking their after-noon beers call out to him as he goes by.

I've spent some time in Stephon's building, and it's not the most pleasant place to come home to after a long practice. It's fourteen stories high and the elevator never works. The long halls stink of urine, and the dark stairwells, where the deal-ers lurk, echo with the low rumble of drug transactions. The apartment doors don't even have numbers on them, though they must have at one time because just outside the Marburys' apartment someone has scrawled violently across the wall, I WANNA FUCK THE GIRL IN 3B CAUSE SHE SUCKS DICK GOOD.

Everyone is hoping that Stephon will keep his head together as his notoriety grows throughout his high-school career and that, more to the point, he or his father won't accept some "gratuity" that raises the interest of the NCAA enforce-ment division. Given the family's circumstances, however, and the lessons they have learned about how this recruiting game is played, one can hardly blame Stephon and his father for wanting theirs—and wanting it now.

NOVEMBER

65 Heading toward Thanksgiving, Lincoln could not have asked for greater success. The team was undefeated, making headlines in all the major New York City dailies, and had received an invitation to play in San Diego in a Christmas tour-nament of the country's top high school teams. Lincoln didn't just win its games either; the team routed its opponents by such lopsided scores that opposing coaches often shook their heads and remarked, "Those guys were high-school players?" Russell was scoring at will—in the team's first scrimmage he turned in an outrageous 46-point performance, missing only three of twenty-four field-goal attempts, then kept to that pace for the next several games. *The Hoop Scoop,* a recruiting newsletter, ranked him the sixth-best player in New York City, and he earned an honorable mention in the magazine *Street & Smith's* nationwide basketball roundup.

Meanwhile Stephon was getting his burn, and then some. He started the sea-son's first game (fifteen points, twelve assists) and every one thereafter. *New York Newsday,* under a half-page picture of the Lincoln team holding their smiling young point guard in their arms, announced the beginning of "the era of Stephon Marbury." Scouting reports were giving Stephon their top rating, and an assistant from Providence College showed up in Coney Island to watch Stephon practice one day, waving discreetly to the freshman—violating the intent, if not the letter, of NCAA rules designed to protect under-classmen from recruiters. "It's never too early to start showing interest," the coach whispered. Word of Stephon's prowess even reached a TV production company, which contacted Stephon about making a commercial, though when the NCAA informed the Marburys that accepting a fee might violate its rules, his father declined.

Off the court, however, there were some unwelcome developments. Stephon was working hard in his classes, hoping to break the pattern of academic failure set by his brothers, but his teachers were noticing that his book reports rarely included a period or a capital letter—not a good omen for the verbal portion of the SATs. As for Russell, he was scoring well on practice SAT exams, but when test day arrived he would panic and forget all his last-minute cramming, shaking his faith that hard work would eventually win the day. Years of bad schooling are coming back to haunt Russell just when he needs his education the most. Leaving the school building now, he looks exhausted, defeated, like a sullen factory worker at the end of a long shift.

Russell took the SATs yet again last weekend. Terry was planning to treat him to a celebratory dinner after the test. As we walk down the school steps, I ask how his date went. "I dissed her good. You should have seen it. Tell him, Corey." Corey says nothing, so Russell goes on. "She came up to me all nice and sweet, and I said, 'Get out of my sight! Don't bother me no more!' "

I'm stunned by this development. The last time I saw them together, Terry was sitting on Russell's lap in study hall, feeding him a bagel bite by bite. "What were you fighting about?"

70   "I don't know. I guess I was just in a bad mood because of the SATs." Russell drapes his arm over my shoulder. "Never let a girl see you sweat. Didn't your mother ever tell you that?" Russell emits a peculiar mirthless laugh. I look at Corey. He shrugs and traces a circle around his temple with his index finger.

The days are getting shorter now. By the time practice is over, the sun has long since dropped into its slot behind the Verrazano Narrows Bridge and the sky at twilight is covered with brooding clouds. Corey's older brother Willie owns a barbershop just off Flatbush Avenue in central Brooklyn, twenty minutes away. After practice Russell, Corey, and Stephon like to hang out there, and I usually give them a lift on my way home. As we drive past the brightly lit bodegas and rice-and-beans joints on Flatbush Avenue, fires rage out of metal drums, circled by hooded men trying to keep warm. Corey looks out the window and says in a high, fragile voice, "Oh no. I just hate it when the Negroes wear those hoods. Scary! Oh! So scary!" Everyone laughs and Corey lifts his own hood over his head. He knows that when he too walks around like that, cops will stop him and pedestrians will turn away from him in fear. "Only in America," he says.

I have yet to hear Corey talk much about colleges, so I ask him where he wants to play. "Oh, I'm thinking about some southern schools: Florida State, North Carolina, maybe Virginia. I hate it when it gets sharp and brisk out like this. My one rule is, I won't go anyplace where I got to wear one of them Eskimo coats."

Corey's recruiting hasn't even begun, but he's already established the proper hedonistic frame of mind.

"Still got to pass those SATs," Russell warns.

"I'm not scared," Corey replies. "I do well on tests. Anyway, this should be our year to relax."

75 "That test is hard," says Stephon from the backseat. "I looked at it once and almost fainted. I read somewhere that David Robinson got a 1300. Is that possible?"

"I heard there are players who get other guys to take the test for them," Russell says. "How do they get away with that? Find someone who looks like them?"

This is not a good sign. One of Russell's friends at Grady, who had scored lower than he on practice tests, suddenly got his 700 and signed with a top program. Some Lincolnites have begun wondering whether Grady players are using standins to take the test.

The NCAA and the college basketball industry have done much soul-searching in recent years over the SAT requirement, as well they should. A combined score of 700 may not seem like a terribly rigorous standard, but given the quality of the Lincoln players' schooling, it's not surprising that they don't know a synonym for panache or how to make the most of what they do know; they've never been told, for example, to avoid guessing and answer only the questions they're sure of—the kinds of test-taking tips suburban kids learn on their first day in a Stanley Kaplan review course. Russell's school average, now over 80, says a lot more about his determination to succeed, but that alone will get him nowhere.

Business is brisk tonight at Willie's shop—either that or a lot of guys are using the place to keep warm. Willie and his partner are cutting with dispatch and still a half dozen guys are hanging out. Willie keeps a basketball in the shop that everyone passes around while watching sitcom reruns on the TV. It's a homey place: taped to the mirrors are photos of the Johnson clan—Corey, Willie, and their six siblings. (The Johnsons are one of the only intact families I know in Coney island: the father lives at home and all the children out of high school have jobs.) A T-shirt commemorating Lincoln's championship last year is pinned to the wall, next to a painting of Jesus, a bust of Nefertiti, and four portraits of Martin Luther King. Willie has also slapped up an assortment of bumper stickers: MORE HUGGING, LESS MUGGING and TO ALL YOU VIRGINS . . . THANKS FOR NOTHING. Outside, darkness has fallen like a black curtain against the shop window, but inside Willie's it's bright and warm.

80 Corey, whistling the theme song to *The Andy Griffith Show,* grabs a razor and stands next to Russell, trimming his right sideburn. (When Russell began dressing for success this season, Corey would remain in the locker room to troubleshoot in case Russell hit any snags knotting his tie.) Corey asks him what's going on with Terry, and Russell admits he's not really angry at her; he's just worried she'll get distant with him if he shows how much he likes her. "What if she decides she don't want to be with me?" he says unhappily. "I would take that hard."

"You just got to tease her a little, is all," Corey says. He moves behind Russell to trim his neck hairs. "Like, instead of kissing her on the lips, kiss her on the nose. Then kiss her on the eyebrow. Give her a kiss on the ear. Before you know it, she'll be beggin' you, 'When you gonna kiss me on the lips?'" Corey laughs and laughs, enjoying his own good advice—he knows it's been thoroughly market-tested. Most Coney Island kids feel utterly lost outside their neighborhood, but Corey goes club-hopping in Manhattan and every time he shows up for a game—no matter where in the city it is—some girl in the bleachers is calling out his name. His shrewdness on a variety of topics—dating, churchgoing, cooking, writing poetry—has earned him the nickname "Future," because, as Russell once explained, "Corey's a future-type guy, crazy-smart, a walking genius. There are no limits to what he can do."

One day in study hall, I watched Corey sitting in the back, bent over his desk, while all around him his classmates wreaked havoc, throwing spitballs and jumping from desk to desk. At the end of the period I asked what he had accomplished and he handed me a poem about life in Coney Island that ended, "A place meant for happiness, sweet love and care—/Something any human desires to share/ Yet it seems to haunt instead of praise/The foundation and center of our bitter days."

When I had finished reading, Corey said to me, "I'm going to be a writer—you know, creative writing, poetry, free-associative stuff. I just play ball to take up time." Corey was tremendously prolific, dashing off a new poem for every girl he met. But having successfully merged his twin passions—writing and romance—he never left time for his homework. He did the assignments he liked, ignored the rest, and, though he never caused trouble in class, had a 66 average and was one failed test away from losing his high-school eligibility. Already Division I coaches had identified him as a gifted player whose grades could be his undoing.

Corey is standing in front of Russell, evening his sideburns. He says, "But whatever you do with Terry, just don't bust inside her. That almost happened to me." Across the room, I hear Willie Johnson snort with disapproval. Willie is cutting Stephon's hair, but mostly he's been keeping a weather eye on his brother. "Corey's smart, but he's stupid too," Willie says to me. "You know what I mean? In junior high, he was a virgin with a 90 average. Now he's got a 65. You tell me." I laugh, but Willie says, "No, I'm serious, man. I try to talk to him. I say, 'Don't you want to go to college? Don't you know you got to sacrifice for things you want?'" Willie is clipping Stephon's hair with growing agitation, and Stephon has sunk low in his chair, hoping to avoid a scalping. "At home Corey's on the phone all night, talking to girls. I say, 'You got a personal problem? Just tell me.'"

85   Willie is speaking in code now. What he's hinting at is the Johnson family's fear that Corey will get one of his girlfriends pregnant. In Coney Island, girls and the distractions of friends represent such a threat to a college career that the neighborhood's talented athletes are often urged to give up the rights and privileges of adolescence and attend a high school far from home. They will be lonely, but they will stay on the straight and narrow. Corey's older brother Louis took this strategy one step further, going into seclusion at an all-boys school, then spending an extra year at a prep school that serves as a sort of academic rehab clinic for basketball players. Not coincidentally, he passed his SATs and became the first of the six Johnson boys to make it to a Division I program, the University of Buffalo.

Louis was so dedicated to his craft that he would practice his shot under the Garden lights until 4:00 A.M. Everyone wishes Corey were equally single-minded. But Corey's sensibility is too quirky for that, and therein lies a danger. If Corey lived twenty-five miles north in, say, Scarsdale, he'd play the offbeat writer whose poor grades earn him a four-year sentence at Colgate, to be served while his classmates all go Ivy. But Corey fools around in an arena where there are no safety schools or safety nets. All of which presents a sad bit of irony: inner-city kids are always accused of doing nothing but throwing a ball through a hoop. Then along comes someone like Corey who takes pleasure in a million other things. (When the Lincoln team runs wind sprints on the outdoor track, Corey gladly takes the outside lane so he can run his hands through the canopy of leaves above his head.) In Coney Island, however, you ignore your basketball talent at great risk—athletic scholarships being significantly easier to come by than those for ghetto poets.

By the time Russell and Corey submit themselves to Willie's shears, it's already late, so I agree to drive them home. All three are tired, and we ride along in a rare moment of quiet. Finally, Russell turns to me and says, "What do you know about Rob Johnson?"

Oh boy.

Johnson is a street agent, a middleman, a flesh peddler. He makes his living getting chummy with high-school players and then brokering them to colleges for a fee—though the coaches who pay it swear they've never heard of him. Lately, Johnson has become entangled in an NCAA investigation, but it hasn't kept him from showing up regularly at the Lincoln gym—a tall black man with an enormous gut, Day-Glo Nikes, and a thick gold chain around his wrist. After practice, he lingers around the players, offering to drive them home or take them to the movies—a particularly appealing figure to broke and fatherless kids like Russell.

90   "Has Rob offered to be your agent?" I ask. Russell looks out the window and says, "He called me last night. Said he liked the way I played. A lot." I tell Russell he might want to check out Rob's reputation, but Russell says, "It don't matter. I've decided to sign with South Carolina. They really want me." Having announced this unexpected decision, Russell pulls out a paper bag with his customary after-practice snack: a plain bagel and a carton of Tropicana.

"You should visit before you make up your mind," Corey advises. He's stretched luxuriously across the backseat.

"But I already know I want to go there," Russell says between mouthfuls.

"Russell, you've never been outside Coney Island! How the hell are you gonna know? Look"—Corey lowers his voice and tries to speak in tones of unimpeachable reasonableness—"Russell, say you're going to marry someone. You going to marry the first girl you sleep with? No. Of course not. You're going to look around, see what the other girls can do for you, and then make your decision. Same with colleges. You got to go up there and have a careful look around."

"Nobody can make me take visits if I don't want to."

95   Corey laughs. "Nobody's gonna make you do anything. But you might as well let them show you a good time. Let them wine you and dine you. When my recruiting starts, I'm going to have me some fun."

Russell, having finished his snack, balls up the paper bag and tosses it out the window with an air of finality: "I don't want to be wined and dined."

As much as he hates Coney Island, Russell has never lived anywhere else, and he often fears that his dark complexion (Corey and Stephon are lighter-skinned) will get him into trouble outside his home turf. That may explain why he doesn't want to take any visits. But something else is up. Corey notes this and changes strategy. "What's your reason? You got to have a reason."

"I'm not like everybody else," Russell replies.

"Yes," Corey says slowly. "This is true."

100 "Look, all the best players sign in the fall. Only the scrubs wait until spring."

"I'm not telling you to sign in the spring," Corey says, "I'm just saying you change your mind every day."

"I'm telling you, Corey, I'm having a great season. And when those schools that lost interest in me come back in the spring, I'm gonna be, like, 'Too late, sucka!' I'm gonna be throwing it all year! Tomahawk jams!" Russell starts thrashing about in the front seat, dunking his orange-juice carton into the ashtray of my car, and now I finally get it—that his decision to dunk in public, like his policy of wearing nice shoes, and now his intention to abruptly sign at a school he's never seen, is Russell's way of propping up his identity, of seizing some measure of control, now that he has realized how easily exchangeable he is for a player with better test scores. Recruiting may be the most important thing in Russell's life, but to the coaches it's just a yearly ritual.

"Man, you are one crazy nigger!" Corey says. "I'm not talking about dunking! I'm talking about whether you should sign at some school you never even seen in your life!"

"Don't matter. It's my decision. And part of growing up is learning to live with your decisions. Even if it turns out to be a nightmare."

105 "But why?"

"Don't push me, Corey." Russell's voice has begun to rise up the scale.

"But why?"

"Because I don't want to talk about it."

"That's not a reason."

110 "BECAUSE I HATE ALL THIS FUCKING RECRUITING!" Russell screams. "All right?"

Corey leans back against his seat, defeated. "Okay, well, at least that's a reason."

DECEMBER

Coney Island never looks quite so forlorn as it does just before Christmas. The amusement park is shuttered, the boardwalk littered with broken glass and crack vials. The cold weather has swept the streets clean of everyone but the most hardened criminals. At night, Christmas lights blink on and off from the top floors of the projects, but few people are around to enjoy them. No one simply passes through Coney Island on the way to somewhere else.

Tonight, Russell and I walk into the deserted lobby of his building and he says, his eyes cast down by shame, "Welcome to the old ghetto." Russell's building is identical in design to the one in which Corey and Stephon live, just a block away—an X-shaped slab of concrete rising fourteen stories into the air. I have always assumed it was no better or worse than theirs. But Russell assures me that looks are deceiving. By the way he peers around the elevator door before getting in, I believe him.

Upstairs, his family's apartment is tiny: a living room, kitchenette, and two bedrooms. His mother has one bedroom, Russell and his two younger sisters share the other. It's Russell's room, though: basketball posters cover the walls from top to bottom and trophies crowd the floor.

115   I notice that Russell is wearing a new ring on his finger and I ask if it's from Terry. He doesn't answer. Instead he says, "Want to see some pictures of Terry and me?" He pulls out a scrapbook filled with newspaper clippings about himself and the Lincoln team. Stuffed in the back are a pile of snapshots. "We been together a long time," he says wistfully. "All those days last summer, picnics, all the stuff we used to do. Maybe someday—way, way off in the future—we'll get married." We're still looking at the photos when Russell hears a key in the front door. He grabs the pictures from my hand and shoves them back in the scrapbook, snapping it shut just as his mother walks through the door.

"You come home right after practice?" she asks anxiously. He nods, and she smiles in my direction. "Russell thinks I'm overprotective, but I have to know where he's at. If he's at practice or at Willie's, okay. But just hanging out on the street? No!" She plunks down a bag of groceries on the kitchen table and lets out a long sigh. The neighborhood's only supermarket is fifteen blocks away. "This is a hard neighborhood, wicked, nothing but drugs out there," says Mrs. Thomas. "Most of Russell's friends are just wasting their lives. You've got to have a strong and powerful will not to go in that direction."

Joyce Thomas certainly has that. She is tall and thin like Russell, and moves around her apartment with fierce efficiency. A burst of what sounds like gunfire erupts outside, but Mrs. Thomas doesn't react. "I always tell Russell, it takes that much"—she spreads two fingers an inch apart—"to get into trouble, and that much"—now two hands shoulder-width apart—"to get out of it." She looks over to her son, but he has vanished from the room. "So far Russell's okay." She raps twice on her kitchen table. "So far."

I start to say something, but Mrs. Thomas cuts me off. "When Russell messes up, I knock him out. I do. I tell him, 'Don't you dog me, boy, I'm all you got!'" She is looking at me forcefully, without blinking. "I don't care how big he is or how much ball he plays, I'll put a ball in his head!"

Russell reappears, this time with his Walkman on and a strange, stricken look on his face. He starts to sing aloud to a slow love song coming from his Walkman—though all we can hear, of course, is Russell's crooning.

120   Suddenly Mrs. Thomas takes in a breath. Looking at Russell, she says, "Did you do it?" Russell keeps on singing, so Mrs. Thomas picks up his hand and examines the ring. "Terry gave it back to you?"

He slides the headphones around his neck. "I took it back," he says. His voice is clotted.

"How did it go?"

He can't think of anything to say. Finally he murmurs, "She was real sad."

Mrs. Thomas doesn't stir. The apartment is quiet, except for the refrigerator's hum. Russell has begun to turn inward and the next words he utters seem to reach us from a great distance. "She was crying, hanging onto my leg, saying, 'Don't go, don't go.'"

125   "Now don't you worry about Terry," Mrs. Thomas says matter-of-factly. "She'll be all right. You just watch out for yourself."

"I'm real sad, too," he says quickly, and now I can see him struggling not to cry.

"Don't be. How long were you together—five, six months? That's not so hard to get over." Mrs. Thomas turns briskly toward her groceries and begins to unpack. Russell stands stock-still in the middle of the living room staring at his feet.

She glances over at me. "I explained to Russell, 'You want friends? Fine. But I don't want you attached to anyone. You will go to college alone, and so will Terry.'" Russell can't bear to hear his mother's words, so he puts on his Walkman and begins his tone-deaf accompaniment. "A girl like Terry could make him do something stupid. He gets carried away. He's very emotional, you know." She speaks with seeming indifference, though it's not hard to hear what lies beneath it: a desperation to get Russell away from Coney Island that is so great she will take away from him the one most stabilizing influence in his life, at a time when he seems to need it the most. "Russell got a second chance on this planet," she says, referring to Russell's suicide threat, "and no one gets that! No one!" She stares at me again, this time with such intensity that I have to fight the urge to look away. "He's got a lot of decisions ahead of him. Important decisions. Business decisions. Without that scholarship, he's nothing. Nothing!" Mrs. Thomas looks to her son to gauge his reaction, but Russell has checked out completely. He's turned his Walkman up to full volume, and he's singing as loud as he can.

A few nights later, Russell, Stephon, Corey, and I are all in my car, making the usual rounds to Willie's. Stephon announces that he's going to get an X shaved into the back of his scalp. Russell is considering a center part like Larry Johnson's, the star of the Charlotte Hornets. As we approach the barbershop Corey says, "Don't be wasting time, all right?" When I ask why, he tells me a gang from a nearby project has been roaming lately. Last week a woman was hit by a stray bullet right outside the shop, so they all want to get their cuts and be gone.

130   To me, Coney Island's desolate project walkways and stairwells have always seemed more threatening than the raucous street life here along Flatbush Avenue. And, in fact, the few Lincoln players who live "across town"—Flatbush or Crown Heights or East New York—won't be caught dead in the Coney Island high rises ever since one of them spent the night at Corey's apartment and someone blew up a car right outside his window. But I am given to understand that in the patchwork of highly distinct neighborhoods that make up Brooklyn, a group of black teenagers will always be at risk outside their own turf. Wherever they go, the three are always scanning to see who might be coming up to them. One of their teammates was shot in the hand a few months ago. Another classmate was stabbed at a party recently; he's still in intensive care. "Something's happening, boy, every day, everyday," says Russell.

As planned, they're in and out of Willie's in a flash and happy to be heading home in my car. Russell has been unusually quiet all evening. When I ask if something is bothering him, he tells me his mother has forbidden him to speak to me anymore. Apparently, she doesn't think it wise for him to talk to a reporter while his recruiting hangs in the balance. I tell Russell that this story won't appear until he's already off to college, but he says, "You don't understand. My mother's crazy!"

Stephon pipes in with some advice for me. "Just greet her at the door and hit her with a hundred. She'll change her mind." He snickers knowingly. "She's no different than my father. He wants to make sure he gets some loot." Lately, Mr. Marbury has been threatening to keep Stephon from talking to me unless I cut him a deal.

At first I think Stephon is missing the point—that Mrs. Thomas's suspicion of me and her desperation to get Russell out of Coney Island are entirely different from Mr. Marbury's demand for money. But Corey sees the connection: "Damn," he says, "your parents must have had a hard life."

"Still do," Stephon replies. "Your father got himself a whole plumbing business. My father and Russell's mother got nothing." Stephon looks at me out of the corner of his eye and says, "You're thinking, What a bunch of niggers, right?"

135   The word just hangs in the air. I can't think of a thing to say. Over the last five months, I realize, I have tried to ignore our racial differences in an attempt at some broader understanding. Stephon's comment may be his way of telling me that understanding begins with race. "You got to think like a black man," he goes on, "got to learn how to say, 'Fuck it, fuck everybody, fuck the whole damn thing.' Now that's life in the ghetto."

"It's true!" Russell exclaims, his mood improving for the first time all evening. "My mother is a nigger! She's a black woman who does not give a damn."

"Man, I'm tired of all this shit!" Stephon slams his hands down hard on his book bag. "Somebody's got to make it, somebody's got to go all the way. How come this shit only happens to us Coney Island niggers?" He shakes his head wildly and laughs. "My father and Russell's mother—yeah, they're crazy, but it's about time there was a little something for the niggs."

"Something for the niggs!" Russell repeats the line with a hoot. "Yeah, Steph! Time to get outspoken!"

"You got it," Stephon says, and laughs again. Then Corey joins in. And they're all three whooping and slapping their knees—laughing at their parents and also, I imagine, at the absurdity of this whole situation.

140   Here they are, playing by all the rules: They stay in school—though their own school hardly keeps its end of the bargain. They say no to drugs—though it's the only fully employed industry around. They don't get into trouble with the NCAA—though its rules seem designed to foil them, and the coaches who break the rules go unpunished. They even heed their parents' wishes—and often pay a stiff price.

Of course none of them is perfect: Russell panics about his SATs and the choices he must make, and has trouble owning up to it; Corey won't apply himself and kids himself into thinking it won't matter; Stephon has—what shall we call it?—an attitude that needs some adjustment. But they operate in an environment that forgives none of the inevitable transgressions of adolescence and bestows no second chances.

Which makes this process of playing for a scholarship not the black version of the American dream, as some would suggest, but a cruel parody of it. In the classic parable you begin with nothing and slowly accrue your riches through hard work in a system designed to help those who help themselves. Here you begin with nothing but one narrow, treacherous path and then run a gauntlet of obstacles that merely reminds you of how little you have: recruiters pass themselves off as father figures, standardized tests humiliate you and reveal the wretchedness of your education, the promise of lucrative NBA contracts reminds you of what it feels like to have nothing in this world.

Jou-Jou, Silk, Chocolate, Spoon, Spice, Ice, Goose, Tiny, T, Stretch, Space, Sky: all of them great Coney Island players, most of them waiting vainly for a second chance, hanging out in the neighborhood, or dead. And here come Russell, Corey, and Stephon in my car, riding down Mermaid Avenue in the bone chill and gloom of this December night, still laughing about "the niggs," hoping for the best, and knowing that in this particular game failure is commonplace, like a shrug, and heartbreak the order of the day.

EPILOGUE: WINTER 1993

In the spring of 1992, near the end of his senior year, Russell signed with Philadelphia's Temple University, whose team in recent years has regularly been among the nation's top twenty. But on his final SAT attempt, his score went down and Temple withdrew its scholarship offer. Rob Johnson brokered Russell into a Texas junior college known on the street as a "bandit" school, where his teammates seemed to carry more guns than schoolbooks. Desperately unhappy, Russell transferred after a week to a junior college near Los Angeles. There, this past winter, he was averaging twenty-six points per game and hoping that after two years he would be recruited by a four-year school and earn his degree.

145   Corey fell short of a 700 on his SATs by ten points. He planned to spend a year at a prep school to brush up on his academics but filed his application for financial aid too late. He went to another junior college in Texas. Away from his girlfriends, Corey earned four B's and two A's in his first semester. He hopes to move on to a four-year school himself.

Stephon is now in his sophomore year. In the summer of 1992, he was among the four youngest players invited to the Nike All-American camp, an all-expenses-paid jamboree in Indianapolis for the 120 top high-school stars in the country. His play, before every Division I coach in the country, looked like a highlight film. Now four inches taller and dunking the ball, he is dominating the PSAL and should have his pick of top programs in his senior year, provided he can score 700 on the SATs and that neither he nor his father violates any recruiting rules.

And at the Garden, some of Coney Island's elders have organized nighttime shooting drills for the neighborhood's schoolchildren—eight years old and up— to prepare them for the road ahead.

▰▰ CRITICAL REFLECTIONS

1. Education—more specifically, school—serves a number of complex purposes for the Lincoln High School players. Based on this reading, how do you think the players featured here would define the purpose of school? What about other people in this article, like the college coaches?

2. Rewrite "The Last Shot" as an example of a narrative (or myth) about American education. Is it a rags to riches trajectory for the players, or something else?

3. "The Last Shot" covers a number of subjects—race, class, school, basketball, aspirations, and violence, to name a few. What is the most important thing that you think this article has to teach readers? How does it contribute to our literacy about something, and what is that thing?

4. Near the end of this article, Frey summarizes the ways that the players in the piece "play by the rules." What are the rules you think they must abide? Are they rewarded for abiding them?

▰▰ MAKING CONNECTIONS

1. Consider the purpose of education for the Coney Island players with what you interpret as the purpose of education and literacy development outlined by Frederick Douglass, Booker T. Washington, W.E.B. DuBois, and Marilyn Nelson writing about George Washington Carver. Do you see parallels between these purposes? How are they similar and/or different?

2. Darcy Frey writes that "A combined score of 700 [on the SATs] may not seem like a terribly rigorous standard, but given the quality of the Lincoln players' schooling, it's not surprising that they don't know a synonym for panache or how to make the most of what they do know; they've never been told, for example, to avoid guessing and answer only the questions they're sure of—the kinds of test-taking tips suburban kids learn on their first day in a Stanley Kaplan review course" (256). Consider this statement alongside arguments by Peter Sacks and Stanley Kaplan about the SATs, as well as your own experiences. Do you find Frey's argument here convincing? Why or why not?

3. In "Literacy Practices," David Barton and Mary Hamilton distinguish between dominant and non-dominant (or "vernacular") literacies. What would you

identify as the dominant and vernacular literacies among the Coney Island crowd? If a national assessment like the one advocated by Nicholas Lemann and Diane Ravitch was developed, which of the players' literacies do you think would be measured by the exam, which would not, and why?

STANLEY KAPLAN

MY 54-YEAR LOVE AFFAIR WITH THE SAT

You've probably heard of Stanley Kaplan—or, more appropriately, the Stanley Kaplan industry of test preparation books, centers, and courses. This chapter comes from a book by the man himself in which he describes his meteoric rise to the top of the standardized testing business. Here, Kaplan explains the moment when he realized that he could prepare students to take a test that was supposed to defy preparation, and his belief in the potential of the SAT and preparation for it.

I'll never forget my introduction to the SAT. It was 1946. I was at the home of a high school junior named Elizabeth, who lived near Coney Island, to help her with intermediate algebra. As we sat down at her kitchen table, she said, "Mr. Kaplan, I need to take an important test. It's called the SAT. Can you help me?"

I had heard of the SAT, then the acronym for Scholastic Aptitude Test, but I had never prepared anyone to take it. The test had been administered since 1926 by the College Entrance Examination Board, a nonprofit organization of member colleges founded at Columbia University in New York City. These member colleges, primarily highly selective schools such as Yale and Princeton, had used the SAT for years as part of their admissions process. Now after World War II, more colleges than ever were using the SAT for admission as increasing numbers of returning veterans wanted to attend college with federally funded tuition. Harvard also used the SAT to award scholarships to needy students based on their intellectual capabilities, not their pedigree or social status.

Elizabeth handed me a booklet published by the College Board that contained a dozen pages of general information about the test, including a description of the test, fees, and test dates. It also included sample questions. These had been added to reduce the element of surprise for the students even though some College Board members had objected to adding the sample questions because they might promote "cramming" at the last minute.

I looked at the sample questions, and a broad smile stretched across my face. It was love at first sight. These questions were different from those on the Regents or other tests for which I had prepared students. For instance, one question asked, "Approximately 820 tons of water per second fall over each of the 11 gates of the Grand Coulee Dam. If the same total amount of water were to fall over only 5 gates, how many tons per second would fall over each gate?" I could see that the questions were designed to test students' knowledge and application of basic concepts, not their ability to regurgitate memorized facts. There were no pat answers. A student could take this test with an open textbook and still not answer the questions easily or correctly.

5   As I scanned the information booklet, my eye glanced at a statement that said "cramming or last-minute reviewing" had no purpose and was not advised. I remember thinking. "Not review for a test?" Now I was really interested. I wondered why the College Board would include such a statement.

"Sure, I can help you," I told her enthusiastically. This test was right up my alley, because it was an innovative test based on problem solving, not rote memorization. That was exactly how I liked to teach. I took the booklet home with me, wondering how I could help Elizabeth study for a test I had never seen. I spent the evening and next morning looking over the booklet and creating simulated questions. They were all the same as in the sample booklet, but entirely different because I made up questions on identical topics with new examples. The challenge was exhilarating. I was thrilled with the idea of teaching Elizabeth to think out her answers. Tutoring for the Regents was fun, and students learned a lot. But tutoring for the SAT would be more fun, because Elizabeth would have to think harder and apply a broader range of math and verbal skills.

In 1946, the SAT was a two-and-a-half-hour multiple-choice exam given nationally four times a year on designated Saturday and Wednesday mornings. Students didn't pass or fail but were ranked by scores ranging from 200 to 800 points for each of the math and verbal portions. The scores of each portion were added together so that the lowest possible SAT score was 400 and the highest was 1600. But in 1946, students never learned their test scores. They were sent to the colleges to which students applied and, on special request, to the students' schools with the condition that the scores be withheld from parents and students. A student had no idea of his standing in the application process when a college used SAT scores as part of its admissions consideration. The SAT didn't have the same influence in the admissions process in 1946 as today because the test was still not widely used, but more colleges were beginning to consider using the test scores in the admissions process.

The College Board was promoting the SAT to students, parents, and teachers as a well-honed research product designed to measure students' academic abilities regardless of where in the nation they attended high school. That made the SAT attractive to admissions officials because the quality of schools and grading systems varied so greatly from region to region. Some schools handed out A's like party favors, while others were as stingy with A's as Scrooge on Christmas Eve. And an A from a private school in New York might carry a different weight from an A from a Topeka public school. A student's grade point average (GPA) was a good indicator of a student's academic ability, but the SAT was becoming the nation's new academic yardstick. It could predict how well a student would perform during the first six months of college, and it could safeguard against grade inflation and poor, less demanding curricula.

I could tell from the sample questions that this systematic and demanding test would require a methodical approach to preparation. The SAT required a variety of skills, ranging from familiarity with the multiple-choice format to knowledge on a variety of subjects. I could see that some students would need to learn the information on the SAT for the first time, while others would need to review subjects they had learned years earlier. Elizabeth, for instance, hadn't worked with percentages or decimals since the sixth grade, but percentage questions were on the SAT math section. Few high school students would remember that $.2 \times .2 = .04$ and not $.4$. For her, I would be the Brush-Up Guy—no different from what I had been to other students.

10   The SAT also expected students to know not just the "what" of subjects, but also the more important "how and why." I remember the moment I learned this crucial difference in how we learn. My college science professor Dr. Goldforb was an expert in posing a question, finding an answer, and then reaching one step further. One day, he asked the class a question about a swallowtail's antennae, and I quickly raised my hand to volunteer the answer.

"Very good, Stanley," Dr. Goldforb said. But he didn't stop there. "But tell me why that is the answer."

"Why?" I pondered. "Hmm. Why." Reciting a factual answer was not good enough. *Why* was my answer correct? he asked. And *how* had I reached it? From then on, I encouraged my students to think things out, to think about the hows and whys. Learning to ask the hows and whys of information was essential in preparing for the SAT because it tested students on reading comprehension, problem solving, math concepts, and vocabulary skills with questions that required them to comprehend and understand the subject matter.

Teaching Elizabeth to prepare for the SAT was a challenge because it was different from tests students took at school. I could see from the SAT instruction booklet that there were tricky questions and even trickier answers with more than one good choice. Some of the choices were better than others, but there was only one best choice. Answering SAT questions required focus, reasoning, and practice. Acquiring test-taking skills is the same as learning to play the piano or ride a bicycle. It requires practice, practice, practice. Repetition breeds familiarity. Familiarity breeds confidence. Confidence breeds success. So I gave Elizabeth pages of vocabulary and reading comprehension drills, math problems, and vocabulary questions that I had created to simulate the SAT. I saw the results: she was becoming a powerful problem solver and a more confident test taker.

On test day, she had a clear advantage over the other students. She knew what to expect, and the SAT questions didn't throw her for a loop. She was able to tackle the questions using the strategies I had taught her and finished the test with time to spare. The test was, in her words, "a piece of cake," and she passed the word to her friends. When five of them called to ask for my help to prepare for the SAT, I suggested they all come as a group because I didn't have enough time to teach them individually and the tuition for each student would be much less expensive.

15   It was my first class to prepare students for the SAT, and it charted my path for the future. My first SAT preparation program consisted of four-hour weekly classes lasting sixteen weeks. The cost was $128, a charge that parents were happy to pay compared to what they would be paying for college tuition. "Go to Stanley Kaplan," students passed the word. "He can help you get into the college of your choice." A year after my first set of SAT classes, I had two hundred students enrolled for SAT preparation. Never could I have imagined the impending explosion in standardized testing that would leave me riding the crest of a swelling wave of educational change.

I began to think more about the SAT and how it affected education and students' aspirations. The SAT provided a more level playing field—and I liked that. It could help democratize American education by ushering a larger, more diverse group of students into the world of higher education. It could give students the opportunity to get into the top colleges without attending a prestigious private school or being the child of an alumnus or big contributor. A test like this one might have gained me entry to medical school, and I wanted one aspect of my tutoring business to be preparing students for a test that could help them get into college based on their academic merit.

Gauging academic competency has been the aim of admissions tests since their debut in America in the late 1800s. At first colleges used written essay exams to test the 4 percent of high school graduates who went on to college. But because each college had its own admissions test on specific subjects, it was difficult for students to apply to more than one college without studying for lots of different tests, and high school teachers complained that they couldn't prepare students for such an array of tests. In 1900, a group of twelve college presidents established the College Board, which represented member colleges and universities, to create order out of the chaotic system of testing and admitting students. Its remedy was to create a standard national entry exam that eventually evolved into the Board's most dramatic and enduring product: the SAT.

From its inception, the SAT was a target of criticism. Its creator, Carl B. Brigham, an associate professor of psychology at Princeton University and the Board's in-house psychometrician, had fervently endorsed scientific mental testing as a method to identify intellectual capacity. He issued the following disclaimers at the SAT unveiling: no measures can guarantee prediction, the test should be used as a supplement to other academic records, and placing too much emphasis on test scores is dangerous. Paradoxically, all his warnings ultimately became the same controversial points debated about standardized testing today.

The College Board said that the SAT, with its easy-to-grade format, met the two main criteria for an effective test: reliability and predictability. No matter how many times students took the SAT, their scores would remain about the same, and students' college performance was very close to what the SAT predicted.

20   The first SAT was administered in June 1926 to 8,040 high school students. It was a vastly different test from today's. The questions were grouped into subtests including word analogies and antonyms, number arrangements, logical inference, and paragraph reading. Here's a question from a copy of the original test:

"Premise: None of the doors with latches are fastened. Conclusion: Some of the doors that are fastened have latches." Is the answer "Necessarily true," "Necessarily false," "Probably true," "Probably false," or "Undetermined"? Give up? The correct answer is "Necessarily false." That's enough to make one's head spin. But spin in a good way. It meant students were being forced to think and deduce.

It wasn't until the late 1940s, when America experienced an influx of soldiers returning from war, that the SAT gained a foothold in the admissions process. Added to this was a new group of students who, encouraged by their parents, realized that a college education could lead to greater success. Six times as many students took the exam in the late 1940s as in 1926. The pressures upon the College Board to meet this increasing demand finally prompted the College Board in 1947 to establish the Educational Testing Service (ETS), a private nonprofit organization near Princeton, New Jersey, to write, administer, score, and interpret the SAT.

My tutoring business grew exponentially with the increasing popularity of the SAT. In 1947, I earned enough money to buy my first car—a Super Buick—so I could drive to students' homes for individual tutoring rather than ride the bus or trolley. The Buick had three portholes and an automatic windshield washer I called a spritzer that was a great novelty to show off to my friends.

* * *

My days of driving the Super Buick to students' homes for private lessons were numbered. I began insisting that the students come to me, and soon the mountain was coming to Mohammed. But the apartment where Rita [Kaplan's wife] and I lived was then filled with students—students in the hallway, students in the bedroom, students at the dining room table. Our first daughter, Susan, was born in 1950, and Rita lined the bathtub with pillows to make available the only remaining play space for Susan. I knew then that it was time to move.

In 1951, we bought a two-story brick-and-stucco house on Bedford Avenue about a mile from my parents and one block from my alma mater, James Madison High School. The house was roomy, with two sun porches—front and back—a large dining room and living room, and a big basement. The house was perfect for a growing family and a school. And I had a new business associate in Rita. She was methodical, organized, and insightful—all the business skills I lacked to give focus and direction to my endless stream of ideas and ambitions. It was only natural that she would step in to help out, because we had daily demands right under our nose to keep the business books and tutor students. That's what happens when you run a business from your home. We all had big plans for the business. Rita and I gradually renovated the basement, converting it into classrooms lined with bookshelves. We installed a separate outdoor entrance for the seemingly endless stream of students.

25   They bubbled with excitement as the smiling bespectacled professor they had heard so much about took them to a never-never land of learning adventures. I gave the students name tags so that I could remember each one's name. Saying "Hi, Mary Beth" was much more meaningful and friendly than just saying "Hi." Encouraging and caring words could go a long way in reaching our mutual goals. The name tags were also useful in one class where one student was named

Virginia Bruce and another was named Bruce Virginia. And the name Rhoda Ruder caused quite a laugh.

My challenge as a teacher was to give students the tools they needed to get the job done. I had to keep students interested, keep them learning, keep them laughing, and—above all—build their confidence that they could succeed. I was the gentle nudger. I wanted them to love learning as much as I loved teaching. I used everything imaginable to stimulate the students—arguing, joking, teasing, cajoling, listening, deciphering, and probing. I dug deep into my bag of tricks and pulled out mnemonic devices, monetary rewards, flash cards, scrawled blackboard diagrams, and flailing animated gestures. "If you get this question right, you'll win a dime," I'd tell students. Hands would shoot up in the air. Sometimes I'd give them a really difficult question. "This one is worth fifty cents," I'd tempt. Then pandemonium would break loose as they struggled to get the answer. But to earn fifty cents, a student needed to be able to explain the *how* and *why* behind the answer. Pocketing Kaplan coins became a symbol of pride and accomplishment for my students.

The classroom was my laboratory. If I listened carefully to a student's question, I could always detect the student's problem and tailor a solution. It was usually not a lack of ability but poor study habits, inadequate instruction, or a combination of the two that jeopardized students' performance. Not all students could grasp concepts with simple verbal explanations. Some needed visual associations. For instance, learning about geometric portions of a circle was easier if I drew a rectangular backyard and told my students to visualize the space a dog could cover if it was tied to a rope from a corner fence post. Suddenly intangible math concepts such as angles and radii came alive. Squishy math ideas took solid form.

My method, as it evolved, really was quite simple: Teach the students to be critical thinkers. My classes were not cram courses. Test-taking tricks and strategies would get the students only so far. They had to know the material, analyze the information, and think out the answer. I wasn't preparing them for only a Saturday-morning test; I was preparing them for a lifetime of critical thinking. It's like riding a bicycle: once you learn how to ride it, the skill is yours for life. And once you get the knack of taking a test like the SAT, it's also yours for life.

To learn a student's capabilities and deficiencies and to familiarize the student with the SAT, I created "quickie" tests or practice tests that simulated the real thing. I nicknamed these verisimilar tests based on the level of difficulty to tickle the students' fancy. When I opened a class with the Quickie Test NSAT, the students asked, "What's that?"

30   "This is an easy test. That's why I call it the Nursery School Admissions Test." Then came groans and premature sighs of relief—premature because it wasn't easy. A Quickie Test Eek evoked groans because it was rife with difficult questions. The name sounds awful, and the test was even worse. But I could tell from the quickie tests how a student would most likely perform on the SAT. My predictions were rarely wrong.

For instance, if students correctly answered ten out of fifteen questions on the NSAT, they would probably score the equivalent of 500 on the SAT. I also used the scores to separate students into classes. Sometimes, however, I relented in the face of passionate pleas from girlfriends and boyfriends who wanted to be assigned to the same class.

If I taught students a basic principle and they practiced applying that principle, they could answer most SAT questions. This was particularly true with basic vocabulary. "Memorize the word first," I told students, "then use it. See how it is used in different ways. You'll never forget it." I told students to go home and tell their parents, "I am impecunious. My allowance is paltry, and I need an augmentation." That left quite a few parents wide-eyed or scurrying to the dictionary.

I told students to think of all the words a young lady could use to call her boyfriend stubborn: obstinate, mulish, stiff-necked, pigheaded, bullheaded, contumacious, persistent, headstrong, obdurate, pertinacious, inexorable, intransigent, or intractable. "It's easier to memorize the meaning of those words because they have basically the same meaning," I told them, "and they all describe my wife." That prompted laughs. "If it helps to call me contumacious, fine. Whatever works."

Each week I instructed students to cut out ten newspaper articles and underline all challenging words. The more they read, the more powerful their vocabulary became. "Underline the words. If you don't know the meaning of a word, look it up in the dictionary," I told them. "Keep using the word. You can reinforce the meaning by seeing exactly how the word is used in the article. Use the word often enough, and it's yours."

35   I also taught them to use word roots, prefixes, and suffixes to help figure out the meanings of words. The prefix "eu," for instance, means "good" or "pleasant," such as the euphonious tone of a violin or a eulogy, meaning a positive speech about someone. "He was a bum all his life, but he was eulogized at his funeral," I told them. "So what does euphemism mean?" I asked the students. "I'll give you a hint. It has something to do with good." A euphemism is an expression describing something as being more pleasant than it really is. A garbage collector can be euphemistically described as a sanitary engineer. When a teacher catches a student with crib notes during a test and asks, "What are these?" the student can euphemistically describe them as "student reference cards."

Words can be fun, depending on how you use them. And understanding how to use words is one reason why reading is so important. I always encouraged my students to read anything they could get their hands on—magazines, newspapers, books, and advertisements. The more they read, the more they would want to read.

I encouraged my students to ask as many questions as needed. "You're allowed four hundred questions before I cut you off," I said jokingly. But seriously, I would have granted them four hundred-plus questions if needed. "Remember, there's only one kind of stupid question. That's the one you don't ask." Homework was essential. I developed pages of vocabulary lists, reading passages, practice tests, and math problems—à la the SAT—for students to work on outside class. "I am serving up success," I said. "Come and get it."

My SAT classes, although small, were sometimes loud and raucous when I threw out vocabulary words for a round-robin quiz. "She was a plucky girl to cross the street alone. What does 'plucky' mean? Look it up or you've made an egregious error," I told them. "Are screaming babies taciturn?" I asked the students. I hoped that from that day forward they would remember "taciturn" every time they heard a screaming baby.

The lessons worked. Here is a poem written to me by several students who attended one of my Sunday-morning SAT preparatory classes:

Every time that he calls us contumacious

We forgive him because he is so sagacious

And even perspicacious, never fallacious

His basic Quickies we shun as an aggregation of aggravation

Due to this we sometimes hold back admiration

Now last but not least after the SATs we'll have fun

Having reached our zenith—and shown our perfection!

CRITICAL REFLECTIONS

1. Kaplan's affection for the SAT is clear throughout this chapter. What are the reasons he felt it was a good test?

2. Describe the methods that Kaplan used to help students prepare for the SAT. Do they reflect his understandings of why the SAT was a good test?

3. Kaplan writes that his method was to "teach the students to be critical thinkers" (270). How do you think Kaplan is defining "critical thinkers" here?

MAKING CONNECTIONS

1. Go to www.collegeboard.com, click on "SAT Test Preparation," and look at the Mini-SAT (you will need to choose a username and password to see the mini-test, but it is free). Choose two or three questions from the mini-SAT to use as a "test" for Kaplan's argument. Consider what Kaplan says about the kinds of questions asked, thinking strategies required to respond to each, and possible responses. Based on *your* analysis, do you find his interpretation of the SAT convincing? Why or why not? Use evidence from the chapter and from the exam to support your response.

2. In "Do No Harm: Stopping the Damage to American Schools," Peter Sacks argues that standardized testing and state-sponsored standardized assessments have inflicted a variety of hardships on American schools. Consider Kaplan's and Sacks's positions against your own experiences with the SAT, ACT, or state-sponsored assessments. Do you agree with one or the other? Neither? What, in your experience, leads you to the assessment you have reached?

3. Stanley Kaplan writes that he believes

The SAT provided a more level playing field—and I liked that. It could help democratize American education by ushering a larger, more diverse group of students into the world of higher education (268).

Put Kaplan's statement side-by-side with one or more of the readings here that focus on student experiences, such as "Fierce Intimacies," "I Just Wanna Be Average," "The Last Shot," "Becoming Literate," or another reading of your choice. Do you agree with Kaplan's statement that a standardized test could level the playing field for the main characters in these narratives in the way that he describes?

NICOLAS LEMANN

THE PRESIDENT'S BIG TEST

This interview with Nicholas Lemann was conducted in conjunction with the broadcast of a documentary on the Public Broadcasting System (PBS) show *Frontline* called "Testing Our Schools." Lemann was interviewed because he has long written about education and assessment practices for publications like the *New Yorker* (where he is Washington correspondent), the *New York Times, Harper's,* and others. Lemann is also the author of a book, *The Big Test: The Secret History of the American Meritocracy.* In it, he chronicles the history, creation, and dissemination of the Scholastic Aptitude Test (SAT) and shows how the SAT was designed to validate the knowledge of those already designated as the smartest and most worthy.

The web site where this interview is found is an invaluable source for investigations of standardized testing and assessment. It includes interviews with administration officials like former Secretary of Education Rod Paige, discussions with supporters and critics of standardized assessments, video clips from the *Frontline* documentary, and a state-by-state map describing standardized assessment practices and providing links to additional resources. The site is located at www.pbs.org/wgbh/pages/frontline/shows/schools/.

March 28, 2002

Writing in the *New Yorker* last July, with President Bush's landmark education bill [No Child Left Behind] in danger of being watered down by House and Senate negotiators, Nicholas Lemann suggested that "the next month will be a pure test of Bush's level of energy, commitment, attention to detail, political skill, and courage on the issue that took him to the White House and that he cares about most."

Nobody foresaw then that the Sept. 11 terrorist attacks would sweep nearly all domestic issues off the table and into legislative limbo. Education was one of the few exceptions. Soon after Sept. 11, the president and the leaders of both parties in Congress announced that education reform, as the nation's top domestic priority, would go forward.

While it didn't exactly steal headlines away from the war on terrorism, the education bill, now officially known as the No Child Left Behind Act of 2001, was signed into law in early January, having emerged from the House-Senate conference in December with Bush's priorities essentially intact. In fact, if the overwhelming bipartisan support for the president's bill is any indication, the idea of enforcing standards and accountability for schools turned out to be less controversial than one might have expected—at least on Capitol Hill. (The issue remains plenty controversial, of course, within the education establishment and in some communities around the country where parents and students have staged protests against high-stakes tests.) The true test now, it seems, is whether the Education Dept. will be able to implement the new law as intended and hold firm with states whose governors fought to weaken the bill's accountability measures.

We recently asked Lemann, who writes the "Letter from Washington" column for the *New Yorker* and is a nationally recognized expert on education politics and policy, to talk about the debate over this bill and its outcome. What were the major issues? Who were the real winners and losers? What are the obstacles to its success? And what did the president achieve with his first major legislative victory, the most significant federal education-reform act since 1965?

5   Lemann is the author of *The Big Test: The Secret History of the American Meritocracy* (1999), about the creation of the Scholastic Aptitude Test and its impact on American society, and *The Promised Land: The Great Black Migration and How It Changed America* (1991), which was the basis for a PBS documentary. He is also known to PBS viewers by his appearances in such documentaries as "School: The Story of American Public Education" (2001) and *Frontline*'s "Secrets of the SAT" (1999). Before joining the *New Yorker* in 1998, Lemann spent 15 years as the national correspondent for the *Atlantic Monthly,* and from 1981 to 1983 he was the executive editor of *Texas Monthly.* He spoke with Wen Stephenson, managing editor of *Frontline*'s website, on March 11, 2002.

Let's talk about Texas. You've written that the Bush education plan—the "No Child Left Behind" plan that has now, more or less, been passed and signed into law—was basically the Texas model applied on a national scale. And we know that education reform is the issue that really made Bush president—at least, one can make a strong case that that's true.

You can make the same case for Clinton, by the way.

How much credit does Bush deserve for what happened in Texas?

It clearly was a sort of consensus effort in Texas that predates Bush's governorship, and spans both parties. The first reform stuff was done under [Democratic] Governor Mark White, who appointed the Perot Commission in the early '80s, which by today's standards was kind of rudimentary education reform. The first of the modern education reform, the first big bill, was passed by [Democratic Governor] Ann Richards. So it's definitely true that Bush was signing on to a movement that was already going on.

On the other hand, to Bush's credit, most people would say he sort of "got it" more, felt more passion about it, and moved it forward more forcefully than Richards would have, or did, when she was governor. So most of the education-reform people like Bush. And Bush, at least in those days, was very good about not claiming credit. He was careful, always, to say, "I didn't start this," and so on. And indeed, you can argue also that even in the national bill Bush was building on Clinton's efforts. Some of the features of this bill were put in place in '93 and '94 by Clinton [in the Goals 2000 bill].

Let's move on to the education bill itself. Your New Yorker *article posed the question, "Can the president's education crusade survive Beltway politics?" So the obvious question at this point is, did it? Did Bush's education crusade survive Beltway politics?*

Yeah. It basically did. The main dangers are the underfunding danger, which the Democrats are obviously very attuned to, and then that the Education Department will not enforce it strictly, and they'll grant [the states] a lot of waivers.

10   But there was one actual loophole in the bill that I can see. There was a fight over the question of what they call "comparability." In other words, how do you prevent states from using ridiculously easy tests, or changing tests all the time? The supporters of the bill wanted some kind of national benchmark against which the state results would be measured.

And that's the National Assessment of Educational Progress (NAEP) [a national achievement test given every other year to a statistical sample of students in every state]?

Right. Well, there was a big debate about [NAEP comparability], and when I wrote the article it wasn't settled. A lot of conservatives were actually against it. The administration held firm on the principle of NAEP comparability, which was good. But what happened was, there's no consequence to it. A state can have ridiculous tests. It still has to compare its scores to NAEP, and it has to publish the results, but if its scores keep falling behind NAEP relentlessly, year after year, there's no actual punishment mechanism for that. The idea is that the embarrassment factor will take care of it.

Say what you mean by falling behind NAEP, year after year, in their scores. How does that work?

Let's say, in a hypothetical situation, a state concocts a test where its students show a 5 percent skill gain every year, so at the end of five years its students have gone up 25 percent in skills on its own test. But during the same period they've dropped 10 percent on the NAEP. Well, that tells you that you're rigging the system with your test—as long as you believe the NAEP is legitimate, which I do.

The thing about NAEP is that people trust it. It's a huge issue. There's a lot of mischief that goes on in testing, and NAEP is a trusted professional test, so it's very important to keep that around as a yardstick.

Tell me about the politics that led to that loophole.

There was a lot of politics of all sorts. But on the NAEP, first of all, the test publishers—and they were an important lobby in this whole thing—were against NAEP comparability, for two reasons. One is, it's essentially a test of the quality of their tests. So for the same reason that nobody wants to be held accountable, or evaluated, if given the choice, they didn't want the NAEP. The second reason was that they felt if the NAEP wasn't used, there was hope that they could devise their own. They dreamed of a bidding process on a brand new national test, other than the NAEP, that they could write.

15   The other important group that was against the use of NAEP was the ideological right, which feared that it was a step toward a national curriculum—which it is—and that there would be problems down the road with things like creationism and so on.

You say it's a step toward a national curriculum?

Yeah, it is. I think this whole bill is a step toward a national curriculum—which I applaud, by the way.

Do you want to say anything more about that? I'm not sure that that's really understood, necessarily.

It's not understood partly because Bush has accompanied the bill with standard Republican rhetoric. But, you know, this bill clearly takes federal control over local public education to a heretofore unknown level.

Is that what makes this, as you put it, "the most significant federal legislation on education since 1965"? The expansion of the federal role?

Yes. It vastly expands federal oversight over local education.

And it moves us toward a national curriculum. How much further toward a national curriculum does it really move us?

It's a significant step, because if there are going to be achievement tests, and if they're going to be at least nationally judged—that is, states can choose their own tests, but they're judged against the NAEP—you'll have a great deal of convergence in curriculum.

20   And the truth is, you already do. I mean, these people who are against national curriculum drive me crazy, because we have a national curriculum now. It's just that it's done by the test publishing companies. You know, we have a choice of about three or four flavors—Houghton-Mifflin, [McGraw-Hill], and so on and so forth. But there is not significant, meaningful curriculum difference in high school American history courses depending on where you are in the country. There are just a few standard textbooks, and they're national products, they're not local products. In deciding what textbooks they use, the states are adopting, in effect, a national curriculum.

You mentioned that the test publishers were a major lobbying influence on this bill. How much power do they wield at the state level? If it's fair to say that the public and most politicians don't really understand what makes a good or appropriate test versus a bad test—it just isn't an issue that people are educated on—how do you see it playing out on the state level, in terms of the testing business influencing what kind of tests are adopted?

The test publishers are not rich enough to have a kind of Enron-like political effect, where they're able to be really major financial contributors to any state's politics, and to be able to say, "We've got our people salted through the entire Gray Davis administration." Their power comes largely from the fact that they have superb contacts with state education departments. That's what they do all day, is send people out on the road to talk to state education commissioners. So they have a tremendous amount of access to state education departments. Their voices are heard. And the states have to deal with them, because they don't want to write their own textbooks. The analogy would be the defense contractors' relationship to the Pentagon. The test companies are where the state has to go to buy their equipment, and they have a very close, complicated, intense relationship with the state Ed. Departments, so they tend not to get left out of the process.

In terms of what actually goes on in the classroom, the pedagogical issues, you said in your New Yorker *piece, "As soon as people figure out what the bill does, there will be caterwauling throughout the land." And you list some of the complaints that the parents and educators who are against testing always raise, like the prevalence of drilling and test prepping and "teaching to the test," and "dumbing down the curriculum." How real are these issues? Do you worry about these things, especially when the stakes are so high?*

The overall answer is that there are good tests and there are bad tests. The overarching principle of what is known in the trade as "curricular alignment" is crucially, crucially important. And this is one reason I'm for a national curriculum.

The cart-horse order here is curriculum first, then tests. A lot of the worst stuff that I've seen goes on when for various reasons a school district has to purchase a test as an isolated act, not having to do with any curricular decision. That is when you get into the bad test-prep stuff. I mean, one of my kids was actually in one of these situations, and they actually have a class every day called "Test Prep." But that was because it was a non-curriculum-aligned test. If you have a curriculum-aligned test, what you want to do is create a situation where the test prep is the course itself, so you don't have to worry about test prep as a separate, free-floating thing.

In other words, just teaching the material that's supposed to be learned in a given course is what prepares kids for the test?

Exactly. Right. To give you a simple example, if you're going to be quizzed on Friday on ten French verbs, and I'm your French teacher, I'm going to teach you those ten French verbs during the week, right? Does that count as "teaching to the test"? Yes. And what's wrong with it, if that's what you want the kids to learn?

You don't seem to have major qualms about the effects on the quality of instruction and learning in our country as a result of all this testing.

25 I don't. It's a huge issue, but it's one of these issues that really depends on the details. I'm very suspicious of dealing with this in a kind of "Men Are From Mars, Women Are From Venus" way—that all tests are bad and all tests lead to soulless drilling, or crush the life out of students.

What you're really seeing here, in part, is an iteration of the long, long, long-running—since the early 19th century—progressive education wars, which are well described in Diane Ravitch's book *Left Back* [2000]. It's very similar to the phonics versus whole language fight in reading instruction. It's almost a theological issue. You very quickly get from the arguments you just mentioned to what I think underlies the real views of a lot of the opponents, which is, "Why should children have to learn to spell? Why should children have to learn these meaningless dates in American history? Why should they have to know the names of presidents?"

It gets into this very deep-seated idea of education—which, I guess, begins in Rousseau's *Emile*—that the best education is one that does not focus on facts at all and instead allows the child to be creative, and, of course, the teacher to be creative. I don't want to say that has no place in education, but I do think it's pretty clearly demonstrated that there's a basic set of skills, and if you don't have them, you're screwed economically. The high school diploma is not a meaningless credential. It is a proxy for saying, or should be a proxy for saying, "This person has these basic skills."

To acquire the basic skills, in many cases, you do have to drill at least somewhat. And the purpose of testing is to make sure people are acquiring the basic skills. My argument is, once you've acquired the basic skills, you're a free kid, and you can study whatever you want. You can be creative and you can do all these portfolios and constructed-response projects and authentic assessment and all that stuff. But you need the skills.

And where the testing opponents scare me, actually, is this "just trust us" attitude. There's a faith that if you have no oversight at all, but adequate funding, you can be sure that teachers will do a good job of teaching kids, and kids will learn. And that just makes me feel uncomfortable. I would like to have a check on that, and I can't think of a check other than tests.

30 And also, all these testing people, they do listen to the critics, and they have moved in the direction of constructed-response answers and such. It's not all multiple choice.

The more complicated part is when you get into things like American history. I can't really argue that you need to know American history in order to survive economically. But I would argue that it's good for America to have some kind of national, agreed-upon material that every kid, every high school grad, should know about the history of our country. And once you have that, then you get into some of the territory that the progressives don't like, of dates and wars and presidents, and things like that.

But you're also getting into territory that the conservatives don't like, either.
Exactly. Which is fear of liberal brain-washing.

Right. "Who's going to decide what my child has to learn."
And my argument is, those fights happen anyway in states. And so let's just let them happen nationally instead of in states. We debate a lot of things as a country without falling apart. I just don't buy the argument that that debate will be so brutal and divisive that we can't possibly get to a good result, and so it's better left at the state level.

▰ CRITICAL REFLECTIONS

1. Lemann notes that one of the dangers of nationwide testing is the possibility that states will make their tests easier (so that scores are higher). He suggests that the NAEP (National Assessment of Educational Progress) can counteract this tendency. How do you interpret his argument about the merits of the NAEP and its potential for "leveling" standardized assessments?

2. In making the case for a national curriculum, Lemann argues that curricula are often already standardized by textbook publishers (including the publisher of this reader). Think back on an earlier English or history class you had that used a mass-marketed textbook, and about any experience you have had with a state-sponsored standardized assessment. Were they similar? Different? Does one or the other persuade you that a national curriculum is a good idea? If so, who should write that curriculum? If not, why don't you think it's a good idea?

3. Lemann makes a distinction in this interview between good tests and bad tests. How do you interpret his analysis of the difference between them? What might a good test look like for you, and why is it good?

4. Beginning on page 278, Lemann situates the debate over testing in the longer-running debate about what the purpose of education in the U.S. should be. How do you interpret the positions in this debate? Isolate one or two moments of your own high school or college education and use them to illustrate how the creative and skill-building purposes of education translate into practice in the classroom.

▰ MAKING CONNECTIONS

1. Throughout this article, Lemann makes the case for a centralized national curricula. Juxtapose Lemann's argument here with the framework laid out in "Literacy Practices" and "How They've Fared in Education." How might Barton and Hamilton (the authors of "How They've Fared") and Harry (the subject of "How They've Fared") stand on the issue, and why?

2. Lemann argues that good tests are curriculum-aligned. Do you see the New York State Regents' Exam (the subject of "The Test Mess") as being curriculum-aligned, or non-curriculum-aligned? Why do you make the case you do?

THERESA MCCARTY

COMMUNITY AND CLASSROOM

This chapter comes from a book called *A Place to Be Navajo: Rough Rock and the Struggle for Self-Determination in Indigenous Schooling.* The book's author, Theresa McCarty, calls this book a "critical life history" of the Rough Rock School, the first Indian-controlled school in the country. Before this, stretching from the mid-19th through the mid-20th centuries, Indian children were removed—often forcibly—from their homes to attend Bureau of Indian Affairs (BIA)-sponsored schools where they were literally stripped of their cultures. They were not permitted to speak their native languages, their clothes were replaced by western clothes, their hair was shorn, and they were "educated" in the ways of Anglo-American culture. If they retreated to their previous ways, they were punished severely. When the Rough Rock School opened, the intention was to enact a different model of schooling for Navajo students.

Theresa McCarty was introduced to the Rough Rock School as a graduate student. She spent three years in the early 1980s living in Rough Rock and working side-by-side with local residents involved with the school to develop curriculum. For the school's 30th anniversary in 1996, she was invited to write a history of the school. Her research, which involved interviews, document analysis, photographs, and analysis of the Rough Rock School's development, illustrates both the promise of a culturally-based school and the tensions faced by the school as students and community members navigated between Navajo culture and the dominant white culture. In this chapter, McCarty focuses on the early days of the school, positioning the school-developed curriculum against the TESL (Teaching English as a Second Language) curriculum used at Rough Rock.

On September 12, 1966, the first American Indian community-controlled school opened its doors to 220 students, from beginners (6-year-olds) through sixth grade. Only one child in the two beginners classes, which had a total enrollment of 38, was reported as speaking English (Roessel, 1966b).

"And it was just like, if you're having a dream and you're trying to go someplace and you can't get there," school registrar Benjamin Bennett remembers of those first days of school. A White educator who had taught on the reservation and worked with Robert Roessel at Arizona State University, Ben Bennett arrived at 2:30 p.m. on the school's opening day. He remains school registrar to the time

FIGURE 1

"People were enthused about the school. 'How wonderful!' it was said."—John Dick
(Photograph from RRCS archives, courtesy of Rough Rock Community School.)

of this writing. When we began gathering oral history data in 1996, we were especially interested in his long-range view. "It was interesting," Ben said, "the attitude of the Bureau . . . . We kept hearing things like, 'Rough Rock won't last for 6 months'"—

There were just so many things to do. Finally on September 12, "We're starting whether you're ready or not." Then, the students were all boarding students, with the exception of [one family]—they brought their children in.

"THE WHOLE THING WAS OPEN"

"What was it like, those first days and months?" we wondered as we talked with community members 30 years later. John Dick began—

> People were enthused about the school—those who lived in the area and others from afar. "*Dooládó'da!* (How wonderful!)" it was said . . . . When the school first opened, people thought it was great work that was being accomplished. The school was created to learn everything possible. A great amount of [income] was distributed.

Ben Bennett concurred: "The main thing for the first day and several weeks after," he said, "people wanted jobs. The whole thing was open. People were in and out . . . they wanted to apply for jobs."[1]

5   To understand the demonstration at Rough Rock requires shedding notions of what "doing school" is about. This was not to be a school in the conventional, classroom-focused sense. The whole thing *was*, in fact, open. "This is a community-oriented school, rather than child-oriented," Robert Roessel told a journalist who visited Rough Rock in 1967. "In the past, Indian schools have taken little interest in their communities, but here, we want to involve adults and teenagers, dropouts, people who have never been to school" (Conklin, 1967, p. 8).

And so, those who read or hear about Rough Rock years after its inaugural days must imagine a completely different kind of school. Imagine, for example, a school whose goal was education in the broadest sense—of cultivating the talents and resources of an entire community, fostering a sense of shared purpose and hope, and *creating* a community around the school. In a community with annual per capita cash incomes of $85.00, school jobs and economic development projects were key to this, and an entire school division, Community Services, was devoted to community outreach (see Fig. 7.2). "It was *all* a Navajo program," Robert Roessel reflected when I spoke with him years later—

> We brought the entire community into the school. Many projects were developed to do this—a greenhouse . . . poultry farm, a furniture factory. This was the Navajo Emphasis program, and Navajos were involved in all aspects of it. This was what the school was all about.

The greenhouse Roessel mentions began with the assistance of dormitory students, who planted and tended the seedlings, then sold them to Rough Rock residents. The poultry farm, financed through a Farm Home Administration loan,

---

[1]Between July and the end of September, the school board hired 91 full-time employees, including 45 Navajos, 38 from the local area. In addition, eight parents served as dormitory aides on a 6-week rotating basis, and two community members were hired as part-time management trainees in the dormitories and administration services. Through an arrangement with the Navajo Nation and the University of Utah, 15 Volunteers in Service to America (VISTA) workers came to Rough Rock to assist in the classrooms and dorms (Roessel, 1966b, pp. 1–2).

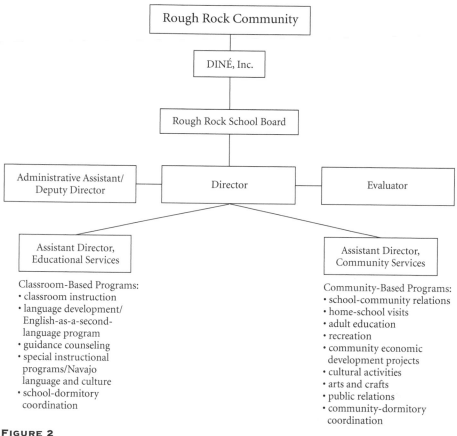

FIGURE 2
Early school organization

operated out of the old day school and sold eggs and chicks to community members and school staff. The toy and furniture factory, financed by OEO, employed three local men; the Navajo Office of Economic Opportunity purchased their products and distributed them to Headstart preschools on the reservation. An adobe home project provided training in adobe brick construction. Local workers completed an adobe building to house the Community Services office and built a science building and several model homes that later were occupied by Rough Rock residents.

The school also sponsored an OEO-funded arts and crafts project, which hired Navajo instructors to teach rug weaving, basket and moccasin making, silversmithing, leather work, pottery making, and dress and sash belt weaving to adults. Participants enrolled in the program for 4 to 9 weeks and received a small stipend. Often, the school purchased participants' finished products, selling them to school staff, visitors, or off-reservation vendors. The goals of this program were to revitalize traditional Navajo arts and crafts, cultivate a cadre of local artisans, and establish new market outlets for their work. Remembered fondly by its participants, the arts and crafts program also nurtured a sense of comradery and communal pride. Hasbah Charley, who continued to work as a weaver for many years, recalled the goodwill the program generated:

> The work we did was good . . . . We learned rug weaving and basket weaving. We also learned to weave sash belts. [The school] asked me to become really involved, and that's what I did. And that was good. To this day, [these activities] are still my teachings and what I talk about.

Now, imagine a school organized around principles of kinship, family, and communalism. Communalism was most evident in the dormitory parent program. Dormitory assistants acted as surrogate parents, watching over the children, providing counseling and moral support, and sharing their knowledge of oral traditions during evening storytelling sessions (Roessel, 1977, p. 2). Lynda Teller explained, "The community parents would stay in the dorm Monday through Friday, helping. Some would work nights . . . . They were doing a lot of crafts in the dorm, and also in the classroom." Dorm parents received a small stipend for their work. To maximize community participation and the distribution of income, they rotated on an 8-week basis.

10   Mae Hatathli worked as a dormitory aide for many years. She remembered how she cared for the children, patching their worn clothes and instructing them on traditional values and behaviors.

> We helped watch over the children there. I did things like make their beds, and I sewed their clothes where they were torn. They [the school board] asked me to talk to them and I did that. I told them to do their best . . . . That's how the school started.

There were other, more subtle applications of the kinship principle. Imagine a school where the informal knowledge residing within extended family households was valued as much or more than that formalized by certificates or degrees. Central to the feeling of "openness," this quality was remarked upon by many people we interviewed. "A lot of these people who worked at the school didn't really have that formal education to be specialized in certain areas," Lorinda Gray pointed out, "but they had jobs. I think that broadened a lot of community interest at the school." Frank X. Begay, who served as a dormitory aide for many years, remembered this about the day he was hired:

> I was asked if I wanted a job. "I didn't go to school—what could I possibly do?" I said.
> "Children are starting at the school and we want you to work there," I was told.
> "I didn't go to school, what could I do there? I don't know how to write," I said.
> "Stop saying that," I was told. "You are going to help us. This is a school run by the community. It is not a BIA school."[2]

---

[2]As part of the goal of opening the school to the community, the school board decided to half the salaries of dormitory and other community aides in order to hire twice as many people. Years later, Robert Roessel explained that he had opposed this policy: "We had to attract good people since we were *demonstrating*," he said, referencing the high stakes attached to a Federally funded experimental program. The board prevailed, however, and many community members obtained jobs and thus participated directly in the school. "The board was right. I was wrong," Roessel acknowledged.

FIGURE 3

Community members building an adobe house, one of the school's economic development initiatives, late 1960s. (Photograph by Marguerite Swift from RRCS archives, courtesy of Rough Rock Community School.)

The kinship principle extended to other, less formal school functions designed simply to bring people together in what historically had been an alien institution. Hasbah Charley reminisced—

> When the school began, we used to hold meetings and potlucks for the community, and everyone donated meat [sheep]. It was a lot of fun. We had people from all over—men, women, and teenagers. That's how it was then.

Besides sponsoring community meetings and dinners, the school functioned almost like a branch of the extended family, assisting community members in times of need. During a severe snowstorm in 1967, school personnel helped open roads, get hay to marooned livestock, and assist Air Force helicopters in bringing food to isolated camps. During spring lambing season, the school purchased lamb starter milk, selling it to community members at discounted rates. The school purchased butane and sold it to community members at cost, rechanneling the proceeds to school projects. During an especially hard winter, the school bought coal from a regional construction company and distributed it free to the community. The school water supply provided stock and domestic water, and the school board and Community Services helped bring a U.S. Public

Health Service clinic to Rough Rock in 1969. In the school's second year, the board petitioned the Bureau to reinstate the Rough Rock Chapter, and that year, a chapter house was constructed near the school. Aside from the new facility itself, construction work on it provided more jobs and wages. "There was a lot of work and the school helped in so many ways," John Dick recalled.

Finally, imagine a school committed to promoting the community's mental health and spiritual life. This was the purpose of the Navajo Mental Health Project, which began in 1967 with funds personally donated by Ruth Roessel. For more than 20 years, the project continued with support from the National Institute of Mental Health. To prepare more Native healers, the Navajo Mental Health Project funded months- and years-long apprenticeships during which aspiring healers trained under locally recognized ritual specialists. Most instruction occurred in the specialist's home or during ceremonies conducted by him.

15   The Mental Health Project helped prepare one of the few local female healers, Mae Hatathli. Mae's father was a well-known medicine man who taught for many years as part of the Mental Health Project. Mae wanted very much to learn the Blessing Way (*Hózhóójí*) ceremony, the core of Navajo religious thought and practice. She recalls her father being selected to study this ceremony. "Then I began to wonder if a woman along with her husband could join the program," Mae said—

> . . . so I asked my uncle, John Dick. "Yes," he said, "It is allowed." So I told him that I wanted to join the men. He said it was acceptable. . . . I joined the group with my father. . . . We [my husband and I] went with him whenever he was asked to do a ceremony. We did that for several years.

THE IMPACTS OF EARLY COMMUNITY-BASED PROGRAMS

Of all the early community development programs at Rough Rock, the Navajo Mental Health Project was the most long-lived, and by community standards, the most significant and successful. This is perhaps because the project tapped into deeply held beliefs that were and are pervasive within the local culture, but also because this project received continuous funding from a single source over many years. Other projects supported by discretionary funds lapsed within a few months or years, and few had economic benefits beyond the provision of short-term wages.

All of these programs cultivated the community's *human* resources, even as they promoted a collective view that Rough Rock was, in fact, the people's school. Virtually all the oral history testimony about the school at this time reiterates the themes of openness, inclusivity, and a sense of belonging and being needed and appreciated by the school. The demonstration project explicitly depended and drew upon the cultural capital of community members—what Norma González, Luis Moll and their associates call the informal, everyday "funds of knowledge" in households and families (González, 1995; González et al., 1995). For many people, the school provided their first wage employment. Local knowledge was rewarded financially and by the social status conferred by school jobs.

As much or more than anything that transpired in the classroom, the validation and use of community-based knowledge held the promise of building a genuinely bilingual and bicultural school culture. I turn now to consider how that promise unfolded in classrooms and the school curriculum.

INDIGENOUS BILINGUAL/BICULTURAL EDUCATION: "WE HAD A LOT OF ACTIVITIES GEARED TO NAVAJO"

In the spring of 1996 I asked Lorinda Gray, a bilingual teacher at Rough Rock Elementary School, how she would describe the school and community in 1966. At that time, Lorinda had just graduated from Chinle High School. "I always wanted to be a clerk-typist," she explained, but she took a job as a bilingual teacher assistant at the new demonstration school. "I think the community really supported the idea of a bilingual school," Lorinda said, "because it seems like the school was open to the community." Parents and grandparents not only worked in the classrooms, dormitories, and school support services, they often visited the classrooms and "they were participating in the arts and crafts and various other activities," Lorinda recalled. "The administration and the school board and that regional board [DINÉ, Inc.]—they were in there as a whole team to support bilingual education," she added. Lorinda laughed that at annual school orientations, there was so much enthusiasm for bilingual education "you could just taste it!"

FIGURE 4

Guy Blackburn's and Lorinda Gray's elementary students painting the metal structure that housed their classroom, c. 1967. (Photograph from RRCS archives, courtesy of Rough Rock Community School.)

20   Bilingual/bicultural education naturally complemented Rough Rock's community development emphasis. "Often in the past," Robert Roessel wrote in the school's first monthly report, "education has been looked upon by Indian parents as a threat"—an either-or proposition that required a choice between two languages and lifeways (Roessel, 1966a, p. 102). In contrast, Rough Rock advocated an additive, "both-and" approach in which students were exposed "to important values and customs of *both* Navajo culture *and* the dominant society" (Roessel, 1977, p. 10).

What did this approach look like in practice? Who were the teachers? How was instruction organized?

In 1966, the number of certified Navajo teachers could be counted on a few hands. Rough Rock hired three of them, all women, to teach the beginner's classes. Although none came from the community, the six teacher assistants hired (also women) had been born and raised at Rough Rock. Lynda Teller, who had recently graduated from high school and was planning to study nursing in Dallas, remembers receiving a letter in the summer of 1966 from her father, John Dick. "My parents wrote to me and told me there was a school that was going to open here in Rough Rock," she said. "And they said, 'Can you come home? We have a job for you here.'"

Lynda Teller became one of those six bilingual teaching assistants. Her mission school literacy in Navajo had never left her, she said, "even though I was away from home a lot. Eventually, word got around that I could read and write Navajo"—

> And so they said, "Well, you're going to teach Navajo to the teachers who don't know how to read or write," and there I was. Anita Pfeiffer [the school's first Educational Services director and a respected leader in Navajo education], said, "I want you to help all these teachers, even the *bilagáanas*, read and write Navajo." I said, "Me? Teach the teachers?" And she said, "Yes!"

In addition to the evening language classes she offered, Lynda Teller rotated between different classrooms as the Navajo language specialist. By the school's second year, four new specialists had been hired to teach Navajo language and social living. Anita Pfeiffer's report of September 1968 gives some idea of how instruction was organized: "Instruction is entirely in Navajo in Phase I where there are bilingual teachers, except for the daily . . . oral English program" (Pfeiffer, 1968, p. 10)[3]

---

[3]By the end of the first year, after teachers expressed dissatisfaction with a graded school system, the school board approved an ungraded system designed to remove "the stigma of promotion and non-promotion while giving importance to individualized instruction" (Pfeiffer, 1967, p. 14). Students were grouped into preschool, beginners, and 15 classes of approximately 11 pupils each in "Phase I" and "Phase II." Phase I students remained in self-contained classrooms throughout the day, receiving instruction from both their classroom teacher and specialists who rotated from class to class. Phase II students moved from a base classroom to specialized classes in Navajo language and social living, physical education, science, industrial arts, and home economics, a class specifically requested by board members who asked that adults also be allowed to take it.

FIGURE 5

Cultural presentation at Rough Rock by Billy Sam of Many Farms, c. 1967. (Photograph from RRCS archives, courtesy of Rough Rock Community School.)

25   Lynda Teller recalled that the school administration encouraged the Navajo staff to use Navajo as much as possible and "to pick up Navajo [literacy] as much as they can." Non-Navajo teachers also participated in periodic live-ins, residing with local families for 2 or 3 days as a way of learning about their students' lives and home experiences. "We had a lot of activities geared to Navajo," Lynda said—

FIGURE 6
Elementary students performing a traditional dance as participants in the Navajo Mental Health project observe, c. 1966. In foreground from left to right: *Project participants John Woody, Jim Hatathli, Mae Hatathli, and Little Laughter. (Photograph from RRCS archives, courtesy of Rough Rock Community School.)*

We had an arts and crafts program in one of the classrooms. Groups of students were taken there, just to watch how everything was done. When they were in the seventh and eighth grades, they could take weaving, silversmithing, sash belt weaving, and leather craft. Then that OEO program [the adult arts and crafts program] would come have workshops with parents, students, and staff. . . .

Accounts such as these provide some sense of the ways in which the demonstration school attempted to blur the lines between classroom and community. With a core staff of teachers, teaching assistants, and parent assistants, classrooms were hubs of activity and personnel. Lynda Teller's recollections help bring those classrooms to life:

We had a lot of teachers in the classroom. We had VISTA workers here, and student teachers paid under the Ford Foundation. We had a students teacher in about every classroom then. We had exchange students from foreign countries, and they would show us the way they make their clothes, and do their cooking. So we had a lot of people in the classroom really helping.

"WE WANTED THE NAVAJO LANGUAGE TO BE WRITTEN"

One of the major obstacles to implementing Rough Rock's "both-and" approach was a lack of bilingual/bicultural teaching materials. Navajo literacy materials at the time consisted of those produced by the BIA in the 1940s and 1950s (including some primers and a dictionary), books for teaching beginning Navajo to non-speakers, translated Biblical works, and scholarly accounts written for an adult, non-Navajo audience (Spolsky, Holm, & Murphy, 1970). Navajo teachers had to improvise, and they complained in their monthly reports that students became bored with the duplication of material. As one teacher reported, the question most often asked by the students was, "What are we going to do next?" (Norris, 1968, pp. 85–86).

With a grant from Title I of the Elementary and Secondary Education Act (ESEA) in 1967, the school established the Navajo Curriculum Center, the first enterprise in the United States to be devoted to the production of Indigenous children's literature. "We said we wanted the Navajo language to be learned. It will be written and there will be books on it," former school board secretary Thomas James maintained. "We wanted books in Navajo and on ceremonial subjects. That is how many books came out."

At first, the Curriculum Center was no more than a workroom off a hallway. "That room was an office for Navajo culture," Lorinda Gray remembered, gesturing to a room adjacent to the bilingual program office in the present elementary school. "We had all these people that told traditional stories," Lorinda went on, "and we had people transcribing, and we had people illustrating. . . . I think that was one of the best highlights of the school."

In its first 4 years, the Curriculum Center produced over a dozen texts, most of them professionally published and beautifully illustrated by local artists. Ethelou Yazzie's (1971) *Navajo History* and Robert Roessel and Dillon Platero's (1968) *Coyote Stories* remain the most popular; they have been reprinted many times and continue to sell briskly around the world. In light of the need for Navajo literacy materials, however, these texts were inadequate; reflecting the priorities of Title I, a compensatory program for English reading and mathematics, nearly all the books were written in English.

30   In later chapters, I revisit the dilemma of Federal funding and its effects on local education control. Here, it should be noted that while Rough Rock's bilingual/bicultural program was born amidst great enthusiasm and promise, the resources to support it in the classroom were slim indeed. Thus, Navajo language instructor and linguist Paul Platero wrote that "the need for adequate instructional materials was constant" (P. Platero, 1968, p. 81). And Dillon Platero, who assumed the school directorship in 1969, agreed: "One of the main difficulties . . . faced in the early days was a lack of suitable texts to teach Navajo language and culture" (Platero, 1969a, p. 5).

▬▬ CRITICAL REFLECTIONS

1. McCarty mentions the principles around which the Rough Rock School was organized—kinship, family, and communalism. Based on evidence from the chapter, how do you see these being enacted in the school?

2. The "both-and" approach to learning is discussed in this chapter. How do you interpret this approach?

3. McCarty writes that one of the goals of the Rough Rock School was to "blur the lines between classroom and community" (290). How do you see that happening here?

4. Think about one portion (a year, a class—some definable unit) of your own schooling, and re-imagine it as being organized around the principles that McCarty cites as central to the Rough Rock School. How would the portion you have chosen be different?

■ MAKING CONNECTIONS

1. Both Booker T. Washington and W.E.B. DuBois were also interested in organizing education around specific principles. How do you think each would respond to the organizing principles for the Rough Rock School? Based on your interpretation of their work included here, why do you think each would respond as you say they would?

2. In "On the Uses of a Liberal Education: II. As a Weapon in the Hands of the Restless Poor," author Earl Shorris says that he explained the Clemente Course to his adult students by saying that "Rich people learn the humanities in private schools and expensive universities. And that's one of the ways in which they learn the political life. If you want real power, legitimate power . . . you must understand politics. The humanities will help" (192). Based on your reading of Shorris's article and this reading, do you see the two approaches to education as opposed to one another? As complementary? As too different to compare? Why do you provide the response you do?

MICHAEL MOFFATT

WHAT COLLEGE IS
REALLY LIKE

This selection, excerpted from a longer chapter, comes from a study by Rutgers University anthropology professor Michael Moffatt called *Coming of Age in New Jersey.* (With the title, Moffatt makes reference to a ground-breaking study published in 1933 by anthropologist Margaret Mead called *Coming of Age in Samoa.*) Conducting field work amidst a different culture, as anthropologists do, Moffatt spent several years in the late 1970s and early to mid-1980s living full- and part-time in the Rutgers University dorms. His research questions reflected those typically posed by anthropologists: What is this culture? What are its customs, its norms? What do its natives do and why? Initially, Moffatt posed *as* a student, developing friendships with his informants (other dorm residents) until he revealed to them that he was studying

them. Here, Moffatt presents what he finds to be students' general understandings of the purpose of college based on data he collected. When reading this selection, it is important to keep in mind that while these findings
sound objective, they reflect Moffatt's interpretation of his observations
and are filtered through his experiences as a researcher and a professor.

My first, most vivid impression from the dorms was how different college looked
from the point of view of the undergraduates. The students' Rutgers was obviously
not the same institution the professors and other campus authorities thought they
knew. The college was a very complicated place, made more complicated by its in-
clusion in a bigger and even more confusing university. Very few administrators
understood all of it—even its formal organization—let alone how it actually
worked. Most campus adults did not even try; they simply did their best to grasp
those small parts of the college and the university that they needed to understand.
The students did the same. And the undergraduates and the professors—and the
janitors and the buildings and grounds men and the campus police and the campus bus drivers and the secretaries and the graduate students and the librarians
and the deans and the administrators and the public relations staff and the president—were all in contact with very different bits of institutional Rutgers.[1]

* * *

Most Rutgers professors would not have known how to do what the students
had to accomplish successfully every semester—how to balance college and major requirements against the time and space demands of Rutgers classrooms,
how to get to their classes on time on the overcrowded campus bus system, and
how to push their academic needs through a half-efficient, sometimes impolite
university bureaucracy. Most faculty members no longer possessed the ability to
sit passively through long lectures without ever once getting a chance to open
their own mouths. Few faculty members could have named the dean of students
at Rutgers College. Most of them had never heard of some of the commoner
terms in undergraduate slang in the 1980s. Almost all of them would have been
confused and uncomfortable in the average dorm talk session, and none of them
would have had any inkling of how to go about locating a good party on the
College Avenue Campus on a Thursday night.

* * *

For most faculty members, *the* purpose of higher education is what goes on in
the classroom: learning critical thinking, how to read a text, mathematical and
scientific skills, expert appreciation and technique in the arts, and so on. Some

---

[1]This language suggests that Rutgers is a big institutional thing existing independently of any particular
actor's perception of it. Rutgers might be redefined more phenomenologically, however, as the sum total
of all those imprecise partial understandings that all the actors who make it up have of it, as the negoti-
ated and changing product of their combined understandings. (Power plays a role, of course; the president's understanding has considerably more impact on the sum total than some untenured assistant professor's. And wider definitions are involved as well. One thing most administrators do when planning
any big change, for instance, is to call their opposite numbers at half a dozen similar institutions to find
out how they do the thing in question.)

educational theorists propose broader, more humanistic goals for a college education, especially for the liberal arts: to produce "more competent, more concerned, more complete human being[s]" (Boyer 1987:1); to give students a "hope of a higher life . . . civilization" (Bloom 1987:336). And, almost all college authorities assume, whatever is valuable about college for the undergraduates is or ought to be the result of the deliberate impact, direct or indirect, of college adults such as themselves on the students.

Professors and other campus authorities do know, of course, that the students get up to other things in college. Many of them remember that they themselves got up to other things in college. But, in their present mature opinions, the "other things" that contemporary students are getting up to at the moment are either to be ignored or to be discouraged. Or they are, at best, the trimmings of a higher education. The main course—the essence of college—is its serious, high-minded goals as articulated and understood by its adult leaders.

5   The Rutgers students I knew in my research agreed that classroom learning was an important part of their college educations. College would not be college, after all, without "academics"—professors, grades, requirements, and a bachelor's degree after four years. Most students also agreed that college should be a broadening experience, that it should make you a better, more open, more liberal, more knowledgeable person. But, in the students' view of things, not all this broadening happened through the formal curriculum. At least half of college was what went on outside the classroom, among the students, with no adults around.

Beyond formal education, college as the students saw it was also about coming of age. It was where you went to break away from home, to learn responsibility and maturity, and to do some growing up.[2] College was about being on your own, about autonomy, about freedom from the authority of adults, however benign their intentions. And last but hardly least, college was about fun, about unique forms of peer-group fun—before, in student conceptions, the grayer actualities of adult life in the real world began to close in on you.

About the middle of the nineteenth century, American undergraduates started calling this side of college—the side that belonged to them, the side that corresponded to late-adolescent development in college the way *they* wanted to experience it—"college life" (Horowitz 1987:23–55, Kett 1977:174–182, Moffatt 1985a). And so they still referred to it in the late twentieth century. American college life was originally a new adolescent culture entirely of the students' own creation, arguably the first of the modern age-graded youth cultures that were to proliferate down to preteens by the late twentieth century. It was a boisterous,

[2]The subjects of these essays are "traditional" college students—in the "college-age" cohort (seventeen to twenty-two years old), residing on campus or, usually as upperclassmen, independently off-campus. Rutgers College served mostly late-adolescent students; adults who attended Rutgers-New Brunswick usually went to University College, the "night school." About one-fifth of the undergraduates at Rutgers College, on the other hand, were commuters with far less access to the pleasures of modern college life than residential students had.

pleasure-filled, group-oriented way of life: hazing and rushing, fraternities and football, class loyalty, college loyalty, and all the other "old traditions" celebrated in later alumni reminiscences.

College life had changed almost out of recognition a century later, however. By the 1980s, it was much closer to the private lives of the students. It no longer centered on the older organized extracurriculum. Nor was it an elite culture of youth any longer. Now it was populistically available to almost all students on campus, and it was for "coed" rather than for strictly masculine pleasures. But college life was still very much at the heart of college as the undergraduates thought of it in the late twentieth century. Together with the career credential conferred on them by their bachelor's degree, it was their most important reason for coming to college in the first place, their central pleasure while in it, and what they often remembered most fondly about college after they graduated. Let us look at its contours in more detail, as the students thought of it and experienced it at Rutgers in the late 1970s and mid-1980s.

WORK AND PLAY

College life, first of all, involved an understanding among the students about the proper relationship between work and play in college, about the relative value of inside-the-classroom education versus extracurricular fun. A century ago, the evaluation was a simple one. Extracurricular fun and games and the lessons learned in the vigorous student-to-student competitions that "made men"—athletics, class warfare, fraternity rushing—were obviously much more important than anything that happened to you in the classroom, as far as the students were concerned.

10   What was the relation between work and play in contemporary student culture, then, and what were the preferred forms of play? Consider an unsophisticated but evocative image entitled "What College is REALLY Like" (figure 1). It comes from a scrapbook a Rutgers freshman put together privately in 1983 for his own enjoyment and apparently for later reminiscence, one of many montages of words and pictures the student had cut out of magazines and newspapers and arranged into his own designs.

Most of the image is obviously about college fun—sexuality, drinking, and entertainment—and, implicitly, about being on one's own to enjoy such things, away from parental controls. Its exemplars, comedian Bill Murray and rock musician Billy Idol, are not collegiate types as they might have been in the early twentieth century, young men in raccoon coats or football players. They are drawn from the national and international youth culture to which most American college students orient their sense of generation in the late twentieth century, a culture that comes to them through popular music, the movies, TV, and certain mass-market magazines. The image also contains references to more local undergraduate culture at Rutgers. The Santa Claus stands for "Secret Santa," a favorite student festivity in the Rutgers dorms in the early 1980s "TKE" is the

What College is REALLY Like

I WANT YOU
To Go to the
bi//y
idol
show
with Me !

OWNER OF a Lonely Heart

Secret Santa

RU Screw 3 WRONG Classes !

college town

Drinkin' buddies.

MAKE IT PERSONAL

12

FIGURE 1

name of the student's fraternity. One of the two references to institutional Rutgers is to its least attractive feature in student opinion, to its bureaucratic inefficiency ("RU Screw"; "Three Wrong Classes!"). The other depicts "Rutgers," together with " '83' Academics," under a mushroom-shaped cloud.

This last image needs interpretation. It did not mean, the student told me a year later, that he had wanted to "blow away" academics during his first year in college. Rather, it depicted what he had feared might happen to his grades when he decided to pledge his fraternity as a freshman. But, he told me proudly, he had kept his "cum" up to a B+. We cannot say, therefore, that the academic side of college was irrelevant to this fun-loving freshman. But it was obviously not a central part of college in his imagery. It was necessary but peripheral, at least at this point in his young college career.

How typical was this college youth? One way to figure out actual undergraduate priorities was to examine a crucial set of student actions: how they budgeted their time in college. Both years in the dorms, I asked hundreds of students to fill out simple time reports: "Please tell me, as precisely as possible, what things you have done, and how long each has taken, since this time twenty-four hours ago." Most of the reports were made on weekdays in the middle of the semester. On these reports, 60 to 70 percent of the students suggested that they studied about two hours a day. Another 10 to 15 percent indicated harder academic work, up to six or seven hours a day—usually, but not always, students in the more difficult majors. And the rest, about a quarter of those who filled out the time reports, hardly studied at all on a day-to-day basis, but relied on frenetic cramming before exams.

How did the students spend the rest of their time in college? They did a surprising amount of sleeping, an average of just over eight hours a day. They spent about four hours a day in classes, on buses, or dealing with Rutgers bureaucracy. A quarter of them devoted small amounts of their remaining free time, one or two hours a day, to organized extracurricular activities, mostly to fraternities or sororities, less often to other student groups. One-eighth worked at jobs between one and four hours a day. One-tenth engaged in intramural or personal athletics. And two-fifths mentioned small amounts of TV watching, less than the average for American children or adults.

15   The students' remaining free time was given over to friendly fun with peers, to the endless verbal banter by which maturing American youths polish their personalities all through adolescence, trying on new roles, discarding old ones, learning the amiable, flexible social skills that constitute American middle-class manners in the late twentieth century. Friendly fun was thus the bread and butter of college life as the undergraduates enjoyed it at Rutgers in the 1980s. It consisted almost entirely of spur-of-the-moment pleasures; with the exception of one type of campus organization (fraternities and sororities—see below), very little of it had to do with the older extracurriculum. Friendly fun included such easy pleasures as hanging out in a dorm lounge or a fraternity or a sorority, gossiping, wrestling and fooling around, going to dinner with friends, having a late-night pizza or a late-night chat, visiting other dorms, going out to a bar, and flirting and more serious erotic activities, usually with members of the opposite sex. And the students managed to find an impressive amount of time for such diversions in college. Across my entire sample, the average time spent on friendly fun on weekdays in the middle of the semester was a little over four hours a day.

On the face of it, then, the students were fooling around about twice as much as they were studying in college. But this is a deceptive conclusion. For from their point of view, college work also included going to classes, and the total of their classroom time plus their study time was about six hours a day. They also almost all worked more and played less around exams or when big papers or other projects were due. It was fairer to say instead that the students acted as if they assumed that academic work and friendly fun were, or ought to be, about equally important activities during one's undergraduate years.

In many ways, they also said that this was the case. Incoming freshmen usually had two goals for their first year in college: to do well in classes and to have fun (or to make friends, or to have a good social life). Older students looked back on college as either an even or a shifting mixture of work and fun. And students in college who were deviating from the ideal balance almost always knew that they were, and sounded defensive about it. Here are two female deviants, in papers written for me in 1986, confessing to the studying styles of a grind and a "blow-it-off," respectively:

> *The Grind:* I am a little too serious about my studies. . . . I often give up extracurricular activities to stay home and study. . . . A few of my friends sent me a "personal" in a recent [student newspaper] which read: "What's more difficult—to get Jane Doe to stop flirting or [name of writer] to stop studying?" This is not to say that I am a "nerd" or some kind of Poindexter.[3] I have a variety of good friends, and I party as much as is feasible. . . . [But] I am the type of person who *has* to study. . . . This inner force or drive has been contained in me since childhood.

> *The Blow-it-off:* I am a female freshman, a once level-headed, driven, and, above all, studious girl [who in college] has become a loafer . . . totally preoccupied with my social life. . . . I spend the great majority of my day in the [dorm] lounge, resulting in my nickname; "lounge lizzette." . . . My new, urgent goal is to combine my old, intellectual self (study habits) with my new social self so I can be a happy, well-rounded person.

20   What was the happy, well-rounded student in the late twentieth century, by contrast? Someone who maintained a healthy balance between academics and college life, obviously. The two halves of college ought to be *complementary* ones in the opinion of modern college students. You came to college for the challenge, for the work, and to do your best in order to qualify for a good career later in life, most students assumed. College life was the play that made the work possible and that made college personally memorable.

YOUTH CULTURE AND COLLEGE CULTURE

In its nineteenth-century origins, college life was a specifically collegiate culture. And up through the middle of the twentieth century, less-privileged American

---

[3]*Poindexter* and *nerd* are two negative stereotypes for socially inept youths. *Poindexter* ("dexter" for short) was the name of a character on a favorite children's TV show, which most of the students had watched when they were much younger. In the late 1980s, the campy musical performer Buster Poindexter had taken his second (stage) name from this old youth cultural meaning. The origins of *nerd* are unknown.

   Note that both terms, by the way, come out of the wider youth culture. They are not specifically collegiate. In past generations, there were college-specific words for such stigmatized students—"throat" at Rutgers in the 1970s, for instance.

youths knew it as the subculture of a college elite—of the more affluent under-graduates, typically from older WASP backgrounds. As [Helene] Horowitz points out, college life did not just distinguish college students from the great masses of less-fortunate young women and men who did not attend college in those days. Many undergraduates were also excluded from it—from the "best" fraternities, for example. Horowitz calls these students "the outsiders," poorer undergraduates who were in college in order to achieve the middle-class status that the more-prosperous students who were enjoying college life took for granted. The outsiders tended to work hard at their studies and to view their professors with respect. Students in the college-life elite often stigmatized them as "grinds" (Horowitz 1987:56–81).

The original college-life culture slowly faded on American campuses during the twentieth century, however, and it virtually disappeared in the sea change that swept over American youth culture in the late 1960s. Between about 1964 and 1968, the casually well-dressed college man (and woman) suddenly became archaic at Rutgers and at other American colleges. All at once the students were part of a common, classless, internationally defined youth culture. And in their new tastes in clothing and in music, they unmistakably stated their new antielit-ist sentiments. Blue jeans had once been working-class garb. Long hair and beards had distinguished cultural bohemians, as had casual drug use. Rock-and-roll music—supplanting collegiate musical tastes such as Peter, Paul, and Mary or "cool jazz"—was recently transformed black music. Army jackets were the clothing of poor draftees into the unpopular Vietnam War (Moffatt 1985b: 174–176, 221–234, 241–243).

Students in the mid-1980s no longer looked like students from the late 1960s. But in the way in which a general youth culture rather than a specifically colle-giate one dominated their lives, and in the way in which this youth culture was available to everyone, not just to an elite, they were still very much the children of the sixties. The old extracurriculum was almost gone. The most fundamental student pleasures were the pleasures of other adolescents: friendship and erotic fun. The students' musical tastes came directly to them out of popular culture, and they recognized the sixties, whose music they now revered as "classic rock," as the *fons et origo* of music as they knew it.

The nearest thing to the older collegiate look in clothing among the students in the 1980s was "preppie," named, with obvious irony, for prep school students rather than for college students. Preppie was one step more formal than "student casual": loafers rather than sneakers, slacks rather than blue jeans, and an Oxford shirt or an Izod shirt rather than a T-shirt or a sweatshirt. Undergraduates said that it was the look of student leaders and of academic straight-arrows. Other clothing fashions—"punk," "gay," "GQ,"[4] "jock"—had nothing to do with col-lege; like music, fashions in clothes also originated in mass adolescent culture. College iconography was only incidentally visible on the walls of student rooms

---

[4]A layered, somewhat European look characteristic of the male fashion magazine "GQ," *Gentleman's Quarterly*.

and on their clothing. Most Rutgers students guessed that no one in a crowd of strangers their own age would be able to guess that they were college students simply by looking at them.

25   There were some collegiate nuances in their otherwise mass-cultural-defined lives, however. Although the students did not show their college identity in any obvious way—that wouldn't be cool, they implied—most of them guessed that other members of their own generation would probably be able to identify them as college students after talking to them for a few minutes. They were likely to sound more intelligent, they thought. They were likely to "talk better." The college transformation was a subtle, inward one, the students implied, not an outer identity to be flashed like a beacon. But almost all of them said that it was important to them that they were in college; privately, "college student" was an identity in which most of them took considerable pride.

Another type of collegiate nuance was exemplified by a category of popular music in the trend-defining periodical *Rolling Stone:* "college albums." College albums were the most sophisticated contemporary popular music—new wave, post-new wave, punk, hard core—the antithesis of Top 40. College albums received their biggest play on college radio stations. What marked them as collegiate was not some class-differentiated identity of their performers, however; they were not sung by buttoned-down preppies, for instance. It was their relatively difficult accessibility as art. Their actual content could be even raunchier than conventional popular music.

COMING OF AGE

The age grading that characterized most of American childhood and adolescence in the 1980s first developed for small numbers of middle-class college students a century and a quarter ago (see Kett 1977:126–128). And with age grading, college students also formulated stereotypical notions of their own physical and mental maturation in college. Drawing on older images of the Ages of Man, late-nineteenth-century undergraduates pretended that they progressed from infancy to maturity during their four short years in higher education. One typical image from Rutgers in the 1880s showed the freshman as a precocious baby, the sophomore as a drunken youth, the junior as a suave ladies' man and the senior as a careworn, middle-aged bourgeois (Moffatt 1985b:57). And for two-thirds of a century, college class histories repeated the same conceits. Freshmen and sophomores were carefree, childish pranksters; juniors and seniors were more manly in body and in mind.

Rutgers students no longer drew such drawings or wrote such histories in the 1980s.[5] But they still had similar concepts of the typical stages of their personal

---

[5]On the deans' initiative rather than the students', the class history was revived in the early 1980s in the form of a student commencement address. It was no longer a collective biography, however, for who could write a biography of about two thousand students? Instead it tended to be a review of local, national, and international events in the four years the class had been at Rutgers and a sanitized account of the ways in which the realities of Rutgers had helped members of the class to grow up in college.

development in college, which they still enacted with some faithfulness. Freshmen were foolish and inexperienced. Sophomores were wild men (and women), the leading troublemakers in the dorms. Then, with a predictability that resembled that of some form of pupating insect, juniors almost always discovered that they had matured beyond the juvenilities of dorm culture. Dorm fun was now dorm foolishness. And the inescapable intimacies of collective living—everyone else knowing almost everything about you—had grown tiresome with time (for changing student images of college in early and later undergraduate years, see figures 2, 3, and 4).

Juniors usually decided that they were ready for something closer to an independent adult existence in the real world, usually an off-campus apartment. Seniors often wanted a maturer life-style still. Or they might typically consider themselves to be "burned out," victims of mild or severe cases of "senioritis," weary of college, apprehensive about what came next. Sexual maturity was no longer peculiar to college upperclassmen in the 1980s. Now it could characterize students in any of the four college classes. But the older you were, the more likely you were to be sexually active.

30   In student opinion, you were pushed through these stages of development in college in the 1980s by the various formal and informal learning experiences that characterized modern undergraduate college life. Students sometimes felt that college adults did have some impact on them in college. Four out of five students in a large class in 1987 said they thought that looking back twenty years after college they would remember a professor or two as people who had inspired them in college, who had made a real difference in what they were today as adults in the real world. But most of the time the students believed that they came of age in college thanks to what they learned among themselves on their own, student to student, or, paradoxically, thanks to what they learned from dealing with precisely the least personal, most uncaring sides of official Rutgers.

College from the students' point of view was a combination of academic and outside-the-classroom education. Academic learning gave you the credentials you needed to progress toward a good career, and perhaps it made you a broader, more knowledgeable person. Outside-the-classroom education, on the other hand, was often the greater influence on your personal development, many of the students believed. About half the same large class in 1987 said that academic and extracurricular education had been "different, but equally important" aspects of college learning for them so far. About one in five of the remaining students considered academic learning more important than extracurricular learning, and about four in five made the opposite judgment. So, for about 40 percent of these students, the do-it-yourself side of college was the most significant educational experience. And for all but 10 percent, extracurricular learning had been at least half of what had contributed to their maturation so far in college.

One form of outside-the-classroom education in college, according to the students, resembled academic learning in content but not in context: the extracurricular intellectual learning that they did among themselves. Like the rest of college life as the students enjoyed it in the 1980s, most of this intellectual fun took

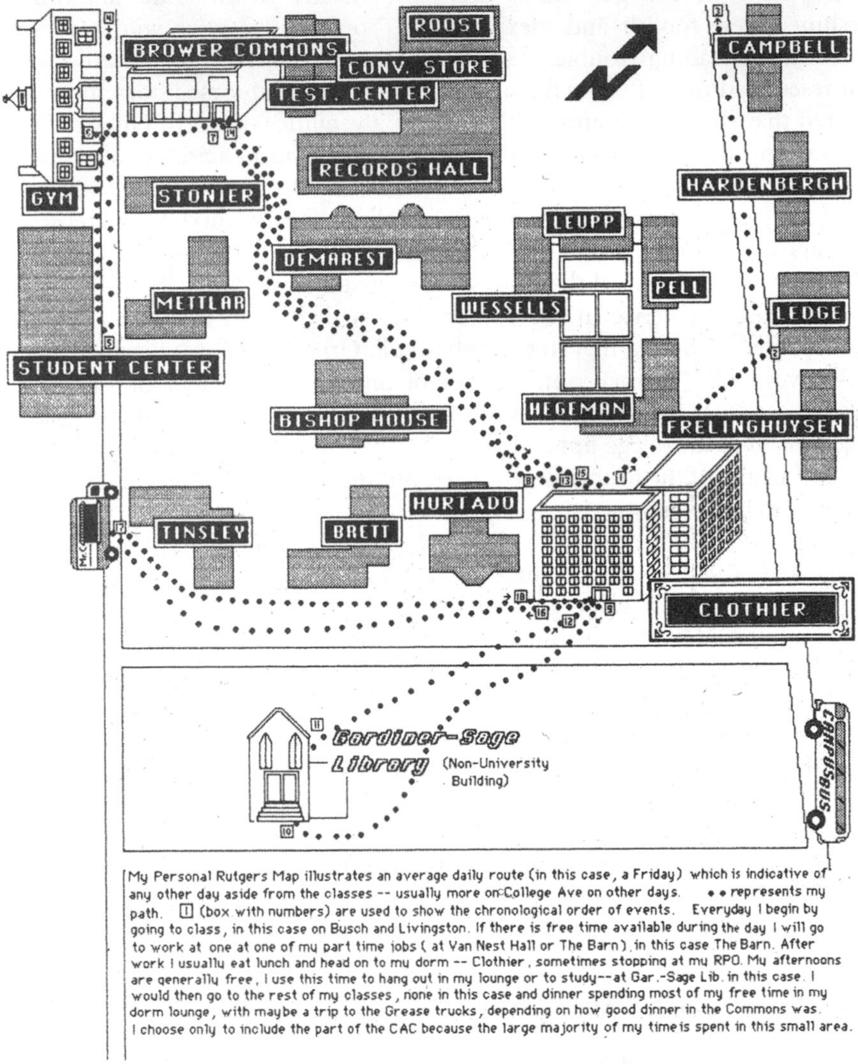
BROWER COMMONS
ROOST
CONV. STORE
TEST. CENTER
CAMPBELL
RECORDS HALL
HARDENBERGH
GYM
STONIER
LEUPP
DEMAREST
PELL
METTLAR
WESSELLS
LEDGE
STUDENT CENTER
BISHOP HOUSE
HEGEMAN
FRELINGHUYSEN
HURTADO
TINSLEY
BRETT
CLOTHIER
Gardiner-Sage Library
(Non-University Building)
CAMPUS BUS
My Personal Rutgers Map illustrates an average daily route (in this case, a Friday) which is indicative of any other day aside from the classes -- usually more on College Ave on other days. • • represents my path. [1] (box with numbers) are used to show the chronological order of events. Everyday I begin by going to class, in this case on Busch and Livingston. If there is free time available during the day I will go to work at one at one of my part time jobs (at Van Nest Hall or The Barn), in this case The Barn. After work I usually eat lunch and head on to my dorm -- Clothier, sometimes stopping at my RPO. My afternoons are generally free, I use this time to hang out in my lounge or to study--at Gar.-Sage Lib. in this case. I would then go to the rest of my classes, none in this case and dinner spending most of my free time in my dorm lounge, with maybe a trip to the Grease trucks, depending on how good dinner in the Commons was.
I choose only to include the part of the CAC because the large majority of my time is spent in this small area.

FIGURE 2

Personal Map of Rutgers, by a Freshman Male

In a class taught in 1986, undergraduates drew college as they knew it at the moment. This younger male's college is typically small in scale and centers on the dorms and the campus buildings immediately surrounding them. It is also clear from his map that this student is an unusually precise, academically oriented youth—the Gardiner-Sage Library is his favorite study spot—and a whiz on the computer.

place in private, in long talks about philosophy, morality, politics, and other serious interests, usually with friends. Some of it also took place due to the extracurricular programming available on campus, the students said, thanks to speakers,

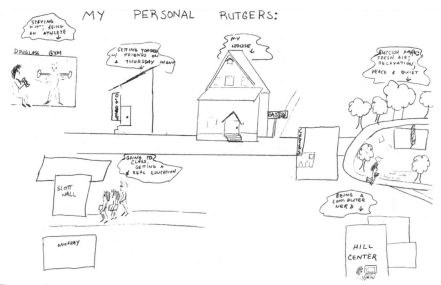

FIGURE 3

Personal Map of Rutgers, by a Senior Female
This older female, on the other hand, draws an upperclassman's image of college, a cute, apparently intentionally naive view centered on off-campus life. Her extracurricular pleasures include athletics, drinking, and relaxing in nature. When she uses the campus, she uses many different parts of it: the gym at Douglass, the computer center at Busch, and only two classrooms on the College Avenue Campus—where she does, despite off-campus distractions, still "get a real education."

concerts, and other performances, thanks to an intellectual environment richer than anything they had typically known in their hometowns and high schools before college.

The students sometimes referred to the rest of extracurricular learning in college as "social learning," as the things you had to know in order to be a competent adult in the real world as you would find it after graduation. And the students' college did prepare them for the real world as well, many of them firmly believed. Moreover, they added, a relatively cheap public college such as Rutgers often did a much better job of this than fancier private colleges were likely to do. You were, first of all, on your own in college, the students pointed out—much more so at Rutgers than at smaller, more personal colleges—and learning to take real responsibility for yourself helped you to grow up as an individual:

Rutgers has helped me to learn what it is like to be on my own and take responsibility for my own actions. . . . The majority of college students find drinking to be

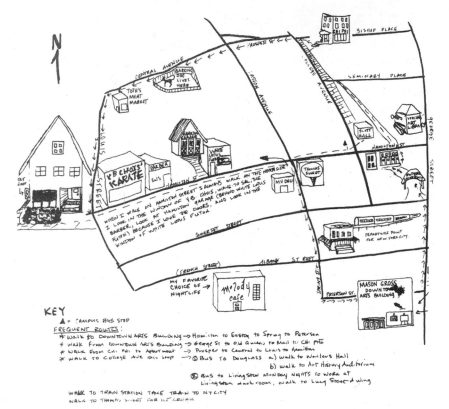

FIGURE 4

Personal Map of Rutgers, by a Sophomore Female
A more cosmopolitan upperclassman, old for a sophomore. She lives farther downtown, goes to a trendier bar (the Melody Cafe), has a sweet tooth, looks at the city more visually, and apparently bugs out regularly for New York. Her College Avenue Campus centers on one classroom, the Art Library, and one fraternity (Chi Phi, top).

> of second nature . . . [but] I do not abuse the freedom obtained by living in college.—Freshman female[6]

> It is up to the individual. No one else at Rutgers cares how he does.—Sophomore male

The academic work was more difficult than it had been in high school. Your teachers no longer knew you personally or cared about you. Guidance counselors were not tracking your every move any longer. Your parents were not sure what you were doing on a daily basis. You had a more flexible schedule and more free time than you had ever had in high school—and more distractions all

---

[6]Unless otherwise indicated, these quotes are taken from self-reports that Rutgers students wrote for me in large classes taught in 1986 and 1987.

around you. It was not easy under these circumstances to remember the serious purposes for which you had probably come to college in the first place. Learning to balance college work against college play was one of the tougher challenges of your college years, the students maintained.

Second, college, and Rutgers in particular, was more like the real world than hometown and high school had been. A century ago the student apologists for college life had claimed that the rich associational activities of the undergraduates had prepared them to be movers and shakers after college, to build business organizations and other voluntary organizations in adult life. Now, in the 1980s, student associations were in eclipse in college, but so, too, were similar activities in the real world beyond the groves of Academe. Now the real world, especially at the professional and middle-management levels toward which most Rutgers graduates were headed, was already highly organized. Now it was an impersonal and bureaucratically complicated place. And now, conveniently, thanks to Rutgers' impersonality and bureaucratic complexity, college prepared you for this aspect of life after college. Smaller, more elite colleges were cloisters compared to Rutgers, the students commonly argued. Rutgers, on the other hand, got you ready for the real world with a vengeance:

> How did Rutgers teach me to deal with the real world? The answer, as ironic as it seems, is through the "RU Screw" . . . through that tortuous, roundabout way of making everything three times more difficult to accomplish, I learned the skills of persistence and determination which I would need for the rest of my days . . . — Junior female

35   Rutgers also mirrored the real world in the diversity of its undergraduate student body, the students often asserted. As a public institution, it brought students together from suburban hometowns and high schools that were often more homogeneous by class, by race, and by ethnic group. And here again, Rutgers resembled the real world much more than fancier colleges did:

> I have an old girlfriend from high school who now goes to Mt. Holyoke. It's all like "high-up Suzie Sorority" there. Like they're all just the *same.* My girlfriend is sheltered from life. I have to deal with more. Because this is a state university, they have to let in all kinds of people. You just can't imagine the *friends* you have at a place like this!—Sophomore male, 1985

The actual ability of Rutgers students to deal with real cultural diversity as I observed it in the dorms was often very limited. Many students could not tolerate it at all, but sealed themselves into little friendship groups of people as much like themselves as they could find. Virtually all the undergraduates believed in the value of diversity, however. For "diversity"—like "friendship" and "community" as they were ideologically defined—was simply one more entailment of late-twentieth-century American individualism. What was the point of being an individualist if everyone and everything was the same? Real choice required a diverse universe within which to choose.

Diversity, moreover, was an easily shared value because it was almost empty of content. Real cultural diversity to an anthropologist might mean the difference between an American middle-class youth from a white ethnic background raised in northern New Jersey and a student who had recently arrived in the United States from a small city in south Asia. To an undergraduate, on the other hand, it might mean a roommate who liked mellow music while you yourself liked punk, a nerdy roommate while you yourself were a jock, or (somewhat more culturally) a friend whose third-generation white ethnic identity was different from yours—Italian versus Irish, for instance.

Nevertheless, undergraduate Rutgers was almost inevitably more diverse than anything most students had known to date, and was probably more diverse than the world in which most of the professors and other college adults lived.[7] At the very least, the students at Rutgers had to learn to get along with people they did not like for reasons of cultural differences. "Archie Bunker would never make it as a Rutgers student," one student commented on a paper in 1987. At best, the students sometimes did learn valuable things at Rutgers about themselves and the world from other students who were really different from themselves.

> All in all I am very glad I came to Rutgers. Many people say it's too big. However, I really believe that is an advantage. There are so many different opportunities here . . . [Also,] being somewhat of a conservative, it was great being exposed to those "damn liberals."—Senior male

> In high school, everyone in my classes was either Irish, Italian or Polish. Here, I go to classes with Asians, Indians, Blacks, Puerto Ricans and many others, from whom I get different viewpoints.—Senior male

> Above all else, college is a breeding ground for interrelationships between students. If nothing else, a college student learns how to interact with his or her peers. The ability to form lasting relationships is of great value to the graduating adult. College is a step in the mental and psychological development of an individual.— Senior female

> One attribute of mine . . . that was well developed through the years I spent at Rutgers . . . is that of being a true partier. . . . —Senior female

> My social development [in college] seemed to help me as much, if not more, than my academic development into shaping me into what I am today. . . . —Senior male

In the end, the students claimed, even the fun of college life was a learning experience. And with this claim, the dichotomy between formal education (work, learning) and college life (fun, relaxation) collapsed entirely for the students. In the end, you learned from everything that happened to you in college, the stu-

---

[7]The diversity of the undergraduate population at Rutgers in the 1980s is suggested by the identity of some of the extracurricular organizations in the college. There were a number of groups for blacks and for Hispanic students; and, beyond groups for these minorities, the ethnic associations included Arab, Armenian, Luso-Brazilian, Chinese, Cuban, Greek, Indian, Islamic, Korean, Lebanese, Pakistani, Filipino, Polish, Turkish, Ukrainian, Vietnamese, and West Indian clubs. (Even if most students were not very active extracurricularly, as was argued above, someone had to care enough about each of these cultural affiliations to serve as officers, to put in regular funding requests to deans, and to talk faculty members into being advisers.)

dents asserted. And, anthropologically speaking, they were not far from wrong. For they did spend those four hours a day in informal friendly fun, working on their real identities through such activities and practicing the "bullshit" necessary to the well-tuned American social self in the real world in the late twentieth century. And they did devote about the same amount of imaginative and real energy to "learning to pick up girls or guys" as they did to seeking out "meaningful relationships" during their college years. All these personal skills would undoubtedly continue to be useful to them long after they graduated from college. In their refinement, in their opinion—as much as in the intellectual learning that they acquired in college—they came of age, they progressed toward something like adult maturity during their four years at Rutgers.[8]

⫸ CRITICAL REFLECTIONS

1. Moffatt writes that Rutgers students "saw [college] was also about coming of age" (294). After reading through the chapter, write a definition of what you think Moffatt means by this. How does it compare with your own idea of what college (both inside and outside of classes) should be?

2. Throughout this chapter, Moffatt uses a variety of adjectives to describe students' work and attitudes toward college. Focusing closely on those descriptive words, how do you interpret Moffatt's attitude toward the Rutgers students whom he studied?

3. In the section on "Youth Culture and College Culture," Moffatt refers to various features—clothing, behavior, language, musical preferences—that identified students as part of a common culture. Do you find that you and your classmates share characteristics that identify you as part of a common campus culture? Why or why not?

4. Based on his interpretation of Rutgers's students lives, what do you think Moffatt would say that these students see as the purpose of education?

5. Moffatt draws on artifacts from students at various points in this excerpt, like time logs kept by students, the collage of student life, and the maps of "my Rutgers" drawn by students. Why do you think Moffatt incorporates this evidence? Does it accomplish what you see as his purpose in the reading?

⫸ MAKING CONNECTIONS

1. This reading, like "Fierce Intimacies," is an outsiders' view of college students—like the author of that article. Moffatt is looking in at the experiences of students (rather than writing about them as a student himself, or writing about his own experiences). Do you find evidence of Moffatt's and Suskind's

---

[8]Actually, only about half of the incoming freshmen at Rutgers passed through college in just four years. Another 20 percent took five to seven years, and about 30 percent never finished—at Rutgers at least.

outsider status in these readings? If you do, where do you? If you do not, how do you think that they cover that status in their writing?

2. What expectations do you think Moffatt believes the Rutgers students whom he studied had for college? How are these similar or different from Cedric's expectations in "Fierce Intimacies"?

NO CHILD LEFT BEHIND
ACT OF 2001

No Child Left Behind is the name given to the Reauthorization of the Elementary and Secondary Education Act, the act which provides government funding for public education and for the Office of the Secretary of Education, by the Bush administration. Although the Elementary and Secondary Education Act was originally passed in the 1960s, NCLB includes requirements that have never been included before. For example, the act includes rewards for schools whose students achieve proficiency on state assessments; however, it also includes penalties (in the form of reduced funding, particularly for students from low-income families) for schools whose students do not achieve proficiency.

What appears here is an executive summary of the full Reauthorization—a précis that captures the bill's main points. The full text of the legislation, in addition to material related to it, can be found at www.ed.gov by searching for "no child left behind." The Office of the Secretary of Education has also created a site for *No Child Left Behind:* www .NoChildLeftBehind.gov. You'll see that the act refers repeatedly to Title 1 schools. Title 1 provides school-wide funding at schools where 40% of the students are identified as coming from low-income families, or funding for specific students identified as coming from low-income where fewer than 40% of the students are not low-income.

These reforms express my deep belief in our public schools and their mission to build the mind and character of every child, from every background, in every part of America.

President George W. Bush

January 2001

Three days after taking office in January 2001 as the 43rd President of the United States, George W. Bush announced *No Child Left Behind,* his framework for bipartisan education reform that he described as "the cornerstone of my Administration." President Bush emphasized his deep belief in our public schools, but an even greater concern that "too many of our neediest children are being left behind," despite the nearly $200 billion in Federal spending since the passage of the Elementary and Secondary Education Act of 1965 (ESEA). The President called for bipartisan solutions based on accountability, choice, and flexibility in Federal education programs.

Less than a year later, despite the unprecedented challenges of engineering an economic recovery while leading the Nation in the war on terrorism following the events of September 11, President Bush secured passage of the landmark *No Child Left Behind Act* of 2001 (NCLB Act). The new law reflects a remarkable consensus—first articulated in the President's *No Child Left Behind* framework—on how to improve the performance of America's elementary and secondary schools while at the same time ensuring that no child is trapped in a failing school.

The NCLB Act, which reauthorizes the ESEA, incorporates the principles and strategies proposed by President Bush. These include increased accountability for States, school districts, and schools; greater choice for parents and students, particularly those attending low-performing schools; more flexibility for States and local educational agencies (LEAs) in the use of Federal education dollars; and a stronger emphasis on reading, especially for our youngest children.

INCREASED ACCOUNTABILITY

The NCLB Act will strengthen Title I accountability by requiring States to implement statewide accountability systems covering all public schools and students. These systems must be based on challenging State standards in reading and mathematics, annual testing for all students in grades 3–8, and annual statewide progress objectives ensuring that all groups of students reach proficiency within 12 years. Assessment results and State progress objectives must be broken out by poverty, race, ethnicity, disability, and limited English proficiency to ensure that no group is left behind. School districts and schools that fail to make adequate yearly progress (AYP) toward statewide proficiency goals will, over time, be subject to improvement, corrective action, and restructuring measures aimed at getting them back on course to meet State standards. Schools that meet or exceed AYP objectives or close achievement gaps will be eligible for State Academic Achievement Awards.

MORE CHOICES FOR PARENTS AND STUDENTS

5 The NCLB Act significantly increases the choices available to the parents of students attending Title I schools that fail to meet State standards, including immediate relief—beginning with the 2002–03 school year—for students in schools that were previously identified for improvement or corrective action under the 1994 ESEA reauthorization.

LEAs must give students attending schools identified for improvement, corrective action, or restructuring the opportunity to attend a better public school, which may include a public charter school, within the school district. The district must provide transportation to the new school, and must use at least 5 percent of its Title I funds for this purpose, if needed.

For students attending persistently failing schools (those that have failed to meet State standards for at least 3 of the 4 preceding years), LEAs must permit low-income students to use Title I funds to obtain supplemental educational services from the public- or private-sector provider selected by the students and their parents. Providers must meet State standards and offer services tailored to help participating students meet challenging State academic standards.

To help ensure that LEAs offer meaningful choices, the new law requires school districts to spend up to 20 percent of their Title I allocations to provide school choice and supplemental educational services to eligible students.

In addition to helping ensure that no child loses the opportunity for a quality education because he or she is trapped in a failing school, the choice and supplemental service requirements provide a substantial incentive for low-performing schools to improve. Schools that want to avoid losing students—along with the portion of their annual budgets typically associated with those students—will have to improve or, if they fail to make AYP for 5 years, run the risk of reconstitution under a restructuring plan.

GREATER FLEXIBILITY FOR STATES, SCHOOL DISTRICTS, AND SCHOOLS

10　One important goal of *No Child Left Behind* was to breathe new life into the "flexibility for accountability" bargain with States first struck by President George H.W. Bush during his historic 1989 education summit with the Nation's Governors at Charlottesville, Virginia. Prior flexibility efforts have focused on the waiver of program requirements; the NCLB Act moves beyond this limited approach to give States and school districts unprecedented flexibility in the use of Federal education funds in exchange for strong accountability for results.

New flexibility provisions in the NCLB Act include authority for States and LEAs to transfer up to 50 percent of the funding they receive under 4 major State grant programs to any one of the programs, or to Title I. The covered programs include Teacher Quality State Grants, Educational Technology, Innovative Programs, and Safe and Drug-Free Schools.

The new law also includes a competitive State Flexibility Demonstration Program that permits up to 7 States to consolidate the State share of nearly all Federal State grant programs—including Title I, Part A Grants to Local Educational Agencies—while providing additional flexibility in their use of Title V Innovation funds. Participating States must enter into 5-year performance agreements with the Secretary covering the use of the consolidated funds, which may be used for any educational purpose authorized under the ESEA. As part of their plans, States also must enter into up to 10 local performance agreements with LEAs, which will enjoy the same level of flexibility granted under the separate Local Flexibility Demonstration Program.

The new competitive Local Flexibility Demonstration Program would allow up to 80 LEAs, in addition to the 70 LEAs under the State Flexibility Demonstration Program, to consolidate funds received under Teacher Quality State Grants, Educational Technology State Grants, Innovative Programs, and Safe and Drug-Free Schools programs. Participating LEAs would enter into performance agreements with the Secretary of Education, and would be able to use the consolidated funds for any ESEA-authorized purpose.

PUTTING READING FIRST

No Child Left Behind stated President Bush's unequivocal commitment to ensuring that every child can read by the end of third grade. To accomplish this goal, the new Reading First initiative would significantly increase the Federal investment in scientifically based reading instruction programs in the early grades. One major benefit of this approach would be reduced identification of children for special education services due to a lack of appropriate reading instruction in their early years.

15 The NCLB Act fully implements the President's Reading First initiative. The new Reading First State Grant program will make 6-year grants to States, which will make competitive subgrants to local communities. Local recipients will administer screening and diagnostic assessments to determine which students in grades K-3 are at risk of reading failure, and provide professional development for K-3 teachers in the essential components of reading instruction.

The new Early Reading First program will make competitive 6-year awards to LEAs to support early language, literacy, and pre-reading development of preschool-age children, particularly those from low-income families. Recipients will use instructional strategies and professional development drawn from scientifically based reading research to help young children to attain the fundamental knowledge and skills they will need for optimal reading development in kindergarten and beyond.

OTHER MAJOR PROGRAM CHANGES

The *No Child Left Behind Act* of 2001 also put the principles of accountability, choice, and flexibility to work in its reauthorization of other major ESEA programs. For example, the new law combines the Eisenhower Professional Development and Class Size Reduction programs into a new Improving Teacher Quality State Grants program that focuses on using practices grounded in scientifically based research to prepare, train, and recruit high-quality teachers. The new program gives States and LEAs flexibility to select the strategies that best meet their particular needs for improved teaching that will help them raise student achievement in the core academic subjects. In return for this flexibility,

LEAs are required to demonstrate annual progress in ensuring that all teachers teaching in core academic subjects within the State are highly qualified.

The NCLB Act also simplified Federal support for English language instruction by combining categorical bilingual and immigrant education grants that benefited a small percentage of limited English proficient students in relatively few schools into a State formula program. The new formula program will facilitate the comprehensive planning by States and school districts needed to ensure implementation of programs that benefit all limited English proficient students by helping them learn English and meet the same high academic standards as other students.

Other changes will support State and local efforts to keep our schools safe and drug-free, while at the same time ensuring that students—particularly those who have been victims of violent crimes on school grounds—are not trapped in persistently dangerous schools. As proposed in *No Child Left Behind*, States must allow students who attend a persistently dangerous school, or who are victims of violent crime at school, to transfer to a safe school. States also must report school safety statistics to the public on a school-by-school basis, and LEAs must use Federal Safe and Drug-Free Schools and Communities funding to implement drug and violence prevention programs of demonstrated effectiveness.

■ CRITICAL REFLECTIONS

1. The NCLB legislation refers repeatedly to how the act will enhance Title 1 schools. Drawing on the definition of Title 1 schools included in the introduction to this reading, interpret, in your own words, they key provisions of this act (each included here under its own separate heading) and how you think these requirements will affect Title 1 schools and students.

2. The Increased Accountability section of this summary describes how statewide standardized assessment will strengthen schools. Reflect on the exam in your state from a perspective appropriate to you (for instance, as someone who took the exam, as someone whose child has taken the exam, or as someone who has read over and analyzed the exam). From that perspective, what do you think the exam accomplished and why?

■ MAKING CONNECTIONS

1. Writing three years before the passage of NCLB, Peter Sacks lists a number of problems associated with standardized assessments. Do you think his concerns have been addressed in the NCLB Act?

2. In "What 'No Child Left Behind' Left Behind," teacher "Wendy Darling" (not her real name) responds to the provisions of the act from the perspective of someone directly affected by it. Write a conversation with a supporter of NCLB, "Darling," and a student (this can be you or another student) focusing on whether this act will help improve education. What positions would each take, and why?

3. "I just wanna be average" was a phrase uttered by one of Mike Rose's classmates that jolted Mike into thinking about his own goals for education. What affect do you think the provisions of this act would have on a student whose goal was to be average, and why do you think so?

"Wendy Darling"

What "No Child Left Behind" Left Behind

"Wendy Darling" (one of the three children who fly away with Peter Pan in J.M. Barrie's book of the same name) is a pseudonym used by the author of this article, which was reprinted in *The Education Digest* in December 2002.

It is the end of August. The 2,000 teachers in my school district are gathering in the civic auditorium for the opening exercises for the school year.

The superintendent has sent us a welcome-back letter that states that "research tells us . . . that what we do as adults at the schools is twice as influential as student demographics." I e-mail her to ask for a citation to justify such an astonishing statement, and she promises to send it along. (After two months, I'm still waiting.)

There's a huge banner above the auditorium entrance that trumpets "Beat the Gap." Some of the teachers hugging old friends wonder what in the world that means, but some of us know: It's that pesky achievement gap.

There's a strange, not-so-funny cartoon on the program. It shows a landscape with a gaping chasm running diagonally from the lower left into the far distance of the upper right. The chasm has been labeled "Achievement Gap." The far side of the chasm seems to be a desert, while the near side has some flowers and an affectionate couple holding outsized books in their arms.

5   The other major feature of this cartoon is a wide bridge made of books that spans the divide. Joyful children are shown sliding or jumping down from this bridge onto the fertile side. The bridge is labeled "Literacy." Ah, literacy is the bridge that allows us to cross the achievement gap.

Finally, and mysteriously, in the far distance, the word "Equity" glows in the sky. It seems to be located at the end of the Achievement Gap, like a pot of gold. This last bit sums up quite succinctly what I think the problem is: The current rhetoric of "reform" touts equity as the goal, when it should be the starting point.

Believing Isn't Everything

Then the motivational speeches begin. The short version of the next two days is that it's all our fault: The achievement gap exists because we teachers "don't believe that all children can learn." There will be no excuses made for why we can't push all of our children across the achievement gap over to the fertile side—and, eventually, to equity, shining in the sky.

The program we're given mentions these specific goals: "Ninety percent of students will read on grade level in third grade. One hundred percent of students will pass the High School Exit Exam in twelfth grade." Is there anyone out there who thinks politicians will be pleased if all our seniors pass the exit exam?

No, indeed. There will be strident demands to "raise the bar" to meet "world-class standards." And how can 90% of our students read at grade level as measured by our norm-referenced test, which was constructed so that 50% of the test-takers will score below grade level (whatever that is).

10   We end the general festivities with an inspirational sing-along, after which we disperse to our schools for another day and a half of training. This consists, first, of reviewing the school handbook, which has 44 pages on the now-mandatory "mission, vision, and goals." (Even my hardware store has its mission posted. Don't we all know what hardware stores are for?)

Then there are sections which carry the headings of "Rules," "Discipline," "Bulletin Boards," "Disaster" (14 pages), "Yard Duty," and "Lifeskills" (37 pages). Then we have our Laser-Like Focus on Literacy (24 pages) and, finally, our K-6 Language Arts Standards (nine pages).

We are also given two packets on the subject of "management," which presume adversarial, disrespectful, manipulative, fast-paced, entertaining, whole-class, frontal teaching. In the Newspeak of school reform, punishments have become "learning opportunities."

Between the district and my school, we have a staggering seven "areas of focus," seven "strategic priorities," seven "core values" (the number happens to be purely coincidental), five "goals for 2005," a "mission statement," four "literacy givens," 15 "life skills," a "Self-Directed Improvement System" (which comes complete with its own trademark sign), and the "six essential elements of an effective literacy program."

On the second day of training, we "analyze the data." We spend nearly two hours examining a grid of our test scores for the last four years for grades 2 through 6. We look horizontally, vertically, and diagonally. We discuss one-and two-point score differences as if they actually mean something.

15   As pointed out by Thomas J. Kane and Douglas O. Staiger in their 2002 Brookings Institution publication, *Volatility in School Test Scores: Implications for Test-Based Accountability Systems,* from 50 to 80 of scores can be attributed to random influences. And, as noted by others elsewhere, scores always improve two to three points a year as a result of innocent teaching to the test.

DATA-DRIVEN, BUT WHITHER?

Nevertheless, we are still told to plan our curriculum around these meaningless numbers. We're certainly data-driven—but whither?

The real analysis comes as we disaggregate the naked numbers. One teacher at my table says, "There were a lot of subs in that fourth grade last year before they got a real teacher." Another teacher complains, "I had four kids transfer into my class in the two weeks before testing, and they were all very low scorers." Still another offers, "Those fifth-graders have always been a very bright group." And one concludes, "You know, the new teachers can't teach to the tests because they didn't see them the year before."

The politicians say that we are giving these tests in order to learn something about achievement. That is, these numbers are supposed to tell teachers something that we can use for the purpose of teaching better. But it takes our preexisting knowledge of our students to explain the numbers. It's the numbers that need us, not the other way around. What's the point?

The point becomes clear as this second day of our teacher training wears on: It's our fault. There are no legitimate reasons that could help explain the gap—there are rather only excuses. There are dozens of schools out there in which 90% of the poor and minority students manage to score above grade level (whatever that is). The key is the teachers' belief system: If we believe, they will achieve.

20   Some of this magical thinking comes straight from the Heritage Foundation's No Excuses propaganda. This was thoroughly debunked by Richard Rothstein in the *New York Times* of January 3, 2001 ("Poverty and Achievement and Great Misconceptions"). It was also thoroughly debunked by Bruce Biddle and Gerald Bracey in their "Review of No Excuses: Lessons from 21 High-Performing High-Poverty Schools," from *Education Policy Project, Education Policy Studies Laboratory,* published July 1, 2000, by Arizona State University.

More recently the Education Trust has published more of the same, and Rothstein has thoroughly debunked these claims, too, in his April 10, 2002, *New York Times* article, "Schools, Accountability, and a Sheaf of Fuzzy Math." These messages are groundless "research by aphorism," and they perpetuate the myth that teachers' beliefs are responsible for the gap in student achievement.

THE MAGIC OF NEVER-NEVER LAND

This myth is a setup. It's "never-never land" magic. As Peter Pan tells the Darling children, "Think of lovely things," and you'll fly. We who teach poor students are simply to think that they can achieve like middle-class students, and it will happen. Even the policy of having external standards (or benchmarks or outcomes or goals—whatever they're being called this year) that are the same for all children is vicious, unless we provide sufficient resources.

But "achieve" in the current reform rhetoric doesn't even mean "learn"; it means "score." And no, I don't believe that the students I teach will ever really score well on tests which have been written by white, middle-class professionals for their white, middle-class children and certainly not on those tests that are referenced to a norm so that half of the children who take them must fail. If they were to reach a point where they began to score well on these tests, then those test writers would change the test, just as the politicians will ratchet up the exit exams if too many students—and particularly my students—do well on them when they take them.

One of the problems that exists with pointing out that perhaps all children can't learn the same stuff on the same timetable is that it sounds so churlish.

After all, don't I have faith in children's capacity? Why am I making excuses? Am I a racist? Those are conversation stoppers—and straw men. The real gap is between the rich and the poor, and it is growing.

25   For instance, Richard Rothstein, in his March 21, 2001, article, "Ambitious but Misguided: Kindergarten Academics," in the *New York Times*, says, "A 1995 study . . . found that parents with professional jobs spoke about 2, 100 words an hour to toddlers. For working-class parents it was 1,300, and for those on welfare only 600."

And Susan Neuman, who serves as the assistant secretary for elementary and secondary education, co-authored a study (see Susan B. Neuman and Donna Celano, "Access to Print in Low-Income and Middle-Income Communities: An Ecological Study of Four Neighborhoods," in *Reading Research Quarterly* for January 2001) that found shocking differences in access to literacy, in which she argued that "high-income children have 4,000 times the number of titles available" to buy in their neighborhoods, compared to poor neighborhoods; high-income school and public libraries have about twice as many books as low-income libraries and are open longer hours; environmental print was from a third to a quarter as readable in poor neighborhoods as in rich ones; and there were many more places to read in rich neighborhoods (e.g., coffee shops with good lighting) and therefore more models. The richest (and, of course, highest-scoring) school in my district has an investment plan to handle all its parent donations, while my students fist-fight over pencils.

THE RESEARCH ISN'T THERE

This school "reform" movement is not just about resources. It's also about control. We need "programs" to teach reading, which are "research-based and scientific." Meanwhile, Elaine M. Garan ("Beyond the Smoke and Mirrors: A Critique of the National Reading Panel Report on Phonics," in March 2001 *Phi Delta Kappan,* as well as her *Resisting Reading Mandates: How to Triumph with the Truth,* published by Heinemann in 2002) and Gerald Coles ("Reading Taught to the Tune of the 'Scientific' Hickory Stick," *Phi Delta Kappan,* November 2001, as well as his *Misreading Reading,* published in 2000 by Heinemann) and many other writers have deconstructed the National Reading Panel's "research" on which the "programs" are based and discovered that it isn't there.

In my school, we are given time weekly for grade-level team meetings, which is good, but the proceedings of each meeting must be written on a "grade-level team meeting record sheet," which specifies by the minute how much time will be spent on purpose (one minute), strategies that worked (five minutes), chief challenge (three to five minutes), proposed strategies (eight to 10 minutes), and action plan (10 minutes). At least we don't have "Open Cult"—I mean Open Court. (Alas, it has been adopted for next school year.)

Our children walk to and from class with their hands clasped behind their backs; they line up at 8:15 and wait in those lines until class begins at 8:30. My job is to tell them to stop playing basketball, soccer, catch, and jump rope and to get in line, like good little soldiers. We say the Pledge of Allegiance and the School Creed every day in unison with the principal over the loudspeaker (along with every house within two blocks, I'll wager).

30   Then, once a week, we have Fun Friday, when the good students get rewarded, and the bad students don't get to play. Fun Friday gives the ruse away, of course: The rest of the week isn't any fun. On Mondays, we are all—adults and children—expected to wear the school uniform colors, navy and white. Look for me in my red skirt and orange blouse.

SCHOOLS AS TEST-PREP FACTORIES . . . WHAT'S THE POINT?

Since the publication in 1983 of *A Nation at Risk,* a Cold War document, the point has been to discredit public schools. The tests and standards "prove" that the schools are bad, and then they are transformed into test-prep factories.

The jewels in the testing crown are the exit exams, which, as we've seen in Chicago and in the Texas Mirage, drive children out of school at unprecedented rates. These ex-students either swell the ranks of the unemployed (thus keeping wages down) or go directly to jail (thus providing cheaper-than-Third-World labor). All of these are among the supposedly "unintended" consequences of reform.

Meanwhile, the National Reading Panel (NRP) report points mutely to Open Cult, Direct Infliction, and Stress for All. This year the reauthorized Elementary and Secondary Education Act (the Leave No Corporation Behind Act) puts muscle behind the NRP report in the form of a billion dollars in Title I blackmail. Open Cult (or its clones) becomes the de facto national reading curriculum. (McGraw-Hill had total sales of $4.6 billion in 2001.) And the scripted programs make teachers superfluous, allowing Edison, Inc.—which hasn't turned a profit yet—and its clones to hire anyone to read the scripts.

The real gap in this nation is between the rich and the poor, and it is obscenely huge. This story's bottom line is the bottom line: money.

35   So teachers, if you and your students are calling in sick from the mold in your portable classrooms, if you're tithing your salary on trade books to humanize your reading "program," if those sisters who live in a parked car down the block are always hungry, if there are eight different languages in your classroom, just stiffen your resolve.

Remember, we can "beat the gap," there are "no excuses" allowed, we're "data-driven and research-based," we have "zero tolerance." And keep in mind that "all children can learn," that we're "leaving no child behind," and that it's not about money and control. Like Peter Pan, "Think lovely thoughts."

NOTE

"Wendy Darling" is a pseudonym for a teacher in a western state who values her principal and so must remain anonymous. Condensed from *Phi Delta Kappan,* 84 (October 2002),

109–111. Published by Phi Delta Kappa International, Inc., 408 N. Union, P.O. Box 789, Bloomington, IN 47402.

⚒ CRITICAL REFLECTIONS

1. Early in this reading, "Darling" discusses the "achievement gap"—the gap between students who do well in school and those who do not. Literacy is supposed to help students cross the gap. Do you think "Darling" concurs with the cartoon's creator that literacy is the answer? What in the article leads you to your response to the question?

2. "Darling" writes that "the current rhetoric of 'reform' touts equity as the goal [of education], when it should be the starting point." What do you think she means by this? (313). Do you agree with her assertion?

3. What experiences do "Darling" and the other teachers she describes have that help them to think about the data they are provided at their workshop? How do you think these experiences lead the teachers to interpret the data differently, and why?

4. The author's biography at the end of this reading states that "Wendy Darling" "is a pseudonym used for a teacher in a western state who values her principal and so must remain anonymous." Reading the article, do you find the author credible despite her anonymity? Why or why not?

⚒ MAKING CONNECTIONS

1. The author of this article used a pseudonym, "Wendy Darling," to refer to herself. After reading the NCLB executive summary, Peter Sacks's "Do No Harm," and Nicholas Lemann's "The President's Big Test," why do you think she felt it necessary to do so?

2. Consider the description of "Darling's" teaching work alongside the description of the typical day of "Mark" in "What High School Is." What similarities or differences do you find between this teacher's description of a student's day and the one Sizer makes? Extending from that analysis, what are the similarities or differences in the approaches to education described in Sizer's text (written in 1984) and "Darling's" (written in 2002)? What is your reaction to the changes, or lack of changes, that you have located?

3. "Darling" and Peter Sacks argue that standardized assessments will only increase the gap between rich and poor students. Stanley Kaplan, however, says that because students can prepare for the exam, he sees the SAT as a great leveler. Based on your own experience with any kind of standardized test or assessment, do you find one of these arguments more compelling? Draw on specific evidence from the readings to explain why or why not.

GARY ORFIELD AND JOHANNA WALD

TESTING, TESTING

This article was written in 1997 in response to then-President Bill Clinton's push for increasingly high-stakes tests—tests that would serve as the only, or one of the only, measures in determining the success of students and schools. In it, Gary Orfield and Johanna Wald recount a number of long-term studies documenting the negative effects of high-stakes testing on students, schools, and curricula. Under President George W. Bush, the push for increasingly high-stakes tests has become even more extreme. Bush's education bill, the No Child Left Behind Act, calls for harsh penalties if schools fail to meet the standards set by the Federal Government.

With education among the electorate's top priorities, the phrase "higher standards" has become ubiquitous in political campaigns across the country. Ever since the publication of the Reagan Administration's *A Nation at Risk* in 1983, the standards-based school reform movement has galvanized a broad coalition from right to left. Conservatives and business leaders are drawn to its pledge to improve the accountability of a public school system they see as an entrenched bureaucracy, as well as to its goal of preparing a more globally competitive work force. At the same time, the movement's underlying premise, that all children can learn at high levels, has won over many liberals and civil rights advocates, who are rightly concerned about teachers and schools lowering their expectations for poor and minority students.

Unfortunately, this movement has all too frequently been reduced to a single policy: high-stakes testing. This policy links the score on one set of standardized tests to grade promotion, high school graduation and, in some cases, teacher and principal salaries and tenure decisions. To date, about twenty-five states have adopted some version of this policy, and the number of legislatures considering similar measures is growing. Both Al Gore and George W. Bush vigorously promote the use of standardized tests. President Clinton recommended in his State of the Union address that test-preparation manuals be made available to all children.

Yet despite the political popularity of the testing "solution," many educators and civil rights advocates are suggesting that it has actually exacerbated the problems it sought to alleviate. They claim that these policies discriminate against minority students, undermine teachers, reduce opportunities for students to engage in creative and complex learning assignments, and deny high school diplomas because of students' failure to pass subjects they were never taught. They argue that using tests to raise academic standards makes as much sense as relying upon thermometers to reduce fevers. Most compellingly, they maintain that these tests are directing sanctions against the victims, rather than the perpetrators, of educational inequities.

The implications of these arguments were serious enough to lead The Civil Rights Project at Harvard University to commission a series of studies on the educational and social impact of high-stakes testing policies from some of the nation's top scholars in this field. Some of their most significant findings include:

- High-stakes tests attached to grade promotion and high school graduation lead to increased dropout rates, particularly for minority students. George Madaus and Marguerite Clarke of Boston College discovered a strong association between high-stakes testing and increased dropout rates. They cite studies showing that in 1986 half of the ten states with the lowest dropout figures used no high-stakes tests. The other half employed testing programs that could be characterized as low stakes. Nine of the ten states with the highest dropout rates used standardized tests in decisions about high school graduation.

  The effects for minority students can be discerned from a study by Aaron Pallas of Michigan State University and Gary Natriello of Columbia University, who examined the racial and ethnic disparities in performance on the Texas Assessment of Academic Skills (TAAS) between 1996 and 1998. By the spring of their senior year, almost twice as many black and Hispanic students as white students had not passed the TAAS exit-level tests required to obtain a Texas high school diploma. The authors concluded that "these tests are, and will remain for some time, an impediment to the graduation prospects of African American and Hispanic youth." In another study, Columbia's Jay Heubert points out that students of color are almost always overrepresented among those who are denied diplomas on the basis of test scores.

- Using tests to retain students in the same grade produces no lasting educational benefits. Robert Hauser of the University of Wisconsin has found that retaining students in the same grade creates huge management problems in the classroom, is extremely expensive for the school system and dramatically increases the likelihood that the retained student will eventually drop out. Moreover, African-American males are disproportionately represented among those who are held back. The Congressionally mandated 1999 National Academy of Sciences report *High Stakes: Testing for Tracking, Promotion and Graduation* cites five other studies that draw similar conclusions about the negative effects of retaining students.

- High-stakes tests narrow the curriculum by encouraging a "teach to the test" approach in the classroom. Most curriculum experts recommend that students approach topics from a variety of perspectives, using all of their senses, over extended periods of time. Many high-stakes tests, however, rely upon multiple-choice questions, ask students to interpret isolated passages unrelated to larger themes or units, and require them to adhere to rigid writing formats that allow little room for deviation. Linda McNeil of Rice University and Angela Valenzuela of the University of Texas argue that while increasing numbers of students in poor schools in Houston may be passing the TAAS reading section, they "are not able to make meaning of literature . . . nor to connect reading assignments to other parts of the course such as discussion and writing." As Clifford Hill of Columbia University wrote recently in a *New York Times* Op-Ed, test preparation has come to "invade" the school day in poor schools in New York City, with worrisome effects: "Learning to take reading and writing tests is not the same as learning to read and write, especially when test prep materials do not meet basic standards."

Moreover, test preparation is far more likely to dominate teaching in high-poverty schools than in affluent ones. Such instruction has all but replaced the curriculum in Houston's poor schools, according to McNeil and Valenzuela's research. Also, high-poverty schools hire a large number of uncertified and inexperienced teachers who tend to focus exclusively on test preparation, as John Lee of the University of Maryland has found.

- There is very little evidence linking test scores with economic productivity. According to Henry Levin of Columbia, the U.S. economy is highly competitive despite the fact that our students lag behind other countries in test performance on some international comparisons. In fact, those countries that do score particularly well on tests may be suffering in the global economy because their curriculum is too narrow and does not yet offer the range of learning opportunities available to students in U.S. schools.

5   Many states are using tests in ways that directly contradict the recommendations of the National Academy of Sciences, the Department of Education's Office for Civil Rights and other experts. The Office for Civil Rights's 1999 resource guide states that "a decision or characterization that will have major impact on a student should not be made on the basis of a single test score." Even one of the nation's most prominent advocates for the standards movement, Robert Schwartz, president of ACHIEVE, wrote recently, "Common sense suggests that states should not rely solely on the results of one-shot assessments." Educational testing service leaders also strongly warn against using test scores alone to make high-stakes judgments about students. Yet many school districts, according to Columbia's Heubert, use tests designed for other purposes to make tracking, promotion and graduation decisions.

If, as all these studies suggest, high-stakes tests both discriminate against poor and minority students and are educationally unsound, we are still left with the dilemma of how to achieve the dual goals of equity and excellence. Dozens of studies offer convincing evidence that children in poor schools make academic gains when they have access to quality early-childhood education programs, when they are taught in small classes by skilled and committed teachers, and when they are given assessments linked to appropriate and immediate responses.

The single most important factor in raising academic performance in poor schools appears to be the presence of experienced, competent and caring teachers. Disadvantaged youths currently are taught by the least prepared and most transient instructors in the system. Devising incentives for recruiting and maintaining highly qualified teachers and for retraining existing staff in high-poverty schools should be the top priority of those serious about raising standards.

Student assessments, of course, are essential to realizing improvements in students and schools. Several groups and individuals, including Clifford Hill, Project Zero at the Harvard Graduate School of Education, the New York Performance Standards Consortium and the Coalition for Authentic Reform in Education (CARE) in Massachusetts, have developed alternative modes of evaluating student performance. These share the following characteristics: (1) they are designed in collaboration with—rather than imposed upon—teachers; (2) they are varied enough to reflect the differing learning styles of students; (3) they address the curriculum actually taught in the classroom; and (4) they provide timely feedback linked to both student remediation, when necessary, and curriculum revisions. Standardized tests can play a role in such a restructured system. As recommended in *High Stakes,* test scores, combined with other assessments, can be very useful in identifying curricular weaknesses and in targeting students in need of additional support.

It is also possible to hold schools accountable for academic performance without penalizing students unfairly. One obvious way is to measure progress as well as outcome. By taking only standardized scores—which are heavily correlated with parents' income and level of education—into account, most current systems automatically reward schools in affluent areas. They also set up a destructive dynamic between teachers and struggling students. With their livelihood and reputations riding on scores alone, faculty are motivated to dismiss low performers in favor of those more likely to score well. One principal in Chicago even admitted that he expelled chronically truant students to boost his schools' test scores. A focus on improvement over outcome will alleviate that dynamic. Tennessee, for example, puts a central focus on the "Value Added" by a school's program.

10   Unfortunately, despite recent revelations of the high numbers of likely student "casualties" to high-stakes testing policies—especially among poor and minority children—many politicians have discovered that vows to bring about "world-class standards" and to "end social promotion" play well on the evening news. For the most part, the media continue to accept at face value claims that high-stakes tests represent a necessary form of tough love for struggling schools. Still, there are indications that the movement to suspend the high-stakes aspect of testing is gaining momentum. It has found an ally in Senator Paul Wellstone, who recently introduced legislation prohibiting the misuse of these tests. Delaware just decided, under intense protest, to postpone its new testing policies, and Virginia, Massachusetts and other states are currently experiencing fierce opposition to their testing requirements. Hopefully such public pressure will lead to the adoption of more effective and equitable uses of assessments within a restructured school reform movement.

NOTE

Gary Orfield is a professor of education and social policy at the Harvard Graduate School of Education and Kennedy School of Government, and co-director of the Civil Rights Project at Harvard University. He recently co-edited *Religion, Race and Justice in a Changing America* (Century Foundation) and *Chilling Admissions: The Affirmative Action Crisis and the Search for Alternatives* (HEPG), and is currently co-editing a book on high-stakes testing. Johanna Wald is a researcher and writer/editor for the Civil Rights Project.

CRITICAL REFLECTIONS

1. It's virtually impossible to have gotten as far as you have in your education without encountering a standardized test or assessment, and almost everyone has a story about their experience taking these tests. What has been your experience? If you have stories, what is the best one, and what is the moral of the story?

2. In your own words, summarize Orfield and Wald's analysis of why standardized testing and assessment has grown more popular since the publication of *A Nation at Risk*.

3. Orfield and Wald identify a number of problems with the current approach to testing. Do you have a stand on these issues? If you do, why do you take the position you do? If you don't, why don't you?

MAKING CONNECTIONS

1. The driving assumption behind the move to standardized statewide assessments like the ones that Orfield and Wald discuss here, and of the national testing program advocated by Nicholas Lemann in "The President's Big Test," is that all students should learn the same things. Yet, one of the points of June Jordan's article "Nobody Mean More to Me than You and the Future Life of Willie Jordan" is that literacy (like using and understanding a dialect of English) is linked to specific communities. Which of these positions do you most agree with? Do you think definitions of literacy (and, therefore, what is taught in schools) should be rooted in specific (local) cultures and knowledges? National? Both? Why do you take the position you do?

2. Orfield and Wald argue that "high-stakes tests narrow the curriculum by encouraging a 'teach to the test' approach in the classroom" (320). Do you think Traub's "The Test Mess" (pp. 339–352) supports or refutes this claim? Why do you make the case you do?

3. Those who argue against high-stakes testing (like Orfield and Wald) believe that assessement is important. Based on your reading, as well as on your experiences

as a student, do you agree with them? Do you think high-stakes testing is the right answer? If yes, why do you? If not, what might be a better assessment system?

PETER SACKS

DO NO HARM: STOPPING THE DAMAGE TO AMERICAN SCHOOLS

Do No Harm comes from Peter Sacks's book, *Standardized Minds.* Sacks, an investigative reporter, explored the culture of standardized testing and ultimately came to the conclusion that state-sponsored assessments, as well as increasing pressure to perform well on tests like the ACT and SAT, had extremely negative consequences for schools. In this chapter, Sacks explores how the increasing trend toward standardized assessments might be reversed. He begins with a discussion of a student who, despite an excellent academic record, was not allowed to graduate from high school in Texas because she could not pass the TAAS (Texas Assessment of Academic Skills), the standardized exam then administered in Texas.

Our inauspicious era of educational crimes and punishments shows no signs of waning. Young people like Kelly Santos, whom we met earlier, aren't isolated examples of the fallout from the national crusade for more "accountable" schools. Texas is among some nineteen states that require high school "exit" tests, and more are in the offing. Dozens of states hold schools, students, teachers, and principals "accountable" on the basis of standardized test scores. "We have been, frankly, inundated with calls from states that are looking at their accountability laws and want to strengthen them," says one official at the Education Commission of the States.[1]

Indeed, states are engaged in an elaborate round of musical acronyms, replacing one testing system for another one, more often than not with one that has significantly higher stakes for all people involved. Some states have abandoned their efforts to try alternatives to standardized tests, such as performance assessments, which strive to permit children to think and perform in deeper and more creative terms than allowed by multiple-choice sound bites, worksheets, and test drills. But such new approaches—promising as they might be to refocus attention on learning instead of scoring—aren't easily fitted into the politically driven objective of school accountability. That objective? Apparently to compare test scores of individual children across the state or the nation and show the public that policymakers are tough on academic standards by punishing those who don't measure up. Some examples:

- In a Hawthornesque variant to the scarlet *A,* Louisiana's accountability law requires school districts to identify and publish the names of all schools scoring in the bottom fifth on the state's standardized test. All Louisiana school districts but New Orleans comply with the 1997 law, pending the outcome of a lawsuit. One of the plaintiffs, a local state representative, ridicules the mandate as tantamount to requiring a public declaration of "Here are the dummy schools."[2]

- In a case of school achievement levels determined simply by which test one chooses to use, school officials in Idaho wring their hands over reading scores of fourth-graders when one exam finds that 60 percent of the children can't read at grade level, while another test indicates just 18 percent cannot. A battle of name-calling, disavowals, and insults ensues over which test was right.[3]

- Illustrative of the newfound lack of concern among some school officials over the educationally dubious practice of "teaching the test," Milwaukee public schools in Wisconsin agree to pay an Arizona consulting firm almost $400,000 for a program called TargetTeach. The firm specializes in getting test scores up in schools "with a problem." The firm, Evans-Newton Inc., promises a 20 to 200 percent surge in test scores in just a year.[4]

- In Chicago, 1 in 10 of Chicago schools' 424,000 students are sent to summer school on the basis of standardized test scores. Thousands of others are forced to repeat a grade even after summer school because of poor showings on a retest. Under the hammer, students at Amundson High School in Chicago spend six weeks of class time on intensive test preparation and coaching for the upcoming test.[5]

- In California, funding for a performance-based assessment system known as CLAS, which had been in place to assess learning without reliance on standardized testing, is vetoed by Governor Pete Wilson. In its place, the state legislature invents STAR, the Standardized Testing and Reporting program, which requires all children in the second through eleventh grades to take a commercial multiple-choice test. A group of several school superintendents from major California cities condemn the plan as educationally regressive, one that "wastes taxpayer dollars and will impede, rather than support, our statewide push toward higher performance."[6]

ADDING THE DAMAGE

Without a doubt, crackdowns such as these on public schools, as well as tales of amazing turnarounds in test results in such locales as Tacoma, Washington, and Northampton County, North Carolina, reflect the good news of American schools for many elected officials, corporate executives, parents, newspaper editorial writers, and others working under the mantle of school reform.

Tales of higher academic standards and achievement test scores beyond expectations sustain popular belief in the reform crusade's holy trinity: standards, accountability, and testing. For many, such stories show that the accountability movement is indeed having the reformers' desired effects:

reinforcing high academic standards, forcing teachers and principals to do their jobs, and providing meaningful incentives for students to achieve.

5   The evidence from the previous three chapters shows just how empty those beliefs are. In fact, while the rhetoric is highly effective, remarkably little good evidence exists that there's *any* educational substance behind the accountability and testing movement. In fact, when one adds up the real costs of the uniquely American model of school accountability and compares them to the minimal or nonexistent benefits, the inescapable conclusion is that the nation's fifteen-year experiment has been an unmitigated failure. Let's sum up the damage:

One: Educational considerations have been subordinate to the political and ideological motivations of politicians, educational bureaucrats, and business leaders. These interests have wielded political power over schools in order to assert their control and to demonstrate preconceived failures of the school system as the means to sustain that power. This was as true at the beginning of the American testing movement in Horace Mann's Massachusetts as it was in Johnson County, North Carolina, in the 1990s.

Two: Blatant and harmful misappropriations of standardized tests for fallacious uses have been a constant of America's historical experience with standardized testing in schools. Zealots, for instance, have taken tests intended to broadly assess achievement at the school, district, or state level, to instead rank and sort individual children. The opposite has also been true: tests intended to evaluate individual achievement have been used to base unfounded conclusions of the educational quality of entire school systems.

Three: In the ongoing struggle between educational equity among social classes and an efficiently managed school system, public policy toward schools has historically tended to side with the latter. Public schools have borrowed the management, surveillance, measurement, and control techniques of American business in order to achieve this efficiency.

Four: The notion of "accountability" itself has been defined in terms analogous to the corporate model, such as profits and returns to shareholders. In practice and in public belief, the educational product of schools has come to be judged almost exclusively by test scores. Borrowing, too, the market-driven ideology of the corporate world, policymakers have created pseudo-market systems of rewards and punishments to schools. Test scores are the currency of these incentives.

10   Five: The modern accountability movement became "federalized," in some decidedly tangible and pervasive ways. The federal government's markings on the accountability movement occurred, not insignificantly, as a result of the federal Title 1 law that has meted out many billions of dollars in federal funding to schools using test scores as a key part of the calculus. Further, prominent national leaders, including three recent American presidents, have ratcheted up the stakes for public schools to that of a national crusade for educational reform, with accountability testing as its linchpin.

Six: The underlying belief in the school reform crusade of the past few decades is that the American way of life was at grave risk because of lax standards and poorly educated schoolchildren. Evidence has proven this belief to be politically convenient mythology, wrong on at least three counts: First, academic achievement was never as horrible as the crusaders made it out to be; next, in the aftermath of an alleged deterioration of American schools, the U.S. economy continued to remain the most productive in the world; and finally, contrary to the implicit assumption that more testing and greater accountability will produce higher academic achievement, states with the most testing and the highest consequences of testing have fared worse on independent measures of achievement than states with no or low stakes to their testing programs.

Seven: Focused on test scores and the means to effect higher scores, the accountability movement has been curiously oblivious to the unintended damage to the learning environment. The movement has ignored the distortions to teaching and learning resulting from teachers, students, and others in the system acting in their own perceived best interest.

Schools and teachers, under intense pressure to boost achievement scores, have discovered the educationally dubious practice of teaching to tests. That, in turn, has narrowed what's taught to material that closely matches items on multiple-choice, standardized tests. Too, teaching to tests has had a dumbing effect on teaching and learning, as worksheets, drills, practice tests, and similar rote practices consume greater amounts of teaching time.

The greater the consequences attached to the test, the more severe these distortions are on teaching and learning. Indeed, a widely discussed international study of math and science performance of twelfth-graders suggests American students' relatively poor performance can be traced to the superficiality of their classroom experiences, which in turn can be linked to the rise of accountability testing.

15　Eight: Schools have also discovered they can boost test scores by drilling students on practice test items, but gains won in this fashion prove to be ephemeral in the long run. In the short run, schools can jack up scores on one standardized test, only to see scores go back down when a new test comes along. Similarly, achievement that is apparently high on the test for which schools have prepared and drilled turns mediocre with a different test for which there was little or no specific preparation.

Nine: An important element of the calculus of school reform, as defined by the modern accountability movement, has been a heavy emphasis on state regulation of schools, similar to other regulatory agencies. State utility regulators, for instance, have historically monitored electric companies to ensure that rates are kept to a reasonable level. Similarly, the new school regulators have tried to ensure the academic integrity of schools through rules on educational "infractions" and punishments to schools and schoolchildren. "Violators," in this sense, have been the children, schools, teachers, and others that perform poorly on standardized achievement tests. Punishments for these "violators" have been severe.

But that seemingly attractive analogy collapses in the end. Whereas determining reasonable rates of profit for electric companies is a relatively straightforward exercise in measurement, assessing educational quality is exceedingly problematic. Is educational quality measured by results on standardized tests? Is it measured by how well students perform on tasks that require them to integrate skills and knowledge from several subjects, such as writing an essay or creating a multimedia presentation? Or does educational quality boil down to the success of graduates in college or in jobs after they leave the school system?

Educational quality may be all these. Even a modicum of justice to this complex, ephemeral concept—and especially for the sake of people whose lives are affected by decisions about what constitutes educational quality—would undoubtedly require an equally complex measurement system. Such a system would have to assess educational quality from a variety of perspectives to be fair, complete, and accurate. But, again, choosing efficiency over equity, Americans through their elected officials have largely chosen to assess quality of schools in exceedingly narrow and often inaccurate terms.

Beyond these social and economic costs of current notions of school accountability, however, is one costly and pernicious piece of damage that framers of the accountability movement have virtually ignored over the past twenty-five years. Obsessed with test results and holding schools accountable for those results, the entire accountability enterprise has studiously avoided confronting the real problems of American schools. I've alluded to the powerful correlations between socioeconomic factors and test scores, taking note, for instance, of the huge economic gaps between communities like Tacoma and Mercer Island, or Northampton County and Chapel Hill. Quite simply, one can't write a book about standardized testing in American schools without confronting the effects of poverty, race, and class on test scores.

20   From *A Nation at Risk* to Bill Clinton's Goals 2000, the accountability crusaders have given no more than lip service to the uncomfortable schism in the American school system between rich and poor, one that in recent years has increasingly resembled the economic and social stratification in the larger society. The accountability movement has sustained, and been sustained by, a big but comfortable lie: that schools themselves are the agent for social and economic change, rather than a reflection and reinforcer of existing social and economic divisions. In practice, this illusion has implied that "fixing" schools—via gains in achievement test scores— will also fix unemployment, crime, and poverty as well as racial and economic inequality. The entire accountability project in the United States over the past two decades has been based on a refusal to even acknowledge the far more difficult prospect that the causal relationships between schools and the larger society might in fact work largely in exactly the opposite direction to that wishful thinking.

As a result of this denial, the accountability machine's damage to children from families that aren't economically comfortable and highly educated or who are African American or Mexican American, has been inestimable, as we saw specifically in Texas, North Carolina, and in Tacoma. In those places and in hundreds more like them across the country, poor and minority schoolchildren have borne the brunt of the accountability machine's punishments.

Indeed, if social engineers had set out to invent a virtually perfect inequality machine, designed to perpetuate class and race divisions, and that appeared to abide by all requisite state and federal laws and regulations, those engineers could do no better than the present-day accountability systems already put to use in American schools.

Inequality in the larger society bleeds through the education system. Rich schools and poor schools match the income levels and occupational status of parents. Compared to rich schools, poor schools, whose children come from homes with incomes of less than $20,000 a year, are more likely to have relatively poorly paid teachers who are also teaching out of their fields of expertise and have less access to special learning tools like the Internet. Quite simply, compared to a rich school district, such as Mercer Island, a relatively poor one like Tacoma is likely to spend significantly less money on each of its students. In one recent year, for example, the nation's richest school districts spent almost 60 percent more per student than the country's poorest schools.[7]

CLASS IS PARAMOUNT

To be sure, inequality may not be on the minds of a lot of parents, except to steer as far away from it as possible when choosing a school. Recall from Chapter 4 how many parents in Boise, Idaho, were known to choose schools for their children based on test scores and child poverty rates; the higher the scores and the lower the poverty, the better the school in the eyes of many parents. Those parents might have been behaving quite rationally—but only up to a point. As it turns out, the economic class of individual children and their parents bears decisively on a child's chances of success in the school system, regardless of a particular school's test scores.

25   Let's digress momentarily to Chuck Lavaroni, the former teacher and school superintendent in Marin County, California, a community of high-achieving, well-paid professionals and schools boasting exceedingly high test scores. At the end of our two-session conversation, Lavaroni somewhat reluctantly confided his hypothesis concerning his Marin County students, which he'd arrived at after years of rumination about his experiences.

"You could take kids (in Marin County) who have grown up in that environment and not send them to school at all and they'd still pass the (standardized) test," Lavaroni told me. "If one of those schools drops below the ninety eighth percentile, they worry."

That was Lavaroni's highly educated guess, after years of experience in education. But he may in fact be close to the sober reality about the powerful relationship of class background and a child's success in test-driven school systems. We can go back to a sweeping 1972 study for some enlightening discoveries along these lines that should still give parents and educators on the edge of the millennium reason to pause. That study suggests Lavaroni's guess is hardly a novel idea nor an unproven supposition. Titled *Inequality: A Reassessment of the Effect of Family and Schooling in America,* the three-year project was led by the sociologist

Christopher Jencks and several other coauthors at the Center for Educational Policy Research at Harvard. The researchers examined how educational "attainment"—whether one obtains, for instance, a high school diploma or a medical degree—is related to such factors as class background, IQ scores, and average test scores of schools attended. As we've already seen, educational attainment is perhaps the most powerful of all indicators of educational quality, because attainment bears most directly on one's economic prospects and well-being.

Contrary to popular belief in the power of a school's average test scores as an indicator of a child's future academic success, the study found that "school quality" measured by scores has in fact a small effect on how much schooling a given child who attends that school will eventually obtain. "We can be almost certain," Jencks wrote, "that a child's going to a grade school with top-drawer test scores will add less than a year to his or her total years of schooling—and probably far less than even that."[8]

Absent any significant effects of schools' average achievement scores on one's years of educational attainment, that leaves such individual characteristics as cognitive abilities, behavioral traits, and the class background a child is born into as possible explanations.

30   As it turns out, the class background of a child's parents, combined with the behavioral traits about school which that class background imparts to children, appear to explain most of the variation in how much schooling someone eventually obtains. According to the Jencks study, a child's social and economic origins, measured by her father's occupational status and income, alone accounts for some 55 percent of her eventual educational attainment. Put another way, upper-middle-class children will obtain a total of four more years of schooling than lower-class kids, simply by virtue of the families they were born into. Further, so-called cognitive abilities, measured by IQ scores, account for less than 10 percent of the variation in the child's educational attainment.

On the other hand, the far more subtle behavioral traits often found in high-achieving households that "nurture the cognitive skills that schools value" have a far more substantial effect—something on the order of 25 percent—than IQ scores in explaining a child's educational achievement. Even then, the authors say, it's not clear that academic aptitude is that important to how much schooling one gets. Rather, attainment could be more related to "coming from the right family." Comparing, for instance, people with significantly different aptitude test scores raised in the same household, the study found that people who were more capable on the tests only attained less than a year of additional schooling. Again, class rules.

"Overall, the data lead us to three general conclusions," Jencks writes. "First, economic origins have a substantial influence on the amount of schooling people get. Second, the differences between rich and poor children is partly a matter of academic aptitude and partly a matter of money. Third, cultural attitudes, values, and taste for schooling play an even larger role than aptitude and money."[9]

INCOME AND POVERTY

Thus, the effects of social and economic class on how much schooling people get are immense, as most parents of schoolchildren implicitly know and understand. Where many parents often get it wrong is in believing that by associating their children with other high-scoring children in top schools, parents can do sort of an end-run around the powerful effects of *family* socioeconomic background. Tragically, this belief in the power of test scores by association sustains the beliefs that schools can either make or break a middle-class child's academic prospects in school or fix the horrendous problems of underachievement in the nation's poor and minority communities. The belief fuels the nation's unhealthy obsession with test scores, while we avoid the underlying problems and inequities.

The uncomfortable truth, however, is that the accountability movement that many states have embraced for their schools has, in fact, accomplished nothing to address the real problems with American schools. Instead of alleviating the problems of schools, which are clearly associated with the vast differences in wealth and privilege, the accountability machine's hard-core system of crimes and punishments has merely stiffened barriers to academic success for many.

35   Indeed, states have erected these barriers with virtually no firmly grounded evidence that they work to anyone's benefit except to those politicians, educators, and policy elites who professionally benefit from the bombardment of bad news about schools and from the engineering of high test numbers.

Besides the high correlation of class background to levels of attainment in the American school system, the relationship between poverty and achievement test scores has been firmly established in various field studies. Consider the Cleveland City School District, where fully 80 percent of schoolchildren are poor, as measured by their eligibility for school lunch programs. In 1990, the Ohio legislature told schools to administer a standardized test to ninth-graders to determine whether students might receive a full-fledged diploma or a down-graded "certificate" at their high school graduation. Students would have to pass all four parts of the test to receive a diploma, and they'd get two chances. James Lanese, of the Cleveland school district, looked into the question that had been troubling some skeptics: Would the state's testing program further punish schoolchildren in places like Cleveland, whose schools and families were already damaged by poverty?

Examining thirty-one school districts of various socioeconomic classes in Cuyahoga County, including Cleveland, Lanese applied the techniques of statistical correlation analysis to find out. Indeed, correlations between poverty levels of a district and success on the statewide tests were considerable. Lanese later told his peers at a meeting of the American Educational Research Association in San Francisco, "The comparison of district level performance on the Ohio Proficiency Test as a function of each district's poverty rates indicates a strong positive relationship exists between the economic status of the district's pupils and their performance on the test."[10]

Perhaps it comes as no surprise, then, that in the initial stages of the new testing program, just one-third of Cleveland students had passed the proficiency test by their junior year in high school. That's compared to three out of four students who had passed statewide. A year after the Lanese report, Michael Gallagher, also of the Cleveland school district, confirmed Lanese's results with slightly greater precision, accounting for more variables that might explain differences in pass rates. Specifically, Gallagher controlled for the confounding effects that occur between school districts, such as curriculum, racial makeup, and per-pupil spending. He looked at both income and poverty rates of the neighborhoods that surround individual schools within the Cleveland school district.

Even then, Gallagher found both household income and poverty were significantly correlated with the chances of passing the Ohio proficiency test. In fact, for every 10 percent drop in the number of pupils eligible for free lunches, a school would produce a 4 percent gain in its passing rate on the standardized test. He also discovered that, as a school approached having almost no pupils eligible for free lunches, the closer to the state average in the rate at which its students passed the test.[11]

40   Hold it a minute, some readers might interject: "But most studies have shown that differences in the *actual funding* of schools don't come close to explaining the yawning gaps of achievement between rich schools and poor ones." Indeed, there have been at least 100 such studies, and few have demonstrated any significant relationship between school funding levels—unequal as they are—and test scores.

And all of those studies may be seriously flawed, taken as a whole. In fact, virtually none have been based on nationwide samples of schools. In perhaps the first study to remedy this shortcoming and investigate the effects on achievement of school funding *on a national basis,* a team led by Bruce Biddle at the University of Missouri compared test scores on three national and/or international studies against the variables of poverty and school funding. Even when controlling for such confounding variables as race and curriculum, the team found the combined effect of poverty and school funding was "mammoth," accounting for the lion's share of differences among average achievement scores in states.

Further, the Biddle team came to a startling conclusion when applying their analysis to the entire pool of nations participating in a recent international comparison of mathematics achievement, on which the American students generally fared poorly. When accounting for economics, the Biddle team estimated that math scores in "advantaged" American schools (those with high funding and low poverty rates) would beat *all* European counterparts and come in second only to Japan. On the other hand, scores for typically disadvantaged American schools would be below all European nations and approach those of many developing countries.

Evidence like this is why the accountability crusade's push for more and more testing persists in going off into left field while the real action is at home plate. Summing up his research team's remarkable findings in *Phi Delta Kappan,* the highly regarded magazine about education, Biddle says:

The effects I report here help us understand why setting higher standards will have so little impact on achievement. If many, many schools in America are poorly funded and must contend with high levels of child poverty, then their problems stem not from confusion or lack of will on the part of educators but rather from lack of badly needed resources. In fact, setting higher standards for those disadvantaged schools can even make things worse. If they are told that they now must meet higher standards, or—worse—if they are chastised because they cannot do so, then they will have been punished for events beyond their control.[12]

Adding fuel to the flames that hurt rather than help children from poorer backgrounds, schools in poor neighborhoods bear the greatest brunt of public and official pressure to raise test scores. At these schools, teachers are most pressured to turn teaching and learning into a rote exercise of practice and drill for the next standardized test. We saw evidence of this disparate burden placed on the poor in Tacoma, Washington, in Northampton County, North Carolina, and in San Antonio, Texas. But further quantitative evidence on a wider scale underscores the observations from those case studies.

45   For example, investigators Joan Herman and Shari Golan examined eleven medium and large school districts in nine states to quantify the effects of big-stakes testing programs. Most noteworthy, the authors said, were the disproportionate effects of such testing on schools with lots of poor children and high numbers of minorities. The poorer the children attending the schools, the more pressure schools place on teachers to raise test scores, and the greater chance that the teachers will focus on the tests in their instruction rather than on deeper understanding.

And to what benefit? In the Herman study, teachers were asked whether the testing programs helped their schools to improve. On a scale of one to five (one corresponding to definite agreement, three to a neutral opinion, and five to definite disagreement), teachers in both wealthy and poor areas were inclined to rate standardized testing as more harmful than helpful for school improvement. Teachers in the poorer areas were least sanguine. "In the minds of teachers," the researchers conclude, "test results are of uncertain meaning and of uncertain value in school improvement."[13]

A PROPOSAL

Judging by the evidence compiled in the previous three chapters, there's abundant reason to believe that the clearest route to raising the achievement levels of schoolchildren, in a real and lasting sense, may be—quite contrary to popular belief—to diminish reliance on standardized testing and high-stakes accountability systems. Instead of helping minority children and children of low and moderate incomes get past already stiff barriers to academic success, the accountability machine has given us bad teaching and perpetuated rather than dampened a powerful structure of economically segregated and unequal schools.

To be sure, that's not the sort of message that flies well in these times, when efforts to attack the problems of schools at the fountainheads of poverty and wealth are frowned on as failed strategies of a bygone era of liberal ideology. Above all, the accountability movement has been incredibly successful at framing the debate about school reform and improvement in the United States, persuading a largely uninformed public that more testing, more standards, and greater accountability for schools and teachers are the panaceas for whatever ails schools. Indeed, a 1997 public opinion poll conducted for Phi Delta Kappa International, the educational organization, showed that two in three Americans highly favored a national standardized test; that well more than half favored Bill Clinton's proposal for a national exam; and that most Americans are content to believe that the massive quantities of standardized testing in their schools is "about right."[14]

Perhaps the public is right in believing that government programs cannot rectify the social and economic inequalities that reproduce more inequality in public schools. But Americans fail to engage a genuine debate over the real problems with their schools at their collective peril. To continue to avoid that debate, to remain out of touch to the hard problems of American schools, means taxpayers will keep throwing good money after bad. They will continue to erroneously believe that more testing and higher consequences for poor test results, enforced by the power of the state, will fix what is wrong with American schools. The public will also be led down a particularly troublesome slippery slope: The nation remains at risk because the standards, testing, and accountability movement never went far enough. Repeating the age-old pattern that the fix for American schools lies in some new technological solution, Americans are likely to be told by the next generation of crusaders about the imperative for *national* standards and a *national* test to measure student performance against those world class standards.

50   Indeed, the next generation was already coming on the scene as I was writing this. About the time of the fifteenth anniversary of the 1983 *A Nation at Risk* report, a prominent group of school reformers and Washington policy elites, led by Ronald Reagan's former education secretary, William J. Bennett, had come out with just that message, in what might be called *Risk II*. Not surprisingly, they dubbed the sequel, *A Nation Still at Risk: An Education Manifesto*.

To be sure, *Risk* was in dire need of an update. Unfortunately for the movement's followers, it had been eclipsed by reality. The American economy's performance relative to all its international competitors was outright defying crusaders' gloomy predictions. Educational attainment was improving, as was student performance on the National Assessment of Educational Progress.

Addressing those difficulties for its message, *Risk II* pleaded that Americans had lapsed into a state of complacency about their schools, and it labeled critiques of the schools-in-crisis mentality as mere "fantasy." Recent poor international showing of American high schoolers on math and science (the so-called TIMSS study dissected in Chapter 6) was a key piece of new cannon fodder for the movement. Also, *Risk II* trotted out the tried-and-true straw men, including my favorite, supposedly held by "many educators" that "some boys and girls—especially those from 'the other side of the tracks'—just can't be expected to learn much." Demonstrating such concern for America's downtrodden provided much needed modernization for the crusaders' message.

Still, the take-home message of *Risk II* was the same as always: The nation's in peril because American schools are in a state of crisis. And the way to fix the problem was also essentially the same, but with some updated wrinkles. Yes, more standards, testing, and accountability—but make them national ones. Additionally, give parents and students more school "choice," permitting "public dollars to . . . follow individual children to the schools they select."[15]

All such solutions, in my view, will do little to address the root causes of the achievement gaps between rich and poor. In fact, these solutions constitute highly flammable rocket fuel that will make the underlying problems all the more severe, wasteful, and tragic.

STOPPING THE DAMAGE

55 The lesson for parents, taxpayers, and policymakers seems clear. Addressing the real problems with American schools means coming to grips with the relationships between academic success and the pervasive influences of class, poverty, and race. I don't mean to be glib, but perhaps the very best way a parent can ensure their children's success in the school system, in terms of achievement and attainment, would be to obtain as much education for oneself as possible. But to do so parents need the help of policymakers. If politicians are really interested in promoting equality, improving schools, and helping the American economy, they would, at a minimum, tear down false barriers to educational attainment that have been erected in the era of school accountability, barriers that have no proven benefit.

Indeed, if government can't feasibly "buy" equality in the schools owing to the political infeasibility of doing so in these neoconservative times, policymakers could try an alternatively novel approach, one of a genuinely conservative bent. How about just *get out* of the nation's classrooms? I'd like to stipulate for policymakers a maxim from the medical profession: First and foremost, *DO NO HARM*. In other words, if policymakers' endless tinkering, controlling, measuring, punishing, and manipulating of schools has failed children, the best thing they could do would be to stop hurting them.

To do that, state legislatures must go back to basics about the role of schools in a democratic society. In a larger society that tends to produce great inequalities between socioeconomic classes and ethnic groups, public schools have little place being a regulatory or credentialing agency that places the Good Housekeeping Seal of Approval on a school system's graduates. Schools should not be hand-maidens to American business interests, which demand cheap and easy—and publicly subsidized—certification of alleged competency through achievement scores. *Public schools ought to have one overarching purpose in a free society: Provide citizens an opportunity to learn and ensure that those opportunities are equal across the lines of class and race.* American citizens ought to begin to question any public policy that does harm to that simple purpose. The public should apply their well-honed skepticism of modern institutions to hold accountable the accountability machine itself.

But a few affirmative, practical steps are in order as well. I would not go so far as to suggest that standardized tests have no legitimate purpose in American schools. In fact, they do; and that purpose is to periodically take the pulse of achievement but do so in a way that doesn't interfere with what should be the real business of schools: teaching and learning for understanding and long-term, sustainable achievement.

That means policymakers need to defang standardized testing programs, exorcizing the punishing consequences of poor test scores for students, teachers, and schools. Schools should compile and report testing data only for broad educational jurisdictions, and do so in terms of running averages over several years. That alone would discourage public and media obsession with meaningless, short-term changes in test results. States should reduce the economic drain of testing programs by rotating schools through the assessment system on a sampling basis. Doing this would also ensure that the test is broad in content, so results are sufficiently reliable and are an adequate indication of broad levels of student achievement. In short, such a test would by guided by the maxim that educational policymakers, first and foremost, *Do no harm.*

60   Alas, it might surprise some readers to learn that such a "test" already exists. In fact, it's been functioning remarkably well as America's educational barometer for some thirty years, and it's called the National Assessment of Educational Progress. Indeed, the NAEP isn't even really a test, in the sense standardized tests have come to mean in the accountability era. In a very real sense, NAEP, known as America's "report card," is simply a regularly conducted national survey of educational achievement in reading, writing, math, science, geography, and U.S. history, of Americans in grade school, middle school, and high school.

A report by the U.S. Office of Technology Assessment reminds us of the beauty of NAEP. "The designers of the NAEP project took extreme care and built in many safeguards to ensure that a national assessment would not, in the worst fears of its critics, become any of the following: a stepping stone to a national individual testing program, a tool for Federal control of curriculum, a weapon to 'blast' the schools, a deterrent to curricular change, or a vehicle for student selection or funds allocation decisions."[16]

Between the politically sensitive lines of that OTA report is a grave and prescient concern over any attempt to tinker with the NAEP that transforms it into a national standardized test along the lines of the Clinton and Bush administrations' proposals, a national test complete with individual scores and the horse-race mentality that invariably accompanies such an approach. Commenting on the safeguards built into the NAEP that recent national testing proposals had threatened to undermine, the University of North Carolina's Lyle Jones, one of the original technical advisers on NAEP's development, says, "Were these features not to have been maintained, I believe that NAEP would have become so controversial that it would not have survived to be the useful indicator of educational progress that it is today."[17]

The NAEP should be left alone, and it should remain the nation's report card. It's the only report card America really needs.

As anybody who's gone to school knows, there's a certain beauty in a report card, that periodic summary boys and girls have taken home to moms and dads since the beginnings of formal public education in the United States. Whether they're compiled in terms of As, Bs, or Cs, in the precise terms of decimal points, or even in narrative form in a teacher's handwriting, a report card is a meaningful thing.

65   A report card is a simple summation of a teachers' intimate and expert knowledge of a child's progress in school to that point. It is a simple answer to simple questions: *How am I doing? How's my child doing?*

And we all know this truth: A teacher knows. Teachers, working day in and day out with a child, who sees, hears, and reads the real work that child has actually accomplished at school, know. When parents really want to know the answer to the question, *How is my child doing?* they also know this: They go to the teacher, and they ask.

Teachers write down what they know about schoolwork of boys and girls in the report card. Parents have always put good report cards on the refrigerator door, and they have always known what a good report card meant. It meant keep up the good work. And they have always known what a bad report card meant. It meant there was room for improvement. It meant "work harder," "study more." Teachers and moms and dads did not need a standardized test or an accountability system to tell them what they already knew. They did not need to put the standardized test scores on the refrigerator door.

ENDNOTES

1. "We have been, frankly, inundated . . ." *Education on the Web,* "The Push for Accountability Gathers Steam," February 11, 1998.

2. All the state's parishes but New Orleans had complied . . . *Education Week on the Web,* "Challenge to La. Accountability Law Heads to Trial," March 13, 1998.

3. In an example of school achievement levels determined . . . *Idaho Statesman,* "Testers rethink kid's reading scores," May 13, 1998, p. A1.

4. Illustrative of a disturbing lack of concern . . . *The Journal Sentinel,* "MPS may hire firm to help 'teach to test,'" April 22, 1998.

5. In Chicago, 1 in 10 of Chicago's school's 424,000 students . . . *Education on the Web,* "The Push for Accountability Gathers Steam," February 11, 1998; and *Catalyst,* "It's test time! IGAP down, CASE, TAP on tap," April 1998, vol. 9, no 7.

6. In California, the performance-based assessment system . . . National Center for Fair and Open Testing, Fair Test, in *Examiner,* "California Adopts Regressive Testing Program,' Winter 1997–1998, p. 8.

7. Compared to rich schools, poor schools . . . ibid, p. 26.

8. "We can be almost certain," writes Jencks . . . Christopher Jencks and others, *Inequality: A Reassessment of the Effect of Family and Schooling in America* (New York: Basic Books, 1972), p. 148.

9. "Overall, the data lead us to three general conclusions . . ." ibid., p. 141.

10. Consider the Cleveland City School District . . . James F. Lanese, "Statewide Proficiency Testing: Establishing Standards or Barriers," paper presented to the annual meeting of the AERA, San Francisco, April 1992.

11. Even then, Gallagher found both income and poverty were significantly . . . Michael Gallagher, "Proficiency Testing and Poverty: Looking Within a Large Urban District," paper presented at the annual meeting of the AERA, Atlanta, April 1993.

12. Summing up his team's remarkable findings in *Phi Delta Kappan* . . . Bruce J. Biddle, "Foolishness, Dangerous Nonsense, and Real Correlates of State Differences in Achievement, " *Phi Delta Kappan,* Internet site, September 1997.

13. To what benefit? . . . Joan Herman and Shari Golan, *Effects of Standardized Testing on Teachers and Learning—Another Look* (Los Angeles: UCLA Center for Research on Evaluation, Standards and Student Testing, 1990), p. 62.

14. Indeed, a 1997 public opinion poll . . . *Phi Delta Kappan,* "The 29th Annual Phi Delta Kappa/Gallup Poll of the Public's Attitudes Toward the Public Schools," August 25, 1997.

15. Still, the take-home message of *Risk II* was the same as its progenitor . . . Center for Education Reform, *A Nation Still at Risk: An Education Manifesto,* April 30, 1998, at the Internet site of the Center for Education reform.

16. "The designers of the NAEP project took extreme care . . . Office Technology Assessment, *Testing in America's Schools: Asking the Right Questions* (Washington, D.C., U.S. Government Printing Office, March 1992), p. 91.

17. Commenting on the safeguards built into the NAEP . . . Lyle V. Jones, "National Tests and Education Reform: Are They Compatible?" William H. Angoff Memorial Lecture Series, Educational Testing Service, 1997.

⚍ CRITICAL REFLECTIONS

1. In the early section of this chapter, Sacks summarizes the damage that standardized assessments have caused to the system of education. Focus on one of these points (you choose which one) and apply it to your own school experience. Does your argument support or refute Sacks's analysis? How does it?

2. Sacks makes the point that "the accountability movement has sustained, and been sustained by, a big but comfortable lie: that schools themselves are the agent for social and economic change, rather than a reflection and reinforcer of existing social and economic divisions" (328).

   Choose one aspect of your previous education, or of the previous education of someone you know well, as a test case for this argument. Focus specifically on one aspect of your education—curriculum, classroom environment, expectations, or something else. What evidence does it provide for or against Sacks's point?

3. Sacks argues that to "do no harm," schools must adopt a new purpose: "Provide citizens an opportunity to learn and ensure that those opportunities are equal across lines of class and race" (329). What would the curriculum in such a school system look like?

⚏ MAKING CONNECTIONS

1. In this chapter, Sacks argues that

> If social engineers had set out to invent a virtually perfect inequality ma- chine, designed to perpetuate race and class divisions . . . those engineers could do no better than the present-day accountability systems already put to use in American schools (329).

Use this quote as a lens for reading one or more of the literacy narratives in this text—choose from Cedric's story or a piece written by Mike Rose, Frederick Douglass, Booker T. Washington, or Lorene Cary. Does reading that experience through this lens lead you to recast it (either from your previous understanding of it, or from the way that it is cast in the chapter)? If it does, how do you recast it, and why? If it doesn't, why doesn't it?

2. "Do No Harm" was written in 1999, three years before the passage of George W. Bush's *No Child Left Behind* Education Act. Review the primary points of that act (found here on pages 308–312). Do you think the act will alleviate or perpetuate the problems raised by Sacks? How?

JAMES TRAUB

THE TEST MESS

"The Test Mess" appeared in *The New York Times Magazine* in April 2002, as students in schools across New York City were preparing to take the Regents Exams for that academic year. As the article notes, the Regents exams have taken on increased importance in New York Schools; students who do not pass the exams do not graduate from high school. Yet, as Traub notes, schools representing a range of students and a range of communities have problems with the exams. Coincidentally, only weeks after this article was published, a New York City parent noticed that the authors of the Regents Exam altered sections of texts—passages from Kofi Annon, Isaac Bashevis Singer, Anton Chekov, Annie Dillard—without permission from the authors or publishers, and without noting the changes.

James Traub is a contributing writer to *The New York Times Magazine* whose work often focuses on educational issues. In 1994, he published *City on a*

Hill, a book questioning whether the City College of New York (CCNY), traditionally an open-admission institution, could effectively educate the diverse students attending its various colleges.

It was late February, and Dee O'Brien was preparing her eighth-grade students for the New York State English language arts exam, which would be administered the following week. O'Brien teaches English at the Hommocks Middle School in the Mamaroneck school district, a comfy corner of the Westchester suburbs. She is not exactly a traditionalist: the kids were sitting in a big circle, and they all talked excitedly at once, addressing her as "Dee." This is not quite the way I remembered junior high, but in recent decades a highly progressive species of education, with interdisciplinary units and history fairs and do-it-yourself science projects, has become an upper-middle-class suburban birthright.

And here O'Brien was drilling her kids to prepare for a test obviously designed for—well, there was no very delicate way to put it. Matt Szabo, a well-groomed kid with wire-rimmed specs and a black-and-white-striped rugby shirt, put this thought as circumspectly as he could: "They give this test all over the state, and we might be smarter than another county, so they have to make it at a level where everyone's going to understand it."

New York's eighth-grade E.L.A. exam, which requires students to listen to a lengthy passage and answer questions and write an essay about its central themes and details, to answer questions about written passages and also write two other essays, is well regarded in the testing world; but nobody in the class, including O'Brien, considered it an intellectually worthwhile exercise. O'Brien just wanted to get back to "Romeo and Juliet." The kids complained that the recited passages were too boneheaded to inspire the required three-page essay; they were doing their best to fill up the pages with material that wasn't too transparently irrelevant. The overall emotional climate of O'Brien's class consisted of a peculiar combination of condescension and acute anxiety. When O'Brien told a story about students last year leaving themselves no time for the "independent essay," there was a collective "Omigod." After about an hour of this teeth-gnashing, O'Brien was ready to move on, but the kids wanted to practice the multiple-choice section one more time. "Dee," one of the students called out, "can you time us?"

Just about every eighth grader at Hommocks, and just about all of their teachers, are dismayed about the state-mandated tests, which include not just English but math, science, social studies and foreign language. Over in Scarsdale, the wealthier suburb next door, the moms are fighting mad; last year, more than half of the eighth-grade parents took their children home when the tests were given. Indeed, in Scarsdales and Mamaronecks all over this great land, educators and parents and, of course, kids are fulminating over a regime of state-administered testing that has now become nearly universal. They believe, of course, in "standards"—the very essence of their culture is high achievement—but they do not like the content of the tests, the number of tests, the way the tests have distorted the curriculum, the way they are scored, the way they are used to judge students, teachers, schools and real-estate value. And they feel as if life is pressured enough as it is; why, now, this?

5   It is, to be sure, highly premature to predict an uprising of the soccer moms. For at least the last decade, few promises have had more appeal to middle-class voters than "I will raise standards." And in December, Congress overwhelmingly passed President Bush's education bill. The new law has some very important provisions designed to increase the number of certified teachers and to promulgate phonics-based reading instruction, but at its core there is a requirement that all states devise standards for English and math and institute tests in Grades 3 through 8 to see that the standards are being met. "Standards-based reform" has thus become the central thrust of federal education policy, as it already was in most states. And evidence has begun to accumulate that low-performing students and schools have higher test scores in the face of more rigorous expectations.

The prospect is for an increasingly stiff dose of testing; and yet the politics of the situation are by no means obvious. The test critics are forever citing the supposed damage that standards-based reform wreaks not only on their own children but also on disadvantaged students. But Amy Wilkins, a policy analyst for the Education Trust, an organization that strongly backs testing as a tool for bringing equity to the schools, says that she finds it infuriating "to hear the soccer moms say these tests are bad for black children." On the other hand, she recognizes the political power of affluent suburbanites. The backlash, Wilkins prophesies, "is only beginning." In February, New Jersey's commissioner of education, William L. Librera, acting on a promise made to voters by the state's new governor, James E. McGreevey, announced the elimination of several mandated tests in Grades 4, 8 and 11. The governor of Virginia, Mark Warner, also vowed in last year's race to modify the state's "standards of learning"; suburban voters are still waiting for him to make good. "Too much testing" is a bandwagon that has only begun to roll.

The United States has never had an "educational system"; what it has had is 15,000 or so school districts, which decide more or less for themselves how and what to teach and what students need to learn in order to move from grade to grade, or to graduate. This nonsystem system has preserved the autonomy of schools and school districts, but it has also had the effect of ensuring that while communities that demand high educational standards have schools that reflect them, communities that care about football get football and communities too careworn or hapless to make demands at all get very little, unless they are lucky.

Americans pretty much took this self-perpetuating system for granted until about 20 years ago, when a series of alarming studies, above all the 1983 report "A Nation at Risk," called attention to how far American students lagged behind the rest of the developed world in virtually all subjects. The difference was quantified easily enough: students in other industrialized nations were taking a far more rigorous academic program than were typical Americans. Our competitors had not only a different kind of academic culture but also a different system. Most had either a prescribed national curriculum or highly specified national standards, with end-of-the-year exams to test whether students had mastered the prescribed material.

The distinctive American answer to this problem was standards-based reform, a not particularly coordinated effort by individual reformers, institutions and states to articulate the academic standards that children should be reaching and then to devise tests aligned with those standards and "accountability" measures to attach consequences to success or failure. Although the most straightforward solution to poor academic achievement might well have been the same kind of national curriculum that seems to work well elsewhere in the world, it became plain early on that our own answer would be neither national nor curricular. The first President Bush tried, and failed, to promulgate a voluntary national curriculum; President Clinton tried, and failed, to create a series of voluntary national tests. (Neither even contemplated a mandatory national system.) And so the action came at the state level. Starting in the mid-80's, individual states, including Texas and California, began to create their own systems of standards or "curriculum frameworks," though in most cases these were pitched at a level of generality that made them close to useless. By now, virtually every state has developed its own version of standards-based reform. Yet according to a recent study by the American Federation of Teachers, none of them have yet created a coherent system of standards, curriculum, tests and accountability measures. We have, in effect, 50 approximations of a European or Asian school system; the new Bush education law is intended not to knit them into one but to ensure that each of them operates in such a way as to improve student performance.

10   New York State is a good example both of the traditional system of autonomy and of the new ethos of high-standards-for-all. For decades, better students in New York had been graduating with a Regents diploma, which signified that they had passed the academic curriculum established by the state Board of Regents; others had received a "local" diploma, which meant they had satisfied bare-bones requirements. In recent years, only 20 percent of New York City students who graduated received a Regents diploma. This meant that an elite slice of kids was being prepared for college, while the rest—and above all minority students— were being coaxed through school on a diet of "business math" and the like. These students were graduating from high school hopelessly unprepared for the demands of the modern workplace. In 1997, the Board of Regents, which oversees education in the state, agreed to phase in a requirement that all students take Regents courses and pass the exams in the major subjects. The Regents would thus become an "exit test" for high-school graduation. At the same time, the state concluded that the only way to end this two-track system was to specify academic standards from elementary school. The Regents approved standards in each grade in the major subject areas.

Tests in math and English language arts in the fourth and eighth grades were administered for the first time in 1999. The initial numbers were grim: only 48 percent of fourth graders passed the English language arts test, though the numbers were higher in math. The test-score rankings were almost indistinguishable from the socioeconomic scale, with wealthy suburbs on top and the big cities on the bottom.

In Mount Vernon, a formerly Italian and now heavily black suburb of New York City, not far south of Scarsdale and Mamaroneck in Westchester County, the students managed to do even worse than their demographics would have suggested: only 36 percent of fourth graders and 24 percent of eighth graders passed the E.L.A. test. The year before, the town hired a new superintendent, Ronald Ross, the first black chief administrator in the city's history; he seized on the dreadful statistics and the sense of anger and humiliation they provoked as a lever to force change in the schools. He won a 10 percent increase in the school budget, and he used the new money to hire assistant principals for the elementary schools, thus freeing principals to focus on the classroom; and he hired a reading specialist, Alice Siegel, from the public-school system in affluent Greenwich, Conn.

Ross decided to concentrate his attentions initially on the fourth grade in one school, the Longfellow School, where 13 percent of children had passed the E.L.A. test. And here, too, Ross used the shocking results for his own purposes. When teachers bridled at change, Ross, an imperious figure with a misleadingly whispery voice, said: "You can leave, or you can try it my way. Why can't we try it your way? Because your way got 13 percent." He and Siegel replaced what had passed for the curriculum with a single-minded focus on the skills required for the test—which is to say that they decided to explicitly *teach to the test.* "The longer and more difficult way," Ross says, "would have been 'Let's decide what to teach.' We never had to have that debate. We analyzed the entire New York State test, and we said, 'What are the broader areas that this test looks at?' "

The academic value of this exercise depends, of course, on whether the test assesses skills important for a fourth grader to master. There seems to be a very wide consensus that the E.L.A. test does just that. Last year's reading comprehension portion, for example, asked students to read both a story and a poem about a whale and expected them to chart the chronology of the story, to understand the imagery of the poem and to write an essay using information from both. The "listening" portion of the test expected students to take notes as they listened to another story and to provide both short answers and a longer essay demonstrating that they understood the narrative.

15   What does it mean to prepare for such a test? Siegel instituted a policy in which every child would take home a book every night and read for at least 30 minutes; the children wrote in every subject, and the teachers drilled into them the difference between an essay that would earn a 4 on the E.L.A. test, indicating "mastery," and one that would merit only a 3, for "proficiency." They learned a graphic system for taking notes. They took lots of sample tests. And it worked: in 2000, Longfellow's pass rate on the English test made a staggering leap to 82 from 13. And since some of these changes had been made system-wide, overall half the fourth graders in Mount Vernon passed. The increase in math scores was almost as steep. And the improvement persisted: last year, 74 percent of students passed the English exam. Fourth graders in Mount Vernon outperformed many of the state's middle-class suburbanites, thus severing the link between socioeconomic status and academic outcome.

In New York, as in many other states, standards-based reform has done more for younger children than for older ones, who suffer the consequences of years of indifferent schooling. The principle certainly holds true in Mount Vernon, where a grand total of 20 percent of eighth graders in Mount Vernon passed the E.L.A. test in 2000. It's reasonable to hope that as the more successful fourth graders reach middle school, they'll do much better; if they don't, Mount Vernon's experiment will have failed. But in the meanwhile, Ross and Siegel have turned their attention to middle school. When I paid a visit to the Davis Middle School, one of Mount Vernon's two junior highs, the principal, Judith Kronin, told me that she had at first assumed that the children would improve their test scores if she assigned more reading and writing exercises. When that failed, it became obvious that the school had to try something new.

Kronin took me over to Mark Molina's eighth-grade English class, where the kids were sitting in the traditional configuration of rows and columns. It was about six weeks before the E.L.A. test, which is given later in eighth grade than in fourth and has much the same design, though of course pitched at a harder level. As I walked in, Molina, a bouncy young guy who keeps a pencil tucked behind his ear, was preparing the kids to write short answers about a sample test passage on Nepal. They talked about possible openings. One girl, Stacy, suggested the sentence. "Using details from the selection, I'm going to describe the geography of Nepal." Molina nodded and then added, "Stay away from 'I.' But using 'The geography of Nepal,' there's another way. You could say, 'The geography of Nepal is,' and then you get in to describe it. Write this down, everybody." And on the blackboard, he wrote, "The geography of Nepal is." Molina then gave the class 12 minutes to actually read the passage, which they hadn't yet done, and to write out a proper answer.

Meanwhile, I leafed through the class textbook. It was titled "Aim Higher English Language Arts, Level H." The book was divided into sections: Test; Pretest; Exam Overview; Listening, Reading and Writing; and Post-test. One chapter even included multiple-choice questions about the coming exam: "Section 1, Part 1 of the English language arts exam deals mostly with. . . . " I looked back up. Molina said, "Five minutes, guys!"

Here was test preparation with a vengeance. The textbook was a training manual, and the curriculum was the test. This was just the kind of "drill and kill" exercise that progressive educators and pamphleteers describe as the inevitable consequence of a regimen of standardized testing. Nobody defends this kind of regimented pedagogy; advocates of standards-based reform insist that the best test preparation is the teaching of a rich curriculum; proponents actually agree with critics that tests that you can prep for aren't worth giving. "There is no such thing as test preparation," as Diane Ravitch, one of the chief intellectual authors of the standards movement, said to me. "The best preparation is to read Charles Dickens or George Orwell or other classic literature which has vocabulary you're not familiar with." That may be the ideal case, but it's not the reality. James Kadamus, deputy commissioner of the New York State Education Department, grudgingly conceded to me that test prep is probably "the norm" in failing districts.

20   It's a truth that might as well be acknowledged, if only because schools under the gun are going to adopt whatever seems like the most expedient policy in order to succeed. More important, test prep—at least good test prep—works. One morning I sat in on the weekly meeting of eighth-grade English teachers at Davis

and listened as they talked about teaching kids to restate a test question, to take coherent notes, to distinguish between a detail and the general statement it supported. One teacher said that she had been working with kids on a story that contained words too archaic for them to recognize—words like "foe." When they finished, I asked the Diane Ravitch question: Why not just teach them Orwell and supply the vocabulary words? Alice Siegel said, "What they're all saying is that with the skill level the kids came in with, we have to take the information and bring it down to their skill level." Most of these students were reading a few grades behind their own level. The fact that they probably couldn't have made sense of Orwell was the symptom, not the problem; the problem was that they had reached eighth grade without mastering the cognitive devices that better-educated children learn unconsciously, as a precipitate of their reading and studying.

It was an ugly form of pedagogy, and I said as much. Siegel is one of those intensely earthbound idealists who often make a home for themselves in the schools. She is a blond, brassy, Rosemary Clooney sort, and dogma makes her eyeballs roll. Now she said: "It's the same thing as whole language and phonics. If you said that you wanted to teach phonics, they said that you hated children. With whole language, it was very nice. You sat there with a big book, and everybody sat there blah blah blah. But everybody needs to know how to attack a word they don't know how to pronounce." In the world of education, a great deal of moral power attaches to practices that are aesthetically appealing; but justice is very often better served by the merely effective.

Siegel will learn if she's right when the test results come back at the end of the year. Even if the kids do better, though, it's fair to ask whether the price has been too high—whether all this test prep has killed whatever residual fondness the kids had for school or learning. Davis held a "Saturday Academy," a euphemism for an extra two hours of voluntary test prep. The teachers insist, implausibly, that the kids show up well before 9 and wait for the doors to open.

I arrived early one cold morning, and there, indeed, were about 50 kids standing on Davis's grand front stairway. About 130 students in all eventually came—almost a third of the grade. They walked into class, yakked with their friends, listened quietly while the teacher told them to underline important details in the story and then got to work on the short-answer portion of a sample test. I talked to a dozen or so kids during the break, and they all said that they came to Saturday academy voluntarily, and most of them said they liked it. The kids in Scarsdale could have been playing tennis, but these children had very little else to do on a Saturday morning. One girl, who kept her red ski jacket on all through the class, said that she so enjoyed the exercise of reading texts and learning to pull meaning out of them that she had started to read more on her own. Many of the kids were reading "Harry Potter" at home. And when they went over the short-answer questions, a good two-thirds of the kids scored 25 out of 25. I may be wrong, but I would have sworn they were having a good time.

The bipartisan enthusiasm that accompanied George W. Bush's education reform bill offered incontrovertible proof of the political appeal of standards-based reform. But many educators and academics view the standards movement as a catastrophic mistake and as a cynical ploy designed to distract attention from "real" reform. Progressive educators believe that neither children nor schools will or even should respond to externally imposed standards and reel in horror at the data-driven, goal-oriented pedagogy induced by the new testing regime. And civil rights advocates argue that it is both unjust and unrealistic to expect disadvantaged students to achieve higher standards until we spend more money on inner-city schools. As Richard Elmore, a Harvard professor of education, writes in the current issue of *Education Next,* a journal of school reform: "Low-performing schools, and the people who work in them, don't know what to do. If they did, they would be doing it already. You can't improve a school's performance, or the performance of any teacher or student in it, without increasing the investment in teachers' knowledge, pedagogical skills and understanding of students."

25   The issue is so profoundly ideological that it is very unlikely that it will be definitively settled by research data. And there is in any case a fierce debate over the data, especially in Texas, which President Bush has pointed to as proof that standards-based reform works. But one reason that the standards-and-testing element of the new education law found such broad support is that many independent scholars and experts have been persuaded that the system does work in Texas. A recent study by the RAND Corporation concluded that Texas and North Carolina, both of which have extensive and relatively longstanding systems of standards and testing, scored significantly better on the National Assessment of Education Progress, a widely regarded test of basic skills, than their demographic makeup would have predicted, and attributed the difference to a combination of prudent spending and standards-based reform. In last year's fourth-grade N.A.E.P. tests in math, black and Hispanic children in Texas outscored black and Hispanic students in every state in the country, while whites in Texas tied Connecticut for the top spot. (Eighth-grade Texans fall closer to the middle.) And of course the success of school systems like. Mount Vernon's undermines the claim that the failures of bad schools are too deep-rooted to be seriously affected by the imposition of new standards (though Ronald Ross, Mount Vernon's superintendent, would agree with civil rights advocates that more spending is crucial).

The new federal law is designed to compel each state to develop its own coherent system of standards-based reform. The states have five years to devise standards and tests. They will be expected to raise all students to "proficiency" levels over the next 12 years, and they will have to administer the N.A.E.P. test every other year in order to provide an external check to their internal measures. But a combination of liberals worried about tests and conservatives worried about federal power blunted the law's bite. Nothing prevents states from designing wishy-washy standards and tests and from defining "proficiency" so modestly that everybody succeeds—though Rod Paige, Bush's secretary of education, argues that the law's highly detailed reporting requirement will shame lagging states into cleaning up their acts. Some of the more ardent bearers of standards worry that the law will turn out to be an anticlimax. "It will tip some states that are on the border of doing the right thing over into the camp of doing it," predicts Chester E. Finn Jr., a former Reagan administration education official. "I don't think it will have any effect on the states that are completely clueless about all this or that don't want to or don't know how to."

Let us stipulate, then, that the strong medicine of standards-based reform can act as a powerful tonic, at least when intelligently administered. The next question is "Is it worth the side effects?" And the answer appears to be "It depends how sick you feel."

Even in Mount Vernon, the teachers felt wistful about the sacrifice of good books, at least until after the test; but that sacrifice often seems intolerable to parents and teachers—and children—in schools where the issue is excellence, not competence. And here we come to the problem created by our nonsystem system, in which matters of teaching and curriculum in any given school or school district reflect not some broadly shared set of principles about schooling but the preferences and standards of that community. Schools that already consider themselves excellent bridle at the idea of being held to standards imposed by state education authorities, not only because it is a nuisance but because it seems pointless. The folks in Scarsdale rebelled only when the state added science and social studies tests in the eighth grade, thus forcing many teachers to miss well over a week of class time in order to prepare for, administer and grade the tests, and to curtail such beloved interdisciplinary, multiweek projects as "the hurricane unit" and "the Colonial fair." One agitated parent said to me: "We in Scarsdale have this state-of-the-art digital science equipment; but the science test used a triple-beam balance. Those triple-beam balances were put away many, many years ago. We had to take them out of the closet and refurbish them. My seventh grader was taught this year to use a triple-beam balance." The parents in Scarsdale have trouble understanding how they can benefit from standards lower than the ones they apply to themselves.

It is not always so clear-cut that the high-performing suburbs are superior to the test. Often the standards, and the tests, assume a kind of traditional pedagogy that has gone out of fashion, especially in liberal suburbs or university towns. Thus when Virginia instituted its "standards of learning" tests in 1998, the failure rate in the suburbs was almost as high as in the backwoods. Roughly 65 percent of students in the state failed the social studies test, which assumed detailed knowledge of dates, places and events. The state is now phasing in a rule accrediting schools when 70 percent of their students pass each test; the first year, 3 percent of state schools qualified for accreditation. Even in wealthy Fairfax County, the figure was only 7 percent. After an interval of shock and soul-searching, teachers realized that they would have to prepare students much more explicitly for the tests. Fairfax is now up to 80 percent; but Daniel Domenech, the county superintendent, says that the new focus "has substantially diverted attention from a broader and richer curriculum." Exactly how unfortunate an outcome this is probably depends on your view of the kind of old-fashioned curriculum the Virginia tests assume. For example, the fifth-grade "Reading/Literature and Research" test expected students to be able to distinguish among rhyme schemes and recognize free verse. Is that so bad?

30   Whatever the merits of the case, Fairfax County parents appear to agree with their superintendent. Last year, Geoffrey Garin, a Democratic pollster, convened focus groups of suburban parents for Mark Warner, the gubernatorial candidate. When he asked a general question about how things were going in the state, parents turned immediately to the standards of learning. "Parents complained bitterly about a curriculum that is structured around teaching to the test and that crowds out other learning," Garin says. Warner got the picture and promised to reform the standards to reflect "real learning," a phrase that is shorthand for a focus on broad skills rather than particular content. Warner's Republican opponent never enthusiastically defended the standards. Garin says that the next frontier may be Florida, where the Democrat Bill McBride has taken to criticizing state tests that are also viewed as hostile to "real learning."

In virtually every state that has both an extensive system of standards-based reform and a network of wealthy suburbs, you can tap a fairly deep vein of disenchantment among parents and, especially, teachers. North Carolina, for example, is widely considered an exemplary state in the world of standards-based reform. Students in every grade from three to eight take tests in the core subjects, and, unlike New York's, the tests have real consequences. Students who fail the benchmark tests in third and fifth grade can be left back, though as a matter of course they rarely are. And schools are judged by how much they increase a student's test performance from year to year; every teacher in a successful school receives a $1,500 bonus. Schools that hit the mark often put up a big sign announcing their status, the way the state soccer champion might elsewhere.

The teachers that I talked to complained about the tremendous pressure from the community—and from their own self-interest—to keep their exalted status. As the writing test was looming, Diane Leusky, who teaches fourth grade at Ephesus Elementary School, a perennially high-scoring school in Chapel Hill, said: "I've spent the last six weeks doing preparation for narrative writing; I focus strictly on the narrative form. The biggest thing I've got is five parent volunteers whom I've trained." Save for the parents, it sounded a good deal like Mount Vernon, with the all-important difference that Leusky couldn't stand it.

Mamaroneck is a perfect example of the suburban conundrum. The town is approximately equidistant from Scarsdale and Mount Vernon, and it falls in between them socioeconomically as well. On the drive eastward from Scarsdale, you pass the immense Tudor clubhouse of the Bonnie Briar Country Club; and Larchmont, one of the two villages that make up the town of Mamaroneck, has high, manicured shrubbery, Land Rovers in the driveways and tennis ladies. But while the other village, which is also called Mamaroneck, has some ritzy neighborhoods of its own, it also houses a sizable black-and-white working and middle class as well as recent Hispanic immigrants. Mamaroneck was the kind of place people moved to for the schools, and there was never any reason to think of the schools as inferior to those in the more glamorous precincts of Scarsdale, Bronxville or Chappaqua. But then New York State administered new tests and also released the results in a format that compared each school with a demographically similar school. And suddenly the Mamaroneck schools didn't look quite so sterling. A quarter of fourth graders failed the E.L.A. test (almost twice as many as in Scarsdale), while the number was much higher in the two more "diverse" schools in the town. Some parents were upset; real-estate agents were mortified. One of them, Liz Sauer, said, "We were getting questions from the people we just sold houses to, people who were coming out from the city." Sherri King, the school superintendent, had to make the rounds of the real-estate agencies to put out the fire. She was asked, as Sauer puts it, "to help us communicate to our customers how to interpret these scores." King appears to have explained, if not in so many words, that the children of the kind of people who worried about their home values did just fine in Mamaroneck.

The general feeling among parents, teachers and administrators in Mamaroneck is that they would like to ignore the tests, but they can't. One fourth-grade teacher, Stefan Kuczinski, said, "My kids do so well on the tests because I reinforce them every day." But then he added, "I don't know anyone who wants to teach fourth grade"—a sentiment that you hear repeated all the time. Mamaroneck appears to harbor very few ideologues, for I met scarcely anybody who objected to standardized tests per se. It wasn't the tests but their effects that troubled the citizenry. The tests brought with them a kind of pressure that made life less pleasant without offering any compensating benefits. One parent, Ellen Payne, said: "If you have a child who's average, you get very, very worried about the test. The test puts an enormous pressure on them, and as a parent I find that very, very upsetting. I was very nervous and anxious about it. Fourth grade is a lot more nerve-racking; it's ridiculous the amount of pressure they put on them."

35   I often wondered, in the midst of these conversations, whether it was the parent or the child who was feeling the most pressure. I asked fourth graders in Mamaroneck and Mount Vernon whether they had felt frightened about the E.L.A. test. And while I found one little girl who said that she had had a nightmare—"I was being chased by a book"—few of them dredged up anything like the trepidation that I heard from adults.

Testing plays into parents' fears about their children and into their sense of status. Edie Roth, a former head of the P.T.A. at Central, a "diverse" school, said that when Central beat out Chatsworth, the town's toniest elementary school, "you'd think we had just been awarded a million-dollar grant to build a new library. It was like this huge breakthrough. It's joked about, because you feel uncomfortable admitting it's important—but it is important."

Mamaroneck complains about the tests much less than Scarsdale, but in some ways it is more affected by them. Parents, teachers and administrators in Scarsdale made a collective decision over the last few years that they would pay as little attention to the tests as possible. Scarsdale could afford to do this because the culture of the schools is the exact opposite of the culture that has brought standards-based reform into being: the internal pressure to succeed according to the highest standards is so intense that external motivations are superfluous. And so in the eighth-grade English class I sat in on at the Scarsdale Middle School in the weeks leading up to the E.L.A. test, the kids were wearing masks and cloaks and performing a scene from "Romeo and Juliet," which they planned on studying for a good eight weeks.

In Mamaroneck, "Romeo and Juliet" turned out to be a luxury that simply couldn't be afforded. Dee O'Brien, the eighth-grade English teacher, was also an actress and theater producer; she had planned a comprehensive unit on the play until she suddenly realized, in December, that the E.L.A. test had been moved up from June to March. As she said to the class the day I was there, "That whole project got knocked to smithereens because we couldn't juggle the time between finishing the project and doing the practice for this exam." And so O'Brien handed out sample tests and had her students give them to one another to evaluate. They had practiced taking notes for the listening section, though they found some of the passages so odd that they had to write down everything in order to make sense of it. They had tried to game the system.

"We all agreed that they would not use Sept. 11," O'Brien said, "but they thought maybe patriotism." O'Brien promised that as soon as the test was over, "we're going to start all over again as if it's a new year." The kids seemed genuinely upset about missing out on Shakespeare. And the very fact that they had to undergo this mind-numbing preparation instead for a test that had absolutely no bearing on their grades or on their ability to get into the highly selective colleges of their choice struck them as cosmically unfair. One student, Beth Shook, complained, "It matters for the school, but not for your future individually." And then her girlfriends chorused, "Like the SAT's!"

40   After class, I asked O'Brien the Diane Ravitch question: Why not just teach Shakespeare? She said, "One of the reasons I prep them is to allay their anxiety." Actually, the prepping seemed to increase their anxiety, but I don't think that O'Brien felt that she could afford to be so blithe with her kids as the Scarsdale teachers did with theirs. There was no compact between parents and teachers allowing her to let the chips fall where they may; and she could not afford to assume that her charges would do just fine on their own. What if other teachers got better results than she did? And so she, too, was teaching to the test, but without much faith in its efficacy. It was something she accepted rather than embraced. And she kept coming back to how much she missed Shakespeare.

In Cambridge, Mass., the epicenter of the anti-testing movement, I sat earlier this year at a breakfast table piled high with leaflets and talked with Jonathan King, father of two, professor of molecular biology at M.I.T. and charter member of the Coalition for Authentic Reform in Education, or CARE. King's children are in the 6th and 10th grades, and last year, like several hundred other students, they did not take the state tests, known as the M.C.A.S., because their parents did not want them to. King said he believed that the tests were turning the schools into "a police state" in which educational drill substituted for education. And while the tests, he said, were a colossal waste of time for his children, they were, he insisted, a catastrophe for minorities, who would soon be dropping out in large numbers as the state began withholding diplomas from students who had not passed the exit tests. "You're going to see in the next few years something that's never existed in the United States," King vowed. "Organizations of parents in defense of public education." It was King's belief that boycotts would soon be breaking out all over the country.

CARE is a most unlikely vehicle for a national campaign against testing: the group's chairwoman, Jean McGuire, described the M.C.A.S. in a recent newsletter as a device for "sorting and labeling," like "the yellow star" and "the N-word." And in fact, CARE was unsuccessful in its initial political campaign, whose goal was to get the State Legislature to repeal the tests. Nevertheless, King is plainly right that graduation tests raise the stakes of standards-based reform to the highest pitch. One reason state-level tests have provoked more grumbling and rumbling than outright protest is that most of the consequences of them fall on schools rather than students. And the same is true of the new federal education law, which provides special opportunities for children who attend failing schools but has no provision for holding back children who fail to pass the tests. But an increasing number of states have come to the conclusion that students should not be permitted to graduate from high school unless they can pass tests in the core subjects. These tests pose very little danger to successful school districts, but they constitute a fearsome reality check in average or below-average school systems.

Texas is one of the few states that have administered exit tests for many years, and opponents of testing have rallied behind findings by Walter Haney, a scholar at Boston College, that the tests have led to enormous numbers of students being held back in ninth grade, before the test, and then dropping out later. (Pro-testing researchers have challenged Haney's conclusions.) When Massachusetts administered its exit tests the year before last, initially to 10th graders, close to 80 percent of black and Hispanic students failed the math portion. That year, the results did not count; the following year, when they did, the number dropped to almost 50 percent. *The Boston Globe* recently noted that "the vision of large numbers of seniors locked out of graduation exercises is starting to fade." But no one is ruling out the possibility of at least a minor train wreck. And if a significant number of minority students are denied diplomas, the politics of standards-based reform could change in a hurry. High expectations might not look like a civil right after all.

Most states have postponed exit tests rather than face the music. When Arizona, to take perhaps the most extreme example, first administered its exit tests to 10th graders in 1999, 88 percent failed math, 72 percent failed writing and 38 percent failed reading. That was scarcely surprising: the state had done little to raise the academic standards of the children reaching 10th grade. Arizona immediately pushed back the day of reckoning when students would have to pass the tests from 2001 to a phased-in period from 2002 to 2004. A consultant then suggested that 2005 might be a more prudent date. The state is now shooting for 2006 and has agreed that students who fail the tests will have "an equivalent demonstration opportunity," which sounds suspiciously like the kind of two-track system that exit tests are meant to abolish. The whole episode is a painful proof of the absurdity of thinking that testing, all by itself, will raise the academic performance of children who have muddled along in school for years. This is the kind of delusion that can make standards-based reform look like a conservative species of naïveté.

45   At the bottom of the conundrum of testing is a problem in the nature of policy, and underneath that a problem in the nature of human understanding. The policy problem is that, for political reasons, you cannot go around making exceptions for people who feel they can do without some given reform. Scarsdale and several other elite school systems have, for example, sought to come up with

an alternative form of assessment to satisfy the state but have been told that they must invent a scientifically sound standardized test of their own—an enormous undertaking. The real point is that New York State is not about to create an exemption for rich suburbs and a few other exemplary schools, whether they deserve it or not. Michael McGill, the Scarsdale superintendent, asks: "So we're taking tests so that everybody will be treated the same? We're not taking tests so that the results will be better?" The answer appears to be "That's right."

The problem of human understanding is that people do not readily grasp a reality radically different from their own. It is, for example, taken for granted among activist Scarsdale parents, as it is among the crusaders at CARE, that testing is even more harmful for disadvantaged children than it is for their own, that "drill and kill" can only crush young minds, that the real problem is money, et cetera. I asked a group of 13 Scarsdale mothers who had gathered to evangelize me if any of them had ever spent a significant amount of time in an inner-city school. There was an embarrassed silence; they hadn't. The truth was that they simply couldn't imagine a school where eighth graders didn't know the meaning of "foe" and hadn't acquired the skills that their children had acquired unconsciously.

And yet the Scarsdales of the world have a reality, too, and that reality is likewise invisible from behind the veil of policy certitudes. Whenever I asked, either in Albany or Washington, about suburban dissenters, I was told that they must have something to hide, that they couldn't face the fact that 10 percent of the kids, or whatever, were failing and that in any case their claims of hardship were preposterously overblown. But that's not so, either. In places like Scarsdale, school is communal identity. Those hurricane units and Colonial fairs are what Scarsdale is about, as those performances of "Romeo and Juliet" are what Mamaroneck is about. These schools are extensions of the community—not of the state. And to one degree or another, the communities see the new doctrine of one-standard-for-all as an assault on their cherished particularity. They see in a reform whose goal is to level students up a threat to level their students down. As one only mildly ironical Scarsdale mother said to me, "It's such an intrusion, and it makes you want to just move to Connecticut."

≋ CRITICAL REFLECTIONS

1. Traub argues that the U.S. has never had an educational system, but local districts which set their own priorities instead. Consider the priorities of your school. Do your experiences support Traub's assertion?

2. Traub explains that standards-based reform was an effort to address concerns rising out of *A Nation at Risk*. What do you think Traub means by "standards-based reform"?

3. Traub describes how Ronald Ross, chief administrator of the Mount Vernon (NY) schools, shifted the curriculum when he arrived. How do you interpret this shift? What is your position on Ross's curricular approach, and why do you take the stand you do?

4. Traub refers to differences between the ideal and the reality of preparation for standardized assessment. Do you agree with his assessment of both? Why or why not?

5. How do you account for the disparity between scores in suburban and inner-city districts? Based on your response, do you think that standardized assessments or standardized tests are fair? Why or why not?

≋ MAKING CONNECTIONS

1. Reflecting on your analysis of the New York State and Texas exams, what is being tested and, therefore, taught? What is not being tested, and therefore not taught?

2. In "My 54-Year Love Affair with the SAT," Stanley Kaplan writes that the SAT is a great leveler among students because everyone is treated equally. The New York State Regents' Exam is intended to act much like Kaplan's version of the SAT, gauging all students equally. Based on reading "The Test Mess," "The Last Shot," and "Fierce Intimacies," do you think that standardized testing and standardized assessment "level the playing field" for students who are graduating from high school and entering college?

3. In the interviews with Nicholas Lemann and Diane Ravitch in this book, both advocate for a national assessment program. Do you find a difference between the kind of testing on the E.L.A. exam and the kind of test that they want? Why or why not?

4. Lemann and Peter Sacks both refer to the National Educational Assessment Program, or NAEP, as a valid test. What do you see as the differences between what they say about the NAEP and what Traub implies about the E.L.A. exam?

5. Summarize Traub's concluding argument in "The Test Mess" and consider it in light of David Barton and Mary Hamilton's "Local Literacies." Do you think that school curricula should help to form, or even reflect, local identities? Why or why not?

BOOKER T. WASHINGTON

THE ATLANTA EXPOSITION ADDRESS

Booker T. Washington (1856–1915) delivered this address at the Atlanta Cotton States and International Exposition in 1895. Washington was the only African-American asked to address the Exposition, which as its name indicated was devoted to the cotton industry in the southern United States.

Washington's appearance at the Exposition raised controversy in the African-American intellectual community, since Washington himself was born into slavery on a plantation and the cotton industry had been supported, sometimes literally, on the backs of slaves.

The Atlanta address in many ways captures some of the many paradoxes of Washington's career. As the founder and director of the Tuskegee Institute, later Tuskegee University, Washington recruited students and worked tirelessly to keep his institution, which was devoted to the education of black people, going. Yet, Tuskegee's purpose was not to educate students to be leaders, but instead to fit into the newly reunited post-Civil War nation. At Tuskegee, therefore, students learned not to advocate for change, but to assimilate. These ideas, embedded in the Atlanta Address, led many to refer to it as the "Atlanta Compromise." At the same time as Washington developed this position, he was a prominent leader in the African-American community. Washington carefully crafted his own image so that he would not seem threatening to whites, who supported his various endeavors, including Tuskegee and the National Negro Business League (which worked for African-American economic independence).

Washington's views on African-American assimilation and education are frequently contrasted with those of W.E.B. DuBois, who held very different beliefs about the role of black citizens in American culture. (DuBois's critique of Washington, "On Mr. Booker T. Washington and Others," appears on pages 222–231.)

The Atlanta Exposition, at which I had been asked to make an address as a representative of the Negro race, as stated in the last chapter, was opened with a short address from Governor Bullock. After other interesting exercises, including an invocation from Bishop Nelson, of Georgia, a dedicatory ode by Albert Howell, Jr., and addresses by the President of the Exposition and Mrs. Joseph Thompson, the President of the Woman's Board, Governor Bullock introduced me with the words, "We have with us to-day a representative of Negro enterprise and Negro civilization."

When I arose to speak, there was considerable cheering, especially from the coloured people. As I remember it now, the thing that was uppermost in my mind was the desire to say something that would cement the friendship of the races and bring about hearty cooperation between them. So far as my outward surroundings were concerned, the only thing that I recall distinctly now is that when I got up, I saw thousands of eyes looking intently into my face. The following is the address which I delivered:—

Mr. President and Gentlemen of the Board of Directors and Citizens.

One-third of the population of the South is of the Negro race. No enterprise seeking the material, civil, or moral welfare of this section can disregard this element of our population and reach the highest success. I but convey to you, Mr. President and Directors, the sentiment of the masses of my race when I say that in no way have the value and manhood of the American Negro been more fittingly and generously recognized than by the managers of this magnificent

Exposition at every stage of its progress. It is a recognition that will do more to cement the friendship of the two races than any occurrence since the dawn of our freedom.

5   Not only this, but the opportunity here afforded will awaken among us a new era of industrial progress. Ignorant and inexperienced, it is not strange that in the first years of our new life we began at the top instead of at the bottom; that a seat in Congress or the state legislature was more sought than real estate or industrial skill; that the political convention of stump speaking had more attraction than starting a dairy farm or truck garden.

A ship lost at sea for many days suddenly sighted a friendly vessel. From the mast of the unfortunate vessel was seen a signal, "Water, water; we die of thirst!" The answer from the friendly vessel at once came back, "Cast down your bucket where you are." A second time the signal, "Water, water; send us water!" ran up from the distressed vessel, and was answered, "Cast down your bucket where you are." And a third and fourth signal for water was answered, "Cast down your bucket where you are." The captain of the distressed vessel, at last heeding the injunction, cast down his bucket, and it came up full of fresh, sparkling water from the mouth of the Amazon River. To those of my race who depend on bettering their condition in a foreign land or who underestimate the importance of cultivating friendly relations with the Southern white man, who is their next-door neighbour, I would say: "Cast down your bucket where you are"—cast it down in making friends in every manly way of the people of all races by whom we are surrounded.

Cast it down in agriculture, mechanics, in commerce, in domestic service, and in the professions. And in this connection it is well to bear in mind that whatever other sins the South may be called to bear, when it comes to business, pure and simple, it is in the South that the Negro is given a man's chance in the commercial world, and in nothing is this Exposition more eloquent than in emphasizing this chance. Our greatest danger is that in the great leap from slavery to freedom we may overlook the fact that the masses of us are to live by the productions of our hands, and fail to keep in mind that we shall prosper in proportion as we learn to dignify and glorify common labour and put brains and skill into the common occupations of life; shall prosper in proportion as we learn to draw the line between the superficial and the substantial, the ornamental gewgaws of life and the useful. No race can prosper till it learns that there is as much dignity in tilling a field as in writing a poem. It is at the bottom of life we must begin, and not at the top. Nor should we permit our grievances to overshadow our opportunities.

To those of the white race who look to the incoming of those of foreign birth and strange tongue and habits for the prosperity of the South, were I permitted I would repeat what I say to my own race, "Cast down your bucket where you are." Cast it down among the eight millions of Negroes whose habits you know, whose fidelity and love you have tested in days when to have proved treacherous meant the ruin of your firesides. Cast down your bucket among these people who have, without strikes and labour wars, tilled your fields, cleared your forests, builded your railroads and cities, and brought forth treasures from the bowels of the earth, and helped make possible this magnificent representation of the progress of the South. Casting down your bucket among my people, helping and encouraging them as you are doing on these grounds, and to education of head, hand, and heart, you will find that they will buy your surplus land, make blossom the waste places in your fields, and run your factories. While doing this, you can be sure in the future, as in the past, that you and your families will be surrounded by the most patient, faithful, law-abiding, and unresentful people that the world has seen. As we have proved our loyalty to you in the past, in nursing your children, watching by the sick-bed of your mothers and fathers, and often following them with tear-dimmed eyes to their graves, so in the future, in our humble way, we shall stand by you with a devotion that no foreigner can approach, ready to lay down our lives, if need be, in defence of yours, interlacing our industrial, commercial, civil, and religious life with yours in a way that shall make the interests of both races one. In all things that are purely social we can be as separate as the fingers, yet one as the hand in all things essential to mutual progress.

There is no defence or security for any of us except in the highest intelligence and development of all. If anywhere there are efforts tending to curtail the fullest growth of the Negro, let these efforts be turned into stimulating, encouraging, and making him the most useful and intelligent citizen. Effort or means so invested will pay a thousand per cent interest. These efforts will be twice blessed—"blessing him that gives and him that takes."

10   There is no escape through law of man or God from the inevitable:—

> The laws of changeless justice bind
>   Oppressor with oppressed;
> And close as sin and suffering joined
>   We march to fate abreast.

Nearly sixteen millions of hands will aid you in pulling the load upward, or they will pull against you the load downward. We shall constitute one-third and more of the ignorance and crime of the South, or one-third its intelligence and progress; we shall contribute one-third to the business and industrial prosperity of the South, or we shall prove a veritable body of death, stagnating, depressing, retarding every effort to advance the body politic.

Gentlemen of the Exposition, as we present to you our humble effort at an exhibition of our progress, you must not expect overmuch. Starting thirty years ago with ownership here and there in a few quilts and pumpkins and chickens (gathered from miscellaneous sources), remember the path that has led from these to the inventions and production of agricultural implements, buggies, steam-engines, newspapers, books, statuary, carving, paintings, the management of drug-stores and banks, has not been trodden without contact with thorns and thistles. While we take pride in what we exhibit as a result of our independent efforts, we do not for a moment forget that our part in this exhibition would fall far short of your expectations but for the constant help that has come to our educational life, not only from the Southern states, but especially from Northern philanthropists, who have made their gifts a constant stream of blessing and encouragement.

The wisest among my race understand that the agitation of questions of social equality is the extremest folly, and that progress in the enjoyment of all the privileges that will come to us must be the result of severe and constant struggle rather than of artificial forcing. No race that has anything to contribute to the markets of the world is long in any degree ostracized. It is important and right that all privileges of the law be ours, but it is vastly more important that we be prepared for the exercises of these privileges. The opportunity to earn a dollar in a factory just now is worth infinitely more than the opportunity to spend a dollar in an opera-house.

In conclusion, may I repeat that nothing in thirty years has given us more hope and encouragement, and drawn us so near to you of the white race, as this opportunity offered by the Exposition; and here bending, as it were, over the altar that represents the results of the struggles of your race and mine, both starting practically empty-handed three decades ago, I pledge that in your effort to work out the great and intricate problem which God has laid at the doors of the South, you shall have at all times the patient, sympathetic help of my race; only let this be constantly in mind, that, while from representations in these buildings of the product of field, of forest, of mine, of factory, letters, and art, much good will come, yet far above and beyond material benefits will be that higher good, that, let us pray God, will come, in a blotting out of sectional differences and racial animosities and suspicions, in a determination to administer absolute justice, in a willing obedience among all classes to the mandates of law. This, this, coupled with our material prosperity, will bring into our beloved South a new heaven and a new earth.

══ CRITICAL REFLECTIONS

1. Throughout this speech, Booker T. Washington uses an extended metaphor: "Cast down your buckets where you are." Working from the early portions of his speech, and considering the context and audience for the talk, what do you think he means in this phrase?

2. Like Frederick Douglass's *Narrative,* this speech was carefully crafted to elicit a response in its audience. After reading, what do you think the desired response is, and why do you think that that is the goal?

══ MAKING CONNECTIONS

1. In both of their selections here, Douglass and Washington discuss the connections between literacy, slavery, and their future aspirations for African-Americans. Douglass writes about the inspiration he found in *The Columbian Orator:*

   > Among . . . other interesting matter, I found in it a dialogue between a master and his slave. The slave was represented as having run away from his master three times. . . . The slave was made to say some very smart as

well as impressive things in reply to his master—things which had the desired though unexpected effect; for the conversation resulted in the voluntary emancipation of the slave on the part of his master (236).

Washington writes about what he sees as the role of African-Americans in the newly reunited nation:

> To those of the white race who look to the incoming of those of foreign birth and strange tongue and habits for the prosperity of the South, were I permitted I would repeat what I say to my own race, "Cast down your bucket where you are." . . . Casting down your bucket among my people, helping and encouraging them as you are doing on these grounds, and to education of head, hand, and heart, you will find that they will buy your surplus land, make blossom the waste places in your fields, and run your factories. While doing this, you can be sure in the future, as in the past, that you and your families will be surrounded by the most patient, faithful, law-abiding, and unresentful people that the world has seen (355–356).

Do you think that Douglass and Washington share a common vision of the purpose of literacy in the lives of African-Americans based on these passages or others in their texts? Why or why not?

2. W.E.B. DuBois's "Of Mr. Booker T. Washington and Others" is a direct challenge to Washington and particularly to the Atlanta Exposition Address (which DuBois calls "The Atlanta Compromise"). What differences do you understand between the purposes of literacy outlined by Washington and DuBois?

PHOTOGRAPHS

Mr. Leatherman's son reading in front of fireplace in dugout. Pie Town, NM (1940)

Boys read storybooks in the shade. Caldwell, ID (1941)

Washington, D.C. Mrs. Ella Watson, a government charwoman, reading the Bible to her household (1942)

Oil field workers taking time out to read the paper, Oil Well, Kilgore, TX (1939)

Construction of houses (reading plans and measuring). Jersey Homesteads, Hightown, NJ (1936)

Greensboro chief of police reading CIO picket sign at a textile mill in Greensboro, Greene County, GA. (sign reads: "Judas Betrayed His Lord for 50 PCS Silver What's your price?") (1941)

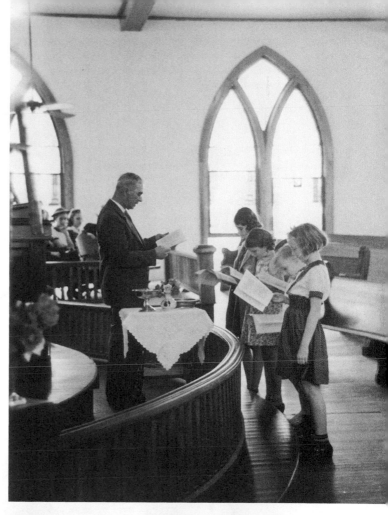

Preacher reading the lesson and instructions before baptism, San Augustine, TX (1939)

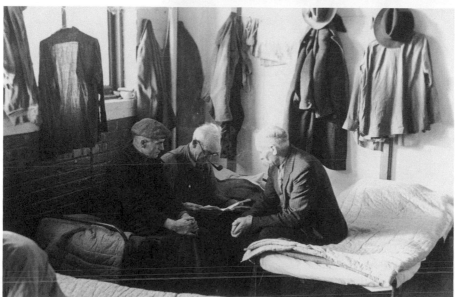

Man reading to fellow inmates, homeless men's bureau, Sioux City, IA (1936)

The photographs on pages 364–367 come from the book School *by Nicholas Nixon and Robert Coles. Nixon is a photographer whose work has documented people in "natural" (as opposed to posed) settings. One series of his photos, for example, is of people on their front porches; another focuses on people coping with the effects of the AIDS virus. Coles is a psychiatrist by training, but his interests are wide and varied. Throughout his long career he has engaged questions about what stories—whether they come from patients, photographs, or teachers—represent.*

For the photographs in School, Nixon focused on three very different schools in Boston, near where he and Coles both live: the Tobin School, a public school; the Boston Latin School, an elite, private, "preparatory" school; and the Perkins School for the Blind, a school for children with special needs.

New York Public Library Grand Reading Room

Reading: Times Square, 2005

Reading building plans

Reading in motion

Modern texts for modern times

Man reading an Arabic newspaper "Reading Culture"

INDEX